Sports Law in the United States

Sports Law in the United States

Third Edition

Matthew J. Mitten

This book was originally published as a monograph in the International Encyclopaedia of Laws/Sports Law.

Founding Editor: Roger Blanpain
General Editor: Frank Hendrickx
Volume Editor: Michele Colucci

Wolters Kluwer

Published by:
Kluwer Law International B.V.
PO Box 316
2400 AH Alphen aan den Rijn
The Netherlands
Website: www.wolterskluwerlr.com

Sold and distributed in North, Central and South America by:
Wolters Kluwer Legal & Regulatory U.S.
7201 McKinney Circle
Frederick, MD 21704
United States of America
Email: customer.service@wolterskluwer.com

Sold and distributed in all other countries by:
Quadrant
Rockwood House
Haywards Heath
West Sussex
RH16 3DH
United Kingdom
Email: international-customerservice@wolterskluwer.com

ISBN 978-90-411-9225-7

e-Book: ISBN 978-90-411-9255-4
web-PDF: ISBN 978-90-411-9289-9

This title is available on www.kluwerlawonline.com

The Author

Matthew J. Mitten is the Executive Director of the National Sports Law Institute and the LLM in Sports Law program for foreign lawyers at Marquette University Law School. He served as the Law School's Associate Dean for Academic Affairs from July 2002 to June 2004. He currently teaches Amateur Sports Law, Professional Sports Law, Sports Industry Sponsorship and Marketing Workshop, and Antitrust Law. He has also taught Comparative Sports Law, International Sports Law, and a Sports Law seminar.

Matt has coauthored a law school textbook titled *Sports Law and Regulation: Cases, Materials, and Problems* (Wolters Kluwer), which is in its fourth edition, as well as an undergraduate and graduate textbook titled *Sports Law: Governance and Regulation* (Wolters Kluwer), which is in its second edition. A leading sports law scholar, Matt has published articles in several of the leading law reviews in the U.S. as well as in medical journals such as *The New England Journal of Medicine*. He is a member of the advisory board for *The International Sports Law Journal*.

He has spoken at more than 175 sports law conferences throughout the U.S. and in Australia, China, England, Korea, and Turkey.

Matthew is an Arbitrator for the Court of Arbitration for Sport (serving on the ad hoc Division for the XXI Winter Olympic Games in Sochi, Russia) and the American Arbitration Association's commercial, consumer, doping, and Olympic sports arbitration panels. He was a Senior Fellow at the University of Melbourne Law School in Australia (2006, 2008, 2010, and 2013) and is a member of the International Advisory Board for its Graduate Diploma in Sports Law program. He also has taught Sports Law courses at the University of Barcelona and the University of Queensland. Matthew is the former President of the Sports Lawyers Association and serves on its Board of Directors. He formerly chaired the American Association of Law Schools' Section on Law and Sports and the NCAA's Committee on Competitive Safeguards and Medical Aspects of Sports and served on the Board of Directors of the Forum for the Scholarly Study of Intercollegiate Athletics.

The Author

Matthew was born in Tiffin, Ohio on April 26, 1959. He earned his BA in Economics from The Ohio State University and his JD, *magna cum laude*, from the University of Toledo College of Law. He is a member of the Order of the Coif and served as a Note & Comment Editor for the *University of Toledo Law Review*'s editorial board. He practiced antitrust and intellectual property law with Kilpatrick Townsend in Atlanta, Georgia from 1984–1989. He taught at South Texas College of Law in Houston from 1990–1999 and has been a visiting professor at the University of Oregon School of Law and University of Toledo College of Law as well as a visiting lecturer in Sports Medicine at The University of Tennessee Graduate School of Medicine.
Significant parts of it are adapted from Matthew J. Mitten, Timothy Davis, Rodney Smith, & Jeremi Duru, Sports Law and Regulation: Cases, Materials, and Problems (Wolters Kluwer 4th ed. 2017) and Matthew J. Mitten, Timothy Davis, Ken Shropshire, Barbara Osborne, & Rodney Smith, Sports Law: Governance and Regulation (Wolters Kluwer 2d. ed. 2016).

Table of Contents

List of Abbreviations

AAA	American Arbitration Association
ADA	Americans with Disabilities Act
CBA	Collective bargaining agreement
CAS	Court of Arbitration for Sport
FBS	Football Bowl Series
IOC	International Olympic Committee
IF	International Federation
MLB	Major League Baseball
MLS	Major League Soccer
NASCAR	National Association of Stock Car Auto Racing
NBA	National Basketball Association
NCAA	National Collegiate Athletic Association
NFHS	National Federation of High Schools
NFL	National Football League
NGB	National Governing Body
NLRA	National Labor Relations Act
NLRB	National Labor Relations Board
NHL	National Hockey League
UAAA	Uniform Athlete Agents Act
USOC	United States Olympic Committee
WADA	World Anti-Doping Agency

General Introduction

Chapter 1. General Background

1. The United States of America is comprised of fifty states, the District of Columbia (where its capital, Washington, DC, is located), and fourteen territories throughout the world. At the beginning of 2016, its estimated population was more than 322 million people.

2. The U.S. has a common law legal system with both federal and state courts. There is one or more federal or U.S. district courts in every state, twelve intermediate appellate or "circuit" courts (each hears appeals from federal district court decisions within its jurisdiction, which encompasses two or more states; one appellate court hears appeals only from District of Columbia federal district court decisions), and the U.S. Supreme Court, which exercises largely discretionary appellate review of circuit court decisions. The Supreme Court is the final authority regarding the interpretation of the U.S. Constitution and all federal laws. Each state has its own independent judicial system consisting of trial courts, intermediate appellate courts, and one highest court generally called the "Supreme Court" (e.g., California Supreme Court), which is the final authority regarding all matters of state law within its jurisdiction.

3. In the U.S., millions of children and adults participate in competitive or recreational sports. The vast majority of competitive or recreational sports leagues and clubs generally are privately organized, funded, and governed. There are thousands of youth sports clubs and/or leagues for many sports, including baseball, basketball, football, ice hockey, soccer, swimming, gymnastics, tennis, and volleyball. Adult recreational sports clubs and leagues are prevalent; millions of adults belong to health and fitness clubs and/or regularly participate in running or cycling races; many adults also participate in marathons or triathlons.

4. Both public and private educational institutions, including colleges and universities, high schools (grades 9–12) and primary schools (grades 1–8) offer and sponsor "amateur" competitive athletics for their students. As part of their general financial support of public educational institutions within their respective jurisdictions, state governments fund competitive sports teams or physical education classes offered by public schools.

5. The federal government encourages the health and physical fitness of the general populace, but it generally does not directly fund or organize athletic competition for children or adults. The mission of the President's Council on Fitness, Sport, & Nutrition's "is to engage, educate, and empower all Americans across the lifespan to adopt a healthy lifestyle that includes regular physical activity and good nutrition."

The Council's twenty-five members are appointed by the President and, among other duties, advise the U.S. Secretary of Health and Human Services on ways to promote regular physical activity, fitness, sports participation, and good nutrition. The Council also functions as a liaison to state, local, and private entities in the effort to achieve these objectives.

6. On June 16, 2009, President Barack Obama announced the formation of a permanent White House Office of Olympic, Paralympic, and Youth Sport to "promote the values of the Olympic Movement and [to] encourage increased youth participation in athletics." He stated, "Sports are an important way to instill values, judgment and teamwork in our nation's kids, and this new office reflects our commitment to giving all our children a chance to thrive."

7. Sport plays a major role in US life, according to a 2010 research report, *What Sport Means in America: A Study of Sport's Role in Society*, which was commissioned by the United States Anti-Doping Agency (USADA). Its survey results indicate that more than 60% of U.S. adults—approximately 162 million people—claim some relationship to sports-related activities, including 25% that are actively engaged in some form of sports activity as participants, parents of children playing sports, coaches, or volunteers. The report's executive summary states:

> Sport offers many positive benefits to society, as the majority of adults agree that sport provides a source of fun and enjoyment (88%), can reduce youth crime and delinquency (84%), can teach valuable life lessons (80%), and can bring people together in ways that strengthen communities (76%). Three-fifths of adults agree that overall sport promotes positive values.

It also states: "Although 60% of spectators spend most of their time watching professional sport, adults believe that professional sport lags behind all other categories of sport in actually promoting positive values, while community-based sport is considered to have the most positive actual influence."[1]

8. Professional and intercollegiate spectator sports are extremely popular in the U.S. According to a January 2014 Harris Poll survey, U.S. sports fans' ten favorite sports are professional football (35%), baseball ("America's pastime") (14%), college football (11%), auto racing (7%), men's pro basketball (6%), hockey (5%), men's soccer (4%), men's college basketball (3%), men's soccer (2%), men's golf (2%), men's tennis (2%), boxing (2%), and swimming(2%). Tennis (1%) and college basketball (1%) are the most popular women's sports. Millions of U.S. citizens attend or watch broadcast sporting events; for example, approximately 167 million persons in the U.S. and millions more worldwide watched the 2012 Super Bowl, the National Football League's (NFL's) championship game. There are several television channels with exclusively sports-related programming (e.g., Entertainment Sports Programming Network (ESPN)). Professional and intercollegiate sports teams that win league or national championships as well as Olympic medalists typically are invited to the White House to meet and be congratulated by the U.S. president.

9. In the U.S., E-sports, which require the rapid movement of fingers on a video controller and eyes on a video monitor, are becoming increasingly popular and arguably

1. . *See* www.usada.org/outreach-research/executive-summary.

satisfy the general characteristics of a "sport."[2] In 2013, the U.S. immigration services determined that "League of Legends" video game players are athletes engaged in a sport who are eligible for visas to enter the U.S. and compete as international athletes. From a consumer perspective, E-sports involve competition with an uncertain outcome, which distinguishes sports from other popular forms of entertainment such as movies, opera, and plays that always have the same content and outcome.[3] The National Basketball Association has created the "NBA 2K Esports" league, in which approximately two-thirds of its member clubs are planning to enter teams, with the objective of becoming a global e-sports league. Several U.S. colleges and universities already have varsity E-sports programs [4] In May 2016, Pac-12 Conference commissioner Larry Scott said that "e-sports is a natural fit for many of our universities located in the technology and media hubs of the country."

2. *See* generally Holden, John T., et. al, *The Future Is Now: Esports Policy Considerations and Potential Litigation*, 27 J. Legal Aspects Sport 46 (2017). In analyzing whether cheerleading is a sport, U.S. courts have identified several relevant factors in making this determination. *Biediger v. Quinnipiac Univ.*, 691 F.3d 85, 105 (2d Cir. 2012) (intercollegiate cheerleading is not a sport because currently there is no "application of uniform set of rules for competition"); *Noffke v. Bakke*, 315 Wis.2d 350, 364–65, 760 N.W.2d 156, 162 (Wis. 2009) (high school cheerleading is a sport because it is "[a]n activity involving physical exertion and skill that is governed by a set of rules or customs").

3. *Bowers v. Fed'n Internationale de L'Automobile*, 489 F.3d 316, 321–22 (7th Cir. 2007) (a spectator is entitled only to "view whatever event transpire[s]" and has no right to a sports event that is "exciting" or during which participants "competed *well*"). However, one U.S. court refused to broadly define "sport" as any "contest involving persons that is viewed by the public." *Davis v. Commonwealth of Kentucky*, 564 S.W.2d 33 (1978) (ruling that a beauty pageant is not encompassed within statute prohibiting sports bribery, which defines "sports contest" as "any professional or amateur sport, athletic game or contest, or race or contest involving machines, persons or animals that is viewed by the public"; statute applies only to "sports contests as are normally understood by the usage of that term").

4. They include Columbia College (Missouri); Robert Morris University (Illinois); University of Pikeville (Kentucky); Maryville University (Missouri); Southwestern University (Texas); University of California, Irvine; Tiffin University (Ohio); Midland University (Nebraska); Southwest Baptist University (Missouri); Indiana Tech; Miami University (Ohio); the University of Utah, and Lourdes University (Ohio).

Chapter 2. Development of Sports Law

10. Although the US has a rich history of sports participation and viewing, the academic study of the laws regulating sports is relatively new. The first US sports law treatises were not published into the late 1970s, and the first sports law textbook was not published until 1990. Many U.S. law schools now offer at least one sports law course, and two law schools (Marquette University and Tulane University) offer sports law certificate programs as part of their JD curricula. Marquette University and St. John's University offer an LLM in Sports Law; Marquette's program currently is open only to those with first law degrees from non-U.S. law schools.

11. There currently is no consensus among U.S. sports law scholars regarding whether "sports law" (like Internet law or health care law) has developed into an independent substantive area of law such as contract, labor, or tort law, or whether it is merely the application of many areas of general law to a unique industry. In an article titled *What Is Sports Law?*[5] One sports law scholar summarized the differing viewpoints:

A. *The Debate*

1. The Traditional View: "Sports Law" Does Not Exist

12. The traditional view is that sports law represents nothing more than an amalgamation of various substantive areas of the law that are relevant in the sports context. According to this perspective, the term *sports law* is a misnomer given that sport represents a form of activity and entertainment that is governed by the legal system in its entirety. … [A]dherents to the traditional perspective argue that "sports law simply entails the application of basic legal precepts to a specific industry" that are drawn from other substantive areas of the law. Consequently, no separately identifiable body of law exists that can be characterized as sports law.

2. The Moderate Position: "Sports Law" May Develop into a Field of Law

13. Other commentators have begun increasingly to question the traditional view that no corpus of law exists that can be characterized as an independent field of law called sports law. … [Some] have staked out what represents a middle ground. Professor Kenneth Shropshire acknowledges that developments, such as state and federal legislation impacting sports (e.g., state statutes regulating sports agents and federal statutes such as Title IX), suggest a "growing sports-only corpus" of law … .

Professor Burlette Carter … argues that sports law is in the midst of an exciting, yet challenging, transformative process. According to Professor Carter, this process parallels the increased focus by law schools on sports, and the growing significance of sports regulation to participants, organizations, and communities. She believes that these developments will better shape the contours of this emerging field of study. This

5. . Timothy Davis, *What is Sports Law?* 11 Marq. Sports L. Rev. 211 (2001).

in turn, will eventually transform sports law from "a course without a corpus" to a widely recognized independent substantive area of law.

3. "Sports Law": A Separate Field of Law

14. [Others] argue that sports law currently exists as a field of law. Adherents to this view emphasize the growing body of case and statutory law specific to the sports industry as evidence of the existence of a separately identifiable body of law. ... Pointing to the increasing body of judicial and legislative law specific to sports, Professor [Simone] Gardiner argues:

> [I]t is true to say that [sports law] is largely an amalgam of interrelated legal disciplines involving such areas as contract, taxation, employment, competition and criminal law but dedicated legislation and case law has developed and will continue to do so. As an area of academic study and extensive practitioner involvement, the time is right to accept that a new legal area has been born—sports law.

15. Commentators also propose that references to sports law as merely an amalgamation of various other substantive areas of the law ignore an important present-day reality—very few substantive areas of the law fit into separate categories that are divorced from and independent of other substantive areas of the law. Doctrinal overlap exists not only within sports law, but within other areas of law as well. According to Professor Carter:

> the field of sports law has moved beyond the traditional antitrust and labour law boundaries into sports representation and legal ethics, sports and corporate structure, sports and disability, sports and race, sports and gender, sports and taxation, international issues in sports law and numerous other permutations.

16. Proponents of the sports law designation and those sympathetic to the view also argue that reticence to recognize sports law as a specific body of law may reflect attitudes regarding the intellectual seriousness of sports. In this regard, they emphasize the tendency to marginalize the study of sports rather than treat it as any other form of business. The intellectual marginalization of sport has been attributed, in part, to the belief that social relations extant in sports were not deemed proper subjects for reconstruction into legal relationships. Thus, private and public law were considered "inappropriate [mechanisms for] controlling the social norms of sport." The competing and increasingly predominant view, however, casts sports as a significant economic activity suitable, like other big businesses, to regulation, whether it be internal or external.

17. In the end, whether sports law is recognized as an independent field of law may turn on the perceptions of those who practice, teach, and engage in scholarship related to sports law. Professor Carter asks that we consider the following:

> But what makes a field a field? The answer is that a field becomes a field not because it is inherently so but because in our public legal dealings we shape it as such, defining the concepts and legal norms that will prevail uniquely in that context. It becomes a field because enough people with power on all sides are so affected by it to require some special treatment of it in the law.

18. Regardless of the position that is adopted regarding the "what is sports law" debate, U.S. sports law scholars agree that matters arising in the sports law context implicate diverse substantive areas of law. Sports-related cases are sculpting a body of law particularly applicable in the sports context and influencing the development of general legal principles:

> On both the federal and state levels, sports related cases have not only had a profound impact on the narrow questions raised by the facts of particular disputes, but have also significantly influenced more general jurisprudential trends. ... The growing body of sports-based legal authority has shaped the face of general legal doctrine in several important areas. In federal law, antitrust and labor doctrines have been significantly shaped by cases originating in the sports industries. In addition, constitutional principles involving drug testing and search and seizure have been influenced by sports law cases. On the state level, important tort doctrine has been and will continue to be affected by disputes arising in the context of sports. Undoubtedly, other areas of the law will be similarly influenced by sports litigation.[6]

19. Relatively few attorneys in the U.S. spend a majority of their time practicing sports law, but many lawyers perform professional services for one or more clients who are part of, or have dealings with, the sports industry. It is a common misperception that the practice of sports law is a narrow field consisting only of lawyers representing professional athletes, sports leagues, or clubs who have specialized expertise in sports-specific laws. To the contrary, "sports lawyers" represent a wide variety of clients who need legal advice and representation that usually requires knowledge of several general areas of law.

20. Virtually every area of U.S. law regulates or is relevant to one or more aspects of youth, high school, college, Olympic and international, professional, or recreational sports. The U.S. sports industry is vast in scope, has millions of athletes (but less than 10,000 major league and top level individual sport professional athletes) and spectators, and generates billions of dollars annually. In addition to amateur and professional players, coaches, referees and officials, leagues, national, regional, state,

6. . Daniel E. Lazaroff, *The Influence of Sports Law on American Jurisprudence*, 1 Va. Sports & Ent. L.J. 1 (2001). *See also* Matthew J. Mitten & Hayden Opie, *Sports Law: Implications for the Development of International, Comparative, and National Law and Global Dispute Resolution*, 85 Tul. L. Rev. 269 (2010). ("The commercialization of sports has given rise to numerous disputes requiring courts to apply several areas of general law (e.g., contract, intellectual property, labour, and antitrust laws) and to reassess their views about external regulation of the sports industry, which has led to the development of important legal precedent with much broader application.").

and local governing bodies, athletics administrators, educational institutions, and sports facility owners and operators are part of the sports industry. Broadly defined, this industry also encompasses sports broadcasters, playing equipment manufacturers, sports medicine care providers, businesses that sponsor athletic events or athletes, concessionaires who serve food and drink to fans at games, and others that provide sports-related goods and services.

21. Because sports law courses are a relatively recent addition to the curriculum at most law schools, lawyers have practiced "sports law" for many years without having taken any sports law courses as part of their formal legal education. U.S. lawyers practicing sports law have varied backgrounds, and most of them did not obtain full-time employment with sports organizations or have a stable of sports industry clients upon graduation from law school. Rather, they gained legal knowledge, skills, and experience representing clients in other industries that have proven to be readily transferable and useful in serving the needs of sports industry clients or handling sports-related matters.

22. The practice of sports law is a very eclectic and interesting field, and lawyers representing sports industry clients must have expertise in several areas of law to represent their clients effectively. Counsel for professional leagues and clubs need general knowledge of contract, labor, private association, antitrust, tort, tax, and intellectual property law. Those representing professional athletes must be familiar with labor and employment, contract, federal and state tax, and worker's compensation laws as well as the multiple layers of athlete agent regulation. It is essential for lawyers representing professional sports industry clients or those doing business with them to have strong contract negotiation and drafting skills. An understanding of the arbitration process is important because most employment-related disputes between professional athletes and the league or their respective clubs are resolved by mandatory arbitration. Representation of individuals, educational institutions, and governing bodies that are part of the youth, high school, college, or Olympic sports industries also requires broad knowledge of several areas of law including contract, private association, tort, and constitutional law as well as arbitration (for Olympic sports).

Chapter 3. Sources of Sports Law

23. In the U.S., there is no federal government sports ministry or council that funds, oversees, or regulates competitive or recreational sports at any level of competition. However, state regulatory agencies oversee some sports such as boxing and mixed martial arts competitions.

24. There are no sports-specific provisions in the U.S. Constitution. Courts generally rule that there is no federal constitutional right to participate in sports at any level of competition. However, various provisions of the U.S. Constitution have been judicially construed to prohibit public educational institutions from infringing the protected rights of college and high school student-athletes by, for example, failing to provide due process or equal protection of the law, or violating their privacy, free speech, or freedom of religion rights. Depending on their individual composition, operation, and degree of delegated authority from a state governmental agency, some sports governing bodies (e.g., certain state high school athletic associations) have been deemed to be a "state actor," which subjects their governing authority to the constraints of the U.S. Constitution. On the other hand, professional sports leagues and individual performer sports governing bodies (e.g., Professional Golfers Association (PGA), Association of Tennis Professionals), the National Collegiate Athletic Association (NCAA), and the United States Olympic Committee (USOC) are private organizations with broad autonomous regulatory authority that is not limited by any provisions of the U.S. Constitution.

25. There are only a few sport-specific federal statutes; for example, the Ted Stevens Olympic and Amateur Sports Act,[7] Sports Agent Responsibility Trust Act,[8] Sport Broadcasting Act of 1961,[9] Equity in Athletics Disclosure Act,[10] Professional and Amateur Sports Protection Act,[11] the Bribery in Sporting Contests Act,[12] Professional Boxing Safety Act of 1996,[13] Muhammad Ali Boxing Reform Act,[14] and the Curt Flood Act of 1998.[15] Similarly, there are only a few sport-specific state statutes, which include laws enacted in virtually all states such as athlete agent statutes based on the Uniform Athlete Agent Act (*see* Part IV, Chapter 2 §3) and statutes establishing concussion protocols for youth/high school sports (e.g., Washington's "Zachary Lystedt Law" (2009)) as well as laws limiting or establishing tort liability standards enacted in some jurisdictions (e.g., Illinois Baseball Facility Liability Act, 745 ILCS §38/10; Wisc. Stat. Ann. §895.525 regarding co-participant liability).

26. With some limited exceptions, sports leagues, clubs, associations, and governing bodies as well as educational institutions that offer recreational or competitive

7. . 36 U.S.C. §§220501 et seq.
8. . 15 U.S.C. §§7801 et seq.
9. . 15 U.S.C. §§1291 et seq.
10. . 20 U.S.C. §1092.
11. . 28 U.S.C. §§3701 et seq.
12. . 18 U.S.C §224.
13. . 15 U.S.C. §§6301 et seq.
14. . 15 U.S.C. §6307a-h.
15. . 15 U.S.C. §26b.

athletics to their students must comply with otherwise applicable general federal statutes. In particular, the federal antitrust, antidiscrimination, and labor laws have significantly shaped the structure, governance, and operation of professional sports. Title IX, a federal statute mandating gender equality in all educational program (including athletics) offered by educational institutions that receive federal funding, has had a significant impact on interscholastic and intercollegiate sports.

27. State common law, particularly contract, private association, and tort law, play a significant role in the regulation of sports. Because of the unique features of sports competition such as the need for uniform rules and competitive balance, this body of law often is applied differently to sports than to other social or business activities. For example, because physical contact among participating athletes is an inherent part of most sports and athletic competitions, tort law permits some on-field contact that would otherwise infringe a person's legal rights. However, to prevent conflicting or unduly burdensome regulation by potentially fifty different states from being imposed on them, the Dormant Commerce Clause of the U.S. Constitution has been judicially construed to prohibit a state from directly regulating the with interstate business activities of national sports governing bodies such as the major professional sports leagues or associations, the NCAA, or the USOC.

Part I. Organization of Sport

Chapter 1. Distinctive General Characteristics of Structure and Governance of U.S. Sports

28. In the U.S. there is no national sports ministry or direct federal government regulation of sports. Rather than a European hierarchical vertical pyramid system of governance, there is a separate governing body for each professional league and level of sports competition. For example, the sport of soccer is regulated at the major league men's professional level by Major League Soccer (MLS) and the Major Indoor Soccer League (which are separate entities governing outdoor and indoor soccer, respectively), at the major league women's professional level by the National's Women's Soccer League (other professional leagues such as the North American Soccer League (NASL) are independently governed); at the Olympic, international, and youth club level by the United States Soccer Federation; at the intercollegiate level by the NCAA; and at the interscholastic level by each state high school athletic association.

29. In contrast to the European model of sports, U.S. major professional sports leagues are "closed" (i.e., the existing league clubs must approve the admission of a new club by majority vote) and there is no promotion and relegation system. Major League Baseball (MLB) and the National Hockey League (NHL) have extensive minor league systems that develop professional players. U.S. colleges and universities serve as a training ground for future National Basketball Association (NBA), NFL, and Women's National Basketball Association (WNBA) players.

30. Intercollegiate, interscholastic, and youth sports competition is based on an "amateur" model, which generally means that athletes must not be professionals or compensated by cash payments for their athletic abilities and skills in order to be eligible to participate. In contrast to the European club sport model, U.S. colleges, universities, and high schools (grades 9–12) provide an extensive system of sports competition for student-athletes enrolled in educational institutions. U.S. Olympic sports competition is privately funded, and there are no government-sponsored organizations that train and financially support athletes.[16]

16. . *See* generally James A.R. Nafziger, *A Comparison of the European and North American Models of Sports Organisation*, in *EU, Sport, Law and Policy: Regulation, Re-regulation and Representation*, 35–55 (Simon Gardiner, Richard Parrish & Robert C.R. Siekmann eds., 2009).

Chapter 2. Structure and Governance of Interscholastic Sports

§1. Historical Overview

31. Beginning in the 1820s U.S. secondary schools began encouraging student athletic activity (e.g., gymnastics) for educational and recreational reasons. During the next several decades physical education classes became a formal part of the educational curriculum for students.[17] In the late 1800s male high school students began participating in self-organized interscholastic competition in sports such as baseball and football. These student-run athletic activities were plagued by economic challenges and a "win-at-all-costs" philosophy.[18] To correct these problems, in 1902, "[t]he 15th Educational Conference of Academics and High Schools … recommended strict faculty control of sports and the establishment of state associations to oversee competition."[19]

32. The first state high school athletic association was formed in Wisconsin in 1896. After the formal organization of the Wisconsin Interscholastic Athletic Association, state athletic associations began to proliferate throughout the U.S. Today, interscholastic athletics are largely regulated under the rules formulated by individual state athletic associations, which are voted upon by the member educational institutions of that state athletic association.

§2. Internal Regulatory Structure, Governance, and Administrative Processes

33. More than 7.8 million high school students participated in interscholastic athletics nationwide; 4,544,574 males and 3,324,326 females in 2015–2016. In an increasingly technology-driven, isolated twenty-first century U.S. society, participation in interscholastic athletics provides a means of establishing social networks with one's peers and developing a community-based identity with corresponding positive academic effects. Finding a link between high school students' sense of identity, patterns of extracurricular involvement, and indicators of successful and risky adolescent development, a 1999 study found that female and male students who participate in high school team sports through the twelfth grade have a school-based identity that correlates to positive academic performance (e.g., an increased twelfth Grade Point Average (GPA) and an increased probability of being enrolled in college full-time at

17. . Mabel Lee, *A History of Physical Education and Sports in the U.S.A.* (1983).
18. . Richard A. Awanson & Betty Spears, *History of Sport and Physical Education in the United States*, 4th ed., (1995).
19. . *Ibid.*, at 199.

age 21.)[20] This highly positive finding is consistent with prior research evidencing that sports participation, relative to participation in other extracurricular activities such as student government and academic clubs, is "linked to lower likelihood of school dropout and higher rates of college attendance."[21]

34. There is no direct federal government regulation or funding of interscholastic athletics, which is an extracurricular activity that is part of the compulsory secondary education traditionally provided and regulated by individual states. Although some general federal legislation (e.g., Title IX, a law requiring gender equity in education) has significantly impacted interscholastic athletics, the internal governance of interscholastic athletics generally occurs on a state-by-state basis.

35. There are few specific state laws directly regulating interscholastic athletics. However, most states have enacted statutory provisions authorizing the participation of home-schooled students in interscholastic athletics, establishing student-athlete academic eligibility rules (e.g., "no-pass, no-play" rules requiring a minimum level of academic performance to participate in high school), or mandating health and safety requirements (e.g., preparticipation medical clearance). Virtually all states have enacted statutes requiring that students with concussion symptoms be removed from competition or practice, and that certain protocols (e.g., medical evaluation and written clearance by a qualified physician) be followed before they are permitted to return to play.[22]

36. Each of the fifty states and the District of Columbia has its own independent regulatory association, whose membership generally consists of all public and private high schools within the state, which has broad authority to promulgate and enforce rules governing interscholastic athletics. Each association establishes student-athlete eligibility requirements as well as regulations to ensure fair and safe play, competitive balance, and ethical conduct consistent with the educational objectives of interscholastic athletics. It also sponsors state championship competitions among member schools and their student-athletes for each sport. The National Federation of High Schools (NFHS) coordinates the efforts of its Member State associations to promulgate uniform rules of the game for each sport and to govern interscholastic athletics in a manner consistent with their member schools' educational objectives and the best interests of student-athletes. The NFHS, however, does not have any direct regulatory authority over interscholastic athletics.

37. A state athletics association's member educational institutions are contractually bound to follow the association's rules (which they have a voice and vote in enacting) and adhere to its interpretation and application of these rules to themselves and their student-athletes pursuant to its plenary authority to govern interscholastic athletics within the state. The failure to do so may result in sanctions such as the ineligibility of the school or its student-athletes to participate in high school sports competitions, or, in extreme cases, expulsion from the association. Thus, state high school athletic associations are able to effectively exercise regulatory authority over student-athletes.

---

20. . Jacquelynne S. Eccles & Bonnie L. Barber, *Student Council, Volunteering, Basketball, or Marching Band: What Kind of Extracurricular Involvement Matters?*, 14 J. Adolescent Research 10 (1999).
21. . *Ibid.*, at 12.
22. . *See* , e.g., Wis. Stat. §118.293.

§3. Judicial Regulation of Interscholastic Athletics

38. As a general rule, courts are very deferential and will provide judicial relief to a party (e.g., a member school or student-athlete) aggrieved by a state high school athletics association only if the challenged rule, application, or enforcement is found to be arbitrary and capricious or violates an applicable federal or state constitutional law provision or statute. For example, in *Brown v. Oklahoma Secondary School Activities Ass'n*,[23] the court explained, "We may not interject ourselves in the Association's internal affairs if the rules are reasonable, lawful, in keeping with public policy, and are interpreted fairly and reasonably and enforced uniformly and not arbitrarily." Regarding the internal affairs, proceedings, rules and orders of a high school athletic association, another court stated: "[w]here there is room for two opinions, and the agency acted honestly and upon due consideration, th[e] court should not find that an action was arbitrary and capricious, even though th[e] court may have reached the opposite conclusion."[24]

39. As a prerequisite to bringing a claim alleging infringement of any federal constitutional right, it must be established that its deprivation occurred as the result of the conduct of a "state actor." Unless a particular state high school athletics association is a "state actor," it is not required to respect the individual rights secured by the U.S. Constitution, and a court will not address the merits of the substantive federal constitutional law issues. The question of whether a state athletic association is a state actor was an unsettled issue for many years, with lower courts reaching different conclusions on this important threshold issue. In a 2001 case, *Brentwood Academy v. Tennessee Secondary School Athletic Association* (*Brentwood I*),[25] the U.S. Supreme Court resolved this issue by adopting a legal standard requiring a fact-specific inquiry to determine the individual status of each state high school athletic association. This is because each high school athletic association's history, composition, and function as well as the nature and scope of its delegated authority from state government differ from state to state. In *Brentwood I*, the Court ruled that the Tennessee Secondary School Athletic Association (TSSAA) is a state actor subject to the constraints of the federal constitution because of "the pervasive entwinement of public institutions and public officials in its composition and workings." 84% of the TSSAA's members are public schools, public school administrators control and perform all of its significant regulatory functions, and Tennessee state board of education officials serve as ex officio members of the TSSAA's board of control and legislative council.

40. Even if a state high school athletic association is a state actor subject to the requirements of the US Constitution, courts will provide the association with significant latitude to effectively govern interscholastic athletics. In *Brentwood Academy v. Tennessee Secondary School Athletic Association*, (*Brentwood II*),[26] the Supreme Court rejected a member private high school's challenges to the TSSAA's anti-recruiting rule, which prohibited pre-enrolment direct solicitation of student-athletes to participate in interscholastic sports, on free speech and due process grounds. The Court acknowledged

23. . 125 P.3d 1219, 1220 (Okla. 2005).
24. . *Jones v. Washington Interscholastic Athletic Assn.*, 2007 WL 293751 at *8 (W.D. Wash. 2007).
25. . 531 U.S. 288 (2001).
26. . 551 U.S. 291 (2007).

the First Amendment protects a school's right to publish truthful information about the excellence of its athletic program in an effort to generate student admissions applications. However, the Court stated that "an athletic league's interest in enforcing its rules sometimes warrant curtailing the speech of its voluntary participants" such as its member schools.

41. Observing that Brentwood Academy "made a voluntary decision to join TSSAA and to abide by its anti-recruiting rule," the Court concluded:

> We need no empirical data to credit TSSAA's common-sense conclusion that hard-sell tactics directed at middle school students could lead to exploitation, distort competition between high school teams, and foster an environment in which athletics are prized more highly than academics. ... [T]he First Amendment does not excuse Brentwood from abiding by the same anti-recruiting rule that governs the conduct of its sister schools. To hold otherwise would undermine the principle ... that [h]igh school football is a game. Games have rules.

42. The Court ruled that the TSSAA did not violate the school's due process rights before imposing disciplinary sanctions for violating its anti-recruiting rule. Brentwood Academy was given appropriate notice of this rule and charges against it and had a fair opportunity to defend itself.

43. Expressing a similar deferential view regarding the nature and scope of the authority of state high school athletic associations and public schools to govern interscholastic sports, courts generally have rejected claims that random suspicionless drug testing of student-athletes constitutes an unreasonable search and seizure in violation of the Fourth Amendment of the U.S. Constitution.[27]

27. . *Vernonia School Dist. 47J v. Acton*, 515 U.S. 646 (1995). However, some courts have ruled that random suspicionless drug testing of student-athletes violates state constitutional law provisions. *See* , e.g., *York v. Wahkiakum*, 178 P.3d 995 (Wash. 2008).

Chapter 3. Structure and Governance of Intercollegiate Sports

§1. Historical Overview

44. The National Collegiate Athletics Association (NCAA) includes over 1,200 colleges and universities divided into three divisions based on the nature of their intercollegiate athletic programs. Division I universities offer full or partial athletic scholarships to their student-athletes and is the highest level of competition in most sports. Division II also offers athletic scholarships and competes at an intermediate competitive level. Division III does not offer athletic scholarships and is the lowest and most student-centered competitive level.

45. There also are other associations engaged in the regulation of intercollegiate athletics. The National Association of Intercollegiate Athletics includes more than 360 colleges and universities and conducts numerous national championships. The National Christian College Athletic Association was incorporated to provide an association for Christ-centered collegiate institutions that are committed to athletic competition as an integral component of education, evangelism, and encouragement. The United States Collegiate Athletic Association, another smaller national organization, was organized for the purpose of holding national championships in a number of sports for very small schools. The National Junior College Athletic Association is made up of more than 500 junior and community colleges throughout twenty-four regions in the U.S. that sponsor men's and women's intercollegiate athletic teams, which compete for national championships in three divisions, based on levels of competitiveness. There are some state-wide governing bodies; for example, California has a community college athletic association that governs athletics within California. Although the rules and governance structures differ among the various national associations that govern intercollegiate athletics, the legal framework applicable to the NCAA's governance of intercollegiate athletics is relevant to all other governing bodies.

46. Students, with some faculty oversight, initially were the major force in organizing intercollegiate athletics. After the deaths of eighteen intercollegiate football players in 1905, President Theodore Roosevelt invited university officials to participate in a White House Conference to review football rules. These efforts to reform football rules led to the formation of a Rules Committee and the formation of the Intercollegiate Athletic Association which, in 1910, was renamed the NCAA.

47. After the Great Depression and the Second World War, with a dramatic increase in access to higher education on the part of all segments of U.S. society, largely through government support for returning military personnel to cover the costs of attending college, public interest in intercollegiate athletics expanded significantly. Commercial pressures intensified with the advent of television, the presence of radio in the vast majority of homes in the U.S., and the broadcasting of major sporting events. These factors, coupled with a series of gambling scandals and recruiting excesses, caused the NCAA to promulgate additional rules, resulting in an expansion of its governance authority over its member educational institutions.

48. Two developments in the 1950s contributed to the transformation of the NCAA into a major regulatory body: (1) Walter Byers became executive director of the NCAA and personally contributed to strengthening the NCAA and its enforcement division; and (2) the NCAA negotiated its first contract to televise intercollegiate football, valued in excess of USD 1 million, opening the door to increasingly lucrative future television contracts.

49. In the 1970s, increased participation by women in intercollegiate athletes gained momentum as women achieved rights under laws requiring gender equity in higher education. The NCAA gained broader rules enforcement power, but found itself caught between two critiques. On the one hand, it was criticized for responding inadequately to the increased commercialization of intercollegiate athletics, with all its attendant excesses. On the other hand, it was criticized for unfairly exercising its regulatory authority.

50. In difficult economic times for higher education in the 1980s, college and university presidents increasingly found themselves caught between the pressures applied by influential members of boards of trustees and graduates, who often demanded winning athletic programs, and faculty, who feared the rising commercialization of athletics and its impact on academic values and their institution's budget. In the mid-1980s, the presidents became increasingly involved in the governance of intercollegiate athletics through the NCAA, taking some of the power away from athletics directors and faculty representatives who had previously largely controlled governance of intercollegiate athletics.

51. The last two decades of the twentieth century have resulted in the increasing commercialization of "big-time" intercollegiate athletics (primarily Division I Football Bowl Series football and men's basketball) and attendant pressures to "win-at-all-costs" along with rapidly increasing costs of producing these sports and a budgetary crisis caused by an economic downturn that has affected both public and private institutions. These economic forces have made it challenging to maintain an effective NCAA enforcement process and a level playing field among Division I Football Bowl Series football and men's basketball teams, while ensuring that student-athletes continue to have an opportunity to obtain an education.

52. University presidents now have primary control of the legislative and administrative processes within the NCAA and athletic conferences. The current and past presidents of the NCAA (Mark Emmert and Myles Brand, respectively) were formerly university presidents. In recent years university presidents became increasingly concerned with cost containment and ensuring that academic values continue to be central to the governance of inter-collegiate athletics. The pressure to produce income largely through the revenue-producing sports of Division I Football Bowl Series football and men's basketball (at some institutions other sports such as women's basketball also produce net revenues) has made it difficult to ensure that academic values predominate. Although the presidents and others have successfully implemented academic reforms that are helping to increase the graduation rates of student-athletes participating in football and men's basketball, cost containment efforts (which are constrained by the federal antitrust laws) have been largely unsuccessful.

53. Intercollegiate athletics is intended to be an extracurricular activity for talented students who attend college for the primary purpose of earning a degree. More than 460,000 student-athletes participate in intercollegiate athletics at NCAA colleges and universities, which provides them with significant academic and future career benefits. As articulated by former NCAA president Myles Brand:

> Participation in athletics has educational developmental value. Student-athletes learn to strive for excellence, to work hard and to work in teams, to be resilient and to persist. A college education should do more than increase disciplinary learning through lectures and textbooks; it should also develop in students the values and character necessary for a successful life and for good citizenship. Participation in college athletics is one very good means to meet these developmental needs.[28]

54. The NCAA"s objective is "to maintain intercollegiate athletics as an integral part of the educational program and the athlete as an integral part of the student body and, by so doing, retain a clear line of demarcation between intercollegiate athletics and professional sports."[29] According to the NCAA, "[s]tudent-athletes shall be amateurs in an intercollegiate sport, and their participation should be motivated primarily by education and by the physical, mental and social benefits to be derived. Student participation in intercollegiate athletics is an avocation, and student-athletes should be protected from exploitation by professional and commercial enterprises."[30]

55. For most sports and most students, this amateur/educational model of intercollegiate athletics still applies. However, today's economic realities have reshaped this idealistic model for sports such as NCAA Division I men's basketball and Football Bowl Subdivision (FBS) football because the tremendous popularity of these sports creates a substantial revenue-generating capacity that has been exploited by television for the benefit of schools that sponsor these sports. In many respects, NCAA universities that offer football and/or basketball at these levels of competition effectively serve as a cost-free system of player development for the NFL and NBA by providing the training environment and playing field for talented football and basketball players to hone their athletic skills for future professional careers. This trend toward commercialism in big-time athletics has continued until today, and intercollegiate athletics is now a multibillion-dollar industry.

56. In August 2014, the NCAA Division I Board of Directors approved a new governance structure that provided the Atlantic Coast Conference, Big Ten Conference, Big Twelve Conference, Pac 12 Conference, and SEC Conference (the "Power Five" conferences because their intercollegiate athletic programs generate the most revenues) with more autonomy. There are two ways in which autonomous legislation applying only to these five conferences can be enacted: 1) When 60% of their collective member institutions (48 votes) and a majority of institutions in three of these five conferences vote for the proposal; or 2) When a simple majority of all member institutions vote for the proposal and a simple majority of institutions in four of the five conferences vote for the proposal. Pursuant to this new autonomy, the Power Five conferences

---

28. . Myles Brand, *Money Not Corruptive If Actions Uphold Collegiate Mission*, the NCAA News 4 (Apr. 25, 2005).
29. 2016–17 NCAA Division I Manual Art. 1.3.1 (2016) [hereinafter NCAA Manual].
30. NCAA Manual, Art. 2.9.

have enacted student-athlete welfare legislation, which includes increasing the economic value of athletic scholarships to the full cost of attendance at their respective institutions.

§2. Internal Regulatory Structure, Governance, and Administrative Processes

57. In an effort to preserve the amateur nature of intercollegiate sports as a component part of higher education and to ensure competitive balance among its members on the playing field, the NCAA exercises plenary power over its members' intercollegiate athletics programs and enacts extensive and detailed rules. For example, it has adopted rules for the recruiting and academic eligibility of student-athletes; standards of amateurism and limitations on financial aid; regulations concerning permissible training, practices, and games; and numerous other requirements applicable to its member universities and student-athletes who participate in intercollegiate athletics. Through its rule-making and enforcement processes, the NCAA controls most essential aspects of the production of intercollegiate athletic competition. The NCAA also sponsors championships in both men's and women's sports, markets its name and logos, and sells the television and radio broadcasting rights for its championship events. In addition, the NCAA's Competitive Safeguards and Medical Aspects of Sports Committee publish a sports medicine handbook that provides guidelines and some requirements for protecting the health and safety of student-athletes and minimizing their risk of serious injury while participating in intercollegiate athletics.

58. Much of the NCAA's rule-making and enforcement efforts have focused on regulating the often fierce competition among member schools for the services of outstanding high school athletes, particularly for the high-revenue-generating sports of football and basketball, and the increasing commercialism of intercollegiate athletics. The current economic realities of intercollegiate sports have spurred a spending spree as universities engaged in "big-time" intercollegiate athletics seek the substantial monetary rewards that come with winning. This economically induced and often insatiable desire to win has led to a corresponding proliferation of NCAA rules violations, along with enforcement actions and sanctions against member universities for their misconduct.

59. Today the NCAA wields regulatory authority over an extremely heterogeneous group of members. There is a marked disparity in the approximately 1,200 individual member schools' total student enrolment, number of intercollegiate sports offered, number of participating intercollegiate athletes, and athletic department budgets. Relatively few university athletic departments—all of which have nationally renowned and popular FBS football programs—generate sufficient revenues to cover their expenses. Despite these significant disparities in athletic department resources, membership in the NCAA is unquestionably an economic necessity if a school desires to participate in "big-time" intercollegiate athletics. Non-members cannot compete in NCAA championship events, do not have the prestige and visibility to consistently attract a large number of quality athletes to their programs, and do not generate the substantial economic revenues from gate receipts and television contracts that NCAA schools do.

60. The NCAA's member universities are contractually bound to follow NCAA rules (which they have a voice and vote in making); to educate their student-athletes, coaches, athletic department personnel, alumni, and representatives of an its athletics interests about NCAA rules; to monitor compliance; and to self-report all rules violations to the NCAA's enforcement staff. They also are required to adhere to NCAA internal rules interpretation and application decisions as well as to accept sanctions for rules violations. Many NCAA rules and regulations are specifically directed toward and indirectly govern the conduct of student-athletes, coaches, athletic department personnel, alumni, and representatives of an institution's athletics interests even though these parties are not members of the NCAA and lack effective representation in the NCAA's rule-making and enforcement process. This indirect regulation is effective because colleges and universities, as part of the NCAA rules enforcement and sanctioning process, may be required not to associate with student-athletes, coaches, boosters, and alumni found to violate NCAA rules.

61. The NCAA has a large administrative enforcement staff at its Indianapolis, Indiana headquarters that investigates and prosecutes rules violations on behalf of its member institutions. Among other things, NCAA rules prohibit academic fraud, unethical conduct, and the provision of an "extra benefit," which is any benefit not expressly permitted by NCAA regulations, to a student-athlete. In general, in order to maintain their "amateur" eligibility to compete in intercollegiate athletics, the only permissible economic benefits that student-athletes are those permitted by NCAA rules. All representatives of member institutions are required to cooperate fully with the NCAA's enforcement staff in connection with its investigation of rules violations.

62. In 1954, to ensure fairness and a level playing field in intercollegiate athletics, the NCAA formed the Committee on Infractions (COI) to interpret NCAA rules and impose penalties on member institutions for rules violations. Concerns were frequently raised regarding the manner in which the COI enforced the rules against member institutions. To address these concerns, a Special Committee to Review the National Collegiate Athletic Association Enforcement and Infractions Process issued a report in 1991 that included a series of recommended reforms designed to bring greater fairness to the NCAA's rules enforcement and infractions processes. The establishment of an internal appellate body, the Infractions Appeals Committee (IAC), was based on one of these recommendations.

63. The mission of the NCAA rules enforcement program is:

> to eliminate violations of NCAA rules and impose appropriate penalties should violations occur. The program is committed to fairness of procedures and the timely and equitable resolution of infractions cases. The achievement of those objectives is essential to the conduct of a viable and effective enforcement program. Further, an important consideration in imposing penalties is to provide fairness to uninvolved student-athletes, coaches, administrators, competitors and other institutions.[31]

64. The COI, the majority of whose members are full-time employees of NCAA member institutions along with some independent representatives of the public, hears

31. . NCAA Bylaw 19.01.1.

cases involving alleged violations of NCAA rules that are not resolved by summary disposition. It makes findings of fact, determines whether violations have been committed by an NCAA member institution, and if so, imposes sanctions. The possible range of sanctions includes a public reprimand and censure; a period of probation; a ban on NCAA postseason championship competition in the subject sport(s); limits on the number of athletic scholarships that may be awarded to student-athletes; limits on off-campus recruiting of student-athletes; disciplinary action against student-athletes, coaches, or other athletic department personnel; fines; and dissociation from a representative of the university's athletics interest. A university's history of NCAA rules violations is an aggravating factor, which when warranted by the particular circumstances, may subject it to the "death penalty" (i.e., a prohibition against participation in a sport for one or more years). This severe penalty historically has been rarely imposed

65. The IAC, whose members consist of NCAA member institution employees (many of whom are law professors) and two public members (often lawyers) functions as an internal appellate body. The IAC may set aside the COI's finding of an NCAA rules violation if: (1) the finding is clearly contrary to the evidence presented to the committee; (2) the facts found do not constitute a violation; or (3) a procedural error affected the reliability of the information that was used to support the finding.[32] The IAC is authorized to reduce or vacate a sanction that is excessive or inappropriate based on all the evidence and circumstances in a particular case.[33]

66. NCAA Divisions I, II, and III have separate rules enforcement and infractions processes, but each division has the same COI and IAC adjudication structure, which includes a wide variety of NCAA member institution employees as well as athletic conference personnel and public representatives (most of whom are attorneys) serve on these committees. Virtually all institutions choose to be represented by legal counsel in proceedings before the COI and IAC. Many institutions are represented by their own internal university legal counsel and by outside law firms.

67. On October 30, 2012, the Board of Directors for Division I adopted major reforms to the Division I rules infractions structure and process, which became effective on August 1, 2013. This reform effort is designed to strengthen a culture among head coaches, the compliance community, institutional leadership, and conferences to assume a shared responsibility for upholding the values of intercollegiate athletics. The new penalty structure provides a four-tier violation hierarchy that ranges from severe breaches of conduct to incidental infractions, which replaces the current two-tier approach (major and secondary violations), with an approach that designates four levels of violations. Level I (severe breach of conduct) is used to designate "[v]iolations that seriously undermine or threaten the integrity of the NCAA collegiate model as set forth in the Constitution and bylaws, including any violation that provides or is intended to provide a substantial or extensive recruiting, competitive or other advantage, or a substantial or extensive impermissible benefit." A university's "lack of institutional control" over its intercollegiate athletics program is a Level I violation that is likely to be harshly punished. Level II (significant breach of conduct), consists of "[v]iolations that provide or are intended to provide more than a minimal but less than a substantial

32. . NCAA Bylaw 32.10.2.
33. . *Ibid.*

or extensive recruiting, competitive or other advantage … or … conduct that may compromise the integrity of the NCAA collegiate model as set forth in the Constitution and bylaws." and encompasses a university's failure to monitor to ensure compliance with NCAA rules. Level III (breach of conduct) consists of "[v]iolations that are isolated or limited in nature; provide no more than a minimal recruiting, competitive or other advantage; and do not include more than a minimal impermissible benefit. Multiple Level IV violations may collectively be considered a breach of conduct." Level IV (incidental issues) consists of "[m]inor infractions that are inadvertent and isolated, technical in nature and result in a negligible, if any, competitive advantage. Level IV infractions generally will not affect eligibility for intercollegiate athletics."[34]

68. Written COI and IAC case decisions are published on the NCAA website at ncaa.org. These cases collectively constitute a growing body of private law that internally governs intercollegiate athletics and has increased the role of lawyers in the NCAA rules compliance and enforcement processes. There is a significant body of scholarly commentary regarding the NCAA's rules enforcement process.[35]

69. Despite its broad constitutional power to regulate interstate commercial activity, the US Congress has not enacted any specific national laws that directly regulate the NCAA. However, some states such as Nevada have passed legislation that would impose certain procedural and fairness requirements on the NCAA's rules enforcement process. To prevent potentially conflicting state legislation from interfering with the NCAA's ability to govern intercollegiate athletics uniformly throughout the U.S., courts have ruled these laws violate the U.S. Constitution's Dormant Commerce Clause, which generally prohibits extraterritorial state regulation of interstate commercial activity, including intercollegiate athletics.[36]

---

34. . NCAA, *New Reform Efforts Take Hold August 1*, available at http://www.ncaa.org/about/resources/media-center/news/new-reform-efforts-take-hold-august-1.

35. . *See* , e.g., Jerry R. Parkinson, Scoundrels: An Inside Look at the NCAA Infractions and Enforcement Processes, 12 Wyo. L. Rev. 215 (2012); Josephine (Jo) R. Potuto, Jerry R. Parkinson, If It Ain't Broke, Don't Fix It: An Examination of the NCAA Division I Infractions Committee's Composition and Decision-Making Process, 89 Neb. L. Rev. 437 (2011); Maureen A. Weston, NCAA Sanctions: Assigning Blame Where It Belongs, 52 B.C. L. Rev. 551 (2011); Glenn Wong et al., The NCAA's Infractions Appeals Committee: Recent Case History, Analysis and the Beginning of A New Chapter, 9 Va. Sports & Ent. L.J. 47 (2009); Gene A. Marsh, A Call for Dissent and Further Independence in the NCAA Infractions Process, 26 Cardozo Arts & Ent. L.J. 695 (2009).

36. . *NCAA v. Miller*, 10 F.3d 633 (9th Cir. 1993) (invalidating a Nevada statute requiring "any national collegiate athletic association to provide a Nevada institution, employee, student-athlete, or booster who is accused of a rules infraction with certain procedural due process protections during an enforcement proceeding in which sanctions may be imposed" because it "would force the NCAA to regulate the integrity of its product in every state according to Nevada's procedural rules").

§3. Judicial Regulation of Intercollegiate Athletics

70. In *NCAA v. Tarkanian,*[37] the U.S. Supreme Court ruled that the NCAA is a private association rather than a "state actor"; therefore, NCAA rules and conduct are not subject to the constraints of the federal constitution. Because it is a private association, courts generally provide considerable deference to the NCAA's broad authority to govern intercollegiate athletics. However, courts will require the NCAA to follow its own rules, to apply them in a consistent and non-arbitrary manner, to provide notice and a fair hearing to those accused of violating its rules before imposing disciplinary sanctions, and to comply with applicable federal and state public laws.[38]

71. Although it is a non-profit association and its members are educational institutions, the NCAA is subject to the federal antitrust laws, which are difficult for courts to apply in a principled manner to alleged anticompetitive conduct[39] arising out of its governance of intercollegiate athletics. Antitrust litigation against the NCAA generally has been brought under §1 of the Sherman Act,[40] which provides that "[e] very contract, combination … or conspiracy in restraint of trade or commerce" is illegal. The NCAA also must comply with §2 of the Sherman Act,[41] which prohibits monopolization or attempts to monopolize interstate trade or commerce, although few §2 claims have been brought against the NCAA (generally without success).[42]

72. The collective adoption and enforcement of NCAA rules by its member universities as well as other agreements concerning the production, marketing, and regulation of intercollegiate athletics constitutes concerted action for purposes of §1 of the Sherman Act. As a result, virtually all NCAA rules and agreements among NCAA members are potentially subject to antitrust challenge. However, §1's broad statutory language has been judicially interpreted to prohibit only unreasonable restraints of trade that have adverse economic effects.

73. In *NCAA v. Bd. of Regents of the Univ. of Oklahoma,*[43] the Supreme Court held that NCAA limits on the total number of televised college football games (which also fixed the price of their broadcasting rights) violate §1. The Court found that the

37. . 488 U.S. 179 (1988).
38. . *See* , e.g., *California State Univ., Hayward v. NCAA*, 121 Cal. Rptr. 85, 88–89 (Cal. App. 1975) ("[i]t is true that courts will not interfere with the disciplining or expelling of members of such associations where the action is taken in good faith and in accordance with its adopted laws and rules. But if the decision of the tribunal is contrary to its laws and rules, it is not authorized by the bylaws of the association, a court may review the ruling of the board and direct the reinstatement of the member. … ").
39. . The purpose of the U.S. antitrust laws is to preserve a competitive marketplace that furthers consumer welfare by resulting in lower prices, better products, and more efficient methods of production than would occur absent vigorous economic competition.
40. . 15 U.S.C. §1.
41. . 15 U.S.C. §2.
42. . *See* , e.g., *Ass'n of Intercollegiate Athletics for Women v. NCAA*, 735 F.2d 577 (D.C. Cir. 1984) (rejecting allegation that NCAA unlawfully used its monopoly regulatory power over men's intercollegiate sports to facilitate its entry into the regulation of women's intercollegiate sports and to force the Association of Intercollegiate Athletics for Women, a competing national governing body, out of existence).
43. . 468 U.S. 85 (1984).

NCAA's college football television plan restrained its member universities' freedom to negotiate and enter into their own television contracts and is a horizontal restraint (i.e., an "agreement among competitors on the way in which they will compete with one another"). Because intercollegiate athletics is "an industry in which horizontal restraints on competition are essential if the product is to be available at all," the Court applied the rule of reason, which requires fact-specific analysis of the net competitive effects of the challenged restraint. The NCAA restriction had the anticompetitive effect of artificially fixing the quantity and price of televised college football games by agreement, thereby precluding their quantity and price from being determined by free market competition. Acknowledging that the NCAA's interest in maintaining competitive balance among its members' college football teams is legitimate, the Court found that the television plan did not actually further this procompetitive objective and that there are less restrictive means of doing so. The Court observed that the NCAA "does not regulate the amount of money that any college may spend on its football programme, nor the way in which the colleges may use the revenues that are generated by their football programmes," so restraints on the number and price of its members' televised college football games will not further its goal of competitive balance.

74. In *Law v. NCAA*,[44] a federal appellate court ruled that fixed maximum salaries for Division I "restricted-earnings" basketball coaches established by an NCAA bylaw violate §1. Characterizing coaching services as a necessary input to produce intercollegiate athletic competition, the court analyzed the legality of this restraint under the same legal standard that *Board of Regents* applied to NCAA restraints on the sale of output (e.g., television rights). The *Law* court described this rule of reason standard as follows:

> Courts have imposed a consistent structure on rule of reason analysis by casting it in terms of shifting burdens of proof. Under this approach, the plaintiff bears the initial burden of showing that an agreement had a substantially adverse effect on competition. If the plaintiff meets this burden, the burden shifts to the defendant to come forward with evidence of the procompetitive virtues of the alleged wrongful conduct. If the defendant is able to demonstrate procompetitive effects, the plaintiff then must prove that the challenged conduct is not reasonably necessary to achieve the legitimate objectives or that those objectives can be achieved in a substantially less restrictive manner. Ultimately, if these steps are met, the harms and benefits must be weighed against each other in order to judge whether the challenged behavior is, on balance, reasonable.

75. Applying this standard to input market restraints, the court ruled that capping the salaries of "restricted-earnings" coaches below the level that free market competition previously had established is horizontal price-fixing with clear anticompetitive effects that are not justified by any countervailing procompetitive benefits. It concluded that "[t]he NCAA's cost containment justification is illegitimate because … [r]educing costs for member institutions, without more, does not justify the anticompetitive effects' of fixing the price of coaches' salaries." The court found "no evidence that limits on restricted-earning coaches" salaries would be successful in reducing deficits, let alone that such reductions were necessary to save college basketball" from being destroyed

44. . 134 F.3d 1010 (10th Cir. 1998).

by overspending. While recognizing that the NCAA's need to ensure competitive balance in intercollegiate athletics is a valid procompetitive justification, the court determined that the NCAA had not proven "the salary restrictions enhance competition, level an uneven playing field, or reduce coaching inequities" among its member schools.

76. On the other hand, in *Adidas America, Inc. v. NCAA*,[45] a federal district court ruled that NCAA limits on its members' potential sources of revenue (e.g., advertising rights) is not an antitrust violation. Adidas, a sporting goods manufacturer, alleged that an NCAA bylaw limiting the size of trademarks on player uniforms and equipment illegally restrains the sale of advertising and promotional rights by NCAA universities in violation of §1. The court found this to be non-commercial regulation not subject to the antitrust laws. Finding the bylaw's purpose to be protecting student-athletes from commercial exploitation and avoiding excessive advertising that could potentially interfere with the basic function of player uniforms, the court explained that the bylaw "is an incidental by-product of the NCAA's legitimate attempt to maintain the amateurism and integrity of college sports, and it does not economically benefit the NCAA or its member institutions."

77. Courts have uniformly held that disciplinary sanctions imposed on NCAA institutions and others such as coaches for violations of NCAA rules do not violate the antitrust laws.[46] In January 2013 the Commonwealth of Pennsylvania filed an antitrust suit against the NCAA, alleging that the unprecedented disciplinary sanctions imposed against Penn State University (including a USD 60 million dollar fine, four year ban on participation in postseason football games, football scholarship limitations) for the role of former university administrators and football coaches in a child molestation scandal constitute arbitrary and capricious punishment not reasonably related to the NCAA's legitimate objectives of maintaining the fairness and integrity of intercollegiate athletics competition in violation of §1 of the Sherman Act. In *Commonwealth of Pennsylvania v. NCAA*,[47] the court granted the NCAA's motion to dismiss this suit because "the complaint is devoid of allegations that [the NCAA] sought to regulate commercial activity or obtain any commercial advantage for itself by imposing sanctions on Penn State." The court observed that "Penn State is not a party to this action and takes no position in this litigation" and that "the complaint limits [its] review to the question of whether [Governor Corbett] has articulated a violation of federal antitrust law." It explained that the complaint "must point to harm directed at commercial activity of the type the Sherman Act is designed to address for §1 to apply to the NCAA's challenged conduct." It ruled this requirement is not satisfied merely by the Governor's allegations that the NCAA sanctions will cripple the ability of Penn State's football program to compete on the playing field or reduce its ability to generate revenues for the university.

45. . 40 F. Supp. 2d 1275 (D. Kan. 1999).
46. . *Bassett v. NCAA*, 528 F.3d 426 (6th Cir. 2008) (dismissing antitrust challenge to sanctions imposed on coach stemming from NCAA enforcement of rules governing recruiting, improper benefits to athletes, and academic fraud because "not within purview of antitrust law as it is not related to NCAA's commercial or business activities").
47. . 2013 WL 2450291(M.D. Pa.).

Chapter 4. Structure and Governance of Olympic Sports

§1. Historical Overview

78. Participation in Olympic, Paralympic, and other international athletic competitions is an important part of U.S. culture. Since the Modern Olympic Games began in 1896, the U.S. has hosted the Games of the Olympiad in 1904 (St. Louis), 1932 (Los Angeles), 1984 (Los Angeles), and 1996 (Atlanta) and the Winter Olympic Games in 1932 (Lake Placid), 1960 (Squaw Valley), 1980 (Lake Placid), and 2002 (Salt Lake City). The U.S. has entered teams each year the Olympic Games have been held with the exception of 1980, when the U.S. boycotted the Moscow Games to protest the Soviet Union's military invasion of Afghanistan. Since 1896, U.S. athletes and teams have won 2,515 medals in the Summer Games (1,023 gold, 788 silver, and 704 bronze) and 281 medals in the Winter Games (96 gold, 102 silver, and 83 bronze).

§2. Internal Regulatory Structure, Governance, and Administrative Processes

79. The USOC is the national Olympic committee authorized by the IOC to represent the U.S. in all matters relating to its participation in the Olympic Games. The USOC, a federally chartered corporation created by Congress, must comply with the Ted Stevens Olympic and Amateur Sports Act (Amateur Sports Act),[48] a federal law that provides a framework for governing Olympic sports in the U.S. It has a statutory obligation to ensure, directly or by delegation to the National Governing Body (NGB) for the various sports (which normally occurs) "the most competent representation possible" for the U.S. in each event of the Olympic, Paralympic, and Pan-American Games.[49] Its Mission is "[t]o support United States Olympic and Paralympic athletes in achieving sustained competitive excellence while demonstrating the values of the Olympic Movement, thereby inspiring all Americans."[50]

80. The Amateur Sports Act authorizes the USOC to select the NGB for each Olympic sport within the United States; this NGB is a member of the corresponding IF that governs the sport on a worldwide level. It gives the USOC exclusive jurisdiction over disputes involving national governing bodies. The Amateur Sports Act establishes arbitration as the procedure for finally resolving disputes regarding which organization

48. . 36 U.S.C. §220501 (2006).

49. . 36 U.S.C. §220503(4). The Stevens Act also requires the USOC to encourage participation opportunities for women, racial and ethnic minorities, and disabled athletes and to provide assistance necessary to achieve this objective. 36 U.S.C. §220503(12)-(14).

50. . United States Olympic Committee, Bylaws of the United States Olympic Committee, §2.1 (2013), available at http://www.teamusa.org/Footer/Legal/Governance-Documents (accessed Jan. 20, 2014).

is entitled to be the NGB for a particular sport, and the USOC is bound to accept a judicially valid confirmed arbitration award.[51]

81. To be eligible to be recognized by the USOC as the NGB for an Olympic sport, an amateur sports organization must provide all amateur athletes with an equal opportunity to participate "without discrimination on the basis of race, color, religion, sex, age, or national origin."[52] Each NGB has an affirmative duty to encourage and support athletic participation opportunities for women and those with disabilities.[53] An NGB's eligibility and participation criteria for U.S. athletes to participate in the Olympic, Paralympic, and Pan-American Games must be consistent with those of the IF for its sport.[54] Athletes must be allowed to compete in international amateur athletic competitions unless the organization conducting the competition does not meet the applicable sanctioning criteria.[55] The Amateur Sports Act requires the USOC to establish a procedure for investigating and resolving complaints by athletes alleging that an NGB has violated these requirements, which adversely affects her or her eligibility to compete.[56] As a condition of being recognized as an NGB, it must agree to submit to binding arbitration to resolve athlete eligibility disputes. If the USOC finds that an NGB is not in compliance with these requirements, it is authorized to place the NGB on probation or revoke its recognition.

§3. Judicial Regulation of Olympic Sports

82. A U.S. athlete has no federal constitutional right to participate in the Olympic Games, Paralympic Games, Pan-American Games, and world championship competitions, which are defined as "protected competitions" under the Amateur Sports Act.[57] In *DeFrantz v. United States Olympic Committee*,[58] a group of athletes selected to be members of the U.S. Olympic team sought injunctive relief enabling them to compete in the 1980 Moscow Olympic Games. The Carter Administration urged a boycott of the Moscow Games to protest the Soviet Union's 1979 invasion of Afghanistan. Faced with political pressure from the federal government, threatened legal action by President Carter, and the possible loss of its federal funding and federal tax exemption, the USOC decided not to enter an American team in the Moscow Games. The court found that, under IOC rules, the USOC has the exclusive and discretionary authority to decide whether to enter a U.S. team in Olympic competition. The court held that, despite being federally chartered, the USOC is a private organization rather than a state actor; therefore, its conduct is not subject to the constraints of the U.S. Constitution. Even

51. . *United States Wrestling Federation v. Wrestling Division of the AAU, Inc.*, 545 F. Supp. 1053 (N.D. Ohio 1982).
52. . 36 U.S.C. §220522(a)(8). However, an NGB has no authority to regulate high school or college athletic competition. 36 U.S.C. §220526(a).
53. . 36 U.S.C. §220524(6)-(7).
54. . 36 U.S.C. §220522(a)(14).
55. . 36 U.S.C. §220524(5).
56. . 36 U.S.C. §220509 (a).
57. . 36 U.S.C. §220509 (a).
58. . 492 F. Supp. 1181 (D.D.C. 1980).

if the USOC's decision constituted state action, the court ruled that athletes have no federal constitutional right to participate in the Olympic Games.

83. In *San Francisco Arts & Athletics, Inc. v. United States Olympic Committee*,[59] the U.S. Supreme Court subsequently confirmed that the USOC is not a state actor. Consistent therewith, lower courts have held that an NGB is not a state actor.[60]

84. The Amateur Sports Act[61] does not create any substantive athletic participation rights that athletes can enforce in a private litigation against the USOC or an NGB.[62] Therefore, courts generally hold that athletes have no private right of action under the Amateur Sports Act and do not recognize claims against the USOC or NGBs seeking injunctive relief or judicial orders regarding their eligibility to compete in "protected competitions."[63] As one federal appellate judge remarked, "there can be few less suitable bodies than the federal courts for determining the eligibility, or the procedures for determining the eligibility, of athletes to participate in the Olympic Games."[64]

85. Consistent with this view, federal courts have ruled that the Amateur Sports Act immunizes an NGB from antitrust liability for rules and decisions that adversely affect an athlete's eligibility to participate in a protected competition. In *Behagen v. Amateur Basketball Ass'n of United States*,[65] the Tenth Circuit noted that the statute expressly authorizes only one NGB to represent the U.S. within each IF and to recommend to the USOC individual athletes and teams to represent the U.S. in the sports it governs. It ruled that implied antitrust immunity is necessary because: "[t]he Act makes clear that Congress intended an NGB to exercise monolithic control over its particular amateur sport, including coordinating with the appropriate international

---

59. . 483 U.S. 522 (1987).
60. . *Behagen v. Amateur Basketball Ass'n of U.S.*, 884 F.2d 524 (10th Cir. 1989); *Harding v. United States Figure Skating Ass'n*, 851 F. Supp. 1476 (D. Ore. 1994), *vacated on other grounds*, 879 F. Supp. 1053 (1995).
61. . In 1998, the original Amateur Sports Act was renamed the Ted Stevens Olympic and Amateur Sports Act and, *inter alia*, amended to expressly provide that, although the USOC may sue and be sued in federal court, nothing in the Act "shall create a private right of action." 36 U.S.C. §220505(b)(9).
62. . *See* , e.g., *Slaney v. IAAF*, 244 F.3d 580 (7th Cir. 2001).
63. . *Martinez v. U.S. Olympic Comm.*, 802 F2d 1275 (10th Cir. 1986); *Oldfield v. Athletic Congress*, 779 F.2d 505 (9th Cir. 1985); *Michels v. USOC*, 741 F.2d 155 (7th Cir. 1984); *Lee v. U.S. Taekwondo Union,* 331 F. Supp.2d 1252 (D. Haw. 2004). But *see* *Sternberg v. USA Nat'l Karate-Do Fed'n, Inc.*, 123 F. Supp.2d 659 (E.D.N.Y. 2000) (athlete allegedly excluded from participating in a protected competition because of her sex has an implied private right of action for damages against an NGB for violating the Stevens Act's prohibition against gender discrimination).
64. . *Michels,* 741 F.2d at 159 (J. Posner, concurring). *See also Abdallah v. U.S. Ass'n of Taekwondo, Inc.*, 2007 WL 2710489 (S.D. Tex. 2007).
65. . 884 F.2d 524 (10th Cir. 1989).

sports federation and controlling amateur eligibility for Americans that participate in sport."[66]

86. In *Gold Medal LLC v. USA Track & Field,*[67] a federal district court ruled that USOC and USA Track & Field regulations restricting commercial advertising on athlete apparel during the Olympic Trials are immune from antitrust challenge because by giving USOC exclusive control over the Olympic marks, "Congress intended to enable the USOC to raise money with which to finance the U.S. Olympic Team").

87. The Amateur Sports Act, which requires that all amateur athletes be given an equal opportunity to participate in protected competitions without discrimination, does not expressly nullify or supersede any applicable federal civil rights statutes that protect Olympic sport athletes against prohibited disability,[68] gender,[69] race,[70] and religious discrimination.[71] However, even if an award of damages against the USOC or an NGB is an appropriate remedy for civil rights violations, courts generally refuse to grant requested injunctive relief that would interfere with the USOC's exclusive jurisdiction regarding all matters relating to eligibility to participate in the Olympics or other protected competitions.[72]

88. Courts have ruled that the Amateur Sports Act preempts state law claims by athletes arising out of eligibility disputes regarding protected competitions except for a breach of contract action to require the USOC or an NGB to follow its own internal dispute resolution procedures.[73] American judges recognize the need for a uniform national procedure for resolving athlete eligibility issues, which is necessary to further Congress' "grant of exclusive jurisdiction to the USOC over all matters pertaining to United States participation in the Olympic Games."[74] Thus, "only a very

---

66. . *See also JES Properties, Inc. v. USA Equestrian, Inc.*, 458 F.3d 1224 (11th Cir. 2006); *Eleven Line, Inc. v. North Texas State Soccer Ass'n, Inc.*, 213 F.3d 198 (5th Cir. 2000). But *see TYR Sport Inc. v. Warnaco Swimwear Inc.*, 679 F. Supp.2d 1120 (C.D. Cal. 2009) (USA Swimming has no implied antitrust immunity from claim it conspired with Speedo, a corporate sponsor, to exclusively promote, to disparage a competing manufacturer's high-end competitive swimwear, and to persuade Olympic-caliber swimmers to switch to Speedo's "LZR Racer" suit).
67. 2016 WL 2757976 (D. Ore.).
68. . *Shepherd v. USOC*, 464 F. Supp.2d 1072 (D. Colo. 2006), *aff'd, Hollonbeck v. USOC*, 513 F.3d 1191 (10th Cir. 2008).
69. . *Sternberg v. USA Nat'l Karate-Do Fed'n, Inc.*, 123 F. Supp.2d 659 (E.D.N.Y. 2000).
70. . *Lee v. U.S. Taekwondo Union*, 331 F. Supp.2d 1252 (D. Haw. 2004).
71. . *Akiyama v. United States Judo Inc.*, 181 F. Supp.2d 1179 (W.D. Wash. 2002).
72. . *See* e.g., *Gatlin v. USADA*, 2008 WL 2567657 (N.D. Fla. 2008); *Lee*, 331 F. Supp.2d at 1260, n. 2. As one court observed, although the Stevens Act requires the USOC and its NGBs to submit unresolved eligibility disputes to binding arbitration, the statute does not require an athlete to do so. *Sternberg*, 123 F. Supp. at 666. Although a court must give effect to both the Amateur Sports Act and a federal civil rights statute if they can be reconciled, judicial application of a federal civil rights law to resolve the merits of an eligibility dispute would conflict with the Stevens Act's grant of exclusive authority to the USOC in such matters. Arbitration, not judicial intervention, is the best means of finally resolving the merits of all athlete eligibility disputes in a timely and efficient manner.
73. . *Pliuskaitis v. USA Swimming, Inc.*, 2017 WL 963202 (D. Utah); *Harding v. U.S. Figure Skating*, 851 F. Supp. 1476 (D. Ore. 1994), *vacated on other grounds*, 879 F. Supp. 1053 (D. Ore. 1995).
74. . *Slaney v. IAAF*, 244 F.3d 580, 594 (7th Cir. 2001), *cert. denied*, 534 U.S. 828 (2001).

specific claim will avoid the impediment to [a court's] subject matter jurisdiction" established by the Amateur Sports Act.[75]

89. In summary, courts hold that the Amateur Sports Act limits the nature and scope of judicial authority in athlete eligibility disputes. The role of the judicial system is to ensure that the USOC and NGBs follow their own rules and provide a minimum level of procedural due process consistent with this federal statute in connection with their internal dispute resolution procedures.[76] The merits of disputes regarding an athlete's eligibility to participate in the Olympic Games and other protected competitions are to be resolved by final and binding American Arbitration Association (AAA) arbitration, a process discussed in Part II, Chapter 3, *infra*, which has res judicata effect that bars the merits from being relitigated in a subsequent judicial proceeding.[77]

90. Pursuant to a series of agreements among the parties, the USOC and its NGBs are required to adopt, apply, and enforce IOC and IF rules that determine or affect American athletes' eligibility to qualify for, or participate in, Olympic or other international sports competitions. For example, the USOC and NGBs must comply with the IOC Charter's athlete eligibility requirements and antidiscrimination provisions protecting athlete participation opportunities. They also must comply with Court of Arbitration for Sport (CAS) awards resolving issues concerning the eligibility of American athletes that arise in connection with the Olympic Games or in disputes with an IF or the World Anti-Doping Agency (WADA). Arbitration before the CAS generally is the agreed forum for resolving eligibility disputes between a U.S. athlete and the IOC or an IF.

91. The New York Convention on the Enforcement of Foreign Arbitration Awards,[78] a treaty to which the U.S. is a party, requires U.S. courts to recognize and enforce valid foreign arbitration awards, including CAS awards that U.S. sports

75. . *Ibid.*, at 595. In *Harding*, a federal district court held that judicial intervention in athlete eligibility disputes: "is appropriate only in the most extraordinary circumstances, where the association has clearly breached its own rules, that breach will imminently result in *serious* and irreparable harm to the plaintiff, and the plaintiff has exhausted all internal remedies. Even then, injunctive relief is limited to correcting the breach of the rules. The court should not intervene in the merits of the underlying dispute." *Harding*, 851 F. Supp. at 1478 (emphasis original). *See USA Track & Field, Inc. v. Leach*, 2016 WL 6584699 (S.D. Ind.) (court refuses to intervene in parties" dispute and grant injunctive relief before pending NGB administrative proceeding has "run its course to a final decision").

76. . The Amateur Sports Act, in relevant part, provides: "In any lawsuit relating to the resolution of a dispute involving the opportunity of an amateur athlete to participate in the Olympic Games, the Paralympic Games, or the Pan-American Games, a court shall not grant injunctive relief against [the USOC] within 21 days before the beginning of such games if [the USOC], after consultation with the chair of the Athletes" Advisory Council, has provided a sworn statement in writing to such court that its constitution and bylaws cannot provide for the resolution of such dispute prior to the beginning of such games." 36 U.S.C. §220509 (a). As one court observed, this statutory provision "is designed to prevent a court from usurping the USOC's powers when time is too short for its own dispute resolution machinery to do its work." *Lindland v. USA Wrestling Ass'n*, 227 F.3d 1000, 1007 (7th Cir. 2000).

77. *Pliuskaitis v. USA Swimming, Inc.*, 2017 WL 963202 (D. Utah).

78. . 9 U.S.C. §201.

organizations or athletes are parties thereto. In *Slaney v. IAAF*,[79] the Seventh Circuit held that a valid foreign arbitration award precludes an American athlete from relitigating the merits of an eligibility dispute in a U.S. court. The court concluded that "[o]ur judicial system is not meant to provide a second bite at the apple for those who have sought adjudication of their disputes in other forums and are not content with the resolution they received." Moreover, a U.S. court may be unable to provide effective relief to an American athlete whose eligibility to participate in sports competition is adversely affected by an IOC or IF rule or decision because its judicial authority is not binding on foreign sports governing bodies outside its jurisdiction.[80]

79. . *Slaney v. IAAF*, 244 F.3d 580 (7th Cir. 2001).

80. . *See* , e.g., *Michels v. U.S. Olympic Comm.*, 741 F.2d 155, 159 (7th Cir. 1984) (noting that an IF "can thumb its collective nose" at the USOC and ask the IOC to disqualify the entire U.S. Olympic weightlifting team if the USOC placed an athlete suspended by the IF on the team; *Gahan v. U.S. Amateur Confederation of Roller Skating*, 382 F. Supp.2d 1127 (D. Neb. 2005) (observing that a U.S. court is unable to effectively protect athletes from decisions of international sports governing bodies).

Chapter 5. Structure and Governance of Professional Sports

§1. Historical Overview

92. Sports as activities, diversions, and cohesive societal events have been a part of U.S. culture since the country's founding in 1776, but sports as professions, businesses, and industries are of more recent vintage. Along with the U.S. industrial revolution in the late 1800s, a sports revolution occurred as well. Recreational sports activity became a business, and business evolved into the modern twenty-first century professional sports industries, which are a significant part of the U.S. economy.

93. The sport of baseball, Americans' national pastime, was the pioneer for U.S. professional players, teams, and leagues. The Cincinnati Red Stockings baseball team is generally acknowledged as the first truly professional team, touring the country in 1869 and taking on all challengers. The National League, the first U.S. professional sports league, was founded in 1876 and is one of the two leagues that today comprise MLB.

94. Decades later than baseball, the other major professional sports leagues eventually emerged. The NHL was formed in 1918, although the "national" designation signified Canada, not the U.S. The first U.S. team, the Boston Bruins, did not join the league until 1924. Today, the number of U.S. clubs significantly exceeds that of Canadian clubs. The NFL, which is currently the most popular U.S. sports league and generates the most revenues (estimated to be approximately USD 13 billion for the 2016 season; in 2016 the average value of an NFL franchise was an estimated USD 2.3 billion), began play in 1920 as the American Professional Football Conference. The NBA was founded in 1946 and was originally named the Basketball Association of America (BAA). Soccer, known to the rest of the world as "football," is truly global in its nature and fan appeal, more so than any other U.S. team sport. However, it has not achieved the same level of popularity as professional baseball, football, basketball, or hockey within the U.S. Although MLS has millions of hardcore supporters, it is not on par with the NFL, NBA, NHL, and MLB in terms of fan interest and revenues generated in the U.S.

95. Tennis and golf are two of the most popular individual performer sports in the U.S. These sports are more global than U.S. professional team sports because the top players in both sports are from throughout the world. Despite loyal and avid followings, the overall level of support for these individual performer sports pales in comparison to team sports in the U.S. Boxing is another sport that historically has had wide fan support, although its popularity has decreased significantly in recent years.

96. Auto racing currently is one of the country's most popular individual performer professional spectator sports. The first Indianapolis 500 Mile Race was held in 1911. The National Association of Stock Car Auto Racing (NASCAR) has been in existence since 1951. NASCAR and the Indy Racing League each sponsor an annual series of auto races at tracks throughout the U.S.

97. Three substantive areas of law, namely, contracts,[81] antitrust,[82] and labor law,[83] historically have been most important to the legal regulation of professional sports in the U.S. The chronology of professional sports leagues reveals a corresponding chronology as to the prevailing legal principles that have helped shape the development of the U.S. professional sports industries during particular periods of time. In the late 1800s and early 1900s state contract law was the body of law that had the most influence. Federal antitrust law concerns became an issue as early as the 1920s, but did not play a major role until the 1950s. Federal labor law first became important, at least as to team sports, in the late 1960s. From the 1970s to the present, the combination of contracts, antitrust, and labor law has significantly influenced the structure, governance, and development of the professional sports industries in the U.S., particularly professional sports leagues and associations. The law of private associations is another important area of state law that regulates the professional sports industries.

§2. Internal Regulatory Structure, Governance, and Administrative Processes

98. Each professional sports league or association has a constitution and bylaws, which establishes a central system of governance with one particular individual given substantial authority to oversee its general operation. This individual is often designated as the commissioner of that particular league or association. The constitution and bylaws, which is a private contract between the parties, constitute the primary authority for the governance of the league or association.

99. U.S. professional sports leagues such as the NFL, NBA, NHL, MLB, and MLS (all of them also have at least one club in Canada except the NFL, so these four leagues are transnational in scope.) as well as individual performer sports associations or governing bodies (e.g., PGA, LPGA) are private entities that are not subject to the constraints of the U.S. Constitution.[84] Courts recognize that private associations must be accorded considerable latitude in rule-making and enforcement in order to accomplish their legitimate objectives. They generally permit professional sports leagues and associations to establish their respective systems of self-governance and are reluctant to interfere with or second-guess their internal decision-making. Their members generally are bound by the terms of the sports league or association's constitution, bylaws, and other governing documents unless there is a breach of fiduciary duty, a conflict of interest, bad faith, or violation of applicable laws such as, for example, federal antitrust law. But otherwise there is broad discretion accorded to a sports league or association to interpret its own rules without judicial intervention,

100. Despite a general judicial reluctance to oversee a professional sports organization's affairs to avoid becoming mired down in areas outside their expertise, courts will provide a forum for resolution of internal governance disputes. At least at

---

81. . *See* Part I, Ch. 5, §2 and Part II, Ch. 4, §3.
82. . *See* Part I, Ch. 5, §3.
83. . Part II, Ch. 4 §2 I.
84. . *Long v. National Football League*, 870 F. Supp. 101 (W.D. Pa. 1994), *aff'd*, 66 F.3d 311 (3d Cir. 1994).

the major league level, a U.S. professional sports league is often without direct competition from another league. Because of the for-profit and monopolistic nature of major professional sports leagues and associations, there is a recognized need for some limited judicial oversight to prevent exploitation and blatant unfairness toward any of the organization's members or participants.

101. A professional sports governing body has a legal obligation to follow its own rules and bylaws; its failure to do so may give rise to a breach of contract claim by an aggrieved member whose interests are harmed. Courts will review the actions of professional sports organizations: "(1) where the rules, regulations or judgments of the association are in contravention to the laws of the land or in disregard of the charter or bylaws of the association and (2) where the association has failed to follow the basic rudiments of due process of law."[85] In addition, courts will intervene if an association's decision-making process is arbitrary or capricious, or is tainted by malice or bad faith. This will occur even if the aggrieved party, prior to the dispute in question, expressly waived its right to judicial recourse.

I. Individual Performer Sports

102. Courts will provide an independent governing body with broad discretion to interpret its own rules. In *Koszela v. National Association of Stock Car Auto Racing, Inc.*,[86] the Second Circuit rejected the claims of a stock car owner and driver that NASCAR misapplied its rules in determining that another car and driver were the winners of two races. The court found that the plaintiffs' membership contract with NASCAR did not provide for an administrative appeal or judicial review of official decisions regarding race procedures or determination of car positions. The court concluded that the plaintiffs had been given an opportunity to be heard by NASCAR officials and had exhausted all available rights. The court affirmed the dismissal of the plaintiffs' claims and held that NASCAR was not in violation of any contractual duties owed to the plaintiffs.

103. In a similar dispute regarding whether NASCAR violated its own procedures in determining the winner of a race, the same court ruled that the proper approach was to defer to an association's interpretation of its own rules absent a showing of bad faith or violation of any state or federal laws. In *Crouch v. National Association of Stock Car Auto Racing, Inc.*,[87] the Second Circuit initially drew a distinction between reviewing the decisions made by private organizations and reviewing the procedures used in reaching those decisions. It recognized the appropriateness of intervening if there were inadequate procedures to safeguard a member's rights, but the plaintiffs did not make any such assertions. Nor was there any allegation that NASCAR violated its own rules or that NASCAR officials acted in bad faith in reviewing the plaintiffs' challenge to the race results. The Second Circuit held that the lower court erred in delving into NASCAR's rulebook and conducting basically an inquiry de novo (i.e.,

85. . *Charles O. Finley & Co. v. Kuhn*, 569 F.2d 527, 544 (7th Cir.), *cert. denied*, 439 U.S. 876 (1978).
86. . 646 F.2d 749 (2d Cir. 1981).
87. . 845 F.2d 397 (2d Cir. 1988).

substituting its judgment for that of the governing body and deciding the merits of the dispute, rather than simply determining whether it complied with its own rules and rendered a reasonable decision).

104. On the other hand, *Gilder v. PGA Tour, Inc.*[88] illustrates that courts will intervene when individuals with vested interests breach their fiduciary duty when governing a professional sports association's affairs. The Ninth Circuit held that touring professional golfers serving on the PGA's board of directors (who had endorsement deals with manufacturers of V-shaped grooved irons) owe a fiduciary duty to act in the best interests of the association and are prohibited from using their position for potential personal gain. Their vote to amend the PGA bylaws' voting procedures, which resulted in U-shaped grooved irons being banned, breached this fiduciary duty.

II. Team Sports

105. The NFL, NBA, NHL, and MLB are each comprised of separate, independently owned and operated for-profit member clubs, which collectively produce their respective brands of athletic competition. Each league was formed in the late 1800s or early 1900s when a group of existing independent clubs banded together to play games against each other and govern their business affairs in an agreed centralized manner. Each league is autonomously governed, and each of their respective member clubs has a voice and vote concerning the league's constitution and bylaws, selection of the league commissioner, and significant internal league governance decisions such as league expansion, the purchase and sale of clubs, and franchise relocations. Unlike the prevailing model of European internal sports governance, there is no national federation that exercises plenary governing authority over all levels of professional competition for each sport within the U.S.

106. In *Professional Hockey Corp. v. World Hockey Association*,[89] a California appellate court ruled that each club's representative on the league's board of directors or governors "owes the league as a whole the traditional fiduciary duties in this commonly shared corporate purpose." It explained:

> The law requires, irrespective of the competitive personal feelings of the various owners of teams may have towards each other, when they or their representatives sit on the board of directors of World Hockey Association (WHA) to the extent they have common corporate goals, they have a duty to make decisions for the benefit of the corporation, the hockey league as a whole.

107. However, in *Oakland Raiders v. National Football League*,[90] another California appellate court subsequently held that the NFL's member clubs do not owe each other a fiduciary duty because they do not share profits and losses like a partnership. Because the NFL is organized as an unincorporated not-for-profit association of its member clubs, this case suggests that each club has no legal duty to place the league's

88. . 727 F. Supp. 1333 (D. Ariz. 1989), *aff'd*, 936 F.2d 417 (9th Cir. 1991).

89. . 191 Cal. Rptr. 773, 777 (Cal. Ct. App. 1983).

90. . 131 Cal. App.4th 621, 32 Cal. Rptr.3d 266 (Cal. App. 2005).

interests ahead of its individual interests in making league rules and governance decisions.

108. Even if a club does not owe a fiduciary duty to vote or act consistently with the league's best interests, courts have imposed implied covenants of good faith and fair dealing in contracts governing the internal affairs of professional sports leagues; for example, in a case arising out of an NFL club owner's request for league approval to relocate the franchise to another city. Applying California law, in *Los Angeles Memorial Coliseum Commission v. National Football League,*[91] the Ninth Circuit ruled that league teams owed each other a reciprocal duty "to refrain from doing anything to injure the right of the other to receive the benefits of the agreement … [and] the duty to do everything that the contract presupposes that he will do to accomplish the purpose." The court held that each club must exercise its contractual right of approval or disapproval and its discretionary power affecting the interests of other league clubs in good faith.

109. The U.S. major professional sports leagues have all adopted a model of organization and governance that places an independent commissioner in control of league internal affairs. This official is generally more powerful than a chairperson of the board of a corporation, and probably wields more power than a typical president of a company. Although selected by and answerable to the league owners and their governing body, a sports league commissioner traditionally has been accorded certain powers and attendant enforcement rights that create a special role.

110. The first commissioner in any sport was Judge Kenesaw Mountain Landis, who assumed that position for baseball in 1920 to ensure that the infamous Black Sox gambling and game fixing scandal arising out of the 1919 World Series would not recur. Reportedly, at his insistence, Judge Landis was accorded the authority to do whatever was necessary to protect the "best interests" of baseball. That same sweeping power—to act in the best interests of the sport—is found in similar terminology in the description of powers and duties vested in all commissioners of the U.S. major professional sports leagues. To that end, the commissioner is delegated disciplinary powers, dispute resolution authority, and decision-making responsibility. Although an employee of the league, the commissioner frequently is granted virtually autonomous authority to govern a significant extent of a league's affairs without direct supervision or control by the member clubs. The commissioner is hired by the owners and can be fired; however, his or her authority is difficult to challenge successfully in a judicial forum.

111. A league's commissioner is an integral part of the league's governance structure whose role often consists of the following functions:

(1) To create a fair and impartial internal authority to resolve disputes within the league and to enforce independently a disciplinary process—these being essential to maintain the game's integrity and provide rudimentary due process protections necessary to avoid judicial oversight of league affairs.
(2) To take action when needed to restrain the unwarranted exercise of power by the league's owners to the detriment of fans and others, again to avoid judicial intervention.

---

91. . 791 F.2d 1356, 1361 (9th Cir. 1986).

(3) To serve as a centralized administrative authority to facilitate efficient decision-making and league governance.
(4) To be a skilful mediator when owners cannot agree.
(5) To be the lead negotiator for league-wide contracts, such as the all-important television deals.
(6) At times, to become involved in labor disputes between the owners and the players—in fact, in some leagues, the commissioner is the lead negotiator on behalf of the owners.

112. Despite having the above powers, a league commissioner does not have unfettered independence or authority. At times, he or she must walk a tightrope to avoid undermining or losing his or her authority. The commissioner, for example, has certain disciplinary authority over the league's club owners and can make decisions adverse to some or even all of them and their interests. Even so, the commissioner's job security is subject to the will of these owners, and a commissioner may be put in the middle of disputes that pose threats to his position. A commissioner may feel compelled to compromise to avoid alienating owners, which could possibly reduce his or her authority or possibly jeopardize his or her continued employment. For example, MLB commissioner Fay Vincent resigned in August 1992 under pressure from MLB club owners after making a series of controversial decisions.

113. A sports league commissioner's authority is contractual in nature and derived from the league's constitution, bylaws, and operating rules. The most sweeping power that a league commissioner is typically granted is the ability to take action deemed necessary to further the best interests of the sport. Interpretation of the nature and scope of the commissioner's contractual authority ultimately is a question for judicial resolution, with courts usually providing substantial deference to the commissioner's judgment if the challenged conduct was contractually authorized.

114. In *Charles O. Finley & Co. v. Kuhn,*[92] a federal appellate court upheld the MLB commissioner's disapproval of the assignments of the contracts of three players by the Oakland Athletics MLB club to two other clubs "as inconsistent with the best interests of baseball, the integrity of the game and the maintenance of public confidence in it." The Commissioner expressed his concern for the debilitation of the Oakland club through the loss of three of its best players and the lessening of the competitive balance in MLB if the more affluent clubs were able to purchase another club's best players for cash. Observing that the commissioner has broad authority to prevent any act, transaction or practice not in the best interests of baseball, the court ruled that he "acted in good faith, after investigation, consultation and deliberation, in a manner which he determined to be in the best interests of baseball" and that "(w)hether he was right or wrong is beyond the competence and the jurisdiction of this court to decide."

115. Similarly, in *Oakland Raiders v. National Football League,*[93] a California court rejected the Oakland Raiders club's claim that the NFL and its commissioner took various actions that were discriminatory towards the Raiders and placed it at a competitive disadvantage vis-à-vis other member clubs. Finding that "the Raiders had

92. . 569 F.2d 527 (7th Cir.), *cert. denied,* 439 U.S. 876 (1978).
93. . 131 Cal. App.4th 621, 32 Cal. Rptr.3d 266 (Cal. App. 2005).

not shown any evidence of a violation of a clear and unambiguous provision of the NFL constitution," the court explained:

> We observe that the rationale of [judicial] abstention from intra-association disputes applies with particular force in this instance. Given the unique and specialized nature of this association's business – the operation of a professional football league – there is significant danger that judicial intervention in such disputes will have the undesired and unintended effect of interfering with the League's autonomy in matters where the NFL and its commissioner have much greater competence and understanding than the courts.

116. However, a court will require a league commissioner to have valid authority to act, to comply with rudimentary notions of due process, to not act in bad faith, and to not contravene any state or federal laws. Although a court will not second-guess a league commissioner's exercise of discretionary judgment, it will require that the commissioner have valid authority to take the challenged action. For example, in *Chicago National League Ball Club, Inc. v. Vincent*,[94] a federal district court held that the MLB commissioner could not order involuntary realignment of the teams in the National League pursuant to his "best interests of the game" authority. The Chicago Cubs successfully challenged Commissioner Vincent's authority to transfer the club to the Western Division of the National League. In 1992, ten National League clubs voted to realign their two divisions so that the Cubs and St. Louis Cardinals would move to the Western Division, and the Atlanta Braves and Cincinnati Reds would move to the Eastern Division. The Cubs and New York Mets voted against the proposed realignment. The National League Constitution required approval by three-fourths of the league's clubs for divisional realignment but provided that no club could be transferred to a different division without its consent. Nevertheless, acting upon the request of several National League clubs to intervene, Commissioner Vincent ordered the proposed realignment in accordance with his "best interests" power. The court preliminarily enjoined the commissioner's order from taking effect based on its finding that he exceeded his authority and impaired the Cubs' contract rights under the National League Constitution, which expressly gave the club the right not to be moved to another division without its consent.

117. When exercising disciplinary authority, courts require that a league commissioner provide due process to the party subject to sanctions. A party is entitled to notice of the alleged misconduct and a fair opportunity to be heard. The league's constitution generally establishes procedural safeguards or enables the commissioner to formulate rules necessary to satisfy the minimum requirements of due process in connection with a disciplinary proceeding. A league commissioner must follow established procedural rules when exercising disciplinary authority and act in an impartial and fair manner without prejudging the disciplinary matter before him. In *Rose v. Giamatti*,[95] a state trial judge temporarily enjoined the MLB commissioner

---

94. . 1992 WL 179208 (N.D. Ill. 1992).

95. . *See* No. A8905178, 1989 WL 111447 (Ct. Com. Pl. Ohio, Hamilton Co. 26 Jun. 1989). Commissioner Giamatti and Rose ultimately entered into a settlement agreement pursuant to which Rose accepted a lifetime suspension from baseball.

from holding a disciplinary hearing to determine whether Pete Rose, the manager of the Cincinnati Reds club, placed bets on MLB games based on evidence that the commissioner was prejudging Rose's guilt, thereby denying him a fair hearing.

§3. External Regulation of Professional Sports

118. In the U.S. there is no federal government body or sports minister that directly regulates individual performer or team professional sports. Although there are some statutes applicable to particular aspects of the professional sports industry,[96] there is no specific federal or state legislation that broadly regulates the U.S. professional sports industries. For the most part, generally applicable federal laws, particularly antitrust law, are the primary means by which the professional sports industries are externally regulated by public law.

I. Antitrust Law Limits on Internal Governance

119. The federal antitrust laws prohibit agreements and collective action that unreasonably restrain trade under §1 of the Sherman Act[97] in order to preserve a competitive marketplace that provides consumers with a wide variety of desired and affordable products and services. In order to produce professional sports competition, numerous agreements between and among a league, its member clubs, and its players are necessarily required, all of which are potentially subject to antitrust challenge under §1. However, traditional antitrust law jurisprudence does not provide a simple means of accurately measuring whether a professional sports league's rules or decisions enhance or harm consumer welfare as represented by the interests of sports fans. Because of the unique nature of professional sports (particularly team sports), it is very difficult for courts to apply §1 in a principled and consistent fashion.

120. Like any other business enterprise, the member clubs of a professional sports league collectively seek to maximize sales of product and profits. However, unlike members of other industries that sell the same product and compete among themselves for consumer support (e.g., oil companies), a professional sports league's member clubs do not have an economic self-interest to drive each other out of business. To the contrary, league clubs have an inherent economic interdependence because a single team cannot survive without other teams as on-field competitors. To further league members' collective economic interests, it is essential that competitive balance exist within the league and that the outcome of games be relatively uncertain to maintain fan interest in the league's product.

121. To offer an attractive product desirable to consumers, a professional sports league must maintain on-field competitive balance among its member teams and preserve the financial viability of each club. In an effort to achieve these objectives, league rules may either prohibit certain conduct by an individual club owner or require

96. . *See* , e.g., Sports Broadcasting Act of 1961,15 U.S.C. §§1291 et seq.; Curt Flood Act of 1998, 15 U.S.C. §26b.
97. . 15 U.S.C. §1.

its approval by a majority of other member clubs to avoid harming the league's collective economic interests. League rules or other clubs' collective decisions may limit an individual club owner's ability to sell or relocate the club, contract with third parties in an effort to maximize the team's revenues, or take other desired action. These rules and decisions have been challenged under §1, but a threshold issue to consider is whether there is an applicable antitrust immunity or exemption.

A. Baseball's Common Law Antitrust Immunity and Other Exemptions

122. In its first case considering the application of federal antitrust law to professional sports, *Federal Baseball Club of Baltimore, Inc. v. Nat'l League of Professional Baseball Clubs,*[98] the U.S. Supreme Court held that professional baseball games, although they constitute business activity, are "purely state affairs." Therefore, the antitrust laws, which regulate only interstate trade or commerce, are inapplicable.

123. In a 1953 case, *Toolson v. New York Yankees,*[99] the Supreme Court reaffirmed *Federal Baseball Club.* The Court reasoned that baseball had been allowed to develop for more than thirty years without being subject to the antitrust laws. The Supreme Court also observed that Congress had not eliminated baseball's antitrust exemption, thereby evidencing its intention that organized baseball not be covered by the antitrust laws.

124. In 1972 the Supreme Court acknowledged that professional baseball's national business activities are interstate in nature, but it continued to recognize its antitrust immunity. In *Flood v. Kuhn,*[100] the U.S. Supreme Court stated:

> Federal Baseball and Toolson have become an aberration confined to baseball. It is an aberration that has been with us now for half a century, one heretofore deemed fully entitled to the benefit of stare decisis, and one that has survived the Court's expanding concept of interstate commerce. It rests on a recognition and an acceptance of baseball's unique characteristics and needs. The Court has emphasized that since 1922 baseball, with full and continuing congressional awareness, has been allowed to develop and to expand unhindered by federal legislative action. Remedial legislation has been introduced repeatedly in Congress but none has ever been enacted. We continue to be loath, 50 years after Federal Baseball and almost two decades after Toolson, to overturn those cases judicially when Congress, by its positive inaction, has allowed those decisions to stand for so long and, far beyond mere inference and implication, has clearly evinced a desire not to disapprove them legislatively.

98. . 259 U. S. 200 (1922).
99. . 346 U.S. 356 (1953).
100. . 407 U.S. 258 (1972).

125. Most courts have broadly construed *Flood* to exempt all aspects of the "business of baseball" from the federal antitrust laws.[101] A notable recent exception is *Laumann v. NHL*,[102] in which the court declined "to apply the exemption to a subject that is not central to the business of baseball . . . namely baseball's contracts for television broadcast rights. Absent an applicable exemption, all other U.S. professional sports generally are subject to federal antitrust law because their respective business activities occur in interstate commerce.[103]

126. The Curt Flood Act of 1998 modifies the Sherman Act to provide Major League Baseball players with the same antitrust remedies as other professional athletes such as football and basketball players.[104] This federal statute gives MLB players the same right to sue under the antitrust laws concerning their employment terms as other professional athletes have in their sports,[105] but it does not provide minor league baseball players with this right.[106] It does not otherwise limit baseball's broad common law antitrust immunity.

127. The Sports Broadcasting Act (SBA) of 1961[107] expressly permits professional sports league clubs to pool and sell or transfer "all or any part of the rights of such league's member clubs in the sponsored telecasting of the games." Congress provided professional sports leagues with this limited antitrust exemption to protect their home game ticket sales, especially those of the weaker clubs, and to facilitate the sharing of television broadcast revenues among clubs, thereby preserving the league's competitive balance, product integrity, and existence. As one court observed, "The purpose of the SBA, as opposed to the purpose of the Sherman Act itself, was not to promote competition. It was to establish the legality of a practice which tends to restrain

---

101. . Courts have extended baseball's antitrust immunity to disputes concerning compensation of minor league franchises for harm to their assigned territories. *Portland Baseball Club, Inc. v. Kuhn*, 491 F. Supp. 1101 (9th Cir. 1974)); exercise of the Commissioner's "best interests of baseball authority" (*Charles O. Finley & Co., Inc. v. Kuhn*, 569 F.2d 527 (7th Cir. 1978)); the minor league player assignment system, franchise location system, and scheduling rules (*Professional Baseball Schools and Clubs, Inc. v. Kuhn*, 693 F.2d 1085 (11th Cir. 1982)); major league club owners' alleged unfair labor practices during players' strike (*McCoy v. Major League Baseball*, 911 F. Supp. 454 (W.D. Wash.1995)); Major League Baseball's alleged interference with a club's efforts to relocate (*City of San Jose v. MLB*, 766 F.3d 686 (9th Cir. 2015)); a state attorney general's investigation of a proposed sale and relocation of a baseball franchise (*Major League Baseball v. Christ*, 331 F.3d 1177 (11th Cir. 2003); *Minnesota Twins Partnership v. Hatch*, 592 N.W.2d 847(Minn. 1999)); a dispute between the Chicago Cubs and rooftop businesses surrounding Wrigley Field (*Right Field Rooftops LLC v. Chicago Baseball Holdings LLC*, 87 F. Supp. 3d 874, 883 (N.D. Ill. 2015)); and terms of a uniform contract for baseball scouts (*Wyckoff v. Office of Comm'r of Baseball*, 2016 WL 5478498 (S.D.N.Y.)).
102. 56 F. Supp. 3d 280 (S.D.N.Y. 2014).
103. . *See* , e.g., *Haywood v. NBA*, 401 U.S. 1204 (1971) (basketball); *Radovich v. National Football League*, 352 U.S. 445 (1957) (football); *U.S. v. Int'l Boxing Club of N.Y., Inc.*, 348 U.S. 236 (1955) (boxing).
104. . 15 U.S.C. §26b.
105. . 15 U.S.C. §27b(c). *See* Part II, Ch. 4, §2D for a discussion of its intersection with the nonstatutory labor exemption.
106. *Miranda v. Selig*, 2015 WL 5357854 (N.D. Cal.).
107. . 15 U.S.C. §1291, et seq.

competition, package sales to the networks."[108] The SBA does not define "sponsored telecasting," which has been narrowly construed by courts to encompass only free television such as "national network and local over-the-air broadcasting provided at no direct cost to viewers," but not satellite or cable television.[109]

128. In *Flood v. Kuhn*,[110] the Supreme Court held that the Supremacy and dormant Commerce Clauses of the U.S. Constitution bar state antitrust law regulation of organized baseball because of its exemption from federal antitrust law. The Court observed that national uniformity is necessary in connection with baseball's reserve system, and that state antitrust regulation would conflict with national antitrust policy.

129. Regarding sports other than baseball that are subject to federal antitrust regulation, courts generally hold that applying state antitrust laws to a professional sports league's interstate activities, such as labor disputes and franchise location issues, violates the dormant Commerce Clause. In *Partee v. San Diego Chargers Football Co.*, [111] the California Supreme Court explained:

> Professional football is a nationwide business. . . . The necessity of a nationwide league structure for the benefit of both teams and players for effective competition is evident as is the need for a nationally uniform set of rules governing the league structure. Fragmentation of the league structure on the basis of state lines would adversely affect the success of the competitive business enterprise, and differing state antitrust decisions if applied to the enterprise would likely compel all member teams to comply with the laws of the strictest state.

B. *Application of §1 of Sherman Act*

1. Concerted Action Requirement

130. The express language of Sherman Act §1 broadly prohibits "[e]very contract, combination in the form of trust or otherwise, or conspiracy" that restrains trade, which literally encompasses virtually all professional sports league rules (which are the product of the agreement among league clubs) and collective governance decisions by league clubs. Nevertheless, as a defense to Sherman Act §1 claims, professional sports leagues (particularly the NFL) have argued that the league and its member clubs collectively produce a single product (e.g., NFL football) that no individual club is

108. . *Chicago Prof'l Sports Limited Partnership v. NBA* (*Bulls I*), 754 F. Supp. 1336, 1352 (N.D. Ill. 1991), *aff'd*, 961 F.2d 667 (7th Cir. 1992).

109. . *Shaw v. Dallas Cowboys Football Club, Inc.*, 172 F.3d 299, 300 (3d Cir. 1999) (package sale of television broadcast rights to satellite distributor not "sponsored telecasting" immune from antitrust scrutiny); *Chicago Prof'l Sports Ltd. Partnership v. NBA* (*Bulls III*), 808 F. Supp. 646, 650 (N.D. Ill. 1992) ("sponsored telecasting not league's pooled television rights contract with cable television programming service").

110. 407 U.S. 258 (1972).

111. 668 P.2d 674, 678 (Cal. 1983).

capable of producing (which became known as the "single entity" defense).[112] Therefore, a professional sports league's rules and member clubs' collective decisions should not be subject to §1 because they are not economic competitors who produce separate products.

131. Some early cases simply assumed without deciding that professional sports league rules or agreements that allegedly reduce or eliminate intrabrand economic competition among league clubs are subject to §1.[113] In a 1975 case, *San Francisco Seals, Ltd. v. National Hockey League*,[114] a California federal district court implicitly accepted the single entity defense in ruling that the NHL's refusal to permit one of its clubs to relocate from San Francisco to Vancouver, British Columbia does not violate §1. The court concluded that, when producing NHL hockey, NHL clubs are "acting together as one single business enterprise, competing against other similarly organized professional leagues."

132. In the 1980s and 1990s most federal appellate courts rejected the single entity defense when directly raised by professional sports leagues in antitrust litigation. For example, in *North American Soccer League v. National Football League*,[115] the Second Circuit held that NFL teams are "separate economic entities engaged in a joint venture" and that the NFL's cross-ownership rule, which prohibits NFL club owners from having a controlling interest in any other major league professional sports team, is subject to antitrust challenge under §1. Rather than focusing on whether the NFL clubs are in fact economic competitors in the alleged relevant market that is restrained (e.g., professional sports capital and entrepreneurial skill), the Second Circuit found they are separately owned and operated legal entities that do not share expenses, capital expenditures, profits, or all revenues with each other.[116]

133. In *American Needle, Inc. v. National Football League*,[117] a 2010 case, the U.S. Supreme Court unanimously held that the NFL clubs' centralized and exclusive licensing of their individual trademarks through a wholly owned league subsidiary is not immune from judicial scrutiny under §1. The Court explained that the key inquiry is whether there is an agreement "amongst separate economic actors pursuing separate economic interests." In other words, "[t]he question is whether the agreement joins together 'independent centers of decisionmaking.'"

134. Acknowledging that NFL clubs must cooperate to produce and market NFL football, the *American Needle* Court determined that their joint conduct satisfies §1's concerted action requirement:

---

112. . For a history of the single entity defense, *see* generally Matthew J. Mitten, *American Needle Inc v. NFL*, Landmark Cases and Decisions in Sports Law 239–253 (Jack Anderson, ed., TMC Asser Press/Springer-Verlag 2013).
113. . *Mid-South Grizzlies v. NFL*, 720 F.2d 772 (3d Cir. 1983) ("In this case there is no dispute about the requisite concert of action among the defendants.").
114. . 379 F. Supp. 966 (C.D. Cal. 1974).
115. . 670 F.2d 1249 (2d Cir. 1981), *cert. denied*, 459 U.S. 1074 (1982).
116. . *See also Sullivan v. National Football League*, 34 F.3d 1091 (1st Cir. 1994); *Los Angeles Memorial Coliseum v. NFL*, 726 F.2d 1381 (9th Cir.), *cert. denied*, 469 U.S. 990 (1984).
117. .560 U.S. 183 (2010).

> Any joint venture involves multiple sources of economic power cooperating to produce a product. And for many such ventures, the participation of others is necessary. But that does not mean that necessity of cooperation transforms concerted action into independent action; a nut and a bolt can only operate together, but an agreement between nut and bolt manufacturers is still subject to §1 analysis. Nor does it mean that once a group of firms agree to produce a joint product, cooperation amongst those firms must be treated as independent conduct. The mere fact that the teams operate jointly in some sense does not mean that they are immune.

135. Construing *American Needle*, in *Deutscher Tennis Bund v. ATP Tour, Inc.*,[118] the Third Circuit concluded that an agreement among the Association of Tennis Professionals' member tournaments regarding the stratification of ATP tennis tournaments is not immune from §1 scrutiny:

> ATP maintained its members do not compete but instead cooperate to produce the Tour, and its adoption of the Brave New World plan was the core activity of producing this product. For their part, the Federations contended ATP operates in the market for top tier men's professional tennis players, and individual tournaments compete to attract top players. They asserted the Brave New World plan was an agreement unreasonably restraining trade in this alleged market … .
>
> [T]he agreement among the ATP's tournament members in the Brave New World Plan might have deprived the marketplace of potential competition. Professional sports teams or tournaments always have an interest in obtaining the best players possible … . The record in this case indicates that the individual tennis tournaments traditionally compete for player talent. An agreement restricting this competition should not necessarily be immune from § 1 scrutiny merely because the tournaments cooperate in various aspects of producing the ATP Tour.

136. In *Laumann v. NHL*,[119] a New York federal district court ruled that alleged agreements among MLB and NHL clubs to create exclusive local television territories and broadcasting rights for each club and to grant their respective leagues the exclusive right to sell television and internet broadcasting rights to those games outside these local territories are subject to §1 scrutiny because the clubs compete for the sale of their respective broadcasting rights.

137. By contrast, in *Washington v. National Football League*,[120] a Minnesota federal district court rejected plaintiffs' assertion that *American Needle* held that the NFL and its teams can "act in concert for the purpose of marketing their collective intellectual property." Distinguishing *American Needle's* facts, the court explained: "Here, unlike in *American Needle*, the intellectual property involved is historical

---

118. . 610 F.3d 820, 835–837 (3d Cir. 2010).
119. . 907 F.Supp.2d 465 (S.D.N.Y. 2012).
120. . Civil No. 11-3354 (PAM/AJB) (D. Minn., 13 Jun 2012) (unpublished opinion).

football game footage, something that the individual teams do not separately own, and never have separately owned. Rather, the NFL owns the game footage, either alone or in conjunction with the teams involved in the game being filmed." The court concluded that the "NFL and its teams can conspire to market each teams" individually owned property, but not property the teams and NFL can only collectively own."

2. Unreasonable Restraint of Trade

138. It is well settled law that the rule of reason is the appropriate standard for analyzing the competitive effects of collective action by professional sports league members or organizations under §1 of the Sherman Act.[121] The production of athletic contests requires many aspects of cooperation and some limits on economic competition among league teams for exciting and appealing playing-field competition to exist. Thus, league member agreements and conduct limiting off-field competition among them are not irrefutably presumed to be anticompetitive and thus per se illegal. Virtually all challenged restraints in the professional sports industry are examined on a case-by-case basis under the rule of reason with consideration of both their anticompetitive effects and procompetitive benefits to determine their net competitive consequences and effect on consumer welfare.

139. Regarding application of the rule of reason to restraints in the sports industry, one court has explained:

> the plaintiff bears the initial burden of showing that an agreement had a substantially adverse effect on competition. ... If the plaintiff meets this burden, the burden shifts to the defendant to come forward with evidence of the pro-competitive virtues of the alleged wrongful conduct. ... If the defendant is able to demonstrate procompetitive effects, the plaintiff then must prove that the challenged conduct is not reasonably necessary to achieve the legitimate objectives or that those objectives can be achieved in a substantially less restrictive manner. ... Ultimately, if these steps are met, the harms and benefits must be weighed against each other in order to judge whether the challenged behavior is, on balance, reasonable.[122]

140. In *American Needle*, the U.S. Supreme Court stated that "teams that need to cooperate are not trapped by antitrust law." The Court noted that the "special characteristics" of the sports industry may justify" a host of collective decisions "necessary to make" the entire league successful and profitable[123] under Rule of Reason analysis. The Court recognized that a professional sports league has a "legitimate and important interest" in maintaining competitive balance among its clubs, which is "unquestionably an interest that may well justify a variety of collective decisions made by the teams."[124]

---

121. . *American Needle v. NFL*, U.S., 130 S. Ct. 2201 (2010); *National Collegiate Athletic Association v. Bd. of Regents of the Univ. of Oklahoma*, 468 U.S. 85 (1984).
122. . *Law v. NCAA*, 134 F.3d 1010, 1019 (10th Cir. 1998).
123. . *Ibid.*, at 2216.
124. . *Ibid.*, at 2217.

141. It is difficult to apply the rule of reason and accurately measure whether a professional sports league's governing rules, agreements, and conduct enhance or harm consumer welfare as represented by the interests of sports fans. Nevertheless, federal antitrust law has played an important role in shaping the structure and governance of the U.S. professional sports industries as illustrated by the following cases.[125]

a. Acquisition, Ownership, and Sale of Sports Club

142. League rules typically require supra-majority approval (e.g., three-fourths) of club owners to approve the purchase and sale of a league club. Rejected prospective purchasers of a club have claimed that such rules and their application constitute a concerted refusal to deal by league club owners in violation of §1 of the Sherman Act league.

143. As illustrated by *Levin v. NBA*,[126] it is difficult for an unsuccessful bidder for an existing professional sports club (even one who has reached an agreement with the current owner to purchase the team) to prove its rejection by the league has anticompetitive effects. In *Levin*, the court ruled that NBA club owners' refusal to approve the sale of the Boston Celtics club to two businessmen does not violate §1. The court explained:

> While it is true that the antitrust laws apply to a professional athletic league, and that joint action by members of a league can have antitrust implications, this is not such a case. Here the plaintiffs wanted to join with those unwilling to accept them, not to compete with them, but to be partners in the operation of a sports league for plaintiffs' profit. Further, no matter which reason one credits for the rejection, it was not an anti-competitive reason. Finally, regardless of the financial impact of this rejection upon the plaintiffs, if any, the exclusion of the plaintiffs from membership in the league did not have an anticompetitive effect nor an effect upon the public interest. The Celtics continue as an operating club, and indeed are this year's champion.

144. As the *Levin* court observed, this refusal simply precludes a particular party from owning a league franchise. It does not reduce the number of league clubs,

125. . Although this section focuses on antitrust issues relating to the internal governance of team sports, the internal regulation of individual performer sports also may give rise to antitrust issues. For example, governing body restrictions on the use of particular playing equipment, *Gunter Harz Sports v. United States Tennis Ass"n*, 511 F. Supp. 1103 (D. Neb. 1981), player eligibility rules, *Toscano v. PGA Tour, Inc.*, 201 F. Supp. 2d 1106 (E.D. Cal. 2002), and player discipline for rules violations, *Blalock v. LPGA*, 359 F. Supp. 1260 (N.D. Ga. 1973) as well as the selection of the tracks hosting auto races, *Kentucky Speedway v. NASCAR*, 588 F.3d 908 (6th Cir. 2009), the stratification of tennis tournaments, *Deutscher Tennis Bund v. ATP Tour, Inc.*, 610 F.3d 820 (3d Cir. 2010), and a requirement that caddies wear bibs with advertising, *Hicks v. PGA Tour, Inc.*, 2016 WL 928728 (N.D. Cal.) have been challenged on antitrust grounds—generally without success by the plaintiffs.

126. . 385 F. Supp. 149 (S.D.N.Y. 1974). See also *Fishman v. Estate of Wirtz*, 807 F.2d 520, 542–44 (7th Cir. 1986) (league's mere selection of one prospective franchise owner over another one is not anticompetitive).

which remains the same as before denial of the proposed transfer of club ownership. Even if the requisite anticompetitive effects can be proven,[127] rejection of a prospective owner based on adequate evidence that the purchaser lacks the minimally necessary financial capital, character and fitness, and/or business skills to successfully operate a league club is a procompetitive means of preventing the league from being weakened with a corresponding reduction in its ability to compete successfully against other forms of entertainment for consumer patronage.[128]

145. One court has suggested that a league rule banning a club owner's sale of a minority interest in a franchise to the public may violate the antitrust laws. In *Sullivan v. National Football League*,[129] the First Circuit held that an NFL policy prohibiting the sale of an ownership interest in a league club through a public stock offering raises a fact question regarding whether it is anticompetitive. The former owner of the New England Patriots franchise claimed he was precluded from selling 49% of his team to the public and thereby forced to sell the club at a depressed price to private buyers. He asserted that, absent the NFL's policy, he would have been able to retain a majority interest in the Patriots and earn future profits from continued ownership of the club.

146. The court observed that the league's public ownership policy "compromises the entire process by which competition for club ownership occurs," rather than merely preventing transfers of club ownership, which do not adversely affect competition. The court rejected the NFL's contention that, as a matter of law, its clubs do not compete against each other for the sale of their ownership interests. It ruled that whether NFL teams are economic competitors in a "nationwide market for the sale and purchase of ownership interests in the NFL member clubs, in general, and in the New England Patriots, in particular" is a fact question. The court found sufficient evidence to support the jury's determination that the NFL's policy against public ownership of franchises is anticompetitive because it interferes with consumer demand for ownership interests in NFL teams and prevents ownership by a class of persons that may be more efficient operators of teams than private owners.

147. However, the First Circuit recognized that the NFL's public ownership policy has a legitimate procompetitive objective. It contributes to the league's ability to effectively function by preventing a potential detrimental conflict of interest between team shareholders' short-term dividend interests and the league's long-term interest in maintaining each club's financial integrity and competitiveness. The court observed, however, that modifying the NFL's policy to permit a club's sale of minority, nonvoting shares of team stock to the public with limits on the size of an individual's holdings may accomplish this objective in a substantially less restrictive manner.[130]

---

127. . Some courts have held that a league's denial of a prospective owner's bid to acquire an existing franchise may have an anticompetitive effect on the market for the purchase and sale of clubs. *See* , e.g., *Piazza v. Major League Baseball*, 831 F. Supp. 420 (E.D. Pa. 1993).

128. . *Nat'l Basketball Ass'n v. Minnesota Professional Basketball Limited Partnership,* 56 F.3d 866 (8th Cir. 1995).

129. . 34 F.3d 1091 (1st Cir. 1994).

130. . The court reversed the jury's verdict in the plaintiff's favor because erroneous jury instructions had been given and remanded the case for a new trial. The retrial of the case resulted in a hung jury, and the parties settled before it was tried for the third time.

148. In *Mid-South Grizzlies v. NFL,*[131] the Third Circuit ruled that the NFL's refusal to provide the owner of a former World Football League team with an expansion club in Memphis, Tennessee does not violate the federal antitrust laws. The court concluded the plaintiff did not prove this refusal was anticompetitive. It did not reduce intrabrand economic competition among NFL clubs because the closest then-existing NFL club was in St. Louis, Missouri over 280 miles away. Nor did it reduce interbrand economic competition among professional football leagues in the U.S. According to the court, "the exclusion was patently pro-competitive, since it left the Memphis area, with a large stadium and a significant metropolitan area population, available as a site for another league's franchise, and it left the Grizzlies' organization as a potential competitor in such a league."

b. Sports Club Relocation

149. The member clubs of the NFL, NBA, NHL, MLB and MLS are geographically dispersed throughout the U.S. Some NBA (Toronto), NHL (Calgary, Edmonton, Ottawa, Montreal, Toronto, Vancouver, and Winnipeg) MLB (Toronto), and MLS clubs (Montreal, Toronto, and Vancouver) are in Canada.[132] Most of each league's respective clubs are given an exclusive home geographical territory (i.e., generally there is only one league club in a city or its 75-mile radius), although some clubs in the same league share a large metropolitan area (e.g., the NFL's New York Giants and New York Jets).

150. It is arguable that there is an undersupply of major league professional sports franchises in the U.S., which does not have the promotion and relegation system prevalent in Europe. There are some U.S. cities that do not have any major league professional sports franchises (or clubs in particular leagues), despite having the population and economic base to support one or more major league clubs. For example, Los Angeles, the second most populous city in the U.S., currently does not have an NFL club.

151. Since the 1950s local communities, including mid-major U.S. cities such as Nashville, Memphis, Charlotte, and Oklahoma City in recent years, have provided multimillion-dollar public subsidies to construct playing facilities to attract major league professional sports franchises. Many other communities have made similar investments of public funds to keep their local sports franchises and prevent them from relocating elsewhere. Courts generally rule that these arrangements are a legitimate use of state and local tax dollars to promote the public good, although these significant public expenditures combined with favorable lease terms provide substantial economic benefits to privately owned professional sports clubs[133] and do not violate the antitrust

131. . 720 F.2d 772 (3d. Cir. 1983).

132. . Currently, the NFL has thirty-two member clubs; the NBA, NHL, and MLB each have thirty clubs. The MLS has nineteen clubs.

133. . *See* , e.g., *King County v. Taxpayers of King County*, 949 P.2d 1260 (Wash. 1997), *cert. denied*, 522 U.S. 1076 (1998); *Libertarian Party of Wisconsin v. State*, 199 Wis. 2d 791 (1996).

laws even if the required public subsidization necessary to retain a team is the product of an alleged anticompetitive conspiracy among league clubs.[134]

152. Depending on the specific circumstances, a sports league's refusal to permit one of its clubs to relocate to another city may violate the antitrust laws. *Los Angeles Memorial Coliseum Comm'n v. NFL* (*Raiders I*),[135] Oakland Raiders' owner Al Davis' antitrust litigation against the NFL, provides an example of a successful case arising out of the league's initial rejection of his 1980 request to move the Raiders from Oakland to Los Angeles.

153. In 1978, the Los Angeles Rams club relocated to a new stadium in Anaheim, California, which left the Los Angeles Coliseum without a major tenant. Coliseum officials then began searching for a new NFL team occupant. After the NFL Commissioner informed them it was not possible to place an expansion franchise in Los Angeles at the time, they negotiated with existing NFL teams in the hope that one might relocate to Los Angeles.

154. After the Oakland Raiders' lease with the Oakland Coliseum expired in 1978, Al Davis, the club's managing general partner, and L.A. Coliseum officials signed on March 1, 1980, a "memorandum of agreement" outlining the terms of the Raiders' proposed relocation to Los Angeles. On March 10, 1980, the NFL club owners voted 22-0 against the Raiders' proposed move with 5 teams abstaining, so the club was prohibited from relocating pursuant to Rule 4.3 of the NFL Constitution. This rule stated:

> The League shall have exclusive control of the exhibition of football games by member clubs within the home territory of each member. No member club shall have the right to transfer its franchise or playing site to a different city, either within or outside its home territory, without prior approval by the affirmative vote of three-fourths of the existing member clubs of the League.

155. In response, the Raiders brought a claim in Los Angeles federal court under §1 of the Sherman Act alleging that the refusal of the NFL and its member clubs to permit the club to relocate to Los Angeles is an unreasonable restraint of trade. This action resulted in a jury verdict in favor of the Raiders awarding USD 11.55 million in damages, which was automatically trebled (i.e., tripled) as a prevailing party in an

134. . *Hamilton County Bd. of County Commissioners v. NFL*, 491 F.3d 310 (6th Cir. 2007) (dismissing local government's antitrust claim against NFL after agreeing to "highly favorable" lease terms to prevent Bengals franchise from relocating, because "county officials knew—or should have known—the NFL was a monopoly during lease negotiations 10 years ago," which is outside applicable statute of limitations). *See also Warnock v. NFL*, 356 F. Supp. 2d 535 (W.D. Pa. 2005), *aff'd*, 154 Fed. Appx. 291 (3d Cir. 2005), *cert. denied*, 547 U.S. 1021 (2006) (Pittsburgh municipal taxpayer has no standing to sue the NFL and its member clubs for allegedly violating the antitrust laws by acting in concert to force league's cities, including Pittsburgh, to build new football stadiums).

135. . 726 F.2d 1381 (9th Cir.), *cert. denied*, 469 U.S. 990 (1984).

antitrust suit.[136] The trial court enjoined the NFL from preventing the Raiders from moving to Los Angeles.

156. On appeal, the Ninth Circuit affirmed the jury verdict finding an antitrust violation and the trial court's injunctive relief. The court rejected the NFL's claim that it is in essence a single economic entity, akin to a partnership or joint venture, precluding application of §1 which prevents only contracts, combinations or conspiracies among business entities with economically separate interests that restrain trade:

> Our inquiry discloses an association of teams sufficiently independent and competitive with one another to warrant rule of reason scrutiny under §1 of the Sherman Act. The NFL clubs are, in the words of the district court, separate business entities whose products have an independent value. The member clubs are all independently owned. Most are corporations, some are partnerships, and apparently a few are sole proprietorships. Although a large portion of League revenue, approximately 90%, is divided equally among the teams, profits and losses are not shared, a feature common to partnerships or other single entities. In fact, profits vary widely despite the sharing of revenue. The disparity in profits can be attributed to independent management policies regarding coaches, players, management personnel, ticket prices, concessions, luxury box seats, as well as franchise location, all of which contribute to fan support and other income sources.
>
> In addition to being independent business entities, the NFL clubs do compete with one another off the field as well as on to acquire players, coaches, and management personnel. In certain areas of the country where two teams operate in close proximity, there is also competition for fan support, local television and local radio revenues, and media space.

157. Recognizing that the unique nature of the business of professional football, which requires agreements among league clubs to produce on-field competition, made application of a per se rule inappropriate, the Ninth Circuit affirmed the jury's finding that the NFL's refusal to approve the Raiders club's relocation to Los Angeles violated the rule of reason. It concluded that Rule 4.3 has the anticompetitive effect of dividing geographical markets among the NFL clubs, precluding the Raiders from engaging in economic competition with the Rams in the Los Angeles NFL market. These exclusive territories insulated each NFL team from economic competition with other clubs, enabling them to set monopoly prices for tickets to the detriment of consumers.

---

136. . In *Los Angeles Memorial Coliseum Comm'n v. National Football League*, 791 F.2d 1356 (9th Cir. 1986) ("Raiders II"), the Ninth Circuit affirmed the jury's finding that the Raiders' gross lost profits from the two-year delay in moving to Los Angeles until 1982 as a result of the NFL's vote against this move amounted to USD 11,554,382. However, the Raiders' damages award was significantly reduced because the court ruled that the value of the Los Angeles market relocation opportunity (which was owned by the NFL) minus the value of the potential relocation opportunity created when the Raiders left Oakland must be offset against the Raiders' lost profits.

158. Regarding the NFL's claim that Rule 4.3 is procompetitive because it helps the league maintain its overall geographical scope, regional balance, and coverage of both major and minor markets, the court acknowledged that:

> Exclusive territories aid new franchises in achieving financial stability, which protects the large initial investment an owner must make to start up a football team. Stability arguably helps ensure no one team has an undue advantage on the field. Territories foster fan loyalty which in turn promotes traditional rivalries between teams, each contributing to attendance at games and television viewing.

159. However, the court determined that the NFL's denial of the Raiders" proposed move did not actually further any of these procompetitive justifications and suggested there was a less restrictive means of achieving them:

> [T]he NFL made no showing that the transfer of the Raiders to Los Angeles would have any harmful effect on the League. Los Angeles is a market large enough for the successful operation of two teams, there would be no scheduling difficulties, facilities at the L.A. Coliseum are more than adequate, and no loss of future television revenue was foreseen. Also, the NFL offered no evidence that its interest in maintaining regional balance would be adversely affected by a move of a northern California team to southern California. To withstand antitrust scrutiny, restrictions on team movement should be more closely tailored to serve the needs inherent in producing the NFL product and competing with other forms of entertainment. An express recognition and consideration of those objective factors espoused by the NFL as important, such as population, economic projections, facilities, regional balance, etc., would be well advised. See L. Kurlantzick, Thoughts on Professional Sports and the Antitrust Laws, 15 Conn. L.R. 183, 206 (1983). Fan loyalty and location continuity could also be considered.

160. Subsequently, in *Nat'l Basketball Ass'n v. SDC Basketball Club, Inc.*,[137] the Ninth Circuit reaffirmed that league rules regarding franchise relocation, including requiring a club to seek league approval before moving, are subject to the rule of reason. The court clarified that, although the objective factors and procedures identified by the *Raiders I* court are "well advised and might be sufficient to demonstrate procompetitive purposes," they are not "necessary conditions to the legality of franchise relocation rules."

161. In *In re Dewey Ranch Hockey LLC*,[138] a bankruptcy court rejected the efforts of a prospective purchaser of the Phoenix Coyotes NHL club to use the federal bankruptcy laws to avoid required NHL approval to purchase and relocate the club to Hamilton, Ontario in Canada. Relying on section 363(e) of the bankruptcy code, "which requires that [a] court "shall prohibit" any sale, where the interests sought to be removed by the proposed sale free and clear of such interests, cannot be adequately protected," the court ruled it "cannot find or conclude that the interests of the NHL can be adequately

137. . 815 F.2d 562 (9th Cir. 1987).
138. . 414 B.R. 577 (D. Ariz. 2009).

protected if the Coyotes are moved to Hamilton without first having a final decision regarding the claimed rights of the NHL and the claims of the debtors and PSE."

162. A professional sports league can avoid antitrust liability if its franchise relocation rules are carefully tailored and properly applied to achieve legitimate procompetitive objectives such as franchise financial stability, competitive balance among its member clubs, and an appropriate geographical distribution of its teams. On the other hand, rather than prohibiting a club from relocating, a league may condition the move upon payment of a relocation fee that is divided pro rata among its clubs. This practice has given rise to thus far unsuccessful antitrust litigation against the league by a relocating club's new host community.

163. In *St. Louis Convention & Visitors Commission v. National Football League*,[139] the Eighth Circuit affirmed the dismissal of the St. Louis Convention & Visitors Commission's (CVC) antitrust claims against the NFL arising out of the Rams franchise's relocation to St. Louis and lease to play its games in the Trans World Dome. NFL club owners approved the Rams' move only after its club owner agreed to pay the NFL a USD 29 million relocation fee, USD 20 million of which CVC agreed to reimburse to the Rams' owner. CVC contended that the application of the NFL's relocation rules and the league's imposition of an unreasonably high relocation fee discouraged other NFL teams from moving and bidding on the Trans World Dome lease. This allegedly forced CVC to give the Rams more favorable lease terms than it would have in a competitive market, which caused CVC damage in an amount between USD 77 million and USD 122 million. The court found that CVC had not proven the existence of a conspiracy among NFL clubs to prevent competitive bidding on the Trans World Dome lease, or that the NFL's alleged anticompetitive acts caused its economic harm. There was no explicit NFL rule or policy that banned or limited NFL clubs from engaging in competitive bidding for available stadium leases. There was no evidence that the NFL's relocation rules had precluded league clubs other than the Rams from bidding on the Trans World Dome lease, and CVC did not solicit other NFL teams to move to St. Louis.

164. The relocation of professional sports franchises frequently causes great upset among the local populace and has spawned antitrust litigation against club owners by their respective former host cities, states, or local governing bodies.[140] Such litigation is motivated by the potential loss of economic benefits to a city and its local businesses, outstanding bond indebtedness to finance the departing club's playing facility, and wounded community pride resulting from the loss of a major league professional sports franchise. These lawsuits, which usually are unsuccessful, have sought to prevent loss of the franchise, to keep the local team from moving before its stadium lease expires and without an opportunity to retain the franchise, or to require the league to provide a replacement franchise.

165. A well-drafted stadium lease is the most effective means of protecting a host community's public investment in the playing facility that houses a local team and ensuring that the local populace receives the full benefit of its contractual bargain for publicly subsidizing a sports facility. For example, expressly authorizing a court

139. . 154 F.3d 851 (8th Cir. 1998).

140. . *See* , e.g., *State v. Milwaukee Braves, Inc.*, 1966 Trade Cas. (CCH) P 71,738 (Wis. Cir. Ct.), *rev'd on other grounds*, 144 N.W.2d 1 (Wis. 1966).

to enjoin a club from relocating prior to the expiration of its lease[141] and/or requiring a relocating club to pay agreed liquidated damages of several million dollars for breach of a playing facility lease are important playing facility lease provisions necessary to protect a host community's interests.

c. Restrictions on Sports Club's Licensing and Sales of Intellectual Property Rights

166. The NFL, MLB, NBA, NHL, and MLS are geographically dispersed throughout the U.S. and Canada. Their respective clubs are located in cities with vastly different populations and economic bases; for example, large market metropolitan areas such as New York City, Los Angeles, and Chicago, as well as much smaller markets like Kansas City, Milwaukee, and Pittsburgh. Thus, league clubs' respective local revenue-generating potential from ticket sales (including personal seat licenses), concessions, parking fees, sponsorships, merchandising rights, and game broadcasts within differing local markets varies considerably.

167. As a means of preventing significant disparities in local revenue streams from inhibiting or destroying on-field competitive balance and fan interest in league games, the NFL, MLB, NBA, and NHL have implemented varying degrees of revenue sharing among their member clubs. MLS clubs also share revenues, although the league is structured as a single entity pursuant to which its clubs are owned and operated by its investors. In each league, national television and broadcasting rights revenues are shared equally among league clubs. Individual clubs' trademarks and logos are collectively licensed by a central league authority, with revenues distributed to league clubs on a pro rata basis. A recent trend is for leagues to require their clubs' Internet rights to be consolidated and centrally licensed (rather than, or with limits on, an individual club's licensing of its marks) with revenues shared among league clubs. Gate receipts from individual ticket sales frequently are also shared between the home and visiting teams in an agreed percentage.

168. The NFL currently has the most significant degree of revenue sharing among its member clubs, which provides the Green Bay Packers, located in a metropolitan area of approximately 100,000 people, with the financial resources to compete effectively on the field with large market clubs such as the Chicago Bears. Except for designated local advertising and facility-related revenues, NFL clubs share virtually all other revenues in an effort to jointly produce exciting games between closely matched teams that attracts fan interest.

169. In testimony before Congress, former NFL commissioner Pete Rozelle stated "revenue sharing is the key to maintaining geographic and competitive balance in professional football … and ensure[s] that each club, irrespective of the size of its community, stadium, or television market, has a comparable opportunity to field a

---

141. . *See* , e.g., *Metropolitan Sports Facilities Comm'n v. Minnesota Twins Partnership*, 638 N.W.2d 214, 225 (Minn. Ct. App. 2002) (court issues injunction requiring the Minnesota Twins MLB club to comply with its lease by playing its 2002 home games in its home stadium and prohibiting MLB from interfering with this contractual obligation).

championship team."[142] The exclusive licensing or sale of pooled intellectual property rights by a central league marketing arm, along with corresponding restrictions on individual clubs, is designed to (and often does) maximize their aggregate economic value and total revenues generated by the league. However, the pro rata revenue shares received by the most popular individual league clubs or those in the largest markets may be significantly less than the percentage of league revenues generated by the intellectual property associated with those clubs. In an effort to enhance its individual revenues, a club may attempt to circumvent league intellectual property licensing restrictions, which may force the league to litigate to protect its clubs' collective economic interests and exclusive sponsorship agreements with third parties from being harmed.[143]

170. In some instances, individual clubs or third parties seeking trademark licensing rights from individual clubs have asserted that league-wide exclusive trademark licensing violates the antitrust laws.[144] In *Major League Baseball Properties, Inc. v. Salvino, Inc.*,[145] the Second Circuit held that a §1 antitrust claim challenging Major League Baseball Properties" (MLPB) centralized trademark licensing program must be evaluated under the full rule of reason. It rejected plaintiff's claim that MLBP's refusal to grant a trademark license violated the "quick look" rule of reason (which does not require pleading and proving reduced competition in the relevant market, a complicated and costly analysis).

171. The Second Circuit noted that the U.S. Supreme Court "has applied quick-look analysis only "to business activities that are so plainly anticompetitive that courts need only undertake only a cursory examination before imposing antitrust liability," and that "if an arrangement "might plausibly be thought to have a net precompetitive effect, or possibly no effect at all on competition," more than a "quick look" is "required"." The MLB clubs" agreement establishing MLBP as the exclusive licensor of their trademark rights did not expressly limit or necessarily reduce the number of licenses issued to third parties. In fact, there was record evidence that the total number of licensees increased substantially after the formation of MLBP, thereby having the procompetitive effect of increasing the quantity of trademarked MLB merchandise available to consumers. The Second Circuit affirmed summary judgment in favor of MLBP because the rejected licensee did not prove that its centralized licensing program was anticompetitive or that MLBP had market power because there were no reasonable substitutes for products bearing MLB clubs" trademarks.

---

142. . *See* William J. Hoffman, Comment, "Dallas" Head Cowboy Emerges Victorious in a Licensing Showdown with the NFL: *National Football League Properties v. Dallas Cowboys Football Club*, 7 Seton Hall J. Sport L. 255, 262 (1997).
143. . *NFL Properties, Inc. v. Dallas Cowboys Football Club, Ltd*, 922 F. Supp. 849 (S.D.N.Y. 1996).
144. . *Dallas Cowboys Football Club, Ltd. v. NFL Trust*, 1996 WL 601705 (S.D.N.Y. 1996) (alleging that NFL Trust and Licensing Agreements create price-fixing cartel that precludes free competition in pro football sponsorship and merchandising markets). *See also, e.g.,* Complaint, *New York Yankees Partnership v. Major League Baseball Enterprises, Inc*, 97-1153-CIV-T-2513 (M.D. Fla. Filed May 19, 1997) (asserting that MLB Properties is a "cartel organized at the behest of a large group of the less successful Major League Clubs" that illegally restrains trade). Both cases settled before being judicially resolved on the merits.
145. . 542 F.3d 290 (2d. Cir. 2008).

172. In *American Needle, Inc. v. NFL,*[146] a hat manufacturer alleged that the NFL's exclusive trademark licensing program, which resulted in the termination of its trademark license, and corresponding restrictions on its member clubs" ability to enter into sponsorship agreements with third parties violate §1 of the Sherman Act. In contrast to *Salvino*, the challenged conduct at issue in this case is the validity of a league trademark licensor's granting of product category exclusivity to a single licensee for a fixed, up-front licensing fee.

173. In defense, the NFL argued that its member clubs function as a single economic entity in jointly producing NFL football and collectively licensing their intellectual property, which does not constitute the requisite concerted action under §1. Since 1963, the NFL teams have licensed their trademarks collectively through NFL Properties (NFLP), an independently managed separate corporation that distributes most of its revenues to NFL clubs on a pro rata basis.

174. A unanimous Supreme Court ruled that "the NFL's licensing activities constitute concerted action that is not categorically beyond the coverage of §1" because the challenged "agreement joins together 'independent centres of decision-making'" Observing that each NFL club is an independently owned and operated business that owns its individual trademarks, the Court concluded that the clubs are at least potential competitors with each other in the sports trademark licensing market. It held the agreement's legality "must be judged under the Rule of Reason" and remanded the case to the trial court for further proceedings consistent with its opinion. On remand, the trial court refused to apply the "quick look" Rule of Reason.[147] The parties subsequently reached a settlement pursuant to which the NFL paid an undisclosed sum to American Needle, and NFLP's exclusive product licensing regime remained intact.

175. Consistent with the foregoing cases, courts have held that other league restrictions on its member clubs' intellectual property rights are subject to scrutiny under the full rule of reason.[148] In *Madison Square Garden, L.P. v. NHL,*[149] the Second Circuit ruled that the owner of the New York Rangers NHL club could not use the "quick look" rule of reason to prove that requiring the club to migrate its website to a common technology platform managed by the NHL, rather than allowing its independent operation, violated §1. It affirmed the lower court's finding that the challenged conduct has several plausible procompetitive effects, including a standardized

146. . 560 U.S. 183 (2010).

147. *American Needle, Inc. v. New Orleans Louisiana Saints*, 2014 WL 1364022 (N.D. Ill.). *See also Dang v. San Francisco Forty Niners*, 964 F. Supp. 2d 1097 (N.D. Cal. 2013) (allegation by a consumer that he paid an "anticompetitive overcharge for his purchase" of an item of apparel bearing an NFL team's logo because of the NFL's current exclusive license with Reebok; case subsequently settled).

148. . *Chicago Professional Sports Limited Partnership v. National Basketball Association*, 95 F.3d 593 (7th Cir. 1996) (holding that the NBA is sufficiently integrated that full rule of reason analysis, which requires the plaintiff to satisfy the difficult burden of proving the challenged restraint substantially reduces economic competition in a properly defined relevant market, should be applied to its television superstation broadcasting limits by the lower court on remand); *Laumann v. NHL*, 907 F.Supp.2d 465 (S.D.N.Y. 2012), (alleged agreements among MLB and NHL clubs limiting the telecasting of professional sports games are subject to rule of reason analysis).

149. . 270 Fed. Appx. 56, 2008 WL 746524 (2d. Cir.).

web-site layout to attract national sponsors and advertisers interested in uniform exposure across the NHL.com network, which is a key element of the NHL's strategy to enhance its national brand to better compete against other sports and entertainment products.[150]

176. In *Laumann v. NHL*,[151] the court refused to dismiss §1 claims by a group of consumers alleging that agreements among MLB and NHL clubs limiting the telecasting of league games outside of assigned geographical territories violate antitrust law and explained: "Plaintiffs have adequately alleged harm to competition with respect to the horizontal agreements among individual hockey and baseball clubs, as part of the NHL and MLB, to divide the television market. Making all games available as part of a package, while it may increase output overall, does not, as a matter of law, eliminate the harm to competition wrought by preventing the individual teams from competing to sell their games outside their home territories in the first place. And plaintiffs in this case—the consumers—have plausibly alleged that they are the direct victims of this harm to competition."

II. Antitrust Limits on Dominant Sports League's Response to Formation of a Rival League

177. There has been a historical tendency toward a single American major professional league for the most popular North American team sports of baseball, football, basketball, and hockey. Throughout the twentieth century, competition among rival leagues in the same sport has never continued for any appreciable period of time.[152] Most recently, two competing women's professional basketball leagues, the American Basketball League (ABL) and the WNBA, began play in the late 1990s. The ABL, despite having some of the best women's basketball players on its clubs' rosters, ceased operations after only a few years of existence because of its inability to market its product and finance its operations as well as the WNBA, many of whose clubs are owned and operated by the NBA teams in their respective locations. Unlike most U.S. industries in which there are multiple producers of similar products, there is currently only one U.S. professional league that produces baseball (MLB), basketball (the NBA), football (the NFL), hockey (the NHL), and soccer (MLS) at the major league level.

178. To be economically viable, a major professional sports league needs several resources, including: (1) franchise owners with the financing and business acumen to successfully operate its member clubs; (2) teams in several large cities throughout the country with the population and economic base to support them; (3) access to adequate playing facilities; (4) major league-quality players; and (5) a national television broadcasting contract. Even if a new league is able to satisfy these minimum requirements, its long-term survival as a profitable independent entity is not ensured. Upstart leagues often fold after a relatively short period of existence because of financial problems or

150. . *Madison Square Garden, L.P. v. NHL*, 2007 WL 3254421 (S.D.N.Y.) at *6.
151. 907 F.Supp.2d 465 (S.D.N.Y. 2012).
152. . *See* generally Paul Weiler, *Leveling the Playing Field: How the Law Can Make Sports Better for Fans*, 324–328 (2001) (analyzing history and economic reasons for this phenomenon).

improper management and strategic business decisions, or fans may choose to support an established league rather than a new league.

179. The formation of a new league challenges an established league's dominance of a major professional league sport and threatens its popularity and profitability. Whether the threat is actual or simply potential, the established league may be tempted to react in ways that are anticompetitive and raise antitrust concerns. On several occasions during the twentieth century and with mixed results, a new league has brought antitrust litigation against the pre-existing dominant league for allegedly restricting access to one or more of the essential inputs necessary to produce competing professional team sports in a national or local market in the U.S.

180. Most antitrust challenges have been brought under §2 of the Sherman Act,[153] which prohibits monopolization or attempted monopolization. Unlike §1 that governs only concerted action, §2 applies to unilateral conduct such as a professional sports league's conduct in response to the formation of a rival league. Monopolization requires proof that: (1) the defendant possesses monopoly power in the relevant market; and (2) the defendant has willfully acquired or maintained that power rather than having grown or developed power as a consequence of a superior product, business acumen, or historic accident.[154] Attempted monopolization requires proof: "(1) that the defendant has engaged in predatory or anticompetitive conduct with (2) a specific intent to monopolize and (3) a dangerous probability of achieving monopoly power."[155] Although the elements of monopolization and attempted monopolization are different, both require analysis of the defendant's degree of control over the relevant market and a determination of whether its conduct is legal, fair competition on the merits, or is illegal exclusionary conduct with anticompetitive market effects.

181. The mere fact that there is only a single major league for a particular sport in the U.S. does not violate §2 of the Sherman Act because there may be certain inherent conditions in the professional sports industries that predispose each sport to dominance by one league at the major league level. One potential reason for this phenomenon is that fans may prefer a single champion for the highest level of competition within the sport. If so, over time, fans will prefer the product of one league over that of another, thereby leading to the demise of the disfavored league. There is no §2 violation if a league's market dominance results from winning the off-field competitive economic struggle by providing a superior entertainment product that is most desirable to sports fans.

182. On the other hand, this phenomenon may be the result of an established league's efforts to illegally exclude a rival league in violation of §2, which reduces interbrand competition among sellers of different brands of products that are reasonable substitutes from the perspective of consumers, thereby harming them by reducing available entertainment options and increasing their cost.[156] For example, this encompasses

153. . 15 U.S.C. §2.

154. . *United States v. Grinnell Corp.*, 384 U.S. 563, 570–71 (1966).

155. . *Spectrum Sports, Inc. v. McQuillan*, 506 U.S. 447, 456 (1993).

156. . *See* generally Stephen F. Ross, *Antitrust Options to Redress Anticompetitive Restraints and Monopolistic Practices by Professional Sports Leagues*, 52 Case W. L. Rev. 133, 158–65 (2001) (providing historical description of dominant leagues' successful predatory practices to achieve and maintain monopoly power).

competition between professional leagues in the same sports (e.g., NFL and United States Football League (USFL) football) or other sports with overlapping seasons (e.g., soccer and football), as well as competition between clubs in a different sport within the same geographical area (e.g., Chicago Bulls NBA team and Chicago Blackhawks NHL team).[157] Similar antitrust issues may arise if monopolistic practices by the dominant organization reduce competition between promoters of individual performer sports.[158]

183. Determining whether a professional sports league has monopoly power for Sherman Act §2 purposes is similar to the process for measuring a league's market power for purposes of Sherman Act §1 under the full rule of reason, which requires definition of both the relevant product and geographical markets and calculation of the defendant(s)' market share in order to evaluate the actual or potential anticompetitive effects of the challenged league rules or conduct. Although courts generally require at least a 70% market share to justify a finding of monopoly power, no rigid mathematical approach is used in §2 sports antitrust cases. Rather, the dispositive issue is whether the relevant market is appropriately defined, which determines whether the league has monopoly power and the corresponding ability to exclude rivals and prevent economic competition.

184. For example, in *American Football League v. National Football League*,[159] the Fourth Circuit ruled that the NFL, the dominant US major professional football league, did not have sufficient control of the market to prevent a newly formed rival from competing with it:

> The relevant market is nationwide, though the fact that there are a limited number of desirable sites for team locations bears upon the question of [the NFL]'s power to monopolize the national market. The District Court's finding that [the NFL] did not have the power to monopolize the relevant market appears plainly correct. In 1959, it occupied eleven of the thirty-one apparently desirable sites for team locations, but its occupancy of some of them as New York and San Francisco-Oakland was not exclusive, for those metropolitan areas were capable of supporting more than one team. Twenty of the thirty-one potentially desirable sites were entirely open to American. Indeed, the fact that the American League was successfully launched, could stage a full schedule of games in 1960, has competed very successfully for outstanding players, and has obtained advantageous contracts for national television coverage strongly supports the District Court's finding that [the NFL] did not have the power to prevent, or impede, the formation of

---

157. . A sports club's efforts to unfairly reduce or prevent competition from a rival club in its locality violates the antitrust laws. *Hecht v. Pro-Football, Inc.*, 570 F.2d 982 (D.C. Cir. 1977), *cert. denied*, 436 U.S. 956 (1978) (refusal to permit club in competing football league to play in and share usage of stadium owned and leased by the federal government).
158. . *See* , e.g., *Deutscher Tennis Bund v. ATP Tour, Inc.*, 610 F.3d 820 (3d Cir. 2010); *Kentucky Speedway, LLC v. Nat'l Ass'n of Stock Car Auto Racing, Inc.*, 588 F.3d 908 (6th Cir. 2009); *Volvo No. Am. Corp. v. Men's Int'l Prof'l Tennis Council*, 857 F.2d 55 (2d. Cir. 1988); *Elite Rodeo Ass'n v. Prof'l Rodeo Cowboys Ass'n*, 2016 WL 429886 (N.D. Tex.).
159. . 323 F.2d 124 (4th Cir. 1963).

the new league. Indeed, at the close of the 1960 season, representatives of the American League declared that the League's success was unprecedented.

185. A large market share or monopoly power does not alone violate §2. Even a monopolist is not prohibited from fairly competing on the merits for consumer support. The antitrust laws do not prohibit the dominant professional sports league from winning a competitive marketplace struggle by producing a product that is highly desirable to consumers (e.g., NFL football). In *American Football League*, the court held that the NFL could expand its business operations in response to increasing consumer demand for its product and compete with the AFL for the best available remaining geographical areas in which to place a professional football franchise.

186. The essence of illegal monopolization is conduct that excludes actual or potential rivals from the market by unfair or predatory means. To draw the line between lawful competition on the merits and unlawful exclusion or predation, it is important to consider the effects of a monopolist's challenged conduct on consumers. For example, a dominant league's clubs are permitted to compete fairly with an upstart rival league's clubs for the services of the best available players and to enforce valid, existing player contracts, thereby preventing their players from switching leagues before their respective contracts expire. As one court explained, "[n]obody has ever thought, so far as we can find, that in the absence of some monopolistic purpose everyone had not the right to offer better terms to another's employee so long as the latter is free to leave."[160] On the other hand, in *Philadelphia World Hockey Club, Inc. v. Philadelphia Hockey Club, Inc.*,[161] the court ruled that the NHL's efforts to control the supply of major league professional hockey players through a series of agreements with Canadian and U.S. amateur and minor professional leagues was illegal monopolistic conduct designed to prevent the WHA from competing in the North American major league professional hockey market.

187. If a new league successfully proves the dominant league has engaged in monopolization or attempted monopolization in violation of §2 of the Sherman Act, the typical remedies are an injunction against the illegal practices and damages. In *Philadelphia World Hockey Club*, the court enjoined the NHL from enforcing or attempting to enforce its reserve clause to prevent players from signing new contracts with WHA clubs after their NHL contacts expired. In *United States Football League v. NFL*,[162] the Second Circuit affirmed the jury's award of only nominal damages (i.e., USD 1, which is automatically trebled under the antitrust laws) to the USFL. Although the jury found that the NFL had monopolized the U.S. major professional football market, it determined that the USFL's bad, self-destructive business decisions were the primary cause of its inability to compete successfully against the NFL.

188. In *USFL*, the court rejected the USFL's proposed judicial restructuring of major league professional football as a remedy for the NFL's antitrust violation, which included its request that all USFL clubs be granted membership in the NFL, separation of the NFL into two leagues with each league being limited to one network television

160. . *Washington Capitols Basketball Club, Inc. v. Barry*, 419 F.2d 472, 478 (9th Cir. 1969).
161. . 351 F. Supp. 462 (E.D. Pa. 1972).
162. . 842 F.2d 1335 (2d Cir. 1988).

contract, or a prohibition on the NFL from broadcasting its games in more than one afternoon time slot on Sunday. The court explained:

> Absent a showing of an unlawful barrier to entry, however, new sports leagues must be prepared to make the investment of time, effort and money that develops interest and fan loyalty and results in an attractive product for the media. The jury in the present case obviously found that patient development of a loyal following among fans and an adherence to an original plan that offered long-run gains were lacking in the USFL.

Chapter 6. Liability for Sports-Related Injuries

§1. Injury to Spectators

189. The common law liability of a sports facility operator to spectators turns on the legal characterization of the parties' relationship. Sports event spectators generally are characterized as "invitees," meaning they are invited to enter a venue to view a game or event (usually as a paying customer). Thus, "the owner of a public facility has a duty of reasonable care under the circumstances to invitees,"[163] which requires a facility owner or operator to maintain the premises in a reasonably safe condition to prevent spectator injury from normal use of the facility. For example, in *Gray v. Louisiana Downs*,[164] a racetrack owner/operator was found liable for a patron's fall caused by its failure to reasonably inspect for and remove discarded concessions, packing materials, and other debris on the floor of its venue.

190. The general duty of a facility owner to exercise reasonable care to protect invitees does not extend to protecting spectators attending sporting events against risks inherent to a particular sport. Regarding the liability of a sports facility operator, club, or player to an injured spectator, some courts have adopted what is frequently referred to as the "limited duty" rule. Pursuant to this rule, "there is no legal duty to protect or warn spectators about the 'common, frequent, and expected' inherent risks of observing a sporting event such as being struck by flying objects [such as baseballs] that go into the stands."[165] Generally, a facility owner complies with the limited duty rule if it offers seating accommodations in a screened area to spectators who desire such seating. Regarding the limited duty rule in the context of baseball, in *Allred v. Capital Area Soccer League, Inc.*,[166] the court stated:

> When an operator of a baseball facility provides some seating which has a screen to protect patrons from errant baseballs, they are held to have discharged their full duty to spectators in safe-guarding them from the danger of being struck by thorn or batted balls[.] This rule applies even if there is an unusually large crowd, and patrons desiring screened seating are unable to obtain it.

191. One commentator has succinctly explained that "[g]iven the plaintiff's awareness of danger and choice of seat, the sports operator's only duty is to provide some reasonably safe accommodations."[167] A rationale frequently articulated in support of the limited duty rule is that spectators assume injury causing risks that are an inherent part of the activity in question. Another rationale rests on the protection of consumer preference. Proponents of this view argue that not imposing a duty on facility owners

163. . *Allred v. Capital Area Soccer League, Inc.*, 669 S.E.2d 777 (N.C. App. 2008).
164. . 585 So. 2d 1238 (La. Ct. App. 1991).
165. . *Jones v. Three Rivers Mgmt. Corp.*, 394 A.2d 546, 551 (Pa. 1978).
166. . 669 S.E.2d 777 (N.C. App. 2008).
167. . *See* generally, Dan B. Dobbs, *The Law of Torts* §215 at 547 (West Group 2000).

for risks inherent in the game promotes allowing owners to construct facilities that enhance consumer choice. Consumers may elect to sit in protected seats or find seats in unprotected areas where their view may be unobstructed and they can become more intimately involved in the particular game.

192. Applying the limited duty rule, in *Thurmond v. Prince William Professional Baseball Club, Inc.*,[168] the Virginia Supreme Court dismissed a spectator's negligence claim against a professional baseball club seeking recovery for a serious injury from being struck in the face by a foul ball while watching a game:

> [The assumption of the risk] doctrine requires us to consider whether a particular plaintiff fully understood the nature and extent of a known danger and voluntarily exposed herself to that danger. Thus, we hold that when a particular adult spectator of ordinary intelligence is familiar with the game of baseball, that spectator assumes the normal risks of watching a baseball game, including the danger of being hit by a ball batted into an unscreened seating area of a stadium.
>
> We conclude that reasonable persons could not disagree that Thurmond, who conceded that she remained alert throughout the game and observed hitters and batted balls for more than seven innings before being injured, was familiar with the game of baseball, knew the risk of being injured by a batted ball, and voluntarily exposed herself to that risk by remaining seated in an unscreened area.

193. In *Sciarrotta v. Global Spectrum*,[169] the New Jersey Supreme Court rejected the plaintiff's argument that the limited duty rule should not apply during pre-game warm-ups because "[t]o demand separate and distinct duties of care in respect to the same peril in this same area based solely on the temporary goings-on on the field of play is impractical and not grounded in reason."

194. Other courts have adopted a broader rule of legal liability for spectator injuries caused by "the play of commercial baseball." In *Edward C.v. City of Albuquerque*,[170] the New Mexico Supreme Court ruled:

> an owner/occupant of a commercial baseball stadium owes a duty that is symmetrical to the duty of the spectator. The spectator must exercise ordinary care to protect himself or herself from the inherent risk of being hit by a projectile that leaves the field of play and the owner/occupant must exercise ordinary care not to increase that inherent risk.

The court determined that the defendant stadium owner/operator may be liable for an injury to a 4-year-old boy who was struck in the head by a batted ball during pregame

168. . 574 S.E.2d 246 (Va. 2003).
169. . 944 A.2d 630, 638 (N.J. 2008). *See also Allred v. Capital Area Soccer League, Inc.*, 669 S.E.2d 777 (N.C. App. 2008) (the rule that spectators assume risk inherent in a sport extends to preliminary and warm-up activities).
170. . 241 P.3d 1086 (N.M. 2010).

batting practice that began without warning when he was in a picnic area with tables positioned perpendicular to the field of play.

195. Lowe v. California League of Professional Baseball[171] provides another illustration of how courts have applied the legal rule requiring sports facility operators not to increase the inherent risks of spectator injury from watching a game or athletic event. In this case, the plaintiff was facing forward and watching a baseball game when the team mascot, a seven-foot-tall caricature of a dinosaur, suddenly and without warning, began touching him from behind with a tail protruding from his costume. As plaintiff turned to see what was touching him, he was struck in the face by a foul ball and suffered serious injury. The court found that the presence of a team mascot is not an integral part of the game of baseball. It held that the mascot's antics in hitting plaintiff with his tail, while the game was being played, created a triable issue of fact as to whether the club increased the inherent risks of watching a baseball game by distracting plaintiff and preventing him from seeing and protecting himself from injury by a batted ball.[172]

196. Judicial development of the nature and scope of the legal duty of care owed to spectators attending sports events other than baseball continues to evolve. Courts initially refused to hold that spectators assumed the risk of being hit by hockey pucks that flew into the stands. However, one court observed that now "it is undisputed that ice hockey spectators face a known risk of being hit by a flying puck."[173] In a 2008 case, a North Carolina appellate court refused to apply the limited duty rule in a case in which a spectator was hit by a soccer ball that left the field of play. It determined that the evidence failed to establish that plaintiff or a reasonable person attending a soccer match would have knowledge of the risk of being injured by a soccer ball leaving the field of play.[174]

197. Some jurisdictions limit sports facility owner and operator liability by statute. For example, the Illinois Baseball Facility Liability Act requires a spectator injured by a baseball or bat to provc that the screen or backstop behind which he or she was sitting is defective (in a manner other than width or height) because of the facility owner or operator's negligence or that his or her injury was caused by willful or wanton conduct.[175] The Illinois Hockey Facility Liability Act creates a similar immunity for spectator injuries caused by being hit by a hockey stick or puck.[176]

198. A facility owner may be liable for failing to use reasonable care in regulating crowd control and fan conduct during sporting events, although it should be noted that the doctrine of sovereign immunity may preclude a negligence suit against a public

171. . 65 Cal. Rptr. 2d 105 (Cal. App. 1997).

172. . *Gil de Rebollo v. Miami Heat Assns, Inc.*, 137 F.3d 56 (1st Cir. 1998) (club liable for mascot's negligent antics during timeout entertainment routine that caused injury to spectator).

173. . *Nemarnik v. L.A. Kings Hockey Club, L.P.*, 127 Cal. Rptr. 2d 10, 15 (Cal. App. 2002); *Hurst v. East Coast Hockey League*, 637 S.E.2d 560, 562 (S.C. 2006) ("risk of being injured by a foul ball at a baseball game and the risk of being injured by a flying puck at a hockey game are similar risks").

174. . *Allred v. Capital Area Soccer League, Inc.*, 669 S.E.2d 777 (N.C. App. 2008).

175. . 745 ILCS § 38/10 (West 2008).

176. . 745 ILCS § 52/10 (West 2008). Other states adopting sport-specific legislation include Arizona, Ariz. Rev. Stat. § 12-554 (West 2003), Colorado, Colo. Rev. Stat. § 13-21-120 (2002), and Utah, Utah Code Ann. § 78B-4-508 (LexisNexis 2008).

entity for inadequate crowd control or policing of spectator conduct.[177] Some courts have held that injury caused by fellow spectators while pursuing a ball that goes into the stands as a souvenir is not an inherent risk of attending and observing a game. In *Hayden v. University of Notre Dame*,[178] the court ruled that a university has a legal duty to protect spectators against a foreseeable risk of such harm:

> We find that the totality of the circumstances establishes that Notre Dame should have foreseen that injury would likely result from the actions of a third party in lunging for the football after it landed in the seating area. As a result, it owed a duty to Letitia Hayden to protect her from such injury. Notre Dame well understands and benefits from the enthusiasm of the fans of its football team. It is just such enthusiasm that drives some spectators to attempt to retrieve a football to keep as a souvenir. There was evidence that there were many prior incidents of people being jostled or injured by efforts of fans to retrieve the ball.

§2. Injury to Athletes

I. Tort Liability

A. Co-participant Liability

199. Injuries frequently occur during all levels of athletic competition and are an inherent risk of participating in sports, which participants generally assume and must bear the resulting costs. Inherent risk would include all of the ordinary harms reasonably expected to occur while engaged in a particular athletic activity. An athlete may be liable for tortious conduct during a sports event that injures another athlete or player during a game or sports event.

200. Most jurisdictions permit recovery in sports injury cases between co-participants only for intentional or reckless conduct because vigorous participation in competitive sporting events "likely would be chilled if liability were to be imposed on a participant on the basis of his or her ordinary careless conduct"[179] and to prevent a flood of litigation arising out of sports injuries caused by negligent conduct. A minority of courts apply a negligence standard that is premised on the duty of reasonable care that one person owes to guard against foreseeable injuries to others. One of the significant differences between the application of the intentional/recklessness and negligence standards is that mere careless or rough play does not establish liability under the former standard.

201. Under the intentional or reckless conduct liability standard, the defendant's violation of a sport's safety rules that causes injury to a co-participant will not necessarily result in liability (which would be much more likely under a negligence standard). As one court observed:

177. . *See* , e.g., *Eneman v. Richter*, 577 N.W.2d 386, 1998 WL 50414 (Wis. App. 1998).
178. . 716 N.E.2d 603, 606 (Ind. App. 1999).
179. . *Knight v. Jewett*, 834 P.2d 696, 710 (Cal. 1992).

> Policy reasons also justify the holding that rules violations, by themselves, are insufficient to impose liability in a contact sport: Even when a participant's conduct violates a rule of the game and may subject the violator to internal sanctions prescribed by the sport itself, imposition of legal liability for such conduct might well alter fundamentally the nature of the sport by deterring participants from vigorously engaging in activity that falls close to but on the permissible side of, a prescribed rule.[180]

202. Most jurisdictions permit recovery in sports injury cases between co-participants only for intentional or reckless conduct regardless of the level of competition, age, or experience of the participants, or organizational structure of the sport. The judicial trend is to apply this liability standard to both contact (e.g., football, soccer, basketball) and noncontact (e.g., golf) sports and to focus on whether the injury causing risk is inherent in the particular sport. In *Thompson v. McNeill*,[181] the Ohio Supreme Court observed: "Analyzing liability for injuries inflicted in sports in terms of a continuum along which the standard of care rises as the inherent danger of the sport falls is more useful than distinguishing sports by applying a black-and-white distinction between contact and non-contact sports." In *Shin v. Ahn*,[182] after surveying precedent from several jurisdictions, the California Supreme Court held that "golfers owe a limited duty of care to other players, breached only if they intentionally injure them or engage in conduct that is 'so reckless as to be totally outside the range of the ordinary activity involved in the sport.'"

203. Prior to the widespread adoption of comparative fault principles in most U.S. states, the focus was on the plaintiff's assumption of the risk (i.e., subjective awareness of the inherent risks of injury from voluntarily participating in a sporting event), which was an affirmative defense barring a negligence action. In most jurisdictions, the focus now is on the nature of the defendant's legal duty to protect a co-participant from injury during competition, which is part of plaintiff's prima facie case. As one legal scholar has explained:

> Primary assumption of the risk focuses not on whether the plaintiff voluntarily assumed a known risk, but on the question of duty. Did the defendant possess a duty to protect the plaintiff from the risk of harm resulting in injury? If the risk causing the injury is an inherent part of the activity, the defendant owed no duty to the plaintiff, and there is no liability.[183]

204. Regarding amateur sports, in *Mark v. Moser*,[184] an Indiana appellate court explained that:

---

180. . *Karas v. Strevell*, 884 N.E. 2d 122, 133–134 (Ill. 2008) (emphasis in original).
181. . 559 N.E. 2d 705, 709 (Ohio 1990).
182. . 64 Cal. Rptr. 3d 803, 813–14 (Cal. 2007).
183. . Timothy Davis, *Avila v. Citrus Community College District: Shaping the Contours of Immunity and Primary Assumption of the Risk*, 17 Marq. Sports L. Rev. 259, 270 (2006).
184. . 746 N.E.2d 410 (Ind. App. 2001).

> voluntary participants in sports activities assume the inherent and foreseeable dangers of the activity and cannot recover for injury unless it can be established that the other participant either intentionally caused injury or engaged in conduct so reckless as to be totally outside the range of ordinary activity involved in the sport.

It explained:

> Applying the foregoing standard, liability will not lie where the injury causing action amounts to a tactical move that is an inherent or reasonably foreseeable part of the game and is undertaken to secure a competitive edge. Thus, where a baseball pitcher throws the ball near the batter to prevent him from crowding the home plate, and the ball ends up striking the batter and causing injury, the pitcher's conduct would not be actionable. Similarly, there would be no tort liability where the defense in a football game strategically blitzes the opposing team's quarterback resulting in injury, or where one basketball team is leading by a point and, seconds from the end of the game, a member of that team chooses to foul the opponent when he drives the lane for a slam dunk, thereby forcing him to try to win the game at the free throw line.

> In contrast, if a co-participant vents his anger at another player by means of a physical attack, such conduct would be actionable. Instances of such tortious conduct would be where one boxer bites his opponent's ear during a boxing match, or where a soccer or football player punches another player after a tackle. Similarly, if a baseball batter in a fit of anger intentionally flips his bat towards the opposing team's dugout and injures one of the players, liability might attach for such recklessness.

205. The intentional or reckless standard generally also applies to liability for co-participant injuries occurring in professional sports.[185] In *Hackbart v. Cincinnati Bengals, Inc.*,[186] the Tenth Circuit rejected the lower court's determination that there should be no tort liability for injuries occurring during professional football because "NFL has substituted the morality of the battlefield for that of the playing field, and the 'restraints of civilization' have been left on the sidelines."[187] The Tenth Circuit ruled "there are no principles of law which allow a court to rule out certain tortious conduct by reason of general roughness of the game or difficulty of administering it." The court observed:

> The general customs of football do not approve the intentional punching or striking of others. That this is prohibited was supported by the testimony of all of the witnesses. They testified that the intentional striking of a player in the face

185. . *Turcotte v. Fell*, 502 N.E.2d 964 (N.Y. 1986); *McKichan v. St. Louis Hockey Club, L.P.*, 967 S.W.2d 209 (Mo. App. 1998); *Averill v. Luttrell*, 311 S.W.2d 812 (Tenn. App. 1957).
186. . 601 F.2d 516 (10th Cir. 1979).
187. . *Hackbart v. Cincinnati Bengals, Inc.*, 435 F.Supp. 352 (D. Colo. 1997).

or from the rear is prohibited by the playing rules as well as the general customs of the game. Punching or hitting with the arms is prohibited. Undoubtedly these restraints are intended to establish reasonable boundaries so that one football player cannot intentionally inflict a serious injury on another. Therefore, the notion is not correct that all reason has been abandoned, whereby the only possible remedy for the person who has been the victim of an unlawful blow is retaliation.

B. Sports Medicine Care Provider Malpractice Liability

1. Team Physician

206. Professional teams and collegiate educational institutions generally hire a physician or group of physicians to provide medical care to their athletes. Many high schools also select a physician to provide pre-participation physical examinations and emergency medical care to athletes participating in interscholastic athletics.

207. A "team physician" provides medical services to athletes that are arranged for, or paid for, at least in part, by an institution or entity other than the patient or his parent or guardian.[188] The team physician's primary responsibility is to provide for the physical well-being of athletes. The team physician must provide medical treatment and advise consistent with an individual athlete's best health interests because there is a physician-patient relationship between them. Although one of the team physician's objectives is to avoid the unnecessary restriction of athletic activity, his paramount responsibility should be to protect the competitive athlete's health.[189] Team physicians may face extreme pressure from coaches, team management, fans, or the athlete to provide medical clearance to participate or treatment enabling immediate return to play.

208. There are relatively few reported cases discussing the appropriate standard of care for physician malpractice in the sports medicine setting. In malpractice suits involving a medical specialist, the trend is to apply a national standard of care because national specialty certification boards exist to ensure standardized training and certification procedures. Team physicians generally are internists, family practitioners, or orthopedic surgeons. Other specialists such as cardiologists and pediatricians also provide sports medicine care to athletes. Team physicians generally have a legal duty to conform to the standard of care corresponding to their individualized specialty training. Historically, courts ruled that sports medicine is not a separate medical specialty, because no national medical specialty board certification or standardized training previously existed.[190] This judicial view is likely to change as sports medicine becomes a recognized and accepted area of specialization within the medical profession. The American Osteopathic Association has a certification board for sports medicine,

188. . *See* generally Joseph H. King, Jr., *The Duty and Standard of Care for Team Physicians*, 18 Hous. L. Rev. 657, 658 (1981).
189. . *See* generally Matthew J. Mitten, *Team Physicians and Competitive Athletes: Allocating Legal Responsibility for Athletic Injuries*, 55 U. Pitt L. Rev. 129, 140–141 (1993).
190. . *See* , e.g., *Fleischmann v. Hanover Ins. Co.*, 470 So.2d 216, 217 (La. Ct. App. 1985) (refusing to recognize subspecialty in sports medicine).

and the specialty boards for family practice, internal medicine, emergency medicine, and pediatrics within the American Board of Medical Specialties now recognize sports medicine as a subspecialty.

209. Some sports medicine malpractice cases adopt an "accepted practice" standard of care in determining physician liability.[191] For example, in *Mikkelsen v. Haslam*,[192] a Utah appellate court upheld a jury verdict imposing liability on an orthopedist who advised a patient with a total hip replacement that snow skiing was permissible "is a departure from orthopedic medical profession standards." Under this standard, acceptable or reasonable medical practices (rather than what has been customary) define the boundaries of a physician's legal duty of care in treating athletes.[193] In a malpractice action, expert testimony regarding the appropriate standard of physician sports medicine care generally is required to prove liability. In *Gibson v. Digiglia*,[194] the court affirmed the dismissal of an athlete's malpractice claim because there was "no evidence to establish the standard of care required of a "team medical director/coordinator" nor have they presented any evidence to support a claim that [the physician's] actions fell below the standard of care for that alleged subspecialty of physicians."

210. The team physician must have an athlete's informed consent before providing any medical treatment. This requirement is based on the principle of individual autonomy, namely that a competent adult has the legal right to determine what to do with his body, including accepting or refusing medical treatment. A competent adult athlete can provide consent to medical care, but consent for treatment of athletes who are minors generally must be obtained from a parent or guardian. Consent may be implied under the circumstances, such as when an athlete has been rendered unconscious during play and needs emergency medical treatment. In these cases, the law generally assumes that if the injured athlete had been aware of his condition and was competent mentally, then he would have authorized appropriate treatment.

211. In addition to following accepted or reasonable sports medicine practices in providing diagnosis and treatment of athletic injuries and in making medical eligibility recommendations, the team physician must fully inform an athlete of any material risks of playing a sport in light of his physical condition. Failure to do so may expose the team physician to liability based on intentional tort or negligence principles.

212. Courts have held that a team physician's intentional or negligent failure to provide an athlete with full disclosure of material information about playing with his medical condition or the potential consequences of proposed treatment is actionable. In *Krueger v. San Francisco Forty Niners*,[195] a California appellate court held that a professional football team's conscious failure to inform a player that he risked a

191. . *Classen v. Izquierdo*, 520 N.Y.S.2d 999, 1002 (N.Y. Sup. Ct. 1987) (physician who treats an athlete must "practice in accordance with good and accepted standards of medical care").

192. . 764 P.2d 1384, 1386 (Utah Ct. App. 1988).

193. . *See* generally, Matthew J. Mitten, *Emerging Legal Issues in Sports Medicine: A Synthesis, Summary, and Analysis*, 76 St. John's L. Rev. 5 (2002) (providing overview of team physician malpractice liability issues).

194. . 980 So.2d 739 (La. App. 2008).

195. . 234 Cal. Rptr. 579 (Cal. Ct. App. 1987). Krueger ultimately was awarded USD 2.36 million in damages, but settled his claim for between USD 1 million and USD 1.5 million.

permanent knee injury by continuing to play was fraudulent concealment. The court found that the plaintiff was not informed by team physicians of the true nature and extent of his knee injuries, the consequences of steroid injection treatment, or the long-term dangers associated with playing professional football with his medical condition. The court found that the purpose of this nondisclosure was to induce plaintiff to continue playing football despite his injuries, thereby constituting fraud.

2. Athletic Trainer

213. Athletic trainers typically provide a variety of sports medicine services to athletes, such as physical conditioning, injury prevention, emergency medical care, and injury rehabilitation, which may give rise to legal liability if rendered improperly contrary to their professional standard of care.[196] In *Searles v. Trustees of St. Joseph's College*,[197] the Maine Supreme Court held that an athletic trainer "has the duty to conform to the standard of care required of an ordinary careful trainer" when providing care and treatment to athletes. The court ruled that a trainer may incur negligence liability for failing to communicate the severity of a player's injuries to the team's coach, or for failing to advise an athlete that he should not continue playing with his medical condition. In *Jarreau v. Orleans Parish School Board*,[198] a Louisiana appellate court upheld a jury finding that a high school football team's trainer negligently failed to refer a player with a wrist injury to an orthopedist until after the season ended. The athletic trainer's delay in referring the player for treatment of his fracture necessitated an extended period of treatment and caused a permanent disability.

214. An athletic trainer, like any other provider of sports medicine care, is not negligent merely because the treatment provided exacerbates an athlete's injury. In *Gillespie v. Southern Utah State College*,[199] the Utah Supreme Court held that a student athletic trainer was not liable for treating a basketball player's ankle injury that ultimately would have healed by itself without medical treatment. The court ruled that the athletic trainer's liability depended upon proof of negligent treatment contributing to the athlete's enhanced injury.

3. Athlete's Contributory Negligence

215. An athlete has a legal duty to use reasonable care to protect his own health and safety. For example, he must truthfully disclose his medical history and physical

196. . *See* , e.g., *Howard v. Missouri Bone and Joint Center, Inc.*, 615 F.3d 991 (8th Cir. 2011) (expert testimony establishes athletic trainer's negligence in conducting workout program that caused injury to college athlete); *Williams v. Athletico Ltd.*, 2017 IL App (1st) 161902
(requiring plaintiff alleging athletic trainer's negligent failure to assess and evaluate him for a concussion to prove his failure "to employ the degree of knowledge, skill, and ability that a reasonable athletic trainer would employ under similar circumstances").

197. . 695 A.2d 1206, 1210 (Me. 1997).

198. . 600 So.2d 1389 (La. Ct. App. 1992).

199. . 669 P.2d 861 (Utah 1983).

symptoms to the team physician.[200] In *Jarreau v. Orleans Parish School Board,*[201] the court, applying contributory negligence principles, found an injured high school football player to be one-third at fault for failing to consult his own physician or requesting that he be referred to a school physician.

216. An athlete generally may rely upon the recommendations of the team physician or his designated consulting specialists regarding when it is appropriate to return to play after an injury without seeking a second medical opinion. His reliance on the team physician's recommendations ordinarily is considered reasonable because of the doctor's sports medicine expertise, and the athlete is not required to obtain a confirming medical opinion.[202]

217. On the other hand, an athlete's failure to follow his physician's instructions constitutes contributory negligence that may reduce or bar his recovery. In *Gillespie v. Southern Utah State College,*[203] a college basketball player was found to be solely responsible for aggravating an ankle injury by not following physician instructions concerning proper treatment and rehabilitation.

C. Educational Institution Liability

218. A high school, college, or university acts through the conduct of its employees and generally is responsible for harm caused by their tortious conduct that injures student-athletes. Absent applicable tort immunity or a valid contractual waiver of tort liability, an educational institution may be liable for the tortious conduct of employees such as coaches, athletic trainers, and administrative personnel.

1. High School

219. Negligence is the theory traditionally relied on by student-athletes who sue their high schools for sports-related injuries. A high school is not an insurer of a student-athlete's safety and is not strictly liable for his or her injuries, including those resulting from the inherent risks incident to customary or normal participation in a sport (e.g., being hit by a batted or thrown ball while playing baseball). To recover for an injury, a high school athlete is required to prove negligence or more culpable tortious conduct (i.e., grossly negligent, reckless, willful and wanton, or intentional) on the part of a school district or its employees. For example, in *Beckett v. Clinton Prairie*

200. . *See McGee v. Covington County Sch. Dist.*, 2012 WL 48026 (Miss. App.) (absolving nurse practitioner, who conducted pre-participation physical examination of high school student-athlete who later died during practice, from liability where athlete and his mother failed to truthfully disclose the athlete's medical history).
201. . 600 So.2d 1389 (La. Ct. App. 1992).
202. . *Mikkelsen v. Haslam*, 764 P.2d 1384 (Utah Ct. App. 1988); *Krueger v. S.F. Forty Niners*, 234 Cal. Rptr. 579 (Cal. Ct. App. 1987).
203. . 669 P.2d 861 (Utah 1983). *See also Holtman v. Reese, 460 S.E.2d 338 (N.C. Ct. App. 1995)* (engaging in high-impact aerobics, snow skiing, and waterskiing contrary to chiropractor's advice. *Starnes v. Caddo Parish Sch. Bd.*, 598 So.2d 472 (La. Ct. App. 1992) (playing volleyball without wearing knee brace against doctor's advice).

Sch. Corp.,[204] the court held that high school personnel have a duty to exercise ordinary and reasonable care for safety of student athletes under their authority.

220. Although coaches generally have a legal duty to use reasonable care and not to increase the risks of injury inherent in a sport, some courts recently have ruled that a coach is liable only for intentionally injuring a student or engaging in reckless conduct that is "totally outside the range of the ordinary activity" involved in teaching or coaching the sport.[205] These courts have reasoned that applying an intentional/ reckless standard is appropriate because a significant aspect of a coach's job is to push athletes to advance their skills and athletic performance, which requires encouraging them to attempt more difficult tasks. Coaches generally are held liable under a negligence theory for not adequately informing high school athletes of the need to wear protective equipment,[206] requiring an athlete to continue play notwithstanding the coach's knowledge of an existing injury,[207] and not obtaining prompt emergency medical treatment for an injured athlete[208] or providing it improperly.[209]

221. Under the doctrine of sovereign immunity, a public educational institution, as a subsidiary agency of the state, may be immune from tort liability for negligent acts of its employees such as coaches, athletic trainers, and sports administrative personnel that cause injury to a high school athlete.[210] The scope of sovereign immunity, which may be statutory or common law, varies on a state-by-state basis.

222. The doctrine of qualified immunity may protect public school employees (e.g., coaches and athletic trainers) from negligence liability when they are exercising a discretionary act but not a ministerial act. A discretionary act involves exercising personal deliberation or judgment, such as examining facts, weighing options, and reaching an independently reasoned conclusion that is not specifically directed. Conversely, the required execution of a specific action given a specific situation is a ministerial act. In *Prince v. Louisville Municipal School Dist.*,[211] the Mississippi Supreme Court distinguished between a coach's discretionary and ministerial function when exploring the parameters of this defense. A high school football player alleged he suffered a heat stroke during practice as a result of his coaches' negligent failure to properly monitor his health and condition, to provide necessary liquids, and to provide necessary medical care in a timely manner. The court ruled that the qualified immunity doctrine immunized the coaches from negligence liability because they were engaged in a discretionary function while conducting practice

---

204. 504 N.E.2d 552, 553 (Ind. 1987). *See also Benitez v. New York City Bd. of Educ.*, 541 N.E.2d 29, 543 N.Y.S.2d 29 (1989) (high school owed student-athlete voluntarily competing in interscholastic football game a duty to protect against injuries arising from unassumed, concealed, or unreasonably increased risks).
205. *Kahn v. East Side Union High School Dist.*, 75 P.3d 30 (Cal. 2003). *See also Kelly v. McCarrick*, 841 A.2d 869 (Md. Ct. Spec. App. 2004)
206. *Moose v. Massachusetts Inst. of Tech.*, 683 N.E.2d 706 (Mass. App. 1997).
207. *Limones v. Sch. Dist. Of Lee County*, 161 So. 3d 384 (Fla. 2015).
208. *Mogabgab v. Orleans Parish Sch. Bd.*, 239 So. 2d 456 (La. App. 1970).
209. *Gahan v. Mineola Union Free Sch. Dist.*, 660 N.Y.S.2d 144 (N.Y. App. Div. 1997).
210. *See* , e.g., *Evans v. Oaks Mission Pub. Sch.*, 945 P.2d 492 (Okla. 1997); *Grandalski v. Lyons Township High Sch. Dist. 204*, 711 N.E.2d 372 (Ill. App. Ct. 1999).
211. 741 So. 2d 207 (Miss. 1999).

223. Pre-injury contracts pursuant to which a person agrees to release a school district or its employees from liability for negligent failure to use reasonable care to protect the health and safety of students during athletic activities may be referred to by many names, including exculpatory clauses, releases, covenants not to sue, and hold harmless agreements. If enforceable under applicable state law, these waivers of liability bar a plaintiff's ability to seek recovery from the defendant for harm caused by negligent conduct. Some courts, which represent the majority view, have refused to enforce pre-injury waivers on grounds that they violate public policy.[212] A minority of jurisdictions have adopted a position that permits parents to sign a release that binds both the parent and minor.[213]

2. *University*

224. In *Kleinknecht v. Gettysburg College,*[214] the Third Circuit ruled that a university has a legal duty to use reasonable care to provide prompt and adequate emergency medical care to student-athletes injured while participating in intercollegiate athletics. Drew Kleinknecht was a 20-year-old sophomore student at Gettysburg College, which had recruited him for its Division III intercollegiate lacrosse team. During practice, Drew, who had no history of heart problems, collapsed and suffered cardiac arrest. At the time Drew was stricken, there was no athletic trainer or other person qualified to perform cardiopulmonary resuscitation or provide emergency medical care present. No telephone was readily available to call for help; rather, coaches and other student-athletes had to run to an off-field site on campus to summon help. Despite resuscitation efforts, which allegedly were delayed by the college's failure to have an appropriate emergency medical plan, he died of cardiac arrest. The Third Circuit held that "a special relationship existed between the College and Drew that was sufficient to impose a duty of reasonable care on the College" for the following reasons:

> Drew chose to attend Gettysburg College because he was persuaded it had a good lacrosse program, a sport in which he wanted to participate at the intercollegiate level. Head Trainer Donolli actively recruited Drew to play lacrosse at the College. At the time he was stricken, Drew was not engaged in his own private affairs as a student at Gettysburg College. Instead, he was participating in a scheduled athletic practice for an intercollegiate team sponsored by the College under the supervision of College employees.

225. Courts have held a university owes a general duty to use reasonable care to protect the health and safety of their student-athletes, although some courts refuse to extend this duty beyond the context of emergency medical care under the factual

212. *Wagenblast v. Odessa School Dist.*, 758 P.2d 968 (Wash. 1988).
213. *Sharon v. City of Newton*, 769 N.E.2d 738 (Mass. 2002).
214. 989 F.2d 1360 (3d Cir. 1993).

circumstances in *Kleinknecht.*[215] In *Searles v. Trustees of St. Joseph's College,* [216]the Maine Supreme Court held "that a college has a legal duty to exercise reasonable care towards its students," which encompasses the duty of college coaches and athletic trainers to exercise reasonable care for the health and safety of student-athletes. A basketball player sued his coach alleging that, notwithstanding medical advice that he should not continue to play basketball with a knee injury, the coach required him to continue playing, thereby causing an aggravated and permanent knee injury. The court concluded there was sufficient evidence to raise an issue of material fact regarding the coach's breach of his duty to exercise reasonable care for the plaintiff's health and safety.[217]

226. Like public high schools and their employees, public universities and their employees may be immune from negligence liability for injuries to intercollegiate athletes pursuant to the doctrines of sovereign immunity[218] and qualified immunity,[219] respectively. A university or employee's sovereign immunity from tort liability may be waived to the extent that negligent conduct arising out of a public university's sports program is covered by insurance.[220]

227. Because intercollegiate athletes generally are adults (unlike high school athletes who usually are minors), courts are more likely to upheld pre-injury liability waivers absolving universities from negligently caused injuries.[221] However, in *UCF Athletic Assoc. v. Plancher,*[222] the court refused to enforce an exculpatory clause, which it construed to cover only injuries inherent in the sport, because its language did not clearly inform an athlete that he was contracting away his right to sue the university for negligence.

---

215. *Orr v. Brigham Young Univ.*, 960 F. Supp.1522 (D. Utah 1994), *aff'd*, 108 F.3d 1388 (10th Cir. 1997).
216. 695 A.2d 1206 (Me. 1997).
217. *See also Lamorie v. Warner Pacific College,* 850 P.2d 401 (Or. Ct. App. 1993) (appellate court ruled that a jury could reasonably find that the player's re-injury of his eye was a foreseeable risk of being directed to resume playing basketball, for which the university could be held liable).
218. *Ward v. Michigan State Univ.,* 782 N.W.2d 514, 520 (Mich. App. 2010) *appeal denied,* 798 N.W.2d 766 (Mich. 2011). However, one court held that sponsoring revenue-generating sports such as intercollegiate football is a proprietary function of a public university that is not protected by sovereign immunity. *Brown v. Wichita State Univ.*, 540 P.2d 66 (Kan. 1975).
219. *Lennon v. Petersen*, 624 So. 2d 171, 173–175 (Ala. 1993).
220. Shriver v. Athletic Council of Kan. State Univ., *564 P.2d 451 (Kan. 1977);* Wallace v. Broyles, *961 S.W.2d 712 (Ark. 1998) (holding that an athletic trainer may be liable for negligence to the extent of his insurance coverage).*
221. *Roe v. Saint Louis University*, 2012 WL 6757558 (E.D. Mo.) (upholding waiver that releases university of liability for negligence that "may rise by or in connection with [student-athlete's] participation in any activities related to Saint Louis University intercollegiate athletic teams."
222. 121 So. 3d 1097 (Fla. App. 2013).

D. League and Governing Body Liability

1. Professional League

228. Federal labor law exclusively governs lawsuits for breach of a collective bargaining agreement (CBA), and section 301 of the Labor Management Relations Act preempts state law contract and tort claims for personal injuries predicated on such agreements.[223] Section 301 preempts tort claims that would frustrate its federal labor-contract scheme. A state law claim is preempted by section 301 when it is "substantially dependent" on analysis of a CBA. . . . Stated alternatively, "[i]f the plaintiff's claim cannot be resolved without interpreting the applicable CBA . . . it is preempted."

229. In *Duerson v. NFL*,[224] the family of deceased former Chicago Bears safety Dave Duerson sued the NFL for wrongful death claiming that his suicide resulted from brain damage he suffered while playing NFL football. The court ruled that their claims were preempted because they were "substantially dependent on the interpretation of CBA provisions." Noting the factually intensive nature of Section 301 preemption questions, it stated "[a]s one would expect in case-by-case analysis, in some situations preemption is found and in others it is not" and identified other suits brought against the NFL involving health and safety that were not preempted.[225]

230. In *Dent v. NFL,*[226] a group of former NFL players sued the NFL, asserting that to keep players in games, NFL teams routinely supplied players with large amounts of powerful pain-killing drugs without regard for the medical complications such dosages could ultimately cause. The court dismissed their complaint because "preemption does not require that the preempted state law claim be replaced by an analogue claim in the collective-bargaining agreement . . . . Nevertheless, the types of claims asserted in the operative complaint are grievable in important respects under the various CBAs."

231. In a pending case, a group of more than one hundred former players filed suit against the National Hockey League alleging it failed to warn them of the adverse effects of repeated concussions and head trauma. In 2016, U.S. District Judge Susan Nelson denied the NHL's motion to dismiss their complaint because factual discovery is necessary to elucidate the nature of the players'" claims, when they accrued, and which—if any—CBAs were in effect at accrual. She observed that preemption would likely be appropriate if discovery revealed both that the plaintiffs' claims accrued while a CBA was in effect and are substantially dependent on the CBA's interpretation.[227]

232. In 2011, the first lawsuit regarding concussions suffered by retired NFL players was filed, which alleged numerous causes of action including negligence,

223. *Allis-Chalmers Corp. v. Lueck*, 471 U.S. 202 (1985).

224. 2012 WL 1658353 (N.D. Ill. May 11, 2012).

225. *See* , e.g., *Brown v. National Football League*, 219 F. Supp. 2d 372, 387 (S.D.N.Y. 2002) (holding that a player's negligence claim against the NFL for failing to appropriately monitor a referee who threw a penalty flag into his eye was not preempted because the NFL rules he cited regarding the scope of the league's duty to train referees were not part of the CBA).

226. 2014 WL 7205048 (N.D. Cal.),

227. *In re National Hockey League Players' Concussion Injury Litigation*, 2016 WL 2901736 (D. Minn.).

fraud, strict liability based on design defect and manufacturing defects, failure to warn, and loss of consortium. Shortly thereafter, a number of other suits were filed, including *Easterling v. NFL*, the first concussion-related class action lawsuit filed against the NFL. In June 2012, these cases were consolidated and titled *In re National Football League Players' Concussion Injury Litigation.* In this litigation, the plaintiffs alleged the NFL was aware of the concussion risks associated with the sport, but intentionally ignored or concealed information pertaining to these risks. Plaintiffs also alleged that the NFL knew or should have known of the increased susceptibility to a variety of medical conditions, including concussions, associated with playing NFL football. In July 2013, judicially ordered mediation resulted in a settlement, which included the NFL's payment of USD 675 million for compensatory claims for players with certain neurological symptoms, USD 75 million for baseline testing, and USD 10 million for medical education and research. In 2014, the settlement agreement was modified to remove the monetary cap on payment for claims, and it was judicially approved in April 2015. This settlement does not preclude lawsuits by persons who opted out of the class, current NFL players, or NFL players who retired on or after July 7, 2014.

2. National Collegiate Athletic Association

233. The NCAA has a legal duty to use reasonable care when promulgating rules to protect athletes' safety. In *Sanchez v. Hillerich & Bradsby Co.,*[228] a California appellate court ruled that the NCAA may be liable for approving the use of a particular baseball bat during intercollegiate games if its performance capabilities are proved to increase unreasonably a pitcher's inherent risk of being hit by batted ball). On the other hand, in *Lanni v. NCAA*,[229] an Indiana appellate court "conclude[d] that the NCAA's regulation of the field of play and other rules and policies with respect to safety issues [and] compliance checks . . . do not rise to the level of assuring protection of the student-athletes from injuries that may occur at sporting events." It determined that "[a]ctual oversight and control cannot be imputed merely from the fact that the NCAA has promulgated rules and regulations and required compliance with those rules and regulations."

234. Intercollegiate student-athletes have filed concussion suits against the NCAA, which alleged it was negligent in safeguarding them from the risks of concussions and were consolidated into *In re Nat'l Collegiate Athletic Ass'n Student-Athlete Concussion Injury Litigation.*[230] The presiding judge granted preliminary approval to a settlement agreement in which the NCAA will pay USD 50 million to set up a fifty-year medical monitoring program for college athletes and another USD 5 million to start a program to research the prevention and treatment of concussions. The settlement's medical monitoring program will allow for medical screenings and evaluations for all current and former NCAA student-athletes, not limited by when they played, what sport they played, how long they played, where they played, or their age. The settlement also imposes requirements on colleges and universities such as requiring that medical personnel trained to diagnose and treat concussions be present at games involving

228. 128 Cal. Rptr. 2d 529 (Cal. App. 2002).
229. 42 N.E.3d 542 (Ind. App. 2015).
230. No. 13 C 9116, 2014 WL 7237208 (N.D. Ill. Dec. 17, 2014).

contact sports. It permits individual plaintiffs to file tort lawsuits against the NCAA, athletic conferences, and schools to recover damages for concussion-related injuries.

3. State High School Athletic Associations

235. State high school athletic associations often promulgate competition and equipment rules for interscholastic sports played within their respective jurisdictions. Courts have held that these governing bodies have a legal duty to exercise reasonable care when formulating safety rules governing high school athletic competition and may be liable for personal injuries to high school athletes if this duty is breached.[231] However, courts have expressed a reluctance to impose liability on a state high school athletic association for an alleged failure to adopt rules to reduce the inherent risks of injuries from participation in interscholastic sports. In *Pierscionek v. Illinois High School Association,* [232] an Illinois trial court dismissed a complaint seeking an injunction requiring a state high school sports governing body to establish particular rules to minimize the risk of a concussion while playing high school sports and to improve the management of student-athlete head injuries by its member schools. The court ruled that plaintiffs' request that it "impose policy and enact legislation by way of the grant of an injunction" is improper because "determining policy and enacting legislation lies within the distinct province of the legislature." It rejected plaintiffs' negligent rulemaking claim because "there is no precedent in Illinois for a private party to bring a negligence claim against a governmental entity for failure to promulgate laws or otherwise act."

4. Olympic Sports Federations

236. To date, there has been little personal injury litigation against Olympic sports federations that has been judicially resolved. In *Mehr v. FIFA,* [233] the court dismissed negligence claims against worldwide, national, and state soccer governing bodies because "[p]laintiffs have alleged no basis for imputing to any defendant a legal duty to reduce the risks inherent in the sport of soccer, or to implement any of the 'Consensus Statement' guidelines or concussion management protocols, and have alleged no facts showing that any defendant took any action that increased the risks beyond those inherent in the sport," In *Mayall v. USA Water Polo, Inc.,*[234] the court ruled that the national governing body for water polo has no duty to adopt return to play guidelines for athletes who sustained concussions.

231. See, e.g., *Mohr v. St. Paul Fire & Marine Ins. Co., 674 N.W.2d 576 (Wis. App. 2003); Wissel v. Ohio High Sch. Athletic Assn., 605 N.E.2d 458 (Ohio App. 1992).*
232. 2015 WL 6550826 (Ill. Cir. Ct.).
233. 2015 WL 4366044 (N.D. Cal.).
234. 2016 WL 1254034 (C.D. Cal.).

II. Criminal Liability

237. Criminal prosecutions for injuries occurring during athletic competition in the U.S. are rare, with convictions for alleged crimes even rarer.

238. In *People v. Fitzsimmons*,[235] the court instructed the jury as follows in a case involving the prosecution of a professional boxer for a blow that killed his opponent during a sparring exhibition:

> The public has an interest in the personal safety of its citizens, and is injured where the safety of any individual is threatened, whether by himself or another. A game which involves a physical struggle may be a commendable and manly sport, or it may be an illegal contest. This depends upon whether it is a game which endangers life. Thus, in the prosecution for a death which was caused accidentally in playing the game of football, it was left to the jury to say whether the game was dangerous; for, if so, consent on the part of the players to submit to what the game had in store for them would not protect a player from prosecution.
>
> In other words, gentlemen, nine men, or whatever constitutes a team of football, cannot lawfully engage in a contention upon the green with the idea that the result may terminate in the death or serious injury of one-half of them; but, if the rules of the game and the practices of the game are reasonable, are consented to by all engaged, are not likely to induce serious injury, or to end life, if then, as a result of the game, an accident happens, it is excusable homicide.
>
> No rules or practice of any game whatever can make that lawful which is unlawful by the law of the land, and the law of the land says you shall not do that which is likely to cause the death of another.

The jury acquitted the defendant of manslaughter.

239. Modern cases illustrate that U.S. law regarding criminal liability for deaths or serious injuries occurring during athletic competition has remained essentially the same since *Fitzsimmons*. In *People v. Schacker*,[236] the court ruled that "the interest of justice" requires dismissal of the charge of assault in the third degree against defendant for injuring a member of the opposing team during an adult recreational ice hockey game. The facts giving rise to this prosecution were as follows:

> … [A]t the Superior Ice Rink … the defendant Robert Schacker during an ice hockey game and after a play was over and the whistle had blown, did come up behind Andrew Morenberg who was standing near the goal net and did strike him on the back of the neck and caused him to strike his head on the crossbar of the net, causing him to sustain a concussion, headaches, blurred vision, and memory loss.

---

235. . 34 N.Y.S. 1102, 1109 (1895).
236. . 670 N.Y.S.2d 308 (N.Y. Dist. Ct. 1998).

240. The court ruled:

> [I]n order to allege a criminal act which occurred in a hockey game, the factual portion of the information must allege acts that show that the intent was to inflict physical injury which was unrelated to the athletic competition. Although play may have terminated, the information herein does not show that the physical contact had no connection with the competition. Furthermore, the injuries must be so severe as to be unacceptable in normal competition, requiring a change in the nature of the game. That type of injury is not present in this case. Firstly, the physical injury resulted from hitting the net, not from direct contact with the defendant. Secondly, the hospital records do not indicate severe trauma to the complainant.
>
> The idea that a hockey player should be prosecuted runs afoul of the policy to encourage free and fierce competition in athletic events. The People argued at the hearing that this was a non-checking hockey league. While the rules of the league may prohibit certain conduct, thereby reducing the potential injuries, nevertheless, the participant continues to assume the risk of a strenuous and competitive athletic endeavor. The normal conduct in a hockey game cannot be the standard for criminal activity under the Penal Law, nor can the Penal Law be imposed on a hockey game without running afoul of the policy of encouraging athletic competition.

241. Similar to tort law, physical contact resulting in even death or severe injury to a participating athlete is not criminal if it is "part of the game." Consent is a defense to alleged criminal assault, and it is necessary to determine "whether the conduct of defendant constituted foreseeable behaviour in the play of the game" and whether a plaintiff's injury "occurred as a by-product of the game itself."[237] Courts have affirmed criminal convictions for injuries caused by intentionally thrown punches during basketball and football games.[238] As one court noted, "There is nothing in the game of basketball, or even rugby or hockey, that would permit consent as a defence to such conduct."[239]

242. Criminal prosecutions of U.S. professional athletes rarely occur, but a Canadian court found Marty McSorley guilty of assault with a weapon for intentionally striking Donald Brashear in the head with his hockey stick during a February 21, 2000 NHL hockey game. Evidence in the case established that deliberately striking a player in the head with a hockey stick is prohibited by the rules of hockey and violates the unwritten code of conduct that is impliedly agreed to by NHL players and referees. The court determined that McSorley "had an impulse to strike [Brashear] in the head. His mindset, always tuned to aggression, permitted that. He slashed for the head. An

237. . *State v. Shelley*, 929 P.2d 489, 493 (Wash. Ct. App. 1997).

238. . *See* e.g., *State v. Floyd*, 466 N.W.2d 919 (Iowa Ct. App. 1990); *People v. Freer*, 381 N.Y.S.2d 976 (N.Y. Dist. Ct. 1976). *State v. Floyd*, 466 N.W.2d 919 (Iowa Ct. App. 1990); *People v. Freer*, 381 N.Y.S.2d 976 (N.Y. Dist. Ct. 1976).

239. . *Shelley, supra.*

NHL player would never, ever miss. Brashear was struck as intended." It imposed a conditional discharge on McSorley for eighteen months (i.e., he was given probation) and prohibited him from engaging in any future sporting event against Brashear.[240]

243. With some exceptions,[241] most recent U.S. criminal prosecutions have arisen out of death or serious injuries caused by a participating athlete to another athlete during non-professional competitive or recreational sports. In *People v. Hall,*[242] the Colorado Supreme Court held that Nathan Hall must stand trial for reckless manslaughter. While skiing, Hall flew off of a knoll and collided with Allen Cobb, who was traversing the slope below him. Cobb sustained traumatic brain injuries and died as a result of the collision. The court stated:

> We hold that under the particular circumstances of this case, whether Hall committed the crime of reckless manslaughter must be determined by the trier of fact. Viewed in the light most favorable to the prosecution, Hall's conduct – skiing straight down a steep and bumpy slope, back on his skis, arms out to his sides, off-balance, being thrown from mogul to mogul, out of control for a considerable distance and period of time, and at such a high speed that the force of the impact between his ski and the victim's head fractured the thickest part of the victim's skull – created a substantial and unjustifiable risk of death to another person. A reasonable person could infer that the defendant, a former ski racer trained in skier safety, consciously disregarded that risk. For the limited purposes of a preliminary hearing, the prosecution provided sufficient evidence to show probable cause that the defendant recklessly caused the victim's death.

244. The jury found Hall guilty of criminally negligent homicide, which verdict was upheld on appeal.[243] He was sentenced to ninety days in jail, ordered to perform 240 hours of community service, and was barred from drinking alcohol and recreational skiing during a probationary term.

245. In September 2000, a 16-year-old Illinois high school hockey player was sentenced to two years' probation, ordered not to participate in any contact sports during that time, and required to perform 120 hours of community service after entering an Alford plea (no admission of guilt, but acknowledgement that sufficient evidence to convict exists) to a misdemeanor battery charge. As a high school hockey game was ending, he cross-checked an opponent from behind, causing him to crash headfirst into the boards and permanently paralyzing him from the chest down.

246. In February 2000, Tony Limon, a Texas high school basketball player, was sentenced to five years in the state penitentiary for deliberately elbowing an opponent in the face (who suffered a concussion and fractured nose) during a game. This conduct

240. . In 1988 Minnesota North Star player Dino Ciccarelli was sentenced to one day in jail and fined USD 1,000 for striking an opposing player several times in the head with his stick during a National Hockey League game.

241. . David Stinson, the former head football coach at Pleasure Park High School in Kentucky, was prosecuted for the death of a player from heat stroke during an August 2008 practice. On Sep. 17, 2009, the jury acquitted him of reckless homicide and wanton endangerment charges.

242. . 999 P.2d 207 (Colo. 2000).

243. . *People v. Hall*, 59 P.3d 298 (Colo. Ct. App. 2002).

was unrelated to any ongoing play, but no foul was called. Limon had previously pled guilty to burglary and was given four years' probation, but had no prior history of violent behavior.

Part II. Sports and Status

Chapter 1. Interscholastic Student-Athletes

247. Courts grant substantial deference to high school sports governing bodies and educational institutions when considering student-athletes' challenges to rules and regulations precluding or limiting their eligibility to participate in interscholastic sports. These rules and regulations are promulgated both at the state-wide level by state interscholastic athletic associations and at the local level by individual schools and school districts. State athletic associations, which typically are comprised of public and private member high schools, promulgate and enforce student-athlete eligibility rules to achieve legitimate objectives of broad concern to their members such as academic integrity, competitive balance, and health and safety. Unlike college sports, direct recruiting of students by member high schools for athletics-related reasons is prohibited. As a means of achieving this objective, transfer rules often restrict the eligibility of student-athletes to participate immediately in inter-scholastic athletics after transferring from one school to another or from one school district to another. Eligibility rules created and enforced at local levels by individual schools or school districts often address more discrete matters, such as those conditioning a student-athlete's eligibility to participate in sports on complying with conduct or grooming standards.

248. Although courts generally defer to sports governing bodies and schools in administering or interpreting their rules, they will require them to follow their own rules. In *Mississippi High School Activities Ass'n v. R.T.*,[244] the Mississippi Supreme Court held that student-athletes are the intended beneficiaries of high school athletic programs and the rules that govern them. Therefore, student-athletes have standing to seek judicial relief requiring a state governing body or high school to comply with its athletic eligibility rules.

249. Student-athletes must exhaust state interscholastic athletic association or educational institution internal administrative processes before seeking judicial recourse. Student-athletes who have received adverse internal eligibility determinations have sought judicial relief, for example, in cases involving rules relating to their inability to participate in either an interscholastic or club sport as well as ineligibility to participate because of one's status as a home-schooled child, misconduct, transfer from one school to another, exceeding maximum age limitations, and/or failing to meet minimum academic requirements (e.g., no-pass, no-play rules).

244. 163 So. 3d 274 (Miss. 2015).

§1. No Property or Liberty Interest in Interscholastic Athletic Participation

250. Even if the requisite state action necessary to trigger federal constitutional protection exists,[245] the prevailing judicial view is that participation in interscholastic athletes is not a protected property right or liberty interest.[246] *Brands v. Sheldon Community School*,[247] which upholds a public high school's disciplinary action rendering a student-athlete ineligible for interscholastic athletic competition for violating its good conduct rules,[248] illustrates the majority view. In *Brands*, a student-athlete was declared ineligible to participate on his high school's interscholastic wrestling team (which prevented him from defending his state wrestling championship) because he and three other male students engaged in multiple acts of sexual intercourse with a 16 year old female student. School officials suspended him from interscholastic athletic participation because his conduct was "detrimental to the best interests" of the school district.

251. In attempting to set aside his suspension, the student-athlete argued, *inter alia*, that he had been deprived of his federal constitutional due process rights, which require a fair hearing and rationally-based decision. To be entitled to due process, the court stated he must first have a protected property right or liberty interest in interscholastic sports participation, not merely an expectation he will be permitted to do so. Consistent with the majority view, the *Brands* court found that he has only a conditional privilege, not a right, to participate in school-sponsored athletics. His speculative claim that he may be offered a college athletic scholarship based on how he performed in the state wrestling championship was insufficient to establish a property interest, which requires a legitimate claim of right. Although the high school's policies and administrative rules may create a property interest by requiring that certain conditions be satisfied before taking away his athletic eligibility, his suspension was in accordance with the school's administrative rules and policies, so there was no legitimate basis for successfully asserting he was deprived of a property interest. Although he has a constitutionally protected liberty interest in his personal privacy, this right was not infringed by the school under the circumstances.

---

245. . *See* Part I, Ch. 2, §3.
246. . *See* e.g., *Brown v. Oklahoma Secondary Sch. Activities Ass"n*, 125 P.3d 1219, 1227 (Okla. 2005) (rejecting plaintiff's assertion he possessed right to participate in interscholastic athletics).
247. . 671 F.Supp. 627 (N.D. Iowa 1987).
248. . "'Good conduct rules' refer to school rules that attempt to govern out-of-school conduct, as well as in-school conduct by students engaged in extracurricular activities." Larry D. Bartlett, *The Courts View of Good Conduct Rules for High School Student Athletes*, 82 Ed. L. Rep. 1087, 1088 (1993). Such rules typically are directed at prohibiting certain behavior such as consuming alcohol or using illegal drugs and tobacco as well as requiring students to abide by community standards of decency as a condition to participation in extracurricular activities including sports.

§2. Judicial Deference And Academic Abstention

252. Courts generally provide interscholastic athletic associations and educational institutions with considerable deference regarding their internal resolution of athletic participation disputes.[249] Even when student-athletes assert that a state high school athletic association or public school has infringed independent and traditionally recognized federal constitutional rights (e.g., freedom of speech, expression, privacy, or religion) that adversely affect their athletic participation interests, courts generally apply only rational basis scrutiny absent discrimination or exclusion based on race, ethnicity, national origin, or gender.

253. For example, in *Wildman v. Marshalltown School District*,[250] a federal appellate court rejected a student-athlete's claim that a public high school infringed her free speech rights by conditioning her continued participation on the basketball team on her apologizing for writing a letter containing one profane word that criticized the coach. Concluding that "coaches deserve a modicum of respect from athletes, particularly in an academic setting, the court ruled that school's disciplinary action was 'reasonable'"

254. Regarding an interscholastic student-athlete's right of religious freedom, one scholar has explained:

> [A]thletic participation and religious observance appear to be two of Americans' most cherished endeavors. When these endeavors collide, and when the collision is due partly to a governmental regulation or policy, the Free Exercise Clause may very well dictate how this conflict between competition and conscience is resolved. The First Amendment's principal message in this regard is that regulations must be religiously neutral and generally applicable, and that religious requests for accommodation must be treated with at least the same solicitude that administrators display towards nonreligious requests (although more favorable treatment is in many instances permissible as well). The government may also have to bend its regulations where the athlete's predicament implicates not only free exercise, but also a conjunctive constitutional claim such as free speech or the right of parents to direct their children's education. To the extent that governments abide by these norms, the First Amendment otherwise permits them generally to regulate in any rational manner, and pursue any legitimate objectives, which they deem appropriate.[251]

---

249. . In re Univ. Interscholastic League, 20 S.W.3d 690, 692 (Tex. 2000) (holding there is no fundamental right to participate in extracurricular activities, the court reasoned that judicial intervention into the matters of educational institutions do more harm than good).

250. . 249 F.3d 768 (8th Cir. 2001).

251. . Scott Idleman, *Religious Freedom and the Interscholastic Athlete*, 12 Marq. Sports L. Rev. 295, 344–345 (2001). However, he points out that state constitutions and other laws may provide a greater level of legal protection to religious freedom rights: "In some states, e.g., strict scrutiny may apply to government regulations even if they are neutral and generally applicable. In others, the rights of students or student-athletes may be specifically protected. While in others, or in certain interscholastic venues, the regulations themselves may provide for certain forms of religious accommodation." *Ibid.*, at 345.

255. Courts generally defer to schools regarding appropriate grooming rules,[252] although some courts have been less deferential. In *Holsapple v. Woods*,[253] the Seventh Circuit ruled that a student's right to wear hair at any length or in any desired manner is an ingredient of personal freedom protected by the U.S. Constitution. In *Hayden v. Greensburg Community School Corp.*,[254] the Seventh Circuit held: "The [plaintiffs] are entitled to judgment on their Title IX claim for the same reasons we have already discussed with respect to the equal protection claim . . . The hair-length policy is applied only to the boys team, with no evidence concerning the content of any comparable grooming standards applied to the girls team."

256. State constitutional provisions may provide interscholastic student-athletes with more protection than that offered under the federal constitution, in terms of equal protection and other protected rights (e.g., association, education, free exercise, free speech, and privacy). In *Indiana High School Athletic Assn., Inc. v. Avant*,[255] the court acknowledged that the Indiana state constitution provided a higher level of protection to high school athletes than is afforded under the federal equal protection clause.

257. Eligibility rules commonly referred to as "no-pass, no-play" rules were initially promulgated in the early 1980s as state legislatures and athletic associations sought to strike an appropriate balance between academics and athletics. No-pass, no-play rules condition participation in extracurricular activities, including sports, on students achieving a certain academic performance. Students deemed ineligible to participate in interscholastic sports have challenged the legality of no-pass, no-play rules on equal protection and due process grounds. Because participation in extracurricular activities is neither a fundamental right nor an infringement on the rights of a suspect class, courts have applied a rational basis test in addressing equal protection challenges. The application of such a standard invariably leads them to conclude that no-pass, no-play rules are rationally related to their intended goals.[256] Other courts have rejected due process challenges to no-pass, no-play rules because a student's interest in participating in extracurricular activities is not a protected property or liberty interest.[257]

258. A rational basis standard has been applied even when students are denied any opportunity to participate in a school's interscholastic athletics program. For example, courts uniformly have upheld state school board or high school athletic association rules prohibiting otherwise eligible home-schooled students from participating in interscholastic sports. Home-schooling refers to the practice of parents educating their children at home rather than in public or private schools for religious, secular, or pedagogical reasons. Approximately 1.9 million students currently are home-schooled

252. *Davenport v. Randolph County Bd. of Educ.*, 730 F.2d 1395 (11th Cir. 1984).

253. 500 F.2d 49 (7th Cir. 1974).

254. 743 F.3d 569 (7th Cir. 2014).

255. 650 N.E.2d 1164 (Ind. App. 1995),

256. . *Bailey v. Truby*, 321 S.E.2d 302 (W.Va. 1984). *See also Bartmess v. Bd. of Trustees of Sch. Dist. No. 1*, 726 P.2d 801, 805 (Mont. 1986) (denying student-athlete's challenge of academic eligibility rule, court reasons that rule provides incentive for students wishing to participate in extracurricular activities and "promotes adequate study time for those students who have not maintained a 2.0 grade average").

257. . *Spring Branch I.S.D. v. Stamos*, 695 S.W.2d 556, 560 (Tex. 1985); *Thompson v. Fayette County Public Schs.*, 786 S.W.2d 879, 882 (Ky. App. 1990).

in the U.S. Although they elect to opt out of formalized high school education systems, many parents desire that their children receive the educational and other benefits of participating in interscholastic sports offered by local public schools.

259. Absent statutory authorization to participate,[258] *Jones v. West Virginia State Board of Education*[259] illustrates the prevailing judicial response to litigation by home-schooled children seeking to play interscholastic sports. The West Virginia Secondary School Activities Commission ("WVSSAC") denied a home-schooled child's request that he be permitted to join a public middle school's wrestling team. The boy's parents alleged, *inter alia*, their son's exclusion from athletic participation violated his equal protection rights as a home-schooled child. The West Virginia Supreme Court ruled that participation in inter-scholastic extracurricular activities, including sports, is not a constitutionally protected right, much less a fundamental right justifying heightened judicial scrutiny. Deferring to the state athletic association's judgment, the court applied the rational basis test. The court deferred to the judgment of school officials who expressed concerns regarding the potential negative impact on maintaining the academic integrity of its interscholastic programs caused by the differences in curriculum, grading standards, and methods between home-schooled and publicly educated children.

260. Courts have adopted a similar approach in uniformly rejecting legal challenges to "outside competition" rules, which generally prohibit student-athletes from participating on a non-school or club team as a condition of participating in the same sport on a high school team during the same season or academic year.[260] In *Letendre v. Missouri State High School Activities Association*,[261] the court upheld the Missouri State High School Activities Association's ("MSHSAA") outside competition rule and ruled that it did not violate student-athletes' equal protection rights. Finding no violation of any fundamental constitutional right, the court applied rational basis scrutiny. It concluded that the outside competition rule is rationally related to the MSHSAA's legitimate objectives, including preventing conflicts between sports and academics, discouraging an over-emphasis on sports by students, avoiding conflicts in coaching philosophy and scheduling, and promoting competitive equity.

261. In addition to the rational basis review standard, courts implicitly rely on the academic abstention doctrine to provide only limited judicial scrutiny of the merits of student-athlete eligibility disputes pursuant to the law of private associations. In *Indiana High School Athletic Association v. Carlberg*,[262] the Indiana Supreme Court held that the Indiana High School Athletic Association ("IHSAA") is "analogous to a government agency with respect to challenges to its rules and enforcement actions brought by students." Although recognizing that the students are not represented in

---

258. . A majority of states now have laws permitting homeschooled students to participate in interscholastic sports. These rules have been dubbed "Tim Tebow" laws, after Tim Tebow, the 2007 Heisman Trophy winner who had been homeschooled, gained notoriety on the football field, at the collegiate and professional levels. *See* http://aol.sportingnews.com/nfl/story/2012-08-21/tim-tebow-new-york-jets-quarterback-law-home-schooled-students-south-carolina.

259. . 622 S.E.2d 289 (W. Va. 2005).

260. . *See* , e.g., *Burrows v. Ohio High Sch. Athletic Ass'n*, 891 F.2d 122 (6th Cir. 1989); *Zuments v. Colo. High Sch. Activities Ass'n*, 737 P.2d 1113, 1116 (Colo. App. 1987).

261. . 86 S.W.3d 63 (Mo. Ct. App. 2002).

262. . 694 N.E.2d 222, 228 (Ind. 1997).

the association's leadership and do not voluntarily subject themselves to the association's athletic eligibility rules or have any voice in their making, it refused to provide de novo review in disputes challenging their validity or application.

262. The court held that deferential "arbitrary and capricious" review, the standard generally applied in reviewing administrative agency action, is appropriate. According to the court, this:

> is a narrow standard of review and the reviewing court may not substitute its judgment for the judgment of the IHSAA. The rule or decision will be found to be arbitrary and capricious only where it is wilful and unreasonable, without consideration and in disregard of the facts or circumstances in the case, or without some basis which would lead a reasonable and honest person to the same conclusion.

263. It upheld the IHSAA's application of its transfer rule to a student who transferred schools for non-athletic reasons without a change of permanent residence by his parents, thereby rendering him ineligible to participate in varsity inter-scholastic athletics for 365 days after enrolment. The court concluded that the IHSAA's decision was not arbitrary and capricious, although it was "undisputed that his transfer was neither primarily for athletic reasons nor as a result of undue influence" by his new high school. It found that the IHSAA had objective standards for determining an athlete's residence and transfer, which were publicized and applied consistently, and that requiring "a factual inquiry into the motivation for every transfer would impose a considerable burden on both the IHSAA and its member schools."

Chapter 2. Intercollegiate Student-Athletes

264. Courts have granted substantial deference to sports governing bodies such as the NCAA as well as college and universities when considering student-athletes' challenges to rules and regulations precluding or limiting their participation in intercollegiate sports. Although college sports are offered because of their inherent educational benefits to participants, U.S. courts almost uniformly refuse to recognize that a student-athlete has a legally protected interest in intercollegiate athletic participation absent a valid express contractual right to play a sport (which rarely is judicially found to exist). Unless the federal constitution is violated[263] or the NCAA or an educational institution violates federal or state civil rights laws by promulgating and/or applying eligibility rules that deny a student-athlete an opportunity to participate in sports based on race, ethnicity, national origin, gender, or disability[264] courts generally provide only very limited rational basis scrutiny of claims arising out of athletic eligibility disputes.

§1. Legal Nature of the Relationship Between Student-Athlete and University

I. Contractual Aspects

265. An express contract between a student-athlete and his or her institution arises out of several documents, including the National Letter of Intent (NLI), the Statement of Financial Assistance, and university publications such as bulletins and catalogues. These documents collectively define the nature of the respective rights and obligations between colleges and universities and their student-athletes.

266. A key document that defines the student-athlete and university relationship is the NLI. The purposes of the NLI include reducing and limiting recruiting pressure on student-athletes. Several legal obligations flow from a prospective student-athlete signing an NLI. By signing an NLI, a prospective student-athlete agrees for a period of one year to attend the institution named in the Letter of Intent (hereinafter referred to as "named institution"). Thereafter, other institutions must cease all recruiting contacts with the student-athlete. The NLI is not effective unless the student-athlete has received a promise in writing from the named institution to provide financial aid for an entire academic year. Assuming the student-athlete complies with NCAA financial aid eligibility requirements and is admitted to the named institution, the athlete is entitled to a scholarship for one full academic year from the named institution. A

263. . *Hysaw v. Washburn University*, 690 F. Supp. 940 (D. Kan. 1987) (public university's discipline of student-athletes for protesting racial mistreatment may infringe their First Amendment rights).

264. . See e.g., *Garvey v. Unified Sch. Dist.* 262, 2005 WL 2548332 (D. Kan.) (Title VI provides intercollegiate student- athlete with a cause of action for claims of intentional discrimination); *Mercer v. Duke Univ.*, 401 F.3d 199 (4th Cir. 2005) (gender discrimination in violation of Title IX); *Cole v. NCAA*, 120 F. Supp.2d 1060 (N.D. Ga. 2000) (Americans With Disabilities Act claim alleging disability discrimination).

student-athlete who fails to attend the named institution will be penalized by being ineligible to compete in intercollegiate athletics for one academic year and losing one year of athletic eligibility to compete in all sports at the new institution in which he or she enrolls. Finally, a student-athlete's 1-year commitment remains effective even if the coach for whom the athlete anticipated he or she would play leaves the named institution in the NLI.

267. Student-athletes who obtain athletic scholarships sign form documents commonly referred to as Statements of Financial Assistance. Pursuant to a Statement of Financial Assistance, a college agrees to extend financial aid to student-athletes to the extent of tuition, fees, room, board, and books for at least one academic year.[265] The purpose of the financial aid award is to assist and enable student-athletes to pursue a program of study and to participate in the educational process of the institution.

268. Student-athletes and their parents are often unaware of the terms and conditions of athletes' contracts with their schools. For example, many athletes and their parents incorrectly assume that scholarships are guaranteed for a four-year period so long as the athlete remains academically and athletically eligible. Some states have enacted legislation to requiring increased disclosure to student-athletes to help them make wise choices. California's Student-Athletes' Right to Know Act requires university coaches who recruit athletes in California to disclose institutional and NCAA policies regarding payment of student-athlete medical expenses, scholarship renewals, and transfers to other institutions.[266] Connecticut has adopted similar legislation.[267]

269. Although courts generally will not recognize claims alleging negligent admission of an academically deficient student-athlete or educational malpractice, a student-athlete may bring a breach of contract claim against his university for failing to provide him with promised academic support services such as tutoring. In *Ross v. Creighton University*,[268] the court held that a student-athlete stated a valid breach of contract claim based on the following allegations:

> To state a claim for breach of contract, the plaintiff must do more than simply allege that the education was not good enough. Instead, he must point to an identifiable contractual promise that the defendant failed to honor. We read Mr. Ross' complaint to allege more than a failure of the University to provide him with an education of a certain quality. Rather, he alleges that the University knew that he was not qualified academically to participate in its curriculum. Nevertheless, it made a specific promise that he would be able to participate in a meaningful way in that program because it would provide certain specific services to him. Finally, he alleges that the University breached its promise by reneging on its commitment to provide those services and, consequently, effectively cutting him off from any participation in and benefit from the University's academic program. To adjudicate such a claim, the court would not be required to determine whether Creighton had breached its contract with Mr. Ross by providing deficient academic

265. . Effective August 2012, the NCAA permits its member institutions to award multi-year scholarships of up to five years. 2012-13 NCAA Division I Manual § 15.02.7.
266. . West's Ann. Cal. Educ. Code § 67365 (West, Westlaw through Ch. 22 of 2012 Reg. Sess.).
267. . C.G.S.A. § 10a-55k (West, Westlaw through Public Acts approved on or before May 14, 2012).
268. . 957 F.2d 410 (7th Cir. 1992).

services. Rather, its inquiry would be limited to whether the University had provided any real access to its academic curriculum at all.

270. In exchange for the university's commitment to provide financial aid and an opportunity to receive a college education, a student-athlete promises to attend a particular college and to participate in athletics.[269] The student-athlete's right to continue to receive financial assistance is contingent upon the athlete remaining academically eligible to participate in the institution's athletic program.[270] Student-athletes also promise to comply with the rules and regulations of their respective institution, athletic conference (e.g., Big Ten Conference), and governing national athletic association (e.g., NCAA).

271. The terms of the athletic scholarship between a university that is a member of the NCAA and its student-athletes incorporate applicable NCAA regulations (including academic and amateurism eligibility requirements) and become a part of the parties' agreement. NCAA Bylaw Article 15, which governs institutional financial aid to student-athletes, is particularly significant. Athletic scholarships must be valid for at least one year (and may be renewed annually), but cannot exceed a student-athlete's 5-year period of eligibility to participate in intercollegiate athletics at an NCAA member school. NCAA regulations strictly limit the circumstances under which an institution can cancel or reduce the financial value of the athletic scholarship while it is in effect, but an institution has the discretion not to renew an athletic scholarship after its expiration for virtually any reason, including athletic performance-related reasons as well as academic ineligibility or misconduct.[271] The NCAA provides the student-athlete with no administrative recourse to challenge the university's decision not to renew an athletic scholarship so long as the institution complies with the NCAA's deadline for making its decision on or before July 1, prior to the academic year in which it is to be effective[272] and the decision is made by the institution's financial aid authority.[273]

272. Student-athletes whose scholarships have not been renewed have few legal remedies.[274] In *Conard v. University of Washington*,[275] the court upheld the University of Washington's refusal to renew the scholarships of two student-athletes who were involved in a series of incidents that violated its football team rules. The university

269. . *Taylor v. Wake Forest University*, 191 S.E.2d 379 (N.C. App. 1972).
270. . *Williams v. University of Cincinnati*, 752 N.E. 2d 367 (Ohio Misc. 2001) (because student-athlete's academic ineligibility was due solely to his own prior deficient academic performance, court rejects his promissory estoppel claim seeking restoration of his athletic scholarship based on alleged detrimental reliance on his coach's advice).
271. . *Conard v. University of Washington*, 62 Wash. App. 664, 671, 814 P.2d 1242 (1991).
272. . 2013-14 NCAA Division I Manual § 15.3.5.
273. . In some instances, an educational institution's internal rules may provide a student-athlete with certain procedural rights (e.g., a hearing) before a scholarship is not renewed, but this is not currently required by NCAA rules.
274. . *Milo v. University of Vermont*, 2013 WL 4647782 (D. Vt.) (recognizing the contractual nature of the student-athlete and university relationship, the court rejects various theories asserted by an athlete (e.g., duty of good faith and deprivation of due process) in upholding a coach's discretion not to renew the athlete's 1-year scholarship).
275. . 834 P.2d 17 (Wash. 1992).

acknowledged that athletic scholarships were typically renewed for 4 to 5 years absent a finding of serious misconduct. Rejecting plaintiffs' breach of contract claims against the university, the court ruled that "the fact that scholarships are, in fact, normally renewed does not create a "common law" of renewal, absent other consistent and supportive UW policies or rules." The court found plaintiffs not only failed to present evidence of such supportive rules or policies, but they also had failed to establish they had met the terms for renewal given their misconduct.

273. Courts have been very reluctant to expand the rights of student-athletes or legal obligations imposed on institutions beyond those promises expressly stated in the contract documents. For example, in *Jackson v. Drake University*,[276] the court rejected a student-athlete's claim that his financial aid agreement implicitly granted him the right to play basketball at his university. Finding that the clear and unambiguous language of the financial aid agreement does not create this right, the court dismissed the student-athlete's breach of contract claim because he admitted the university had performed all obligations expressly established by the financial aid agreement.

274. Although courts generally will not imply new terms into the written contract between a student-athlete and university, the breach of an express written or oral promise is actionable. Influenced by its reputation as "Quarterback University," Brian Fortay, a highly recruited high school quarterback, decided to attend and play football at the University of Miami. In his lawsuit, *Fortay v. Univ. of Miami*,[277] Brian Fortay maintained that his contract with Miami impliedly obligated the university to provide the guidance necessary to allow him to develop his football talents. Although the court ruled that the Letter of Intent and other contract documents did not give rise to the alleged implied obligations, it determined that Fortay had alleged sufficient facts to support his breach of oral contract claim. These promises allegedly included representations that Miami would provide guidance that would enable Fortay to develop his football skills, that it would not recruit other quarterbacks, and that Fortay would be Miami's starting quarterback by his third year.

275. Notwithstanding the *Fortay* court's ruling, student-athletes will be required to overcome traditional defenses to breach of contract in convincing a court to enforce an oral promise. These defenses include: a lack of definiteness (i.e., the failure of the oral offer to include all of the terms of the contract to be made),[278] the parole evidence rule,[279] and the statute of frauds.[280]

---

276. . 778 F. Supp. 1490 (S.D. Iowa 1991). *See also Soderbloom v. Yale Univ.*, 1992 Conn. Super. LEXIS 256 (the court rejected a student-athlete's argument that the institution's alleged obligation to provide a wrestling program during the athlete's four years at the university arose by implication from the contract documents).

277. . 1994 U.S. Dist. LEXIS 1865.

278. . *Giuliani v. Duke University*, 2010 WL 1292321 (M.D.N.C.); *Searles v. Trs. of St. Joseph's Coll.*, 695 A.2d 1206 (Me. 1997).

279. . *Hartman v. Univ. of Tennessee*, 1998 Tenn. App. LEXIS 620.

280. . *Hairston v. Southern Methodist University*, 2013 WL 1803549 (Tex. App. 2013); *Cooper v. Peterson*, 626 N.Y.S.2d 432 (1995).

II. Constitutionally Protected Property or Liberty Interests

276. Public colleges and universities are state actors because they are state or local government entities; whereas, private colleges and universities are not state actors that are subject to the constraints of the U.S. Constitution. Therefore, student-athletes rendered ineligible to participate in intercollegiate athletics can assert denial of due process claims only against public colleges and universities. The U.S. Constitution prohibits a public college or university from depriving a student-athlete of a property right or liberty interest without due process of law.

277. Courts generally refuse to recognize a constitutionally protected property right or liberty interest in intercollegiate athletic competition[281] and have rejected arguments that such participation is necessary to develop the skills necessary for a future professional sports career. Although many college athletes aspire to a professional career, few achieve their dreams and such aspirations are considered speculative and not subject to constitutional protection under the due process clause,[282] which requires deprivation of a legitimate claim of entitlement under state law to be actionable. On the other hand, courts have held that a student-athlete's contractual right to the economic value of an athletic scholarship during the period in which it is in effect with a public university is a constitutionally protected property interest.[283] However, absent a legally enforceable promise of playing time therein, an athletic scholarship does not create a constitutionally protected property right or liberty interest to participate in intercollegiate sports.[284]

III. Student-Athlete Eligibility for Workers' Compensation Benefits

278. Some student-athletes have claimed that their receipt of an athletic scholarship and other factors justifies characterizing them as university "employees" eligible to recover workers' compensation benefits for injuries suffered while participating in intercollegiate athletics.

279. Workers' compensation laws, which are governed by state law, provide a simple and inexpensive method for employees to obtain compensation and medical expenses for work-related injuries or diseases. The underlying policy of these laws is that industries should bear the burden of industrial accidents as a component of the cost of production. Under workers' compensations legislation, benefits are available

281. . *See Spath v. NCAA*, 728 F.2d 25 (1st Cir. 1984); *Rutledge v. Arizona Bd. Of Regents*, 660 F.2d 1345 (9th Cir. 1981); *Marcum v. Dahl*, 658 F.2d 731 (10th Cir. 1981); *Hall v. NCAA*, 985 F. Supp. 782 (N.D. Ill. 1997); *Lesser v. Neosho County Cmty. Coll.*, 741 F. Supp. 854 (D. Kan. 1990).
282. . *Colorado Seminary v. NCAA*, 417 F. Supp. 885 (D. Colo. 1976), *aff'd* 570 F.2d 320 (10th Cir. 1978).
283. . *Conard v. Univ. of Washington*, 834 P.2d 17, 22–23 (Wash. 1992).
284. . *Hysaw v. Washburn Univ.*, 690 F. Supp. 940 (D. Kan. 1987) (student-athlete has no liberty interest in pursuing a college football career); *Lesser v. Neosho County Cmty. Coll.*, 741 F. Supp. 854, 865 (D. Kan. 1990) (athletic scholarship promised plaintiff financial aid but not a position on the baseball team). *See* Part II, Ch. 2, §1, I.

to injured workers regardless of an employer's common law tort or other statutory liability. These laws, however, generally preclude employee tort actions against employers, and limit the amount of damages that can be recovered. Thus, employees are required to waive tort claims against their employers in exchange for a simplified, but limited, recovery under workers' compensation laws.

280. Generally, a person injured while performing services for compensation is considered an employee if two elements are present: (1) an express or implied contract to hire, and (2) employee status. A contract to hire requires an employer to pay compensation to an employee who performs services, sets forth the place to perform such services and work to be performed, and sets the compensation for the performance of the work. In addition to a contract to hire, there must be an employer-employee relationship.

281. Courts often adopt one of the following tests to determine an employment relationship: (1) the right to control the details of the work test, or (2) the relative nature of the work test. The right to control test examines whether the employer possessed the right to control the manner, means, and details of the worker's performance. Factors that demonstrate the requisite right of control include the terms of the employment agreement, the actual exercise of control, the method of payment, the furnishing of equipment, and the right to terminate the worker. An alternative standard used by an increasing number of courts is the relative nature of the work test. Pursuant to this test, "employees are those who as a matter of economic reality are dependent upon the business to which they render service."[285] This test is likely to be satisfied where a worker performs tasks integral to the employer's regular business and does not provide an independent business or professional service vis-à-vis the employer. The principal consideration under the nature of the work test is the relationship between the services provided and the regular business of the alleged employer.

282. Some states expressly exclude student-athletes from the definition of an employee for workers compensation purposes including California,[286] Hawaii,[287] New York,[288] Oregon,[289] and Vermont.[290] In contrast, although it is not characterized as workers compensation benefits, Nebraska has established an administrative system for providing medical and disability benefits to injured university athletes.[291] Most states, however, do not expressly include or exclude scholarship athletes from coverage under their respective workers' compensation statutes nor provide another system of compensation for injured university athletes. Thus, courts must determine whether or not scholarship athletes are covered "employees."

285. . Leo L. Lam, *Designer Duty: Extending Liability to Manufacturing for Violation of Labor Standards in Garment Industry Sweatshops*, 141 U. Pa. L. Rev. 623, 651 (1992).

286. . Cal. Lab. Code § 3352(k) (Deering Supp. 2011).

287. . Haw. Rev. Stat. Ann. § 386-1 (Michie Supp. 2011) (worker or employee "shall not include a person engaged in amateur sports even if an employer contributes to support of such sports").

288. . N.Y. Workers' Comp. §2(4) (McKinney 2012) ("'[E]mployee' shall not include persons who are members of a supervised amateur athletic activity operated on a non-profit basis … ").

289. . ORS § 656.027(13) (2008).

290. . 21 VSA § 601(14(b)) (LexisNexis 2009).

291. . Neb. Rev. Stat. §85–106.05.

283. As illustrated by *Waldrep v. Texas Employers Insurance Association,*[292] courts generally hold that athletes who suffer injuries while participating in intercollegiate athletics are not entitled to workers' compensation benefits.[293] In 1972, Kent Waldrep agreed to play football for Texas Christian University (TCU). In exchange, TCU agreed to provide him with a full athletic scholarship. While playing football for TCU against the University of Alabama, Waldrep sustained a severe injury to his spinal cord and was paralyzed below the neck. He subsequently filed a workers' compensation claim for his injury.

284. The *Waldrep* court framed the issue before it as "whether, for [Texas] workers' compensation law purposes, a recipient of a scholarship or financial aid from a university" is an employee, which it answered negatively. The court explained:

> It is undisputed that before Waldrep signed the Letter of Intent and Financial Aid Agreement, both he and TCU understood that his recruitment and future football career at TCU would be governed by and subject to the rules of the NCAA. The record indicates that the NCAA's policies and rules in effect at that time exhibited a concerted effort to ensure that each school governed by these rules made certain that student-athletes were not employees. Indeed, the rules declared that the fundamental policy of the NCAA was to maintain inter-collegiate athletics as an integral part of the educational program and the athlete as an integral part of the student body, and, by so doing, retain a clear line of demarcation between college athletics and professional sports. Following its policy, the evidence reflects that the NCAA rules made the principle of amateurism foremost and established several requirements to ensure that the student-athlete would not be considered a professional.

285. The *Waldrep* court also relied on evidence establishing that neither the student-athlete nor TCU treated the financial aid he received as "pay" or "income" (e.g., TCU never placed Waldrep on its payroll), which was not subject to income tax. With respect to the right of control, the court found that TCU exercised control over all athletes participating in its football program, including non-scholarship players. However, it determined that TCU did not have the right to control all aspects of its football players' activities while enrolled at the university or "any extraordinary degree of control over his academic activities."

286. Although student-athletes generally cannot recover workers' compensation benefits for injuries while participating in intercollegiate athletics, the NCAA has a catastrophic athletic injury insurance plan covering student-athletes who suffer serious injuries while participating in intercollegiate athletics at its member institutions. This plan, which provides for a maximum individual lifetime benefit of USD 20 million provides compensation for educational benefits and lost earnings, as well as lifetime rehabilitation, medical, and dental expenses.

---

292. . 21 S.W.3d. 692 (Tex. Ct. App. 2000).

293. . *See also, Rensing v. Ind. State Univ. Bd. of Trs.*, 444 N.E.2d 1170 (Ind. 1983) (student-athletes not entitled to workers' compensation benefits); *Coleman v. W. Mich. Univ.*, 336 N.W. 2d 224 (Mich. Ct. App. 1983) (student-athletes not entitled to workers' compensation benefits).

287. NCAA bylaws permit a university to continue an injured student-athlete's scholarship to complete his education even if he is unable to participate in intercollegiate athletics.[294] Effective with the 2013–2014 academic year, California's "Student Athlete Bill of Rights"[295] requires any California four-year university whose athletic program receives USD 10 million or more in media revenues (currently Stanford University, the University of California, Berkeley, the University of California, Los Angeles, and the University of Southern California) to provide an academic scholarship for up to five academic years, or until he or she graduates, to a student-athlete who suffers a career-ending injury causing the loss of an athletic scholarship.

IV. Student-Athletes as Employees for Purposes of Employment or Labor Law

288. In *Berger v. NCAA*,[296] the Seventh Circuit ruled that student-athletes are not employees under the federal Fair Labor Standards Act because "the long tradition of amateurism in college sports, by definition, shows that student athletes—like all other amateur athletes—participate in their sports for reasons wholly unrelated to immediate compensation ... and have done so for over 100 years under the NCAA—without any real expectation of earning an income." However, in a concurring opinion, Judge Hamilton added "a note of caution" stating:

> The plaintiffs in this case were students who participated in track and field at the University of Pennsylvania. Like other Ivy League schools, Penn does not offer athletic scholarships. Also, as far as I know, track and field is not a "revenue" sport at Penn or any other school. In this case, therefore, the economic reality and the sometimes frayed tradition of amateurism both point toward dismissal of these plaintiffs' claims. , , , Because the plaintiffs in this case did not receive athletic scholarships and participated in a non-revenue sport, they pursued a broad theory. The logic of their claim would have included not only any college athlete in any sport and any NCAA division, but also college musicians, actors, journalists, and debaters. That broad theory is mistaken, as Judge Kanne's opinion explains. I am less confident, however, that our reasoning should extend to students who receive athletic scholarships to participate in so-called revenue sports like Division I men's basketball and FBS football. In those sports, economic reality and the tradition of amateurism may not point in the same direction. Those sports involve billions of dollars of revenue for colleges and universities. Athletic scholarships are limited to the cost of attending school. With economic reality as our guide, as I believe it should be, there may be room for further debate,

289. In *Northwestern University and College Athletes Players Association*,[297] the National Labor Relations Board (NLRB) determined that, even if Northwestern

294. . NCAA Division I Manual §15.3.3.1.
295. . West's Ann.Cal.Educ.Code § 67450.
296. . 843 F.3d 285 (7th Cir. 2016).
297. 362 N.L.R.B. No. 167, 2015 WL 4882656 (Aug. 17, 2015).

University scholarship football players are employees under the NLRA, "it would not effectuate the policies of the Act to assert jurisdiction." The NLRB stated:

> Our decision is primarily premised on a finding that, because of the nature of sports leagues (namely the control exercised by the leagues over the individual teams) and the composition and structure of [Division I] FBS football (in which the overwhelming majority of competitors are public colleges and universities over which the Board cannot assert jurisdiction), it would not promote stability in labor relations to assert jurisdiction in this case.

290. Observing that "this case involves novel and unique circumstances," it explained:

> [S]cholarship players are unlike athletes in undisputedly professional leagues, given that [they] are required, inter alia, to be enrolled full time as students and meet various academic requirements, and they are prohibited by NCAA regulations from engaging in many of the types of activities that professional athletes are free to engage in, such as profiting from the use of their names or likenesses. . . . [E]ven if scholarship players were regarded as analogous to players for professional sports teams who are considered employees for purposes of collective bargaining, such bargaining has never involved a bargaining unit consisting of a single team's players, where the players for competing teams were unrepresented or entirely outside the Board's jurisdiction. . . . As in professional sports. . . . uniform rules of competition and compliance with them ensure the uniformity and integrity of individual games, and thus league competition as a whole. There is thus a symbiotic relationship among the various teams, the conferences, and the NCAA. As a result, labor issues directly involving only an individual team and its players would also affect the NCAA, the Big Ten, and the other member institutions. Many terms applied to one team therefore would likely have ramifications for other teams. . . . [S]uch an arrangement is seemingly unprecedented; all previous Board cases concerning professional sports involve leaguewide bargaining units.

291. Some states have laws that effectively prohibit intercollegiate athletes at public universities from unionizing under state labor laws applicable to public employees.[298] As a result of the *Northwestern University* NLRB ruling and these state laws, intercollegiate athletes currently are not legally characterized as "employees;" therefore, they do not have the legal right to unionize and collectively bargain any of the terms of their athletic scholarships with NCAA universities.

298. *See,* e.g., Ohio Rev. Code Ann. § 3345.56 (West 2016) ("Notwithstanding any provision of the Revised Code to the contrary, a student attending a state university as defined in section 3345.011 of the Revised Code is not an employee of the state university based upon the student's participation in an athletic program offered by the state university."). *See also* Mich. Comp. Laws § 423.201(1)(e)(iii) (2016).

V. Special Relationship for Purposes of Tort Liability

292. Student-athletes have asserted that a "special relationship" with their respective university or college justifies the imposition of an affirmative legal duty to protect them from foreseeable and unreasonable risks of physical harm while participating in intercollegiate athletics. In *Kleinknecht v. Gettysburg College*,[299] the Third Circuit held that a special relationship exists between a university and its recruited athletes, which creates a university duty to have a reasonable medical emergency response plan to aid injured student-athletes. The court found that the defendant university had recruited the plaintiff lacrosse player for its own benefit, hoping that the success of its intercollegiate athletic program would result in favorable publicity and increased applications from potential students, which created a special relationship to use reasonable care to protect him from foreseeable harm (e.g., aggravated harm after his initial injury). Although his incident of cardiac arrest during a non-contact lacrosse practice drill was unforeseeable under the circumstances, the court held that the possibility of severe and life-threatening injury is reasonably foreseeable during contact sports. As a result, the reasonableness of the college's emergency response plan and whether the breach of its duty of reasonable care caused his death were questions of fact for consideration by a jury.

293. Outside the context of emergency medical care, *Kleinknecht* has potentially broad implications regarding the nature and scope of a university's affirmative duty to protect the health and safety of its intercollegiate athletes. However, in *Orr v. Brigham Young University*,[300] the Tenth Circuit refused to extend *Kleinknecht's* holding beyond the scope of emergency medical care. An injured college football player alleged that university officials, placing greater emphasis on winning games than on his health, pressured him to play football with a back injury, resulting in aggravation of this injury. The Tenth Circuit affirmed the district court's holding that the parties' legal relationship is "more of a contractual nature than a custodial nature mandating special duties of care and protection beyond those traditionally recognized under a simple negligence theory of liability" as well as its ruling the university would be liable only for negligent medical care provided to its athletes by its sports medicine personnel.[301] Other courts, however, have held that a university has a general duty of reasonable care to protect student-athletes" health and safety, including the process of permitting injured athletes to return to play.[302]

299. . 989 F.2d 1360 (3d Cir. 1993).
300. . 108 F.3d 1388 (10th Cir. 1997).
301. . 960 F. Supp. 1522 (D. Utah 1994). *See also Sandford v. Long*, 2012 WL 874678 (Cal.App. 4 Dist. Mar. 15, 2012) (rejecting student-athlete's argument that special relationship between university and student-athlete imposed duty of coach to protect athlete against the intentional tortious conduct of a teammate). *See Roe v. St. Louis University*, 746 F.3d 874 (8th Cir. 2014) (finding university not negligent in its treatment of field hockey player's injury).
302. *Searles v. Trustees of St. Joseph's College*, 695 A.2d 1206 (Me. 1997).

§2. Legal Nature of the Relationship Between Student-Athlete and NCAA

294. The NCAA's student-athlete eligibility rules, which have national application and effect, are, designed to maintain academic integrity, the "amateur" nature of intercollegiate athletics, and competitive balance among its member schools and participating student-athletes. Most eligibility disputes arise when a prospective student-athlete fails to satisfy the NCAA's threshold academic or amateurism requirements, a current student-athlete violates one of these requirements, or is denied a requested waiver of a rule or restored eligibility that would enable him or her to participate in intercollegiate athletics. Because it has no direct or express contractual relationship with student-athletes, the NCAA has no authority to enforce directly its eligibility rules, interpretations, and decisions against them. However, the NCAA has the ability to do so indirectly because each of its member institutions has agreed to conduct its athletics program in full compliance with its rules and regulations. The NCAA's eligibility rules are incorporated by reference into its member institutions' respective contracts with each of their student-athletes. Institutions must comply with and enforce the NCAA's student-athlete eligibility rules and determinations.[303] An institution that permits a student-athlete to participate after the NCAA has declared him or her ineligible risks potentially severe sanctions.

295. When a student-athlete violates an NCAA rule, it may be minor, sometimes requiring little more than a waiver of the rule as it applies to the student-athlete in a given instance. It also can be more serious, requiring the imposition of sanctions at the institutional level under NCAA Rules. The NCAA oversees this process to ensure that its member institutions are acting consistently and in a manner that maintains a level playing field for intercollegiate athletics. For example, during the fall of 2015, the University of Georgia suspended its star running back Todd Gurley for four games for accepting more than USD 3,000 in cash from multiple individuals for autographed memorabilia and other items over a two-year period of time. Student-athletes who have been penalized for violating an NCAA rule (e.g., Todd Gurley) will have to seek reinstatement of their intercollegiate athletics eligibility.

296. The NCAA Student-Athlete Reinstatement Committee (SARC) oversees the reinstatement process, which has been summarized as follows:

> The consequences to a student-athlete for committing an NCAA bylaw violation are determined by the [SARC] and its staff. In academic year 2010-11, the last year for which data are reported, approximately 1,850 student-athlete violations were sufficiently serious to trigger the formal involvement of the NCAA student-athlete reinstatement process. Student-athletes are ineligible to compete from the point at which they commit a violation until their eligibility status is resolved.
>
> Even for the most serious student-athlete violations, the NCAA enforcement staff conducts no investigation, makes no allegation of violations, and compiles

303. . *See* , e.g., *Brennan v. Bd. of Trustees.*, 691 So.2d 324 (La. App. 1997) (university suspends student-athlete from competition for one year for failing NCAA drug test).

no evidence to support allegations. Instead, the university at which a student-athlete is enrolled investigates, determines the relevant facts, decides whether a violation was committed, reports any findings of violations to the NCAA enforcement staff, and typically reports those findings to the SARC staff and requests reinstatement to eligibility of the culpable student-athlete. There is no fact-finding by any NCAA committee, no adversarial hearing before an adjudicatory body analogous to the COI, and no appeal of a SARC decision to an internal NCAA appellate body equivalent to the IAC. The exclusive role of the SARC and its staff is to ensure that a university provides a fully developed factual record to support its conclusion as to the seriousness of the violation reported, to assess the degree of student-athlete culpability based on the facts that an institution reports, and to decide whether and under what conditions a student-athlete may be reinstated to competition eligibility.

[Generally matters are disposed of by the staff and member institution]. [T]he SARC hears university appeals from staff decisions. To limit the scope of the reinstatement staff's discretion and enhance the likelihood that cases with similar facts are treated similarly across all NCAA member institutions, the SARC has adopted guidelines that prescribe reinstatement conditions (sanctions) for particular violations. For minor violations, there is no withholding of a student-athlete from competition. Serious violations can result in withholding for a substantial number of competitions (including permanent ineligibility), a decrease in the total number of years (five) a student-athlete has to compete, and sometimes both consequences.[304]

297. Courts generally do not interfere with the merits of NCAA decision-making on student-athlete eligibility issues unless the NCAA fails to provide appropriate notice and a fair hearing, violates its own rules, applies them in an inconsistent, arbitrary, or capricious manner, or violates applicable federal or state law. In *California State Univ., Hayward v. NCAA*,[305] a California appellate court enjoined the NCAA from breaching constitution and bylaws in denying student-athletes the opportunity to participate in an NCAA championship competition. Courts have rarely held that an NCAA student-

304. Josephine (Jo) R. Potuto and Matthew J. Mitten, *Comparing NCAA and Olympic Athlete Eligibility Dispute Resolution Systems in Light of Procedural Fairness and Substantive Justice*, 7 Harv. J. Sports & Ent. L. 1 at 17–20 (2016).

305. 121 Cal. Rptr. 85 (Cal. App. 1975). *See also Gulf South Conference v. Boyd*, 369 So.2d 553 (Ala. 1979) (finding student-athlete is eligible to participate in football under athletic conference's bylaws, which would be breached by its refusal to permit him to do so).

athlete eligibility rule or its application by the NCAA's was arbitrary or capricious.[306] Even when student-athletes have alleged that NCAA eligibility rules or internal decisions have violated federal laws prohibiting gender[307] or race discrimination,[308] courts generally are reluctant to find that these laws are applicable and to use them to constrain the NCAA's governance of intercollegiate athletics.

298. Courts generally defer to the NCAA and its member schools because of their presumed expertise in promulgating intercollegiate athletics policy.[309] Consequently, when examining challenges to NCAA regulations, courts tend to accept the NCAA's characterization of its rules and underlying objectives and presume it is acting appropriately in governing intercollegiate athletics. This is particularly true when a student-athlete challenges an NCAA academic or amateurism eligibility rule or its application.

299. Through its rule-making and enforcement processes, the NCAA articulates values considered fundamental to intercollegiate athletics such the maintenance of academic integrity. Its amateurism principle is a core value and an ingrained feature of its student-athlete eligibility rules. For example, the NCAA's amateurism rules prohibit a student-athlete from accepting compensation for their athletic skills (other than the economic value of permissible university financial aid),[310] entering into contracts with agents (even those post-dated after the student-athlete's intercollegiate athletics ability is exhausted),[311] signing contracts to play for professional teams,[312] and accepting compensation for endorsing commercial products or services.[313]

300. Two recent cases, *Bloom v. NCAA*[314] and *NCAA v. Lasege*,[315] illustrate the extreme deference courts provide to the NCAA in student-athlete eligibility disputes. *Bloom* arose out of the NCAA's decision to declare Jeremy Bloom, a talented snow skier, ineligible to play football for the University of Colorado. He had deferred his

---

306. . A notable exception is *Oliver v. National Collegiate Athletic Assn.*, 920 N.E.2d 203 (Ohio Ct. Common Pleas, 2009), in which a college baseball player sued the NCAA, alleging breach of contract and tortious interference with contractual relations and seeking declaratory and injunctive relief to prevent it from rendering him ineligible for violating its rules. The court held that NCAA bylaws prohibiting an attorney representing a student-athlete from being present during contract negotiations between the athlete and a professional sports team and allowing the NCAA to impose penalties on student-athletes and institutions (i.e., restitution rule) for not complying with it violated the NCAA's contractual obligation of good faith and fair dealing to its member universities' student-athletes, The court's ruling subsequently was vacated pursuant to a settlement between the parties.
307. . *NCAA v. Smith*, 525 U.S. 459 (1999).
308. . *Cureton v. NCAA*, 198 F.3d 107 (3d Cir. 1999). But *see Pryor v. NCAA*, 288 F.3d 548 (3d Cir. 2002) (recognizing Title VI claim against the NCAA alleging that Proposition 16 scholarship and athletic eligibility criteria for incoming student-athletes constitutes intentional discrimination).
309. . W. Burlette Carter, *Student-Athlete Welfare in a Restructured NCAA*, 2 Va. J. Sports & L. 1, 6, 9 (2000).
310. . 2013-14 NCAA Division I Manual, Art. 12.1.2.1.
311. . 2013-14 NCAA Division I Manual, Art. 12.3.
312. . 2013-14 NCAA Division I Manual, Art. 12.2.5.
313. . 2013-14 NCAA Division I Manual, Art. 12.5.1.3(d).
314. . 93 P.3d 621 (Colo. App. 2004).
315. . 53 S.W.3d 77 (Ky. 2001).

education and college football career for a year in order to compete in the 2002 Winter Olympics. NCAA rules permit an athlete to play and accept compensation as a professional in one sport (e.g., skiing), while retaining amateur eligibility to play another sport (e.g., football). As was customary for professional skiers, Bloom contracted to endorse commercial products to pay for his living expenses and Olympics training costs, which violated NCAA amateurism rules prohibiting a student-athlete from accepting payment for product or service endorsements. After the NCAA denied the university's request on his behalf for a waiver of this rule, the trial court denied Bloom's request for an injunction against NCAA enforcement of this rule despite his assertion that "his endorsement, modelling, and media activities were necessary to support his professional skiing career, something which the NCAA rules permitted."

301. Although Bloom had no constitutional or express contractual right to participate in intercollegiate athletics, the Colorado appellate court ruled he was a third party beneficiary of the membership contract governing the relationship between the NCAA and the University of Colorado. It held he had legal standing to assert that the NCAA acted arbitrarily and capriciously in interpreting and applying its eligibility rules by breaching the duty of good faith and fair dealing implied into every contract.

302. Regarding the merits of Bloom's claim, the court ruled that the NCAA's application of its endorsement and media rules to Bloom was rationally related to the legitimate purpose of maintaining a line of demarcation between college and professional sports. Noting that the NCAA serves as the guardian of amateurism in intercollegiate athletics, the court accepted the NCAA's interpretation and application of its amateurism rules to Bloom. Refusing to substitute its judgment for that of the NCAA, the court concluded that the NCAA's application of its bylaws was not "manifestly arbitrary, unreasonable, or unfair," or in breach of the NCAA's duty of good faith and fair dealing.

303. Similarly, in *Lasege*, a student-athlete from Nigeria was declared ineligible by his institution, the University of Louisville, after he compromised his status as an amateur athlete under NCAA rules by entering into a professional basketball contract with a Russian team, signing a representation contract with a sports agent, and receiving certain financial benefits stemming from his status as a student-athlete. The university requested that *Lasege's* intercollegiate athletics eligibility be reinstated based on his ignorance of these regulations at the time he violated them. The NCAA's Student-Athlete Reinstatement Committee declined to do so because it found that his conduct evidenced a "clear intent to professionalize." Recognizing that judicial intervention is warranted only when a "voluntary association acts arbitrarily and capriciously toward student-athletes," the Kentucky Supreme Court found that the NCAA's refusal to restore *Lasege's* eligibility did not violate this standard and rejected *Lasege's* legal claims. The court determined that the NCAA's internal eligibility determination was entitled to a presumption of correctness, particularly because Lasege admitted the violations.

304. In *NCAA v. Bd. of Regents of the Univ. of Oklahoma*,[316] the U.S. Supreme Court acknowledged:

> The NCAA plays a critical role in the maintenance of a revered tradition of amateurism in college sports. There can be no question but that it needs ample

316. . 468 U.S. 85 (1984).

latitude to play that role, or that the preservation of the student-athlete in higher education adds richness and diversity to intercollegiate athletics and is entirely consistent with the goals of the Sherman Act. It is reasonable to assume that most of the regulatory controls of the NCAA are justifiable means of fostering competition among amateur athletic teams and therefore procompetitive because they enhance public interest in intercollegiate athletics. In order to preserve the character and quality of the product, athletes must not be paid, must be required to attend class, and the like. And the integrity of the product cannot be preserved except by mutual agreement; if an institution adopted such restrictions unilaterally, its effectiveness as a competitor on the playing field might soon be destroyed. Thus, the NCAA plays a vital role in enabling college football to preserve its character, and as a result enables a product to be marketed which might otherwise be unavailable. In performing this role, its actions widen consumer choice—not only the choices available to sports fans but also those available to athletes—and hence can be viewed as procompetitive.

305. Courts historically have rejected, as a matter of law, antitrust challenges to the validity of NCAA student-athlete eligibility rules on the ground that "eligibility rules are not related to the NCAA's commercial or business activities" and, therefore, are not anticompetitive.[317] Eligibility rules have been judicially presumed to be a necessary and procompetitive means of preserving amateurism, academic values, and/or competitive balance in intercollegiate athletics. Courts have held that NCAA rules prohibiting a college student-athlete's receipt of any compensation or extra benefits exceeding the value of an athletics scholarship are legal under the antitrust laws.[318] NCAA rules declaring that athletes who have previously been paid to play a sport[319] or who have hired agents or entered a professional league's draft[320] are ineligible in participate in NCAA sports have been judicially upheld. NCAA and athletic conference rules defining athletic eligibility for student-athletes who transfer to other universities also have survived antitrust challenge.[321] Courts also have ruled that NCAA or athletic conference sanctions against member institutions for violating student-athlete eligibility rules do not violate the antitrust laws.[322]

306. In *Banks v. NCAA*,[323] the Seventh Circuit held that the NCAA's "no-draft" and "no agent" rules, which resulted in a Notre Dame student-athlete's loss of eligibility to play college football when he entered the NFL draft and agreed to be represented by an agent in that sport, is not a commercial restraint that causes antitrust injury. It reasoned that "[n]one of the NCAA rules affecting college football eligibility restrain

317. . *Smith v. NCAA*, 139 F.3d 180 (3d Cir. 1998).
318. . *Justice v. NCAA*, 577 F. Supp. 356 (D. Ariz. 1983).
319. . *Jones v. NCAA*, 392 F. Supp. 295 (D. Mass. 1975).
320. . *Banks v. NCAA*, 977 F.2d 1081 (7th Cir. 1992); *Gaines v. NCAA*, 746 F. Supp. 738 (M.D. Tenn. 1990).
321. . *Tanaka v. Univ. of Southern California*, 252 F.3d 1059 (9th Cir. 2001); *Smith v. NCAA*, 139 F.3d 180 (3d Cir. 1998).
322. . *Hairston v. Pac.-10 Conference*, 101 F.3d 1315 (9th Cir. 1995); *McCormack v. NCAA*, 845 F.2d 1338 (5th Cir. 1988).
323. 977 F.2d 1081 (7th Cir. 1992).

trade in the market for college players because the NCAA does not exist as a minor league training ground for future NFL players but rather to provide an opportunity for competition among amateur students pursuing a collegiate education." Similarly, in *Smith v. NCAA*,[324] the Third Circuit dismissed an allegation that the NCAA's postbaccalaureate bylaw, which precluded a graduate student from participating in intercollegiate athletics at a university other than the one at which she earned her undergraduate degree, violates §1. The court concluded that "eligibility rules are not related to the NCAA's commercial or business activities"; therefore, "the Sherman Act does not apply." Relying on *Smith*, the Sixth Circuit, in *Bassett v. NCAA*,[325] held that the "NCAA's rules on recruiting student athletes, specifically those rules prohibiting improper inducements and academic fraud, are all explicitly non-commercial." The court affirmed the dismissal of a §1 claim by a former college football coach who had been disciplined for violating them.

307. In *Agnew v. NCAA*,[326] the Seventh Circuit diverged from (or at least clarified) *Banks* by ruling that "the Sherman Act applies to the NCAA bylaws generally" because despite their nonprofit status, NCAA universities enter into commercial transactions with premier athletes by providing scholarships for their playing services that can generate millions of dollars in revenues. Thus, all NCAA student-athlete eligibility rules and other input market restrictions are commercial restraints. It distinguished between NCAA student-athlete eligibility rules and other forms of NCAA regulation such as limiting the duration of athletic scholarships to one-year and the total number of scholarships a university may award for a particular sport, which have adverse commercial effects on student-athletes and may be challenged as a violation of §1 of the Sherman Act under the rule of reason. The court explained:

> It is true that the prohibition against multi-year scholarships is, in a sense, a rule concerning the amount of payment a player receives for his labor, and thus may seem to implicate the split between amateur and pay-for-play sports. After all, student-athletes are paid, but their payment is limited to reimbursement for costs attendant to receiving an education. For the purposes of college sports, and in the name of amateurism, we consider players who receive nothing more than educational costs in return for their services to be unpaid athletes. It is for this reason, though, that the prohibition against multi-year scholarships does not implicate the preservation of amateurism, for whether or not a player receives four years of educational expenses or one year of educational expenses, he is still an amateur. It is not until payment above and beyond educational costs is received that a player is considered a paid athlete …
>
> The NCAA's limitation on athlete compensation beyond educational expenses … directly advances the goal of maintaining a clear line of demarcation between intercollegiate athletics and professional sports, and thus is best categorized as an eligibility rule aimed at preserving the existence of amateurism and the

324. 139 F.3d 180 (3d Cir. 1998).
325. 528 F.3d 426 (6th Cir. 2008).
326. . 683 F.3d. 328 (7th Cir. 2012).

student-athlete. The Bylaws at issue in this case, on the other hand, are not directly related to the separation of amateur athletics from pay-for-play athletics, as explained in the preceding paragraphs. Nor do they help preserve the existence of the student-athlete (as a facial matter, anyway), since they actually limit the number of athletes awarded financial aid and the amount of financial aid that an athlete can be awarded. Thus, financial aid rules do not always assist in the preservation of amateurism or the existence of student-athletes, so the regulations at issue cannot be presumptively procompetitive simply because they relate to financial aid.

308. Applying *Agnew*, in *Rock v. NCAA*,[327] the court ruled that a student-athlete's antitrust challenge to current NCAA limits on the maximum number of Division I football scholarships its member universities could award (eighty-five for Football Bowl Series (FBS) teams, and sixty-three for Football Championship Series (FCS) teams) and former prohibitions against multi-year scholarships constitute commercial activity subject to §1:

> Agnew held that [i]t is undeniable that a market of some sort is at play in this case. A transaction clearly occurs between a student-athlete and a university: the student-athlete uses his athletic abilities on behalf of the university in exchange for an athletic and academic education, room, and board. In analyzing whether that exchange is commercial in nature, the Seventh Circuit concluded that [n]o knowledgeable observer could earnestly assert that big-time college football programs competing for highly sought-after high school football players do not anticipate economic gain from a successful recruiting program. Despite the nonprofit status of NCAA member schools, the transactions those schools make with premier athletes—full scholarships in exchange for athletic services—are not noncommercial, since schools can make millions of dollars as a result of these transactions.

309. In *Rock*, a former FCS football player sought damages for the non-renewal of his athletic scholarship after his junior year based on his allegation that "in a competitive market not subject to the NCAA's prohibition on multi-year scholarships and the cap on the total number of scholarships per team, he would have received additional or enhanced scholarship offers, including a multi-year scholarship." Applying the rule of reason, the court determined he adequately alleged the subject NCAA bylaws had the requisite anticompetitive effects in a relevant market defined as "the nationwide market for the labor of Division I football student athletes" by "reduc[ing] the overall supply of football scholarships available to student-athletes thereby forcing them to accept far less compensation than they would have received for their labor." It held he had standing to challenge both the FCS and FBS scholarship limits because

327. . 2013 WL 4479815 (S.D. Ind.).

of his allegation that "he would have received more scholarship offers, including from FBS teams."[328]

310. In *Deppe v. NCAA,*[329] a federal district court dismissed a Division I FBS football player's antitrust challenge to the NCAA's "year in residence" bylaw, which requires Division I athletes to fulfill a full academic year residency requirement at the university to which he or she transfers before being eligible to play intercollegiate sports. Based on *Agnew*, the court held that this "eligibility bylaw is presumptively procompetitive and, therefore, does not violate the Sherman Act," which is the same ruling it made in *Pugh v. NCAA,*[330] a prior case challenging the same bylaw.

311. In *O'Bannon v. NCAA,*[331] the Ninth Circuit ruled that NCAA's eligibility rules prohibiting student-athletes from receiving any revenue from videogames and telecasts incorporating their names, images, or likenesses unreasonably restrain (NIL rules) economic competition among its member universities in the college education market in which student-athletes purchase higher education services and sell their athletic services in violation of §1. Disagreeing with *Agnew* and distinguishing *Smith* because the NCAA's postbaccalaureate bylaw (which subsequently was repealed) is "a true 'eligibility' rule akin to" its academic eligibility rules and those limiting the number of seasons student-athletes can play intercollegiate sports, the court held that this particular student-athlete eligibility rule is a commercial restraint subject to §1. The Ninth Circuit also disagreed with the NCAA's assertion that its NIL rules are valid as a matter of law under *Board of Regents* and found *Agnew* "unpersuasive" to the extent it supports this contention, holding that the[se] "'amateurism rules' validity must be proved, not presumed."

312. To determine if the NCAA's NIL rules constitute an unreasonable restraint of trade, the Ninth Circuit applied the following rule of reason analysis: [1] The plaintiff bears the initial burden of showing that the restraint produces significant anticompetitive effects within a relevant market. [2] If the plaintiff meets this burden, the defendant must come forward with evidence of the restraint's procompetitive effects. [3] The plaintiff must then show that any legitimate objectives can be achieved in a substantially less restrictive manner.

313. The Ninth Circuit affirmed the following rulings by the district court: the challenged NCAA eligibility rules fix the price of one element of competition (i.e., NIL rights) at zero in the college education market in which NCAA universities compete for the services of student-athletes; NIL compensation rules serve "the two procompetitive purposes ... [of] integrating academics with athletics, and 'preserving the popularity of the NCAA's product by promoting its current understanding of amateurism'; these rules 'do not promote competitive balance, ... do not increase output in the college education market, and ... play a limited role in integrating student-athletes with their schools' academic communities."

---

328. But *see Rock v NCAA*, 2016 WL 1270087 (S.D. Ind.) (refusal to certify a class of football players "recruited" by Division I schools who didn't receive scholarships for the full duration of their undergraduate education because this definition, including the term "recruited," is impermissibly vague and subjective, making the class unascertainable).
329. 2017 WL 897307 (S.D. Ind.).
330. 2016 WL 5394408 (S.D. Ind.).
331. 802 F.3d 1049 (9th Cir. 2015), *cert. denied*, 137 S. Ct. 277 (2016).

314. Although it recognized that "a restraint that broadens choices can be procompetitive," the Ninth Circuit court rejected the NCAA's assertion that "denying student-athletes compensation apart from scholarships" does. It reasoned that "loosening or abandoning the compensation rules might be the best way to "widen" recruits range of choices." For example, "athletes might well be more likely to attend college, and stay there longer, if they knew that they were earning some amount of NIL income while they were in school."

315. Regarding the less restrictive alternative prong of rule of reason analysis, the Ninth Circuit stated that "plaintiffs must make a strong evidentiary showing" that its proposed alternative is "viable" and "'virtually as effective' in serving the procompetitive purposes of the NCAA's current rules, and without significant costs." The court observed it "must generally afford the NCAA 'ample latitude' to superintend college athletics" and "plenty of room . . . to preserve the amateur character of intercollegiate athletics." Applying this standard, the court ruled that allowing NCAA schools to award full cost of attendance scholarships (which has been permitted by revised NCAA rules since August 2015) is a substantially less restrictive alternative to the NCAA's NIL rules, which would be an effective means of integrating academics with athletics and maintaining amateurism in intercollegiate athletics without significantly increasing their costs. It affirmed the district court's injunction requiring the NCAA to allow its members to provide compensation up to the full cost of attending their respective institutions.

316. The Ninth Circuit majority held that the district court erred in determining that permitting NCAA schools to provide pro rata cash payments to football and basketball players of no less than USD 5,000 for each year of sports participation after they left college or their eligibility expires is also a substantially less restrictive alternative to the NCAA's current NIL rules. The district court reasoned that no evidence established that "consumer demand for the NCAA's product would decrease if schools were permitted to provide such stipends" or that doing so "would hinder any school's efforts to educate its student-athletes or integrate them into the academic community." They disagreed that "allowing students to be paid NIL compensation unrelated to their education expenses, is "virtually as effective" in preserving amateurism as not allowing compensation" because "not paying student-athletes is precisely what makes them amateurs." In reaching this conclusion, they effectively ruled that antitrust law permits the NCAA to prohibit student-athletes from receiving "cash payments untethered to their education expenses."

317. Acknowledging that his disagreement with the majority "largely boils down to a difference in opinion as the procompetitive interests at stake," the dissenting judge characterized the key issue as "whether allowing student-athletes to be compensated for their NILs is "virtually as effective" in preserving popular demand for college sports as not allowing compensation." He cited expert economist testimony that "consumer demand typically does not decrease when athletes are permitted to receive payment, and that this general principle holds true across a wide variety of sports and competitive formats." In his view, this record evidence was sufficient to affirm the district court's finding that a USD 5,000 per year stipend is a substantially less restrictive alternative to achieve this objective.

318. On February 3, 2017, the NCAA agreed to pay USD 208.7 million to settle the *Alston* lawsuit filed by former student-athletes who claimed that capping the economic value of their scholarships to the costs of tuition, room, board, books, and fees violated federal antitrust law, which was preliminarily approved by Judge Claudia Wilken on March 21, 2017. Division I men's and women's basketball players and Football Bowl Subdivision football players who played during the period from March 2010 through the 2016–2017 seasons will receive a payout based on the difference between this amount and the full cost of attendance at their respective schools; these payments will average approximately USD 6,763.[332] Another part of this lawsuit, the so-called *Jenkins* antitrust litigation, which seeks to enjoin the NCAA's cost-of-attendance-based limits on the compensation athletes can receive while playing college sports, is unaffected by this settlement.

319. In *In re: NCAA Athletic Grant-in-Aid Cap Antitrust Litigation,*[333] the district court judge (who was the *O'Bannon* trial judge) denied the NCAA's motion to dismiss the *Jenkins* antitrust litigation because it concluded that *O'Bannon* did not preclude the injunctive relief remedies the plaintiffs were seeking:

> The Ninth Circuit's decision in O'Bannon simply forecloses one type of relief Plaintiffs previously sought: cash compensation untethered to educational expenses. While O'Bannon is binding on this Court, it does not provide the basis for judgment on the pleadings. . . . The Ninth Circuit's decision in O'Bannon limits the types of relief Plaintiffs may seek but it does not provide a basis upon which a judgment on the merits can be rendered.

332. In 2008, the NCAA settled *White v. NCAA*, an antitrust suit by Division I men's basketball and football players making similar allegations, which resulted in the creation of a USD 10 million fund to reimburse qualified members of the class for educational expenses (a USD 500 payment for career development expenses, and a maximum of USD 2,500 a year for three years of future undergraduate, graduate, or certificate education expenses).

333. 2016 WL 4154855 (N.D. Cal. 2016).

Chapter 3. Olympic Sport Athletes

320. The Amateur Sports Act,[334]a federal statute, establishes the legal framework for protecting the participation opportunities of Olympic sport athletes. It mandates that the USOC establish a procedure for "swift and equitable resolution" of disputes "relating to the opportunity of an amateur athlete to participate" in the Olympic, Paralympic, Pan-American Games, and world championship competitions (hereinafter "protected competitions").[335] The USOC is required to hire an athlete ombudsman to provide independent advice to athletes (free of charge) regarding resolution of disputes regarding his or her eligibility to participate in these competitions.[336]

321. Section 9 of the USOC's Bylaws creates both procedural and substantive rights for an "amateur athlete" (defined as "any athlete who meets the eligibility standards established by the [NGB] or Paralympic Sports Organization for the sport in which the athlete competes"), which also includes professional athletes who are eligible to participate in the Olympic Games and other international sports competitions. Section 9.1 prohibits an NGB from "deny[ing] or threaten[ing] to deny . . . the opportunity to participate" to an athlete otherwise qualified to do so, who has the right to file a complaint with it against an NGB that allegedly adversely affected his or her athletic eligibility by denying him or her the opportunity to participate. Pursuant to the ASA, an athlete dissatisfied with USOC's resolution of the complaint may submit the dispute with an NBG to final and binding arbitration in accordance with the Commercial Rules of the AAA, and may be represented by counsel. The athlete must submit a list of persons that may be adversely affected by the arbitration (e.g., other athletes). The arbitration proceeding is held in person or telephonically before a single arbitrator selected by the parties from a closed pool maintained by the AAA (most of whom are U.S. Court of Arbitration for Sport arbitrators). The arbitrator is required to render a timely written and reasoned award, which is published on the USOC's website.

322. For example, *Hyatt v. United States Judo, Inc.*,[337] involved a dispute arising out of United States Judo's rules and process for selecting athletes to compete in the 2014 International Judo Federation (IJF) Junior World Championships, a protected competition under the ASA. Claimant Alex Hyatt, who placed second in the girls' Junior 48 kg weight division at United States Judo's 2014 Scholastic Nationals, contended that the winner of this event, Gabriela Prado, should not have been permitted to compete because she did not make weight by the time established by United States Judo's written rules for this competition. Therefore, as the second-place finisher, she was entitled to represent the U.S. in the girls' 48 kg weight division at the IJF Junior World Championships pursuant to United States Judo's rules. The arbitrator initially observed that "Section 9 jurisprudence requires [Ms. Hyatt] to prove [United States Judo] breached its approved and published Athlete Selection Procedures for the [2014 IJF Junior World Championships], applied them inconsistently to athletes similarly

334. . 36 U.S.C. §220501 et seq.
335. . 36 U.S.C. §220509(a).
336. . 36 U.S.C. §220509(b).
337. AAA Case Number: 01-14-0000-7635 (2014).

situated, acted in bad faith towards or with bias against [her], and/or violated applicable federal or state laws (e.g., Ted Stevens Olympic and Amateur Sports Act) [by a preponderance of evidence]."

Applying de novo review of its decision, the arbitrator determined that United States Judo breached its published athlete selection rules for the 2014 U.S. Junior World Team by granting Ms. Prado a thirty-minute extension of time to make weight and ordered it to name Ms. Hyatt as the U.S. entrant in the girls' 48 kg weight division for the 2014 IJF Junior World Championships Team.

323. A court will provide only limited scrutiny of an AAA arbitration award determining an athlete's eligibility to participate in a sport. In *Gault v. United States Bobsled and Skeleton Federation*,[338] a New York appellate court explained: "[a]lthough we also may disagree with the arbitrator's award and find most unfortunate the increasing frequency with which sporting events are resolved in the courtroom, we have no authority to upset it when the arbitrator did not exceed his authority." However, a court will vacate or refuse to confirm an arbitration award that is "the result of "corruption," "fraud," "evident partiality," or any similar bar to confirmation."[339]

324. In *Walker v. USA Swimming*,[340] a federal district court held that the Federal Arbitration Act[341] does not provide federal question subject matter jurisdiction to review an arbitration award. Rather, there must be an independent basis for its jurisdiction. The court determined that plaintiff's allegation that that both USA Swimming and the arbitrator failed to follow USA Swimming's rules and regulations in imposing a lifetime ban upon him established the basis of its federal question jurisdiction under the Amateur Sports Act because ensuring that an NGB follows its rules for determining athlete eligibility is a narrow exception to the general rule of judicial non-intervention in such disputes.

---

338. . 578 N.Y.S.2d 683, 685 (N.Y. App. Div. 1992).
339. . *Lindland v. U.S. Wrestling Ass'n, Inc.*, 227 F.3d 1000, 1003 (7th Cir. 2000).
340. 2017 WL 782970 (M.D. Tenn.).
341. . 9 U.S.C. §1 et seq.

Chapter 4. Professional Athletes

§1. Introduction

325. For virtually all major league professional athletes, playing their respective sports is their primary occupation and source of income. In team sports, professional athletes generally are employees of their respective clubs who are paid a very substantial salary. For the 2016 season, estimated average annual player salaries in five major U.S. professional sports leagues were as follows: NBA—USD 6.2 million; MLB—USD 4.4 million; NHL—USD 2.9 million; NFL—USD 2.1 million; MLS—USD 308,969.[342] By comparison, the maximum player salary was USD 107,500 and average player salary was USD 75,000 for women's professional basketball players in the WNBA during the 2015 season.[343] Professional athletes who participate in individual performer sports such as golf and tennis usually are independent contractors whose compensation is based on their respective individual performances in competitions.

326. In general, the legal relationship between a producer of professional sports competition and an athlete is established by the terms of their contract, with state contract law and federal labor, antitrust, and civil rights laws limiting its boundaries. United States professional sports leagues and governing bodies are private entities that are not subject to the constraints of the U.S. Constitution,[344] which protect several individual rights, including due process, equal protection, and free speech rights. The U.S. Constitution's Dormant Commerce Clause precludes direct state regulation (other than by contract law) of the legal relationship between a professional athlete and a national or multi-state professional sports league or governing body.[345]

§2. Team Sports

I. Labor Law

327. A landmark 1969 ruling by the National Labor Relations Board (NLRB), *The American League of Professional Baseball Clubs and Association of National Baseball League Umpires*,[346] concerning the right of baseball's umpires to unionize

342. . Kurt Badenhausen, *Average Player Salaries in Major American Sports Leagues* (Dec. 15, 2016) at https://www.forbes.com/sites/kurtbadenhausen/2016/12/15/average-player-salaries-in-major-american-sports-leagues/#6d3191261050.
343. . David Berri, *Basketball's Gender Wage Gap Is Even Worse Than You Think* (Aug. 12, 2015) at https://sports.vice.com/en_us/article/basketballs-gender-wage-gap-is-even-worse-than-you-think.
344. . *See* , e.g., *Long v. NFL*, 870 F. Supp. 101 (W.D. Pa. 1994), *aff'd*, 66 F.3d 311 (3d. Cir. 1994).
345. . *See* , e.g., *Partee v. San Diego Chargers Football Co.*, 668 P.2d 674 (Cal. 1983).
346. . 180 N.L.R.B. 190 (1969).

introduced federal labor law to the professional sports industry. The NLRB ruled that "professional sports are in or affect interstate commerce, and as such are subject to the Board's jurisdiction." As a result, it became firmly established that professional athletes in team sports, as well as umpires and referees, can unionize and take advantage of the protections provided by national labor laws.

328. The *American League of Professional Baseball Clubs* case coincided with the first Collective Bargaining Agreements (CBAs) between players and clubs in the major team sports in the late 1960s. Within months of each other, the NBA, NFL, and MLB all reached formal agreements with the players unions in their respective leagues. The NHL also reached a series of less formal agreements with the NHL Players Association.

329. The federal labor laws have had a profound impact on major league professional sports for more than fifty years. The National Labor Relations Act (NLRA)[347] was enacted by Congress in 1935. It provides the basic legal structure governing management-worker relations in the U.S., including the employment relationship between a professional sports league, its member clubs, and athletes. Section 7 of the NLRA provides three basic rights for workers: (1) the right to form, join, and assist labor organizations; (2) the right to bargain collectively through representatives chosen by the workers; and (3) the right to engage in "concerted activities" such as picketing and strikes to advance and protect their interests.[348]

330. Section 8(a) of the NLRA details prohibited employer conduct, including interference with employees" rights to organize and bargain collectively, domination or interference with the formation or administration of a labor union, discrimination against employees to discourage union membership, retaliation against employees for exercising their rights, and refusing to bargain in good faith.[349] All these prohibited employer actions may constitute unfair labor practices. The NLRA also prohibits unfair labor practices by a labor union; for example, a refusal to bargain collectively in good faith.[350]

331. The oversight and enforcement of these rights is under the jurisdiction of the NLRB and the federal courts. The NLRB enforces the federal labor laws by adjudicating claims of "unfair labour practices" allegedly committed by either management or labor. The NLRB also administers the process that determines appropriate units or groups of employees (e.g., professional team sport athletes) qualified to vote in a union representation election, and that conducts such elections to determine which, if any, union will represent all employees who are part of that unit.

332. The NLRB also determines which issues are subject to negotiation under the labor laws, delving into questions concerning the required scope of bargaining. Under the NLRA, this includes all issues relating to wages, hours, and terms and conditions of employment.[351] Wages include pay, fringe benefits, and bonus payments; hours encompass time spent on the job; and working conditions cover factors influencing the work environment, such as work rules, seniority, and safety. Most importantly,

347. . 29 U.S.C. §§151 et seq.
348. . 29 U.S.C. §157.
349. . 29 U.S.C. §158(a).
350. . 29 U.S.C. §158(b).
351. . 29 U.S.C. §158(d).

these three areas—wages, hours, and working conditions—are considered mandatory subjects of bargaining. If either labor or management requests bargaining on issues that are mandatory under the labor laws, the other side must bargain over these in good faith. A failure to do so is an unfair labor practice that violates §8 of the NLRA. However, what actually constitutes an issue of wages, hours, or conditions of employment is not always certain. In particular, it is not uncommon for labor and management to disagree regarding what is a condition of employment. Such disputes must be resolved by the NLRB.

333. A union that is duly certified by the NLRB pursuant to the prescribed procedures becomes the exclusive bargaining agent for all employees within the unit. As a practical matter, all active players in a U.S. professional sports league come under the authority of the union chosen to represent them. A player is not required to become a member of the union that the NLRB certifies for his or her league, but he or she is bound by the terms of any CBAs that it negotiates with the league and its member clubs.

334. Those who are not currently active players in the league (as defined by the bargaining unit) are not members of the union, and, as such, have no vote and little voice in union affairs. Even so, to a large extent, the actions of the union may affect their rights. For example, college players who want to play professionally usually find that their eligibility to do so or their minimum and maximum compensation is determined by the CBA between the league and the players' union. The same may be true for foreign players and others such as high school graduates seeking the opportunity to play in a unionized U.S. professional league.

335. A labor union representing professional athletes faces unique challenges, and the task of representing them is a difficult one. It must represent the diverse interests of several hundred extremely talented athletes who have overcome difficult odds to rise to the top of a very elite profession. The small number of athletes who ever get the chance to play their sport at the major league level for even a brief period are far outnumbered by those who aspire to do so. Even within their membership ranks are significant divisions, with a spectrum including a relatively few superstars, several very good players, numerous marginal players, and some perennial bench-warmers. The career of a major league professional athlete is, on average, very short in relation to most other professional careers, so players want to maximize their earning potential as quickly as possible.[352]

336. A labor union has a duty to fairly represent all current and prospective players, but only conduct that is "arbitrary, discriminatory, or in bad faith" breaches this duty.[353] In *Air Line Pilots Association International v. O'Neill*,[354] the U.S. Supreme Court held that this standard applies to the collective bargaining process and explained:

352. . Estimated player average career lengths in years are as follows: MLB (5.6); NHL (5.5); NBA (4.8); NFL (3.5); and. MLS (3.2). Frank Doyle, *How to Make Money in Pro Sports-Inforgraphic* (Oct. 24, 2013) at http://news.sportsinteraction.com/sports/how-to-make-money-in-pro-sports-infographic-45774/ (accessed Mar. 11, 2014).

353. . *Peterson v. Kennedy*, 771 F.2d 1244, 1253 (9th Cir. 1985).

354. . 499 U.S. 65, 78 (1991).

> Congress did not intend judicial review of a union's performance to permit the court to substitute its own view of the proper bargain for that reached by the union. Rather, Congress envisioned the relationship between the courts and labor unions as similar to that between the courts and legislature. Any substantive examination of a union's performance, therefore, must be highly deferential, recognizing the wide latitude that negotiators need for the effective performance of their bargaining responsibilities. For that reason, the final product of the bargaining process may constitute evidence of a breach of duty only if it can be fairly characterized as so far outside a wide range of reasonableness.

337. The players union has a duty not to agree to arbitrary or irrational CBA terms that constitute "invidious" discrimination against some players it represents. An exclusionary eligibility requirement does not breach a union's duty of fair representation unless it discriminates against a legally protected class of employees. For example, collective bargaining terms excluding players from employment in a sports leagues based on one's race violates this union duty.[355]

338. Under U.S. law, a minimum age eligibility rule (or a de facto equivalent) for professional athletes[356] that is part of a collective bargaining agreement is not a form of prohibited discrimination that breaches a players union's duty of fair representation. The federal Age Discrimination in Employment Act of 1967 (ADEA)[357] protects only persons who are at least 40 years old. Although the ADEA "forbids discriminatory preference for the young over the old," it does not prohibit "favoring the old over the young."[358] For example, although such eligibility rules categorically exclude young athletes for reasons unrelated to their individual talent, skills, and maturity, these rules generally do not violate federal labor or civil rights laws.

A. Collective Bargaining in the Professional Sports Industries

339. The primary basis for determining legal relationships between owners and players in professional sports is the CBA reached between the players union and the owners' multiemployer bargaining unit, which prevails over a league's rules and the terms of individual player-club agreements. Multiemployer collective bargaining is the prevailing norm in professional team sports because the league is an integrated group of clubs with common labor issues, which exercises a high degree of centralized

---

355. . *Steele v. Louisville & N.R. Co.*, 323 U.S. 192 (1944).

356. . With narrow exceptions, the NBA limits eligibility to players who are 19 years old and one year removed from their high school graduation and the WNBA limits eligibility to players who are 22 years old and four years removed from their high school graduation. The NFL currently requires that three NFL seasons have elapsed since a prospective player graduated or would have graduated from high school to be eligible to play in the league.

357. . 29 U.S.C. §621 et seq. (2006).

358. . *General Dynamics Land Systems, Inc. v. Cline,* 540 U.S. 581, 584 (2004). *See also Detroit Police Officers Ass'n v. City of Detroit*, 214 N.W.2d 803 (Mich. 1974).

control over labor relations.[359] As a result, the terms of the CBA are collectively bargained on behalf of, and are binding upon, all league clubs and players.

340. The primary focus of bargaining between players and owners has shifted since the first CBAs in the late 1960s, which largely concentrated on player job security issues such as minimum salaries, fringe benefits such as health and life insurance, and pension plans. These are still important considerations, but two general issues driven by the changing economics of sports have dictated a shifting focus in collective bargaining negotiations.

341. The first of these issues center around the initial allocation of a player to a club through a draft and limitations on player movement to other clubs through free agency restrictions. The second arises from league concerns that player free agency has greatly increased player salaries and other economic benefits, which implicates club financial stability and league wide competitive balance issues. Thus, leagues have sought restrictions on spending by club owners by constraints such as aggregate team salary caps, competitive balance or luxury taxes, and other devices aimed to discourage excessive spending. These restrictions directly impact players' wages and conditions of employment and thus are mandatory subjects of bargaining, which raise central issues of contention in CBA negotiations and have triggered strikes or lockouts in all of the major professional leagues at one time or another.

342. The NBA was the first league to institute a comprehensive cap on the maximum amount each club could annually pay in player salaries. This occurred in 1983, at a time when the NBA was clearly struggling financially. In an unprecedented move, the league opened its books for inspection by the players union, which reluctantly agreed to a salary cap. The cap was fraught with vagueness, and the parties had contemplated the many ways in which its provisions could be circumvented. The NBA has a "soft cap," because there are many ways by which a team could exceed the cap and still be within its provisions. The chief exception, often used, was to pay salaries to a team's own veteran players that sent the overall team salary far beyond the official league team limit. Since its inception, the NBA salary cap has undergone several collectively bargained revisions, including more explicit limits on both veteran and rookie salaries, but it still remains, in most respects, a "soft" cap approach.

343. Approximately ten years later, the NFL instituted a "hard cap." Each year, a team maximum aggregate salary is determined based on prior and projected league revenues. Each team's total player salaries cannot exceed a maximum amount without exception. It has led to clubs' restructuring of individual players' contracts to attract or retain desired players while complying with the cap. For example, players enter into new contracts wherein their immediate salary is low, but a new signing bonus provides most of the money they would have received under their old contract. The signing bonus, however, is then allocated equally over the years of the new contract, thus reducing the club's immediate salary cap obligations. Another device to change a club's cap obligations is to have the player sacrifice immediate income provided in the old contract for even greater future rewards in a new contract.

359. . *No. Amer. Soccer League v. Nat'l Labor Relations Bd.*, 613 F.2d 1379 (5th Cir. 1980) (upholding the NLRB's certification of "all NASL players of clubs based in the United States" as the appropriate collective bargaining unit). *See also Brown v. Pro Football, Inc.*, 518 U.S. 231 (1996) (recognizing need for multiemployer collective bargaining in professional team sports).

344. MLB does not have a salary cap, but has attempted to curtail some teams' spending by requiring them to pay a tax if a club's spending on aggregate player salaries exceeds certain maximum amounts. Its current CBA creates a "competitive balance tax," requiring clubs above a certain salary level to pay a tax to the league for distribution to lower-income clubs.

345. Until 2005, the NHL had no salary cap or competitive balance tax, which led to sharply escalating salaries (with the club owners' cooperation, of course). After the NHL CBA expired at the conclusion of the 2004 season, Commissioner Gary Bettman declared that some type of salary cap was necessary. The players union announced its unequivocal opposition. In response, the NHL instituted a player lockout that caused the 2004–2005 season not to be played. The parties reached agreement on a new CBA in mid-July 2005, which included a hard salary cap, which continues to exist in its current CBA.

346. Beginning in the 1890s with MLB, U.S. professional leagues and their clubs unilaterally established rules tying players to a particular team through a draft of players initially entering the league, a "reserve clause" that purportedly gave a club perpetual rights to a player even after his contract expired, and other restrictions on player movement to other league teams. In some instances, NBA, NFL, and NHL players successfully challenged these restrictions on antitrust grounds.[360] MLB players gained free agency through a 1976 landmark labor arbitration decision.[361] In modern times, the nature and scope of restrictions on player mobility usually are a contentious part of collective bargaining negotiations in all of the U.S. major professional leagues that are unionized.

347. Each league has a uniform or standard player contract incorporated into its CBA, which is thus an integral part of thereof. Although each league's standard player contract is different, they generally have similar provisions. As a collectively bargained agreement, the terms of the standard player contract (which frequently incorporate specific CBA terms) take precedence over the league's constitution, bylaws, and rules as well as the provisions of individually negotiated contracts between clubs and players.

348. Unless prohibited by the CBA or standard player contract, the following terms in individual player contracts generally are negotiable: (1) basic salary above the collectively bargained league minimum salary and length of contract; (2) individual and team signing, roster, and performance bonuses; (3) guaranteed income clauses; (4) limitations on the assignment of a player's contract rights to other clubs; and (5) additional player injury protections.

349. Because player disciplinary sanctions for on-field and off-field misconduct are mandatory subjects of collective bargaining, the players union is empowered to protect the players' interests by negotiating with a sports league the conduct subject to discipline, sanctions for violations, and grievance mechanisms. In most instances the union is able to limit (at least somewhat) the otherwise broad authority of a club

360. . *See* Part II, Ch. 4, §2 II.

361. . *National & American League Professional Baseball Clubs v. Major League Baseball Players Association*, 66 Lab. Arb. 101 (1976).

or league commissioner to discipline players[362] through effective use of the collective bargaining process. There generally is a collectively bargained range of disciplinary sanctions for on-field or off-field player misconduct that violates league or club rules promulgated to: (1) maintain competitive balance (e.g., doping, use of impermissible equipment); (2) preserve the sport's integrity (e.g., gambling, doping, equipment regulation); (3) maintain the sport's public image (e.g., criminal conduct, domestic violence, doping); (4) protect player health and safety (e.g., violence injuring opposing player, doping); and (5) team unity and appropriate decorum.

350. In an effort to ensure stable, peaceful labor relations, the federal labor laws require the league and its member clubs to maintain the status quo when the CBA expires. In other words, the expired CBA's terms must remain in effect until the parties reach a new agreement, bargaining negotiations reach an impasse, or the collective bargaining process ends by the players' decertification of their union or an extremely long impasse accompanied by the defunctness of the league's multiemployer bargaining unit.[363] If there is an "impasse"[364] in collective bargaining negotiations, which is frequently a recurring part of this process, the league may (but is not required to) unilaterally implement new terms and conditions of player employment "'reasonably comprehended' within [its] preimpasse proposals (typically the last rejected proposals)" if it has bargained in good faith and has not otherwise committed any unfair labor practices.[365] However, if a league does so, it invites the union's filing of unfair practice charges with the NLRB alleging there is no impasse or the league failed to bargain in good faith, and/or a strike by the players. Alternatively, the players may decertify their union and bring an antitrust suit claiming that the league's unilaterally imposed new terms and conditions of employment are an illegal unreasonable restraint of trade.

B. Unfair Labor Practices

351. Section 8(d) of the NLRA imposes a mutual obligation on representatives of both management and labor "to meet at reasonable times and confer in good faith with respect to wages, hours, and other terms and conditions of employment," so-called mandatory subjects of collective bargaining.[366] Either side's failure to do so constitutes an unfair labor practice. However, this obligation "does not compel either party to agree to a proposal or require the making of a concession." U.S. law provides that labor disputes are to be resolved by collective bargaining and/or resort to economic

362. . Absent limits imposed by the collective bargaining agreement, courts generally provide a professional sports league and its clubs with substantial discretion to impose player discipline and are very deferential to their decisions. *See* , e.g., *Molinas v. NBA*, 190 F. Supp. 241 (S.D.N.Y. 1961) (upholding indefinite suspension of player for admittedly gambling on his team's games in violation of his contract and league rules).

363. *Brown v. Pro Football, Inc.*, 518 U.S. 231 (1996).

364. . As "impasse" is "a temporary deadlock or hiatus in negotiations "which in almost all cases is eventually broken, through either a change of mind or the application of economic force." … Furthermore, an impasse may be "brought about intentionally by one or both parties as a device to further, rather than destroy, the bargaining process." *Charles D. Bonanno Linen Service, Inc. v. NLRB*, 454 U.S. 404.

365. . *Brown v. Pro Football, Inc.*, 518 U.S. 231 (1996).

366. . 29 U.S.C. §158(d).

coercion in the form of a strike by players or a lockout by league clubs. In some instances, voluntary mediation has used to reach agreement on a new CBA, but neither private mediation or arbitration nor NLRB intervention is required or occurs in connection with professional sports collective bargaining.

352. The NLRB enforces the requirements of the NLRA and polices the unionization and collective bargaining processes. After an administrative hearing, the NLRB is empowered to order either labor or management to cease and desist from engaging in any unfair labor practice.[367] The NLRB may petition the appropriate federal circuit court for judicial enforcement of its orders.[368] Upon issuance of an administrative complaint alleging that a party has committed an unfair labor practice, the NLRB may petition a federal district court for appropriate interlocutory relief as warranted by the alleged illegal conduct.[369] Failure to comply with an injunction may result in contempt sanctions imposed by the court.

353. In the context of professional sports, unfair labor practices have arisen in a variety of circumstances. For example, a league's interference with the players' rights to unionize, its refusal to recognize an NLRB- certified union as the players' exclusive bargaining representative,[370] or its failure to bargain in good faith by unilaterally implementing new terms constituting mandatory subjects of collective bargaining prior to an impasse in negotiations,[371] or refusing to provide relevant information (i.e., financial records) to substantiate its position on a mandatory subject of collective bargaining (e.g., alleged financial inability to meet the players union's economic demands).[372] League retaliation against union activists (e.g., terminating their employment for union activities) is an unfair labor practice because section 8(a)(3) of the NLRA[373] prohibits an employer from discriminating against an employee to encourage or discourage union membership.[374] Discrimination against players who exercise their right to strike during a labor dispute also is an unfair labor practice.[375]

C. *Labor Arbitration*

354. Most disputes between a league and the players union (or a player and his club) regarding the meaning of terms in the CBA, uniform player contract, or individual player contract are resolved by an independent arbitrator mutually selected by the league and players union for each sport. In contract dispute arbitration, the arbitrator usually is given plenary authority to construe the meaning of the parties' contract(s)

367. . 29 U.S.C. §160(a).
368. . 29 U.S.C. §160(e).
369. . 29 U.S.C. §160(j).
370. . *No. Amer. Soccer League v. Nat'l Labor Relations Bd.*, 613 F.2d 1379 (5th Cir. 1980).
371. . *Silverman v. Major League Baseball Player Relations Committee, Inc.*, 880 F.Supp. 246 (S.D.N.Y. 1995).
372. . *Silverman v. Major League Baseball Player Relations Committee, Inc.*, 516 F.Supp. 588 (S.D.N.Y. 1981).
373. . 29 U.S.C. §158(a)(3).
374. . *Nordstrom d/b/a Seattle Seahawks*, 292 NLRB 899 (1989), *aff'd*, 984 F.2d 479 (D.C. Cir. 1993) (USD 301,000 award of back pay to NFL player for period he would have been employed by the Seattle Seahawks club but for his unlawful termination).
375. . NFL Management Council, 309 N.L.R.B. 78 (1992).

and to grant appropriate relief to the non-breaching party, including damages and/or ordering action necessary to remedy a breach of contract. For example, an arbitrator ordered basketball player Brian Shaw to comply with the terms of his contract with the Boston Celtics by rescinding his contract with an Italian club (which he had a contractual right to do) and not playing for any other club for the duration of his Celtics' contract.[376]

355. Arbitration also is generally used to resolve player legal challenges to discipline imposed by the club or league for on-field or off-field misconduct. The union typically files a grievance on the player's behalf and represents him in the arbitration proceeding (sometimes the player is represented by his agent or attorney). The arbitrator generally determines whether the league or club had "just cause" to impose the challenged disciplinary sanction, which is upheld if this standard has been met, or nullified or reduced if it has not.[377]

356. The players union's agreement to arbitrate disputes arising out of the CBA or uniform player contract effectively will preempt state law claims that are substantially dependent on interpretation and analysis of these agreements (i.e., these claims cannot be asserted by a player against the league or a club in litigation). In *Sprewell v. Golden State Warriors*,[378] the Ninth Circuit explained:

> … The Supreme Court has held that federal law exclusively governs suits for breach of a CBA, while concomitantly preempting state law claims predicated on such agreements. See Allis-Chalmers Corp. v. Lueck, 471 U.S. 202, 210, 105 S.Ct. 1904, 85 L.Ed. 2d 206 (1985). The Court has expanded the preemptive reach of section 301 [of the Labor Management Relations Act] beyond contract claims, holding that section 301 also preempts tort claims which, as applied, would frustrate the federal labor-contract scheme established in § 301. … A state law claim is preempted by section 301 when it is substantially dependent on analysis of a CBA. … Stated alternatively, [i]f the plaintiff's claim cannot be resolved without interpreting the applicable CBA … it is preempted. … [T]he bare fact that a collective bargaining agreement will be consulted in the course of state-law litigation, however, does not require that the state-claim be extinguished. … Nor is a state-law claim preempted merely because the defendant has raised a defense based on the terms of a CBA. …

357. It is often difficult for courts to determine which state law claims are preempted and those that are not. For example, in *Duerson v. Nat'l Football League*,[379] a case in which the family of deceased former Chicago Bears safety Dave Duerson

376. . *Boston Celtics Ltd. Partnership v. Shaw*, 908 F.2d 1041 (1st Cir. 1990) (judicially confirming labor arbitration award).
377. . *See* , e.g., *Owens v. Philadelphia Eagles*, NFL Arbitration (2005) (Bloch, Arb.); *Nat'l Basketball Players Ass"n on Behalf of Player Latrell Sprewell and Warriors Basketball Club and NBA* (May 4, 1998) (Feerick, Arb.).
378. . 266 F.3d. 979, 990 (9th Cir. 2001). *See also Nelson v. National Hockey League*, 2014 WL 656793 (N.D. Ill.) (Illinois tort claims against NHL by a former player preempted by Labor Management Relations Act).
379. . 2012 WL 1658353 (N.D. Ill.),

sued the NFL for wrongful death and alleged his suicide resulted from brain damage he suffered while playing in the league, the court noted the factually intensive nature of section 301 pre-emption questions: "[a]s one would expect in case-by-case analysis, in some situations preemption is found and in others it is not." The court ruled that Duerson's claims were preempted because they were "substantially dependent on the interpretation of CBA provisions," but noted numerous other health and safety suits brought against the NFL and its clubs in which state tort claims were not preempted.[380]

358. Both MLB and the NHL use a collectively bargained arbitration process to resolve salary disputes between teams and individual players, which is available only in limited situations but has far-reaching effects on player salaries within the league. The MLB CBA's salary arbitration provisions apply to players who have between three and six years of credited major league service. One of the most notable aspects of baseball salary arbitration is that it utilizes "final offer arbitration." This means that, without knowing what the other side will submit as a salary figure, the team and the player each submit an amount for a one-year contract. This requires substantial thought by both parties, because the arbitration panel must select one figure or the other. There can be no compromise. Thus, if the matter is decided by arbitration, the end result will be a one-year, nonguaranteed contract (with no bonuses) at a salary submitted by the club or the player. The club may release its rights to the player at any time consistent with the then-applicable CBA.

359. Unlike MLB's final offer arbitration, the NHL's salary arbitration system is premised on a conventional arbitration model. Like MLB's system, the NHL's salary arbitration system contains eligibility requirements that must be met in order for players to seek salary arbitration; procedures are in place for selecting arbitrators, and limitations are imposed on the factors the arbitrator can consider in determining a player's compensation. Because it is based on a conventional arbitration model, the salary determined by the arbitrator can be either the offer of either the player or club or any amount ranging between the two offers. Another notable difference is the binding effect of the arbitrator's award. Generally, the arbitrator's decision is final and binding on the player and club. However, clubs have a limited right to reject a salary award (a walk-away right), which may be exercised no more than three times in two continuous years and not more than twice in the same year. If this right is exercised, the player becomes a free agent. If he does not receive a better offer from another team, he may accept his prior team's last offer prior to becoming a free agent.

380. . *See* , e.g., *Jurevicius v. Cleveland Browns Football Co.*, No. 1:09 CV 1803, 2010 WL 846120, at *12–13 (N.D. Ohio) (holding that a player's negligence claim filed after he contracted a serious infection from using the Cleveland Brown's training facility was not preempted because CBA provisions bearing on player health and safety governed players' physical condition rather than training facility management); *McPherson v. Tenn. Football Inc.*, No. 3:07–0002, 2007 U.S. Dist. LEXIS 39595, 2007 WL 5445124, *16 (M.D. Tenn.) (holding that a player's negligence claim against the NFL's Tennessee Titans related to a mascot running into him with a golf cart during halftime was not preempted because the CBA contained no provisions "concerning [] mascots or field safety for half-time activities."; *Brown v. National Football League,* 219 F.Supp.2d 372, 387 (S.D.N.Y. 2002) (holding that a player's negligence claim against the NFL for failing to appropriately monitor a referee who threw a penalty flag into his eye was not preempted because the NFL rules he cited regarding the scope of the league's duty to train referees were not part of the CBA).

360. The arbitrator's decision is final and binding on the parties, but it is subject to judicial review by a federal court under the Labor Management Relations Act. A court's review of an arbitration award is very limited, and the award will be vacated only on very narrow grounds.[381] In *Major League Baseball Players Association v. Garvey,*[382] the U.S. Supreme Court ruled:

> Courts are not authorized to review the arbitrator's decision on the merits despite allegations that the decision rests on factual errors or misinterprets the parties' agreement. We recently reiterated that if an arbitrator is even arguably construing or applying the contract and acting within the scope of his authority, the fact that a court is convinced he committed serious error does not suffice to overturn his decision. It is only when the arbitrator strays from interpretation and application of the agreement and effectively dispenses his own brand of industrial justice that his decision may be unenforceable. When an arbitrator resolves disputes regarding the application of a contract, and no dishonesty is alleged, the arbitrator's improvident, even silly, fact finding does not provide a basis for a reviewing court to refuse to enforce the award.

361. A highly publicized disciplinary suspension imposed by NFL Commissioner Roger Goodell on New England Patriots star quarterback Tom Brady for violation of league rules illustrates the substantial degree of deference that courts provide to decisions by the parties' agreed arbitrator. During the 2015 AFC Championship game between the Indianapolis Colts and New England Patriots, the NFL discovered that footballs used by the Patriots were underinflated in violation of NFL rules. Based on an independent investigation by attorney Ted Wells that concluded it "was more probable than not" that Brady was "at least generally aware" the footballs used by the Patriots had been deflated below league allowed air pressure, the NFL suspended Brady for four games for "conduct detrimental to the integrity of, and public confidence in, the game of football" under Article 46 of the NFL CBA. Commissioner Goodell, serving as the arbitrator as authorized by the CBA, upheld this discipline based on his finding that Brady had knowing involvement in the deflation of game balls by New England Patriots' equipment personnel during the 2015 AFC Championship game and willfully destroyed his cell phone containing potentially relevant evidence.

362. A New York federal district court vacated the arbitration award, determining that Goodell "failed to draw [his] award from the essence of the collective bargaining agreement" because Brady had no notice that a player's involvement in deflating footballs during a game and failure to cooperate in an ensuing league investigation would result in the same discipline (i.e., a four-game suspension) applied to a player

381. . *See* generally Martin J. Greenberg & James T. Gray, *Sports Law Practice* §2.03 (2nd ed., 2002) (arbitration awards will be vacated by courts in a limited range of circumstances including when the award was procured by fraud or corruption, when partiality on the part of the arbitrator was obvious, or when an arbitrator exceeds his or her power); *National Football League Players Ass"n v. Pro-Football, Inc.*, 857 F. Supp. 71, 75–76 (D.C. 1994) (although arbitration decisions should be afforded deference even if arbitrator makes errors of fact and law, an award will not be upheld if it compels violation of law or conduct contrary to well-established public policy).

382. . 532 U.S. 504 (2001).

who violated the NFL Policy on Anabolic Steroids and Related Substances for the first time.[383]

363. In a 2-1 decision, in *National Football League Management Council v. National Football League Players Association,*[384] the Second Circuit reversed the district court and remanded with instructions to confirm Goodell's arbitration award. The majority observed that the NFL CBA authorized Commissioner Goodell to investigate possible rule violations, impose appropriate sanctions, and to preside at arbitrations challenging his discipline and that the court's "review of labor arbitration awards is narrowly circumscribed and highly deferential." Because Brady and the NFLPA did not contest Goodell's factual findings or dispute his authority to determine Brady's "participat[ion] in a scheme to tamper with game balls" was "conduct detrimental" under Article 46 that justified a four-game suspension, the majority rejected the district court's ruling that Brady did not have adequate notice that deflation of footballs could result in this discipline and concluded "the Commissioner was within his discretion in drawing a helpful, if somewhat imperfect, comparison to steroid users" to suspend him for four games. Noting that "arbitration is a matter of contract, and consequently, the parties to an arbitration can ask for no more impartiality than inheres in the method they have chosen," they explained "[h]ad the parties wished to restrict the Commissioner's authority, they could have fashioned a different agreement."

D. *Statutory and Non-statutory Labor Exemptions from Antitrust Law*

364. One of the more perplexing aspects of labor relations in U.S. professional sports is the intersection of, and the inherent tension between, federal antitrust and labor law. Section 1 of the Sherman Act[385] prohibits agreements that unreasonably restrain interstate trade or commerce. Applied literally, §1 prohibits both employees and employers from engaging in joint activity or making agreements that unreasonably restrain the labor market. Section 1 requires employers in an industry (e.g., league clubs) to compete independently for employees' (e.g., players) services. Similarly, employees must individually compete for employment.

365. On the other hand, labor law permits employees and employers to engage in joint conduct among themselves, and with each other, that otherwise may violate the antitrust laws. For example, labor law permits employees to unionize and collectively bargain, which is an allowable form of anticompetitive behavior. Multiemployer bargaining within an industry, which is similarly anticompetitive, is legal under labor law. Such concerted action among otherwise competing groups of employees (e.g., players) and employers (e.g., league clubs) squarely conflicts with §1 of the Sherman Act.

366. To resolve this conflict, Congress enacted two federal statutes (section 6 of the Clayton Act and the Norris-LaGuardia Act), the combined effect of which is to create a statutory labor exemption, which provides a labor union with immunity from antitrust liability for its unilateral efforts to further its members' economic interests.

383. *National Football League Management Council v. National Football League Players Association*, 2015 U.S. Dist. LEXIS (S.D. N.Y.).

384. 820 F.3d 527 (2d Cir. 2016).

385. . 15 U.S.C. §1.

Thus, in general, union collective bargaining activities over issues of player wages, hours, and conditions of employment as well as strikes, picketing, and boycotts of employers, including a professional sports league and its member clubs, do not violate the antitrust laws.[386] To facilitate the collective bargaining process, courts have held that the activities of multiemployer bargaining units (which are common in the U.S. professional sports industries) to further their members' common interests, such as collective strike insurance and player lockouts, also are protected by the statutory exemption.[387] The statutory labor exemption only applies to unilateral conduct by a players union or the league multiemployer bargaining unit. It does not immunize the terms of the league's CBA from antitrust challenge.[388]

367. Courts have created a broad non-statutory labor exemption, which precludes the parties from challenging the terms of an existing CBA on antitrust grounds, which furthers the strong U.S. labor policy that permits employees, including professional athletes, to unionize and engage in collective bargaining concerning their wages and working conditions.[389] In a series of cases from 1976–1987, federal appellate courts held that the terms of existing CBAs were not subject to antitrust attack by any of the parties subject to its terms, thereby permitting league clubs and the players union to agree to contract terms that otherwise may violate the antitrust laws.[390] Subsequently, the Eighth Circuit ruled that terms of an expired CBA (which labor law generally requires the league to maintain in effect until a new CBA is reached) do not lose their antitrust immunity even if the players' union and league multiemployer collective bargaining unit reach an impasse in their efforts to negotiate a new agreement.[391]

368. In 1996, the U.S. Supreme Court significantly expanded the scope of the non-statutory labor exemption. In *Brown v. Pro Football, Inc.*,[392] the Court held that the exemption shields all restraints on the labor market for players' services (e.g., player drafts, team salary caps, and player free agency restrictions) from antitrust challenge as long as there is an ongoing collective bargaining process between the league and the players union. If there is, federal labor law exclusively governs labor relations between the parties.

369. In *Brown*, the NFL unilaterally established a maximum weekly salary of USD 1,000 for all developmental squad players (i.e., non-roster players) after collectively bargaining to impasse on this important issue (historically, all U.S. major professional sports league player salaries were individually negotiated between a player and his club). The players claimed this conduct was illegal wage fixing in violation of §1 of the Sherman Act, but the Court ruled they could not bring their antitrust claim:

---

386. . *United States v. Hutcheson*, 312 U.S. 219 (1941).
387. . *Kennedy v. Long Island Rail Road Co.*, 319 F.2d 366 (2d Cir. 1963), *cert. denied*, 375 U.S. 830 (1963).
388. . *Mackey v. National Football League*, 543 F.2d 606, 611 (8th Cir. 1976).
389. . *Connell Construction Co. v. Plumbers, Local 100*, 421 U.S. 616, 622 (1975).
390. . *Wood v. Nat'l Basketball Assn.*, 809 F.2d 954 (2d. Cir. 1987); *McCourt v. California Sports, Inc.*, 600 F.2d 1193 (6th Cir. 1979); *Reynolds v. National Football League,* 584 F.2d 280 (8th Cir. 1978); *Mackey v. NFL*, 543 F.2d 606 (8th Cir. 1976).
391. . *Powell v. NFL*, 930 F.2d 1293 (8th Cir. 1989), *cert. denied*, 498 U.S. 1040 (1991).
392. . 518 U.S. 231 (1996).

> the implicit (non-statutory) antitrust exemption applies to the employer conduct at issue here. That conduct took place during and immediately after a collective-bargaining negotiation. It grew out of, and was directly related to, the lawful operation of the bargaining process. It involved a matter that the parties were required to negotiate collectively. And it concerned only the parties to the collective-bargaining relationship.

370. The Court, however, explained that its holding "is not intended to insulate from antitrust review every joint imposition of terms by employers, for an agreement among employers could be sufficiently distant in time and in circumstances from the collective bargaining process that a rule permitting antitrust intervention would not significantly interfere with that process." It suggested that the non-statutory labor exemption would end if the players terminated the collective bargaining process with the league by decertifying their union, which would then permit them to bring an antitrust suit challenging any agreements among league clubs that restrained the market for their services.

371. Unions can be dissolved in two ways: (1) by decertification; or (2) by a disclaimer of interest. Decertification is a more formal and time consuming process involving the National Labor Relations Board, which ultimately requires that at least 50% of the members of the players association vote to decertify the union in an NLRB-supervised election.[393] If a majority of the players vote to decertify the union, they cannot vote to re-unionize (and engage in collective bargaining with the league) before the elapse of a twelve-month period.[394] In contrast, a disclaimer of interest is an informal procedure pursuant to which the union leadership disclaims authority to represent the players based on at least 50% of them indicating they do not desire such representation.[395] A majority of the players can reauthorize the union to represent them at any time, creating the possibility of stepping into and out of a collective bargaining relationship as desired based on the circumstances.

372. In *Brady v. NFL*,[396] the Eighth Circuit refused to enjoin an NFL lockout after NFL players disclaimed their union's authority to represent them in negotiations over a new CBA and filed an antitrust suit claiming that the lockout is an unlawful group boycott among NFL clubs. It ruled that the Norris-LaGuardia Act, which provides that courts do not have jurisdiction to issue injunctions "in any case involving or growing out of a labor dispute" precluded it from doing so:

> The text of the Norris–LaGuardia Act and the cases interpreting the term labor dispute do not require the present existence of a union to establish a labor dispute. Whatever the precise limits of the phrase involving or growing out of a labor dispute, this case does not press the outer boundary. The League and the players' union were parties to a collective bargaining agreement for almost eighteen years

393. . *See* generally Catherine Meeker, *Defining "Ministerial Aid": Union Decertification under the National Labor Relations Act*, 66 U. Chi. L. Rev. 999, 1000–1001 (1999).

394. . 29 U.S.C. §159.

395. . *Powell v. NFL*, 764 F. Supp. 1351 (D. Minn. 1991).

396. . 644 F.2d 661 (8th Cir. 2011). *See* generally Jeremy Davis, ed., *A Roundtable Discussion for the Digital Age: Brady v. NFL*, 29 Ent. & Sports L. 1 (2011).

> prior to March 2011. They were engaged in collective bargaining over terms and conditions of employment for approximately two years through March 11, 2011. At that point, the parties were involved in a classic labor dispute by the Players own definition. Then, on a single day, just hours before the CBA's expiration, the union discontinued collective bargaining and disclaimed its status, and the Players filed this action seeking relief concerning industry-wide terms and conditions of employment. Whatever the effect of the union's disclaimer on the League's immunity from antitrust liability, the labor dispute did not suddenly disappear just because the Players elected to pursue the dispute through antitrust litigation rather than collective bargaining.

373. In *Clarett v. National Football League*,[397] the Second Circuit held that the non-statutory labor exemption immunizes player eligibility requirements that are the product of a lawful collective bargaining process from antitrust scrutiny. The court ruled that the union has the exclusive authority to negotiate the terms and conditions of prospective NFL players' employment (e.g., requiring that "at least three full college seasons have elapsed since their high school graduation"). Eligibility rules are a mandatory subject of collective bargaining between the league and the players' union because they pertain to players" "wages, hours, and other terms and conditions of employment." As part of its efforts to obtain a CBA providing the best overall deal for all NFL players, federal labor law gives their union "the ability to advantage certain categories of players over others, subject to [its] duty of fair representation." The court held that "the NFL and its players' union can agree that an employee will not be hired or considered for employment for nearly any reason whatsoever so long as they do not violate federal laws such as those prohibiting unfair labor practices, or discrimination" (e.g., race, ethnicity, national origin, or disability discrimination).

374. A federal statute, the *Curt Flood Act of 1998*,[398] limits the otherwise broad scope of baseball's common law antitrust immunity by providing MLB players with the same antitrust remedies as other professional athletes such as football, basketball, hockey, and soccer players. This legislation is the product of a joint lobbying effort by the MLB players' union and MLB clubs pursuant to a provision in their 1994 CBA. It is not intended to affect judicial construction and application of the non-statutory labor exemption to baseball players' antitrust claims brought against professional baseball organizations.[399] Thus, unionized MLB players cannot challenge the terms and conditions of their employment arising out of the collective bargaining process on antitrust grounds. However, if the CBA expires and the non-statutory labor exemption is inapplicable because the players terminated the collective bargaining process with MLB by decertifying their union, MLB players could bring an antitrust suit challenging any agreements among MLB clubs that restrain the labor market for their services.[400]

---

397. . 369 F.3d 124 (2d Cir. 2004), cert denied, 544 U.S. 961 (2005). *See also National Hockey League Players' Ass'n v. Plymouth Whalers*, 419 F.3d 462, 474 (6th Cir. 2005) ("any anti-competitive effect of a properly bargained collective bargaining agreement is excluded from antitrust scrutiny by [the] non-statutory antitrust exemption.").
398. . 15 U.S.C. §26b.
399. . 15 U.S.C. §26b(d)(4).
400. . *See* paras 315–317 *supra* .

The Act expressly permits antitrust challenges only to conduct or agreements by those persons "in the business of organized professional MLB directly relating to or affecting employment of MLB players to play baseball at the major league level,"[401] not conduct or agreements relating to employment as a minor league baseball player, the amateur or first-year player draft, or any reserve clause applied to minor league players.[402]

II. Antitrust Law

375. Players in team sports may choose not to unionize or may decertify their union, thereby preventing or discontinuing the collective bargaining process and the applicability of the non-statutory labor exemption. The non-statutory labor exemption has not been applied to individual performer sports, such as tennis, golf, boxing, and others.[403] These professional athletes are not employees who have the right to unionize and engage in collective bargaining activities. Even if athletes in the sport form a players' association and enter into employment agreements with event promoters or organizers, this generally does not constitute collective bargaining under the federal labor laws.

376. Courts generally hold that the non-statutory labor exemption does not bar an antitrust challenge by non-parties to CBA terms that have anticompetitive effects outside the labor market for players' services. In *Philadelphia World Hockey Club, Inc. v. Philadelphia Hockey Club, Inc.*,[404] the court ruled that this exemption does not preclude a rival league's claim that the NHL's reserve clause, which gave league clubs the rights to players for three years after their contracts expire, violates the antitrust laws. The WHA prevailed on its antitrust claim by proving that the reserve clause in the NHL's CBA deprived it from competing for the services of players with the ability to play major league professional hockey. The WHA needed access to these players in order to produce major league professional ice hockey in North America in competition with the NHL.

377. Most litigation seeking to invalidate player labor market restraints involves claimed violations of §1 of the Sherman Act, which requires concerted anticompetitive conduct that unreasonably restrains interstate trade or commerce. Courts generally have rejected the defense that the league and its member clubs function as a single economic entity whose rules are not subject to challenge under §1. For example, in *McNeil v. NFL*,[405] the court held that agreements among league clubs to reduce competition for player services are subject to §1. In *Chicago Professional Sports Ltd. Partnership v. NBA*,[406] the Seventh Circuit observed: "from the perspective of college

401. . 15 U.S.C. §26b(a).
402. . 15 U.S.C. §26b(b)(1). *See Miranda v. Selig*, 2015 WL 5357854 (N.D. Cal.) (holding that baseball's common law antitrust immunity bars minor league baseball players' antitrust claims).
403. . *See*, e.g., *Blalock v. Ladies Prof'l Golfers Ass'n*, 359 F. Supp. 1260 (N.D. Ga. 1973) (finding that golfer's one-year suspension imposed by LPGA with "completely unfettered, subjective discretion" by a group of her competitors violates the antitrust laws).
404. . 351 F. Supp. 462 (E.D. Pa. 1972).
405. . 790 F. Supp. 871 (D. Minn. 1992).
406. . 95 F.3d 593, 599 (7th Cir. 1996).

basketball players who seek to sell their skills, the teams are distinct, and because the human capital of players is not readily transferable to other sports (as even Michael Jordan learned) the league looks more like a group of firms acting as a monopsony."

378. Because the unique features of the professional sports industry require some uniform rules and agreements among competing teams in order to produce on-field competition that is appealing to consumers,[407] courts generally apply the rule of reason on a case-by-case basis to determine whether particular restraints affecting the market for player services violate the antitrust laws.[408] Some agreements among league clubs regarding the permissible scope of competition for player services is necessary to jointly produce games, which is an important factor is to be considered when assessing the reasonableness of the challenged player restraints.[409]

379. Applying the rule of reason to player restraints requires complicated analysis and balancing of several different factors and their economic effects. Considering the validity of the NBA's then-current draft eligibility rules, one court observed:

> The primary disadvantages of the rule of reason are that it requires difficult and lengthy factual inquiries and very subjective policy decisions which are in many ways essentially legislative and ill-suited to the judicial process. For instance, in the present case, a complex economic inquiry would be required to determine the economic necessity of action of this type. In addition, the court would be required to determine a standard which could be used to weigh the various public policy goals which might be alleged as justification by the NBA. The court would further be forced to determine whether the boycott was genuinely motivated by the purposes given or by other reasons. Frequently, these motives are closely intertwined.[410]

380. Under the rule of reason, a player must prove that the challenged restraint reduces economic competition among the defendants for player services. For example, agreements among league clubs to fix players' wages, which thereby eliminate individual salary negotiations, have clear anticompetitive effects.[411] Because their adverse economic effects are not as direct and less clear, other labor market restraints such as player drafts, free agency restrictions, and other forms of allocating players among league clubs may require detailed market analysis to determine their effects on economic

407. . *American Needle, Inc. v. NFL*, 130 S. Ct. 2201, 2216 (2010) ("When 'restraints on competition are essential if the product is to be available at all,' *per se* rules of illegality are inapplicable, and instead the restraint must be judged according to the flexible Rule of Reason."); *National Collegiate Athletic Association v. Board of Regents of the University of Oklahoma*, 468 U.S. 85, 101 (1984) ("refusing to apply per se rule to sports industry because some horizontal restraints are necessary 'if product to be available at all'").

408. . *See* , e.g., *Smith v. Pro-Football Inc.*, 593 F.2d 1173, 1182 (D.C. Cir. 1978) ("legality of NFL draft should not be governed by per se rule. legality of player restriction in professional sports should be governed by the rule of reason"); *Mackey v. NFL*, 543 F.2d 606, 619 (8th Cir. 1976) ("unique nature of the business of professional football renders it inappropriate to mechanically apply per se illegality rules" to challenged league free agency restrictions).

409. . *McNeil v. NFL*, 1992 WL 315292 (D. Minn. 1992).

410. . *Denver Rockets v. All-Pro Management*, 325 F. Supp. 1049, 1063 (C.D. Cal. 1971).

411. . *McNeil v. NFL*, 790 F. Supp. 871, 877 (D. Minn. 1992).

competition. In such cases, the players must prove the league and its clubs have a sufficiently large market share to adversely affect competition in the relevant labor market for their services. The relevant market has both a product and geographical component. The product market includes all prospective purchasers of player services that are reasonable substitutes from the players' perspective in terms of earning potential, prestige, and other economic factors.[412] The geographical market is the geographic area "to which players can turn, as a practical matter, for alternate opportunities for employment" as professional athletes.[413]

381. If the players prove the requisite anticompetitive effects, the league and clubs must prove the challenged restraint furthers a legitimate procompetitive justification. Some courts have held that the anticompetitive effects of labor market restraints cannot be justified by procompetitive effects in a different market.[414] More recently, other courts, including the U.S. Supreme Court, have ruled that procompetitive effects in a closely related market (i.e., those that enhance a professional sports league's ability to more effectively compete with other forms of entertainment) should be balanced against a restraint's anticompetitive effects.[415] In *American Needle, Inc. v. NFL*,[416] the Supreme Court recognized that a professional sports league's interest in maintaining competitive balance among its member clubs is "legitimate and important," which is "unquestionably an interest that may well justify a variety of collective decisions made by the teams."

382. A labor market restraint may be invalidated if there is a less restrictive means of achieving the league's procompetitive objective. For example, in *Smith v. Pro Football, Inc.*,[417] the court held that the NFL's then-existing sixteen-round draft violated §1 because "significantly less anticompetitive alternatives" exist to maintain league-wide competitive balance among its clubs such as draft with fewer rounds.

383. As an illustration of how courts have applied the rule of reason to labor market restraints, in *Mackey v. NFL*,[418] the court explained:

> The focus of an inquiry under the Rule of Reason is whether the restraint imposed is justified by legitimate business purposes, and is no more restrictive than necessary. …
>
> In defining the restraint on competition for players' services, the district court found that the Rozelle Rule [which required Commissioner Rozelle to award compensation in the form of players and/or draft choices from the club that

412. . *Smith v. Pro Football, Inc.*, 593 F.2d 1173, 1185 n. 48 (D.C. Cir. 1979) (finding that employment in Canadian Football League is not reasonable substitute for employment with an NFL team).
413. . *Fraser v. Major League Soccer, LLC*, 284 F.3d 47, 63 (1st Cir. 2002), *cert. denied*, 537 U.S. 885 (2002) (upholding jury finding of an international market for the services of professional soccer players).
414. . *Smith v. Pro Football, Inc.*, 593 F.2d 1173 (D.C. Cir. 1979).
415. . *Sullivan v. NFL*, 34 F.3d 1091, 1111–13 (1st Cir. 1994).
416. . 130 S. Ct. 2201, 2217 (2010).
417. . 593 F.2d 1173, 118 (D.C. Cir. 1979).
418. . 543 F.2d 606 (8th Cir. 1976).

contracted with a free agent player to his former club if they could not agree on compensation for the lost player] significantly deters clubs from negotiating with and signing free agents; that it acts as a substantial deterrent to players playing out their options and becoming free agents; that it significantly decreases players' bargaining power in contract negotiations; that players are thus denied the right to sell their services in a free and open market; that as a result, the salaries paid by each club are lower than if competitive bidding were allowed to prevail; and that absent the Rozelle Rule, there would be increased movement in interstate commerce of players from one club to another.

We find substantial evidence in the record to support these findings. Witnesses for both sides testified that there would be increased player movement absent the Rozelle Rule. …

In support of their contention that the restraints effected by the Rozelle Rule are not unreasonable, the defendants asserted a number of justifications. First, they argued that without the Rozelle Rule, star players would flock to cities having natural advantages such as larger economic bases, winning teams, warmer climates, and greater media opportunities; that competitive balance throughout the League would thus be destroyed; and that the destruction of competitive balance would ultimately lead to diminished spectator interest, franchise failures, and perhaps the demise of the NFL, at least as it operates today. Second, the defendants contended that the Rozelle Rule is necessary to protect the clubs' investment in scouting expenses and player development costs. Third, they asserted that players must work together for a substantial period of time in order to function effectively as a team; that elimination of the Rozelle Rule would lead to increased player movement and a concomitant reduction in player continuity; and that the quality of play in the NFL would thus suffer, leading to reduced spectator interest, and financial detriment both to the clubs and the players. Conflicting evidence was adduced at trial by both sides with respect to the validity of these asserted justifications.

The district court held the defendants' asserted justifications unavailing. … The court further concluded that elimination of the Rozelle Rule would have no significant disruptive effects, either immediate or long term, on professional football. In conclusion the court held that the Rozelle Rule was unreasonable in that it was overly broad, unlimited in duration, unaccompanied by procedural safeguards, and employed in conjunction with other anticompetitive practices such as the draft, Standard Player Contract, option clause, and the no-tampering rules.

> We agree that the asserted need to recoup player development costs cannot justify the restraints of the Rozelle Rule. That expense is an ordinary cost of doing business and is not peculiar to professional football. Moreover, because of its unlimited duration, the Rozelle Rule is far more restrictive than necessary to fulfill that need.
>
> We agree, in view of the evidence adduced at trial with respect to existing players' turnover by way of trades, retirements and new players entering the League, that the club owners' arguments respecting player continuity cannot justify the Rozelle Rule. ...
>
> In sum, we hold that the Rozelle Rule, as enforced, unreasonably restrains trade in violation of §1 of the Sherman Act.

384. Although federal antitrust law may be used by players to invalidate labor market restraints that have not been collectively bargained, it is only prohibitory rather than remedial in nature. In other words, although antitrust law prohibits league clubs from unreasonably restraining the market for player services, it does not require them to agree to or implement any particular terms and conditions of employment, including those that are "reasonable." Court's ruling that various restraints violate the antitrust laws has observed that the collective bargaining process is the best means of resolving labor disputes between players and clubs. In *Mackey*, the court recognized that "[t]he parties are far better situated to agreeably resolve what rules governing player transfers are best suited for their mutual interests than the courts." As a result, even if the players' antitrust suit is successful, the league and the players union often subsequently agree to a modified system of player restraints that is incorporated into a new CBA, which is immune from antitrust challenge by the non-statutory labor exemption.[419]

III. Worker's Compensation Law

385. Like other athletes, professional athletes assume the inherent risks of injury while participating in their respective sports. However, major league CBAs and standard player contracts generally establish the contractual right of professional athletes to receive team-provided or paid medical care and rehabilitation for injuries suffered during games, practices, and training. Major league professional athletes also have contractual injury protection guarantees and benefits for career-ending injuries and sport-related disabilities.[420] Disputes between a player and team concerning the parties' respective rights and responsibilities under these agreements generally must be submitted to binding arbitration.[421]

419. . *See* Part II, Ch. 4, §2, I, D.
420. . An athlete also may be entitled to receive league-provided disability benefits depending upon the terms of the pension benefit plan and the circumstances giving rise to the player's disability.
421. . *Sherwin v. Indianapolis Colts, Inc.*, 752 F. Supp. 1172 (N.D.N.Y. 1990).

386. As employees, professional team sport athletes, including those playing minor league sports, also may be eligible to recover state workers' compensation benefits for injuries or illnesses arising from playing a sport. In general, a professional athlete may recover workers' compensation benefits if: 1) he or she is an "employee" under the applicable state statute; and 2) the injury or illness arose out of or in the course of his or her employment with the team, which includes during games, practices, and training.[422] Workers' compensation laws enable employees to obtain compensation and medical expenses for work-related injuries and illnesses. The theory underlying these laws is that industries should bear the burden of industrial accidents as a component of the cost of production. Thus, workers' compensation is premised on the idea that workplace accidents are a cost of doing business and therefore should be borne by the company for whom the employee was working when the injury occurred. In this sense, workers' compensation is a transfer of economic losses from injured workers to industry and, ultimately, to the public.

387. Under workers' compensation legislation, benefits are available to injured workers without having to prove breach of an employer's common law tort or other statutory liability. In other words, workers' compensation systems are a form of strict liability. A professional athlete may receive workers' compensation benefits for aggravation of an injury caused by improper treatment by the team's medical personnel.[423] Aggravation of a player's existing injury caused by a professional team's requirement that the player continue or resume playing is compensable damage under workers' compensation law.[424] Affirmative defenses available in common law tort actions, such as contributory negligence and assumption of risk are unavailable to employers in workers' compensation actions. The removal of such requirements enables injured employees to avoid the legal impediments that left many workers uncompensated under the traditional common law tort doctrines.

388. Employees (e.g., professional team sport athletes) obtain the security of workers' compensation benefits on a no-fault basis in exchange for relinquishing rights to pursue tort actions against their employers (e.g., clubs or teams). A worker who accepts workers' compensation benefits or has successfully prosecuted a workers' compensation claim is barred from bringing a common law tort action against his employer or a co-employee.[425] Limitations are also imposed on the amount of compensation that workers can recover. For example, workers' compensation statutes generally preclude employees from recovering for pain and suffering or punitive damages. Available remedies are typically limited to compensation for disability,

---

422. *See* , e.g., *Norfolk Admirals v. Jones*, 2005 WI 2847392 (Va. App. 2005) (professional hockey player entitled to receive workers' compensation benefits for injuries suffered in a fight with an opposing player during a game ordered by his coach); *Dandenault v. Workers 'Compensation Appeals Bd.*, 728 A.2d 1001 (Pa. Comm. Ct. 1999) (professional hockey player's participation in a summer hockey league to get into shape for upcoming season was not with scope of his employment because his team did not require or encourage him to engage in this activity).

423. . *DePiano v. Montreal Baseball Club, Ltd.*, 663 F. Supp. 116 (W.D. Pa. 1987); *Bayless v. Phila. Nat'l League Club*, 472 F. Supp. 625 (E.D. Pa. 1979).

424. . *DePiano v. Montreal Baseball Club, Ltd.*, 663 F. Supp. 116 (W.D. Pa. 1987).

425. . *Stringer v. Minnesota Vikings Football Club, LLC*, 705 N.W.2d 746 (Minn. 2005); *Hendy v. Losse*, 819 P.2d 1 (Cal. 1991); *Lotysz v. Montgomery*, 766 N.Y.S.2d 28 (N.Y. App. Div. 2003); *Daniels v. Seattle Seahawks*, 968 P.2d 883 (Wash. App. Ct. 1998).

medical, death, and burial expenses. Thus, employees waive tort claims against their employers in exchange for a simplified but limited recovery under workers' compensation laws.

389. State statutes are the source of employee rights to workers' compensation benefits. Absent a specific exclusion under a particular state's law, injured professional athletes normally are eligible to receive workers' compensation benefits. A few states expressly exclude professional athletes from the definition of employee for workers' compensation purposes or otherwise limit the extent to which workers' compensation benefits are available to professional athletes.[426] To prevent professional athletes from receiving benefits for the same injury from two different sources, some states limit the amount of recoverable workers' compensation benefits if contractual injury compensation is provided.[427]

390. Rather than seeking the no fault fixed benefits provided by workers' compensation, an injured player instead may prefer trying to obtain an uncertain, but potentially much larger, judgment for damages in tort litigation. The exclusive remedy provisions of workers' compensation laws usually will not bar a tort action against an employer for harm caused by conduct that is intended to injure an employee. If the requisite intent is established, an employee may elect to either receive workers' compensation benefits or bring a tort claim. In jurisdictions that recognize the intentional injury exception to the exclusivity effect of workers' compensation laws, courts are rather strict with regard to the burden of proof imposed upon the employee. In *DePiano v. Montreal Baseball Club, Ltd.*[428] the court ruled that a player must prove that his club intended to injure or aggravate an injury by requiring him to continue playing, which he could not do by simply showing it did so because of its desire to win games.

391. Even if a club did not intend to injure a player, in some jurisdictions the club may be subject to tort liability for fraudulent concealment of material medical information concerning a player's fitness to play. In *Krueger v. San Francisco Forty Niners*,[429] the court held that a professional football team fraudulently failed to disclose that a player risked permanent disability by continuing to play with a chronic knee condition. Evidence established that the team "consciously failed" to disclose that the player's knee lacked the anterior cruciate ligament, that steroid injection treatments might have adverse effects, and that he risked permanent injury by continuing to play without surgery. The exclusivity provisions of the California workers' compensation statute were inapplicable because they expressly permitted the recovery of tort damages if the employee's injury was aggravated by the employer's fraudulent concealment of the existence of the injury.

426. . *See* , e.g., Fla. Stat. Ann. §440.02(17)(c)(3); Mass. Gen. Laws Ann. Ch. 152, §1(4)(b); Wyo. Stat. Ann. §27-14-102(vii)(F). The Florida and Wyoming statutes provide coverage for professional athletes when their team purchases insurance for the specific purpose of providing workers' compensation benefits for its athletes.

427. . *See* , e.g., Tex. Lab. Code Ann. § 406.095 (athletes are required to elect to receive workers' compensation benefits or benefits available pursuant to contract or collective bargaining agreement where applicable).

428. . 663 F. Supp. 116 (W.D. Pa. 1987).

429. . 234 Cal. Rptr. 579 (Cal. Ct. App. 1987).

§3. Individual Performer Sports

392. Individual performer sport athletes such as golfers, tennis players, and boxers are independent contractors rather than employees, so they are not permitted to unionize under the federal labor laws and generally are not eligible for workers' compensation benefits under state laws. Because there is no union to collectively bargain on their behalf, the sport's governing authority or the event organizer generally establishes the conditions of participation unilaterally. To maximize an individual performer sport's commercial appeal to fans and spectators, a professional sports governing authority has a strong economic incentive to encourage and permit participation by the most highly skilled athletes without discriminating based on non-performance related factors. Absent violation of a professional athlete's federal or state civil rights, courts generally are reluctant to invalidate athlete eligibility rules established by an independent sport's governing body or event organizer.[430] For example, it is permissible to adopt non-discriminatory, unbiased eligibility rules or methods for evaluating an individual performer sport athlete's playing ability and skills.[431]

393. Courts will enforce valid contracts entered into by individual performer sport athletes and may grant injunctive relief to enforce negative covenants to prevent irreparable harm to the non-breaching party. For example, in *Lewis v. Rahman*,[432] Lennox Lewis, the then-former heavyweight champion of the world, claimed a contractual right to fight a rematch against Hasim Rahman, the then-current heavyweight champion of the world, within 150 days of an April 21, 2001 match in which Rahman defeated Lewis and sought to enjoin Rahman from fighting another opponent before the rematch occurred. Granting the requested injunctive relief, the court stated:

> I find that Lewis would suffer irreparable harm were he denied the opportunity to regain his championship title. It is undisputed that the heavyweight championship is the most prestigious title in professional boxing. The opportunity to fight for the heavyweight championship, and especially the opportunity to regain the championship, cannot be measured in money. Because of his age, Lewis has only a limited time to regain his title and restore his reputation. Rahman, in contrast, is only 28 years old. Even if he chose not to box for 18 months, he would still have several productive years left in his career. Rahman concedes that he has a contractual obligation to fight Lewis in a rematch eventually, although he prefers to fight an interim bout. When asked if he wished to fight Lewis immediately, he said, I don't have a problem with it. … A preponderance of the credible evidence shows that Lewis will not be able to fight for more than the next two years. Even during the next two years, his boxing abilities may diminish. An injunction for 18 months provides an effective remedy for Lewis' irreparable harm and does not unfairly impede Rahman.

---

430. . *See* , e.g., *Toscano v. PGA Tour, Inc.*, 201 F. Supp.2d 1106,1113 (E.D. Cal. 2002) (rejecting antitrust challenge to Senior PGA Tour's per-event limit of seventy-eight golfers and its eligibility rules limiting the ability of new and non-exempt players to compete in its events).
431. . *Deesen v. Prof'l Golfers' Ass'n of America*, 358 F.2d 165 (9th Cir. 1966).
432. . 147 F. Supp. 2d 225 (S.D.N.Y. 2001).

394. There is no collectively bargained disciplinary process and range of sanctions for athletes participating in individual performer professional sports. Player discipline for violations of the sport's rules, including suspension from competition, generally is imposed by an independent commissioner or governing authority. Under contract or private association law, courts will provide limited judicial review to ensure that an appropriate level of procedural process is provided, contract rights are respected, and that disciplinary decisions are not arbitrary, capricious, or made in bad faith.[433] Some athletes (e.g., tennis players who are members of the Association of Tennis Professionals) may have a contractual right to have an independent arbitrator review a disciplinary sanction for a doping offence imposed by the sport's governing authority.

395. Because there is no collective bargaining relationship between individual performer sport athletes and the sport's organizer or governing body, the non-statutory labor exemption[434] is inapplicable and these professional athletes retain their antitrust law rights and remedies. For example, in *Blalock v. Ladies Professional Golfers Association,*[435] the court ruled that a professional golfer's one-year suspension imposed with "completely unfettered, subjective discretion" by a group of her competitors was an unreasonable restraint of trade that violates the antitrust laws. The court observed that this suspension was imposed by a group of competing golfers who would gain financially from her exclusion from all tournaments sponsored by the Ladies PGA. However, it suggested that the association's legitimate self-policing activities and reasonable disciplinary sanctions against member golfers who violated its rules would not violate the antitrust laws.

§4. Taxation Issues

396. U.S. professional team and individual performer sport athletes are required to pay federal income, social security, and Medicare (a fund to pay for the health care needs of elderly citizens) taxes based on their income (e.g., salary and bonuses, prize money, and product endorsements) earned within the U.S. and in foreign countries.[436] They also are subject to state and local income tax based on income earned within the particular taxing authority's jurisdiction. For example, a baseball player for a club in California may be required to pay state and local income taxes on the proportionate amount of income earned from playing home games in California and away games where other league clubs are located as well as to the state and city in which he resides. A tennis player income is subject to state and local income tax by taxing authorities in the geographical area in which it is earned (e.g., both the State of New York and

433. . *See* , e.g., *Crouch v. NASCAR*, 845 F.2d 397 (2d Cir. 1988); *Koszela v. NASCAR*, 646 F.2d 749 (2d. Cir. 1981).

434. . *See* Part II, Ch. 4, §2, I, D, *supra* .

435. . 359 F. Supp. 1260 (N.D. Ga. 1973).

436. . *See* generally James A.R. Nafziger, *International Sports Law* (2d ed., Transnational Publishers 2004). For a discussion of international taxation issues involving U.S. citizens or residents who earn income from playing professional sports outside of the U.S., *see* Carole C. Berry, *Taxation of U.S. Athletes Playing in Foreign Countries*, 13 Marq. Sports L. Rev. 1 (2002).

New York City may tax prize winnings from a New York City tournament) as well as to the state and city in which he resides.

Chapter 5. Legal Protection against Race Discrimination

§1. Historical Perspective

397. During the early years of professional and collegiate sports, a period extending from after the Civil War to the late 1800s and early 1900s, African-Americans participated in organized sports at the amateur and professional levels, including boxing, horse racing, baseball, and cycling. The opportunity to participate during this period was not accompanied by equality of treatment. African-Americans were both exploited for their athletic ability and subjected to the indignities that flowed from racial discrimination.

398. The early years of inclusion in amateur and professional sports, albeit limited, were followed by a period during which formal (e.g., prohibitions against blacks attending white colleges and universities and statutes prohibiting any form of athletic competition between whites and African-Americans) and informal rules (e.g., "gentlemen's agreements" that prohibited blacks from participating in league contests and quotas that restricted the slots open to black players on a team) excluded blacks from collegiate sports. Even those athletes who had the opportunity to play were subject to the indignities of racism. This period of segregation was followed by what some have coined as the reintegration of sports. By the end of the Second World War, virtually every major collegiate program outside the South had opened its doors to permit at least one African-American player to compete for it. Southern colleges and universities resisted this fundamental change in college sport and continued after the Second World War to exclude African-American student-athletes. The integration of college sport at predominantly white colleges in the South did not occur until the latter part of the 1960s, during which time the numbers of African-American players competing for these institutions significantly increased.

399. Prior to the Second World War, the experiences of racial and ethnic minorities in professional sports largely paralleled those of their amateur counterparts. For example, it is estimated that approximately twenty-four blacks played in organized professional baseball during the 1880s. By the 1890s, however, segregation of professional baseball emerged pursuant to a gentleman's agreement that resulted in the total exclusion of black and dark-skinned Latino players from MLB. Seeking alternative venues in which to play baseball, blacks and dark-skinned Latinos played in the Negro Leagues and Latin America, and also informally played games with white players. This period of segregation was followed by what some have coined as the reintegration of sports. Baseball, for example, would remain segregated until Jackie Robinson joined the Brooklyn Dodgers in 1947. The formal desegregation of baseball would not occur, however, until 1959, when the Boston Red Sox, the last MLB team to field an all-white team, promoted Pumpsie Green to the major leagues.

400. During the latter half of the twentieth century a confluence of social, political, and economic variables resulted in the integration of professional sports and broader American society. Significant among these variables are (1) expectations for desegregation created by the "democratic idealism spawned by World War II," (2) opportunities created by a shortage of players due to the Second World War's decimation of the talent pool of white athletes, (3) political activism by blacks and their white allies demanding the desegregation of professional sports, (4) U.S. Supreme Court desegregation decisions, and (5) enactment of federal civil rights legislation. Additional factors converged to provide incentives for colleges and universities to recruit African-American student-athletes, including political decisions, such as congressional passage of the G.I. Bill (which increased the presence of African-Americans on college campuses) and the increased professionalism of college sports following the Second World War.

401. To satisfy strong public demand for competition among a sport's best athletes, producers, and organizers of intercollegiate and professional sports events have a strong economic incentive to select athletes based on their individual ability, skill, or proficiency and not to exclude athletes from participating based on their race (which is now clearly prohibited by federal civil rights laws). Currently, the majority of players in the NFL and NBA are African-American. During the 2015–2016 season, African-Americans constituted 74.3% of NBA players and 68.7% of NFL players. A disproportionate number of male student-athletes who played Division I football and basketball during this timeframe are African-Americans, 53.4% and 55.6%, respectively. By contrast, African-Americans constituted only 2.9% of student-athletes who participated in Division I baseball. The disproportionate presence of African-Americans in basketball and football is misleading to the extent it suggests that race has become a nonissue in U.S. sports. To the contrary, the debate regarding race has merely shifted from the question of distributive justice (e.g., participation opportunities for African-Americans in the major sports) to other matters, including: (1) opportunities for minorities in administrative and coaching positions; (2) the under representation of racial minorities in sports other than football and basketball; and (3) the implications for sport when issues relating to race converge with those relating to gender, globalization, and economic exploitation.[437]

§2. Interscholastic and Intercollegiate Athletics

I. Treatment of Student-Athletes

402. Public educational institutions must comply with the U.S. Constitution's Equal Protection Clause, which prohibits race discrimination. Different treatment of student-athletes based on race is subject to strict scrutiny by courts, which requires a compelling state interest and that it is applied in the least restrictive manner.[438] In

437. . *See* generally Timothy Davis, *Race and Sports in America: An Historical Overview*, 7 Va. Sports & Ent. L. J. 291, 307–311 (2008) (identifying other present-day manifestations of the role of race in sports, including recent studies suggesting that race may influence officiating in the NBA and MLB, the convergence of race and economics to create impediments to access in certain sports such as golf, and media racial insensitivity in sport).
438. . *Priester v. Lowndes County*, 354 F.3d 414 (5th Cir. 2004).

Hysaw v. Washburn University,[439] a group of African-American student-athletes were removed from the football team after protesting alleged unequal financial aid and treatment based on their race. The court ruled that the student-athletes would have a viable federal constitutional law claim for violation of their free speech rights if they could prove that they were disciplined for protesting racial mistreatment.

403. In *Heike v. Guevara*,[440] a Caucasian student-athlete alleged that her basketball coach refused to renew her scholarship because she was white. Regarding her race discrimination claims, the court applied the *McDonnell Douglas*[441] framework that allows a plaintiff to establish a violation of her constitutional equal protection rights either by presenting direct evidence of discrimination or indirect evidence of discrimination. Applying this framework, the court held that the coach's alleged statements that she preferred "thug" or "ghetto" players and that plaintiff was not her "type" failed to establish direct evidence of racial discrimination. The court reasoned that to adopt plaintiff's logic would countenance the perpetuation of stereotypes because it assumes that only black players can be "thug" or "ghetto." The court also found that plaintiff failed to present indirect evidence of racial discrimination. Analogizing the college's failure to renew plaintiff's one-year scholarship to a one-year employment contract renewable at will, the court stated that "[t]o subject run-of-the-mill coaching decisions to class-of-one equal protection challenges would be to expose collegiate athletics to an unprecedented, unjustified and unjustifiable level of judicial oversight."

404. Title VI of the 1964 Civil Rights Act, a federal statute applicable to entities that receive federal funds that covers virtually all public and private educational institutions in the U.S., also provides a remedy for student-athletes who are the victims of race discrimination. In *Garvey v. Unified School Dist.*,[442] in determining who would be selected for the team, a coach evaluated high school basketball players based on both objective criteria (e.g., shooting and dribbling) and subjective criteria (e.g., heart and character). Plaintiff, a minority player who was cut from the team, alleged that the public high school engaged in racial discrimination. The court found that the plaintiff could sue for intentional race discrimination under Title VI,[443] but the statute does not permit a discrimination claim based on the disparate impact that the defendants' conduct has on the members of a particular race.

405. In *Cureton v. NCAA*, 198 F.3d 107 (3rd Cir. 1999), plaintiffs alleged that NCAA Proposition 16 had a disparate impact on African-American intercollegiate athletes. Proposition 16 is an NCAA academic eligibility requirement, based on standardized test scores and GPA in core classes, that student-athletes must meet to

439. . 609 F. Supp. 940 (D. Kan. 1987).

440. . 519 Fed. Appx. 911(6th Cir. 2013).

441. *McDonnell Douglas Corp. v. Green*, 411 U.S. 792 (1973).

442. . 2005 WL 2548332 (D. Kan. 2005).

443. . *See also Scott v. State of Hawaii Dept. of Educ.*, 2009 WL 564709 (D. Hawaii) (African-American athlete kicked off of high school football team failed to present evidence establishing disciplinary rules were applied to him in a discriminatory manner—other students received less harsh punishment for similar violations—and, therefore, could not sustain a Title VI racial discrimination claim); *Williams v. U.S. Tennis Assoc.*, 2009 WL 5088727 (N.D. Cal.) (tennis player and her mother failed to allege facts sufficient to support their claim that the daughter was a victim of racial discrimination based on the defendant association's failure to respond to hostile comments made by another player and her mother).

be eligible to play Division I sports. The Third Circuit held that Title VI applied only to specific educational programs or activities receiving federal funds and not the educational institution or entity as a whole. Because the NCAA program allegedly receiving federal funding was not affected by Proposition 16 and the NCAA did not exercise controlling authority over its member institutions' ultimate decisions about student-athletes' eligibility to participate in athletics and thus had no real control over a program receiving federal funding, Title VI is inapplicable.

406. However, in *Pryor v. NCAA*,[444] the Third Circuit subsequently held that the plaintiffs' allegation that Proposition 16 constitutes intentional discrimination against incoming student-athletes states a valid Title VI claim:"[t]he NCAA purportedly tried to improve graduation rates among black student athletes by adopting Proposition 16, a facially neutral rule that establishes scholarship and athletic eligibility criteria for incoming student athletes. As a result of these criteria, Plaintiffs allege, Proposition 16 has caused increased numbers of black student athletes to lose eligibility for receiving athletic scholarships and for participating in intercollegiate athletics during their freshmen year. Plaintiffs further alleged that defendant knew of these effects and intended them. And thus, Plaintiffs suggest that the NCAA actually adopted Proposition 16 to 'screen out' more black student athletes from ever receiving athletic scholarships in the first place, with the asserted goal of increased graduation rates serving as a mere 'pretext.' . . .."

II. Coaching and Administrative Opportunities

407. In 2005, the NCAA created the Diversity and Inclusion Department, which "is responsible for leading the Association in the development and implementation of strategies, policies and programmes that promote diversity and inclusion throughout intercollegiate athletics." A program that now falls under the umbrella of the Diversity and Inclusion Department and was launched in 2003 is the NCAA Football Coaches Academy, which seeks to enhance the skills required for advancement in football coaching. It has three components, the first of which is an advanced coaching program that consists of workshops that address skill development in areas including communications, booster/alumni relations, fiscal responsibility, moral and ethical considerations, and interview preparation. Another important component of the program is a mentoring initiative that pairs program participants with experienced head football coaches, athletic directors, and conference commissioners. Through its Diversity and Inclusion Department, the NCAA has developed other program aimed at addressing the shortage of senior-level ethnic minorities in administrative positions at its member institutions.

408. In 2008 the Black Coaches Association (BCA) asked the NCAA to initiate a college version of the NFL's Rooney Rule, which requires that each NFL team hiring a head coach interview at least one candidate of color before filling the position. In addition, the BCA threatened legal action to redress what it characterized as the continued segregation of college football at the head coach position. Although the NCAA has not done so and the BCA has not instituted any litigation, in 2008 the

444. . 288 F.3d 548 (3d Cir. 2002).

Division I-A Athletic Directors Association voluntarily created a Rooney Rule-like "best practice" for all Division I FBS head football coaching searches.[445] These efforts have proven successful. Between 2008 and 2011, the percentage of FBS head football coaches of color increased from 6.7% to 12.6%, by far the most substantial increase among NCAA college football's four divisions.[446] However, a period of stagnation has followed because the percentage of FBS head football coaches of color at the beginning of the 2014–2015 football season was virtually unchanged from 2011.

409. State legislators from around the country, inspired by the Rooney Rule's impact, have expressed interest in requiring their state universities to interview at least one candidate of color when making hires in their athletic departments, and one state, Oregon, has passed legislation to that effect. In July 2009, Oregon passed a law requiring its seven public universities to interview minority candidates before hiring a head coach or athletic director, and in 2015 passed a law requiring that the state's Higher Education Coordinating Commission more closely monitor the universities' compliance with the interview protocols.

410. Although these developments are promising, head football coaching positions continue to be difficult for minorities to obtain.[447] Overall, coaching opportunities for racial minorities in college sports are very limited. For the 2014–2015 season, the racial demographics of combined head coaching positions in all Division I men's sports were as follows: Whites, 87.1%; African Americans, 7.9%; Latinos, 1.8%; Asian Americans, .08%; and Native Americans, 0.3%. Similar numbers are present in all Division I women's sports, where Whites hold approximately 85.7% of head coaching positions, African Americans 7.3%, Latinos 2.0%, and Asians 1.5%. Minority representation in the head coaching ranks is even lower for both men's and women's Division II and III sports. Minorities also are underrepresented in various other intercollegiate athletics administrative positions, including athletic directors, league commissioners, and faculty athletics representatives (FARs). For example, the Institute for Diversity and Ethics in Sport's *2015 Racial and Gender Report Card: College Report* (Richard Lapchick, ed.) (April 7, 2016) notes, that in 2014–2015, whites held 89.1% of FBS FAR and 100% of the FBS conference commissioner positions.

411. When minority college or high school coaches have alleged racial discrimination in hiring and promotion in sports, they have relied on Title VII and section 1981 of the 1964 Civil Rights Act. Title VII prohibits discrimination in employment. Under Title VII, a plaintiff is likely to assert claims premised on disparate

445. . N. Jeremi Duru, *Call in the Feds: Title VI as a Diversifying Force in the Collegiate Head Football Coaching Ranks*, 2 Wake Forest J. L. & Pol'y 143, 151 (2012).

446. . *Ibid.*, at 152. ("The percentage of Football Championship Subdivision (formerly Division I-AA) collegiate head football coaches of color increased by only one percentage point during that time, from 5.9% to 6.9%. And the percentage of head football coaches of color in divisions II and III actually dropped during that time: from 4.5% to 3% and from 3.7% to 2.9%, respectively").

447. *See* generally N. Jeremi Duru, *Call in the Feds: Title VI as a Diversifying Force in the Collegiate Head Football Coaching Ranks*, 2 Wake Forest J.L. & Pol'y 143, 152 (2012) ("The percentage of Football Championship Subdivision (formerly Division I-AA) collegiate head football coaches of color increased by only one percentage point during that time, from 5.9% to 6.9%. And the percentage of head football coaches of color in divisions II and III actually dropped during that time: from 4.5% to 3% and from 3.7% to 2.9%, respectively").

treatment (which focuses on intentional racial discrimination) and/or disparate impact (which focuses on the use of facially neutral employment practices) that unjustifiably discriminate against members of a protected group. Section 1981 prohibits intentional discrimination and is broader in scope in that it applies to the making, performance, and enforcement of all contracts, not just employment contracts. The significant proof required in order to establish a cognizable Title VII or section 1981 claim limits the effectiveness of these federal antidiscrimination laws for those seeking redress for alleged racial discrimination.[448]

412. In general, courts afford employers considerable latitude in establishing neutral employment qualifications, so race discrimination claims are difficult to prove. In *Jackson v. University of New Haven*,[449] James C. Jackson, an African-American with no collegiate coaching experience, brought an action against the University of New Haven that alleged, among other things, racial discrimination in hiring in violation of Title VI and Title VII. Title VI prohibits discrimination on the basis of race, color, or national origin by programs and activities that receive federal financial assistance. Title VII prohibits discrimination by employers on the basis of race, color, religion, sex, or national origin. When the university hired a new head football coach, they posted the position, and "successful collegiate coaching experience" was among the requirements. Of the thirty-six applicants, the university interviewed six people, all of whom had college coaching experience. Jackson was not interviewed, nor was any other African-American applicant.

413. For both his Title VI and Title VII disparate treatment claims, which have the same elements, Jackson needed to first establish a prima facie case by proving: (1) membership in a protected class, (2) qualification for the employment, (3) an adverse employment decision, and (4) circumstances that give rise to an inference of discrimination. The court rejected both claims because he failed to show he was qualified for the university's head football coach position because he did not meet the express condition of having collegiate coaching experience.

414. For his Title VII disparate impact claim, Jackson needed to: (1) identify a policy or practice, (2) demonstrate that a disparity exists, and (3) establish a causal relationship between the two. Statistical evidence often is an important part of establishing a sufficient causal link between the employment criterion and the impact on the protected class. However, exceedingly small sample sizes often result in statistically unreliable evidence, which was the case here because there were only fourteen applicants who identified their race on their application, so Jackson could not establish his prima facie case of disparate impact.

415. On the other hand, some coaches have successfully proven racially motivated employment discrimination. For example, in *McBryde v. Ritenour*,[450] a coach succeeded on a race discrimination claim under the Missouri Human Rights Act by establishing that he did not receive his coaching contract until mid-season, while another employee always received his contract before the season began, and by proving that white coaches

448. . *See* Neil Forester, Comment, *The Elephant in the Locker Room: Does the National Football League Discriminate in the Hiring of Head Coaches?*, 34 McGeorge L. Rev. 877 (2003) (outlining the elements of Title VII and sec. 1981 claims).

449. . 228 F. Supp. 2d 156 (D. Conn. 2002).

450. . 207 S.W.3d 162.

were disciplined with verbal reprimands while he received an immediate suspension for improper conduct. The court found that this proof of disparate treatment, as well as the inconsistencies in the evidence, could have led a reasonable jury to find that the coach established illegal race discrimination.

§3. Professional Athletics

416. Although there have relatively few recent claims of race discrimination made by professional athletes,[451] race has been identified as a factor historically limiting access to coaching and administrative positions and promotion opportunities for African-Americans and other minorities in professional sports. Minorities are beginning to make inroads in coaching and senior-level administrative positions in U.S. professional sports, but progress in the coaching ranks has generally outstripped progress at the senior administrative level. For example, at the end of the 2015–2016 NBA regular season, people of color held 30% of the league's head coaching positions, but only 15.3% of the CEO/President positions.

417. On September 20, 2003, attorneys Johnnie Cochran and Cyrus Mehri released *Black Coaches in the National Football League: Superior Performance, Inferior Opportunities*, a report concluding that African-American football coaches are victims of discrimination with respect to hiring and firing notwithstanding their superior coaching performance. Following the report's release, Cochran and Mehri suggested that the NFL would be sued if it failed to take concrete steps to increase the number of African-Americans who are head coaches of the league's thirty-two clubs. Shortly thereafter, an NFL Committee issued guidelines as a part of its policy to foster greater opportunities for African-Americans to gain head coaching positions. The guidelines, commonly known as the Rooney Rule, include provisions that require at least one person of color be interviewed as a candidate for coaching vacancies and documentation of each interview.

418. For several years following its adoption, the Rooney Rule was quite successful in increasing the numbers of NFL head coaches of color. Over the ten years between 2001 and 2011, the number of minority NFL head coaches increased from two to eight, and while no team in any of the first forty Super Bowls were led by a head coach of color, Super Bowls XLI, XLIII, XLIV, and XLV (played in 2007, 2009, 2010, and 2011, respectively) featured head coaches of color. These diversity gains, however, began tapering considerably in 2012. According to an ESPN study published in July 2016, whereas 21.2 % of head coaches hired between 2007 and 2011 were of color, only 13.9% of those hired between 2012 and 2016 were of color. The numbers

451. . See, e.g., *Moran v. Selig*, 447 F.3d 748, 758 (9th Cir. 2006) (rejecting retired Caucasian and Latino professional baseball players" claims that Major League Baseball violated Title VII by excluding them from medical and supplemental income plans for former Negro League players, because "providing a remedy for past discrimination only to those who have been discriminated against does not constitute discriminatory conduct"). In November 2013, Miami Dolphins offensive lineman Richie Incognito allegedly harassed and racially abused his teammate, Jonathan Martin, calling him, among other things, a "nigger." *See Slurs in Incognito's Message* ESPN.com, Nov. 5, 2013, http://espn.go.com/nfl/story/_/id/9926139/.

for first-time head coaches of color are even worse. Whereas 26.9% of first time head coaches hired between 2007 and 2011 were of color, only 4.5% of those hired between 2012 and 2016 were of color. Moreover, the study painted a bleak picture of the future, finding that as of 2016 very few of the league's assistant coaches of color held positions that tended to eventually lead to head coaching positions: offensive coordinator, quarterbacks coach, and offensive line coach.[452] Although the Rooney Rule has helped the NFL diversify its leadership positions, this increased diversity has highlighted the stagnation with respect to diversity in other professional sports leagues. For instance, the Atlanta Braves' May 2016 firing of Fredi Gonzalez left MLB—a league in which nearly 30% of the players are Latino—with no Latino managers and only two managers of color. Overall, in U.S. professional sports leagues, people of color continue to be underrepresented in administrative positions (e.g., general managers, coaches, team vice presidents) and club ownership.[453]

452. Mike Sando, *Rooney Rule in reverse: Minority coaching hires have stalled*, ESPN.com, Jul. 19, 2016, http://espn.go.com/nfl/story/_/id/17101097/staggering-num-bers-show-nfl-minority-coaching-failure-rooney-rule-tony-dungy.

453. *See* generally the racial report cards for each major professional sport league generated annually by the Institute for Diversity and Ethics in Sport at the University of Central Florida.

Chapter 6. Legal Protection against Gender Discrimination

§1. Historical Perspective

419. In the U.S., males historically have enjoyed many more athletic participation opportunities than females at all levels of sports competition. Some progress towards gender equality in athletics has occurred, but it has been a slow, incremental process that began in the early 1970s in response to a federal law mandating gender equity in education that continues today. The 1972 enactment of Title IX gender equity legislation[454] by Congress provided significant momentum for increased participation for women in organized athletics at the interscholastic and intercollegiate levels. Although it is not sports-specific legislation, Title IX required the promulgation of federal regulations to achieve gender equity athletics. These regulations became effective on July 21, 1975 and are enforced by the federal Department of Education's Office of Civil Rights (OCR).[455] By 1978, the number of female high school student-athletes increased from 300,000 to more than 2,000,000. Women's participation in intercollegiate athletics doubled from 32,000 participants in 1971 to more than 64,000 participants in 1977.

420. In the 1980s, women began successfully challenging gender discrimination in intercollegiate athletics on a program-wide basis on federal and state equal protection grounds.[456] Although Title IX was enacted in 1972, its application to intercollegiate and interscholastic athletics was not clearly established until 1987. The Civil Rights Restoration Act of 1987, a federal statute, reversed the Supreme Court's 1984 *Grove City College* ruling that Title IX applies only if a specific educational program receives federal funds. As a result, college and university as well as high school athletic programs now are covered by Title IX if any part of the educational institution directly or indirectly receives federal funds.[457] Because almost all educational institutions receive some federal funding, virtually all high school and college athletics programs are covered by Title IX. Olympic sports organizations and professional sports leagues, clubs, and organizations generally do not receive any federal funding, so they are not subject to the gender equity requirements of Title IX.

421. In a 1992 case, *Franklin v. Gwinnett County Public Schools*,[458] the Supreme Court ruled that prevailing plaintiffs can recover monetary damages and attorney fees for intentional violations of Title IX. The *Franklin* decision, coupled with increased

454. . 20 U.S.C. §1681.

455. . 34 C.F.R §106.41(a)-(c).

456. . *See* , e.g., *Haffer v. Temple Univ.*, 678 F. Supp. 517 (E.D. Pa. 1987); *Blair v. Wash. State Univ.*, 108 Wash.2d 558, 740 P.2d 1379 (1987).

457. . For cases considering whether an athletics governing body is subject to Title IX, *see NCAA v. Smith*, 525 U.S. 459 (1999); *Horner v. Kentucky High School Athletic Ass"n*, 43 F.3d 265 (6th Cir. 1994); *Alston v. Va. High Sch. League, Inc.*, 144 F. Supp. 2d 526 (W.D. Va. 1999).

458. . 503 U.S. 60 (1992).

enforcement activity on the part of OCR, contributed to a significant rise in the number of Title IX cases in the athletics context over the past twenty years.[459]

422. Title IX currently is the law most frequently utilized to remedy gender discrimination in interscholastic and intercollegiate athletics.[460] Thus far, Title IX litigation involving interscholastic sports has occurred with less regularity than litigation in the intercollegiate athletics context, but it is anticipated that this federal law will be invoked by private parties at all levels of athletic participation with greater regularity in the future. To date, most college cases have involved claims that women are not being provided with equal athletic participation opportunities in comparison to men. At the high school level, most litigation thus far has involved claims that female athletes are not provided equivalent treatment and benefits such as playing fields, equipment, and game scheduling vis-à-vis male athletes.

423. Private litigation and government enforcement activity under Title IX has resulted in increased athletic participation opportunities for women and more equitable treatment since this law's enactment in 1972, but the goal of gender equity in athletics has not been fully achieved yet. Women continue to be underrepresented in intercollegiate and interscholastic athletics participation opportunities, and they still do not have access to equivalent athletic facilities, equipment, and other resources. For the 2015–2016 school year, 3,324,326 girls participated in interscholastic athletics; by comparison, 4,544,574 boys participated in interscholastic athletics. During the 2015–2016 academic year, 275,075 men (56.5% of total participants) participated in NCAA intercollegiate athletics; whereas, 211,784 women (43.5% of total participants) did so.

424. Today, U.S educational institutions face legal, political, and social pressure to increase sports participation opportunities for female athletes and to enhance overall gender equity in athletics. As more women have been given the opportunity to participate in athletics, the demand for new revenue resources to cover the cost of expanding opportunities has increased dramatically. This pressure to achieve gender equity in athletics has been affected by reduced government funding for education. With declines in state tax revenues, many public institutions of higher educational have faced significant cuts in their overall budgets with corresponding cuts in their athletics programs, placing increasing pressure on those programs to generate more revenues to cover existing expenses and the costs of expanding opportunities for female athletes. High schools and colleges continue to struggle with difficult practical and legal issues in their efforts to comply with Title IX's mandate of gender equity in interscholastic and intercollegiate athletics.

459. . *See* generally Paul M. Anderson & Barbara Osborne, *A Historical Review of Title IX Litigation*, 18 J. Leg. Aspects Sport 127 (2008).

460. . Federal constitutional law (if the requisite "state action" exists) and state constitutional law also may provide a basis for remedying gender inequities in interscholastic or intercollegiate athletics. *See* e.g., *Williams v. School District of Bethlem, PA*, 998 F.2d 168 (3d Cir. 1993); *Haffer v. Temple University of the Commonwealth System of Higher Education*, 678 F. Supp. 517 (E.D. Pa. 1987); *Blair v. Washington St. University*, 108 Wash.2d 558, 740 P.2d 1379 (1987). *See also Richards v. United States Tennis Ass'n*, 400 N.Y.S.2d 267 (N.Y. Sup. Ct. 1977) (use of Barr body test as sole criterion of gender, which excludes transsexual from qualifying to participate in the United States Open Tennis Tournament, violates New York's Human Rights Law).

425. Title IX is also increasingly being relied upon in litigation against educational institutions for failure to report and punish acts of sexual violence on campus, usually committed by male student-athletes against female students. In *Williams v. Board of Regents of the University System of Georgia*,[461] a female student was allegedly gang raped by three male student-athletes in an on-campus dormitory. The plaintiff argued that the university was liable under Title IX because the coach, athletics director, and university president were all aware that one of the student-athletes who attacked the plaintiff had a history of sexual assault before he was recruited and admitted to the university. The Eleventh Circuit held that given the past history of the recruited student-athlete, the institution had "before the fact notice" and should have made efforts to prevent future harassment from occurring.

426. The issue of how gender is determined for purposes of athletic eligibility to participate in unisex sports at all levels of competition is also fast becoming a significant issue in the twenty-first century and requires exploration of the corresponding medical, legal, and policy issues. The issue of "verification" of gender—what methods are used to define a woman for the purpose of participation in women's sports—is increasingly controversial. On November 30, 2010, the Ladies Professional Golfers Association changed its "female at birth" requirement to allow transgender membership in response to a federal lawsuit filed by a transgendered woman in a California case.[462] In April 2017, USA Volleyball approved the participation of Tia Thompson, a male-born transgender athlete, as a female volleyball player. USA Volleyball issued the following statement regarding its decision: "USA Volleyball supports the inclusion of transgender athletes in USA Volleyball events in the gender in which they self-identify, yet also prioritizes a fair and competitive landscape. As such, subject to applicable laws and regulations, all athletes over the age of 12 wishing to participate in the gender that differs from their birth gender are required to provide medical documentation to the USAV Gender Committee demonstrating that their testosterone levels do not exceed the upper limit of the normal reference range in their desired gender of play for their age group. The USA Volleyball transgender guidelines do not apply to athletes desiring to represent the United States in the Olympic Games, Paralympic Games and all other international competitions which are under the control of the relevant governing body." In March 2017, Mack Beggs, a transgender boy, won a Texas state high wrestling championship. Because of the state high school athletic association's rules requires all student-athletes to participate on sports teams that match the sex identified on their birth certificate, Beggs was not allowed to wrestle on the boy's team despite his desire to do so.

§2. Equal Athletic Participation Opportunities Under Title IX

427. Title IX states that its general prohibition against gender discrimination shall not "be interpreted to require any educational institution to grant preferential or disparate treatment to the members of one sex on account of an imbalance which may exist" between the total number or percentage of persons of that sex participating in

461. 477 F.3d 1282 (11th Cir. 2007).

462. *Lawless v. LPGA et al.*, Case No. 4:10CV04599 (N.D. Cal. 2010).

any federally supported program or activity, and "the total number or percentage of persons of that sex in any community, State, section, or other area."[463] However, this statute "shall not be construed to prevent the consideration in any … proceeding under this chapter of statistical evidence tending to show that such an imbalance exists with respect to the participation in, or receipt of the benefits of, any such program or activity by the members of one sex."[464]

428. The OCR's Title IX regulations state that a covered educational institution that "operates or sponsors interscholastic, intercollegiate, club or intramural athletics shall provide equal athletic opportunity for members of both sexes."[465] In determining whether equal opportunities exist, the OCR considers the following factors:

(1) whether the selection of sports and levels of competition effectively accommodate the interests and abilities of members of both sexes;
(2) the provision of equipment and supplies;
(3) scheduling of games and practice time;
(4) travel and per diem allowance;
(5) opportunity to receive coaching and academic tutoring;
(6) assignment and compensation of coaches and tutors;
(7) provision of locker rooms, practice, and competitive facilities;
(8) provision of medical and training facilities and services;
(9) provision of housing and dining facilities and services;
(10) publicity.[466]

429. Because the OCR's regulations pertaining to gender equity in athletics have been judicially found to be a reasonable interpretation of Title IX, courts generally afford them considerable weight. In addition, courts provide substantial deference to the OCR's Policy Interpretations that reasonably interpret these regulations.

430. Regarding Title IX's application to athletics participation opportunities, in *Cohen v. Brown University*,[467] the First Circuit explained:

> Title IX does not mandate strict numerical equality between the gender balance of [an educational institution's] athletic program and the gender balance of its student body. [W]hile evidence of a gender-based disparity in an institution's athletics program is relevant to a determination of noncompliance, a court assessing Title IX compliance may not find a violation solely because there is a disparity between the gender composition of an educational institution's student constituency, on the one hand, and its athletic programs, on the other hand.

431. In order to evaluate whether equal athletics participation opportunities exist for both genders in high school and college sports, courts have adopted a 1978 OCR Policy Interpretation of Title IX that establishes a three-prong test, which has

463. . 20 U.S.C. §1681(b).
464. . *Ibid.*
465. . 34 C.F.R. §106.41(c).
466. . *Ibid.*
467. . *Cohen v. Brown University*, 101 F.3d 155 (1st Cir. 1996), *cert. denied*, 520 U.S. 1186 (1997).

been uniformly adopted by federal courts: (1) substantial proportionality; (2) a history and continuing practice of program expansion; and (3) full and effective accommodation of the underrepresented gender's athletic interest.[468] A school can prove compliance with Title IX by independently fulfilling the requirements of any one prong of this test. In a July 11, 2003 public letter, the OCR reaffirmed that "[e]ach of the three prongs is thus a valid, alternative way for schools to comply with Title IX."

432. The first prong, substantial proportionality, requires that the proportionate participation in athletics at the relevant level of competition (intercollegiate, club, or intramural sports) by each gender be very close to the corresponding proportion of undergraduate enrolment for each gender at that educational institution. For example, if a university's undergraduate student enrolment is 52% male and 48% female, then approximately 52% of the participants in its athletics program at each level of competition should be male and 48% female. Exact proportionality is not required, but whether a disparity is substantially proportionate is determined on a case-by-case basis. In determining compliance with this prong, the total number of athletic participants for each gender is the controlling factor, not simply the number of athletic teams for each gender. This prong is often very difficult to satisfy, particularly in the current era of rising female university undergraduate enrollment and if an institution has a football program (which typically has a significant number of male participants). Courts have ruled that this prong "entails a fairly close relationship between athletic participation and undergraduate enrolment," which is not satisfied as a matter of law by a 10.5% disparity between undergraduate enrolment and athletic participation for women.[469] One court ruled that a 1% gender disparity between an institution's undergraduate enrolment and intercollegiate athletic participation opportunities complies with the substantial proportionality test.[470] Another court held that whether a 6% disparity between female undergraduate enrolment and intercollegiate athletic participation opportunities satisfies this test is a fact question to be resolved at trial.[471]

433. An important developing issue is what constitutes a "sport" for purposes of determining the athletic participation opportunities provided by an educational institution. According to the National Federation of State High School Associations, more than 128,000 female and male students participated in competitive cheer in 2015–2016. A majority of state high school athletic associations recognize it as a sport. However, in 2012, in *Biediger v. Quinnipiac University*,[472] the Second Circuit held that competitive cheer is not an intercollegiate sport because, among other reasons, no uniform set of rules applied to intercollegiate cheerleading and Quinnipiac University's team competed against "a motley assortment" of teams rather than only varsity intercollegiate competitive cheer teams. The court noted there is a presumption that a

468. . *See* , e.g., *Cohen v. Brown University, supra* ; *Pederson v. La. State Univ.*, 213 F.3d 858 (5th Cir. 2000); *Horner v. Ky. High Sch. Athletic Ass'n*, 43 F.3d 265 (6th Cir. 1994); *Roberts v. Colo. State Bd. of Agric.*, 998 F.2d 884 (10th Cir.), *cert. denied*, 510 U.S. 1004 (1993); *Oliver v. Sweetwater Union High School District*, 604 F.Supp.2d 1264 (S.D. Cal. 2009).

469. . *Roberts v. Colo. State Bd. of Agric.*, 998 F.2d 824, 830 (10th Cir. 1993), *cert. denied*, 510 U.S. 1004 (1993).

470. . *Miller v. University of Cincinnati*, 2008 WL 203025 (S.D. Ohio 2008).

471. . *Brust v. Univ. of Calif.*, 2007 WL 4365521 (E.D. Cal.).

472. . 691 F.3d 85 (2d Cir. 2012).

sport qualifies for Title IX purposes if it is recognized by the NCAA, which it was not at the time, In an August 16, 2011 news release, the NCAA Committee on Women's Athletics stated it "will watch for continued growth and development in a new sport that combines elements of gymnastics and competitive cheerleading after two different groups requested emerging-sport status for slightly different versions."[473] The NCAA currently recognizes equestrian, rugby, and sand volleyball as emerging sports, but not competitive cheer.

434. To determine compliance with the second prong, an examination of the entire history of an educational institution's women's athletics program must be made in evaluating whether it has a history and continuing practice of program expansion responsive to the developing interests and abilities of the underrepresented gender. In *Boucher v. Syracuse University*,[474] a federal district court cited a January 16, 1996 OCR letter entitled "Clarification of Intercollegiate Athletics Policy Guidance: The Three Part Test" and stated that the following three factors should be considered:

(1) the institution's record of adding intercollegiate teams, or upgrading teams to intercollegiate status, for the underrepresented sex;
(2) an institution's record of increasing the number of participants in intercollegiate athletics who are members of the underrepresented sex; and
(3) an institution's affirmative response to requests by students or others for addition or elevation of sports.

435. Applying these factors, the *Boucher* court found that Syracuse University had a sufficient history of expanding athletic participation opportunities for its female students because it added women's teams from 1971–1982 and increasing the number of female participants in varsity sports by 47% between 1982 and 1995. It concluded that Syracuse demonstrated a continuing practice of program expansion by monitoring and gathering information regarding female students' developing athletics participation interests and abilities. Thus, Syracuse satisfied the second prong of OCR three part test.

436. The prong two requirement of demonstrating a history and continuing practice of athletics program expansion cannot be satisfied by cutting sports participation opportunities for the disfavored gender. As one court explained:

> We recognize that in times of economic hardship, few schools will be able to satisfy Title IX's effective accommodation requirement by continuing to expand their women's athletics programs. Nonetheless, the ordinary meaning of the word "expansion" may not be twisted to find compliance under this prong when schools have increased the relative percentages of women participating in athletics by making cuts in both men's and women's sports programs. Financially strapped institutions may still comply with Title IX by cutting athletic programs such that

473. . Michelle Brutlag Hosick, *NCAA Committee Looks Into New Sport*, NCAA.com, Aug. 16, 2011, http://www.ncaa.com/news/ncaa/2011-08-16/ncaa-committee-looks-new-sport.

474. . 1998 WL 167296 (N.D.N.Y. 1998), *vacated in part and appeal dismissed in part*, 164 F.3d 113 (2d. Cir. 1999).

> men's and women's athletic participation rates become substantially proportionate to their representation in the undergraduate population.[475]

437. Given the difficulties of proving prongs one or two of the three part test, universities are increasingly attempting to prove compliance by establishing their existing sports program fully and effectively accommodate the athletic participation interests of the underrepresented gender (almost always women athletes), which satisfies the third prong. Compliance with this prong also is difficult and requires proof that the total range and competition level of sports participation opportunities are fully consistent with and satisfy the underrepresented gender's athletics interests and abilities (i.e., all desired sports are being offered by the university). Under this prong, educational institutions have an affirmative obligation to gather information regarding current and prospective students' athletic participation interests and may be required to add new sports or upgrade existing ones to higher levels of competition (i.e., from intramural or club sports to intercollegiate sports) in response to the underrepresented gender's developing interests.

438. Courts uniformly have rejected the argument that females generally are less interested in sports participation and lesser athletes relative to males, and therefore that Title IX only requires educational institutions to provide athletic participation opportunities for women relative to their interests and abilities vis-à-vis males.[476] In *Neal v. Board of Trustees of the California State University*,[477] the Ninth Circuit explained:

> [this] interpretation of Title IX would have allowed universities to do little or nothing to equalize men's and women's opportunities if they could point to data showing that women were less interested in sports. But a central aspect of Title IX's purpose was to encourage women to participate in sports: The increased number of roster spots and scholarships reserved for women would gradually increase demand among women for those roster spots and scholarships. … Title IX is a dynamic statute, not a static one. It envisions continuing progress toward the goal of equal opportunity for all athletes and recognizes that, where society has conditioned women to expect less than their fair share of the athletic opportunities, women's interest in participating in sports will not rise to a par with men's overnight.

439. Courts generally are very deferential to a school's chosen means of remedying a Title IX violation. In *Cohen v. Brown University*,[478] the First Circuit ruled:

---

475. . *Roberts v. Colo. State Bd. of Agric.*, 998 F.2d 824, 830 (10th Cir. 1993), *cert. denied,* 510 U.S. 1004 (1993). *See also Mansourian v. Regents of Univ. of California*, 816 F.Supp.2d 869 (E.D. Cal. 2011) (prong two not satisfied if the number of women given the opportunity to participate in a university's intercollegiate athletics program declines significantly).
476. . *See* , e.g., *Cohen v. Brown University*, 101 F.3d 155 (1st Cir. 1996), *cert. denied*, 520 U.S. 1186 (1997).
477. . 198 F.3d 763 (9th Cir. 1999).
478. . 101 F.3d 155 (1st Cir. 1996), *cert. denied*, 520 U.S. 1186 (1997).

> Brown [University] may achieve compliance with Title IX in a number of ways: It may eliminate its athletic program altogether, it may elevate or create the requisite number of women's positions, it may demote or eliminate the requisite number of men's positions, or it may implement a combination of these remedies. I leave it entirely to Brown's discretion to decide how it will balance its program to provide equal opportunities for its men and women athletes. I recognize the financial constraints Brown faces; however, its own priorities will necessarily determine the path to compliance it elects to take.

440. Although cutting programs for the overrepresented gender is disfavored, this is a permissible option for complying with Title IX. Courts have uniformly held that cutting men's sports in an effort to achieve substantial proportionality in athletic participation opportunities does not violate Title IX or male athletes' equal protection rights under the U.S. Constitution.[479] As the *Neal* court observed:

> An extensive survey of Title IX's legislative history and the regulations promulgated to apply its provisions to college athletics concluded that boosters of male sports argued vociferously before Congress that the proposed regulations would require schools to shift resources from men's programs to women's programs, but that Congress nevertheless sided with women's advocates by deciding not to repeal the HEW's athletics-related Title IX regulations. Mary Jo Festle, Playing Nice: Politics and Apologies in Women's Sports 171-76 (1996). Congress thus appears to have believed that Title IX would result in funding reductions to male athletic programs. If a university wishes to comply with Title IX by leveling down programs instead of ratcheting them up, as Appellant has done here, Title IX is not offended.

§3. Equal Benefits and Treatment Under Title IX

441. A student-athlete only has standing to assert claims to remedy specific harm that arises out of his or her current past or future participation in the school's athletic program.[480] Without any individualized harm, he or she does not have standing to broadly challenge inequitable treatment or the discriminatory provision of benefits on the basis of gender in connection with a school's entire athletics program.[481]

442. As is done in evaluating whether proportionately equal athletic participation opportunities are provided to both genders, determining whether an educational institution is in compliance with Title IX requires a comparison of boys' and girls' sports on program-wide basis. Identical athletics benefits and treatment are not required;

479. . *See* , e.g., *Miami Univ. Wrestling Club v. Miami Univ.*, 302 F.3d 608 (6th Cir. 2002); *Chalenor v. Univ. of N. D.*, 291 F.3d 1042 (8th Cir. 2002); *Neal v. Board of Trustees of the California State University*, 198 F.3d 763 (9th Cir. 1999); *Boulahanis v. Bd. of Regents*, 198 F.3d 633 (7th Cir. 1999); *Kelly v. Bd. of Trustees*, 35 F.3d 265 (7th Cir. 1994).

480. . *See* , e.g., *Boucher v. Syracuse University*, 164 F.3d 113 (2d Cir. 1999); *Cook v. Colgate Univ.*, 992 F.2d 17 (2d Cir. 1993).

481. . *Pederson v. La. State Univ.*, 213 F.3d 858, 871–872 (5th Cir. 2000).

a school will be in compliance if its athletic program-wide benefits and treatment of both genders are equivalent (i.e., the overall effect of any differences is insignificant). As one court observed:

> Schools thus have considerable flexibility in complying with Title IX. For example, a school that provides better equipment to the men's basketball team than to the women's basketball team would be in compliance with Title IX if it provided comparably better equipment to the women's soccer team than to the men's soccer team.[482]

443. An educational institution's provision of proportionately unequal funding for its men's and women's athletics programs violates Title IX.[483] However, simply providing the same funding mechanism for both programs does not alone ensure compliance with Title IX's requirement that schools provide equal athletic participation opportunities for both genders. In *Daniels v. School Board of Brevard County, Florida,*[484] the court rejected a high school's assertion that inequities between its boys and girls athletics program could be justified because each engages in separate booster fund-raising activities and it "cannot be held responsible if the fund-raising activities of one booster club are more successful than those of another." In response, the court ruled it is the school's "responsibility to ensure equal athletic opportunities, in accordance with Title IX," and that it is responsible for the consequences of the funding system it established.

444. A disparity in one athletic program component can alone violate Title IX if it is substantial enough in and of itself to deny equality of athletic participation opportunity to student-athletes of one gender. Disparate treatment of male and female teams for the same sport may violate this law. For example, courts have ruled that the cumulative effects of inequalities in the playing facilities for boy's baseball and girls' softball (e.g., scoreboard, signage, field maintenance, and lighting) violate Title IX.[485] Courts also have held that a high school district's decision to schedule girls' soccer in the spring and boys' soccer in the fall, which deprives girls but not boys of the opportunity to compete for a state championship in soccer, violates Title IX without any offsetting comparable advantage to female athletes or disadvantage to male athletes.[486] Similarly, always scheduling boys' basketball games on Friday and Saturday nights, while scheduling girls' basketball games only on Monday-Thursday evenings may violate Title IX because "[n]on-primetime games result in a loss of audience, conflict with homework, and foster feelings of inferiority."[487]

---

482. . *McCormick v. School District of Mamaroneck*, 370 F.3d 275 (2d Cir. 2004).
483. . *See* , e.g., *Barrett v. West Chester Univ. of Pa.*, 2003 WL 22803477 (E.D. Pa. 2003) (spending less money on recruiting for women's teams and coaches' salaries than for men's teams violates Title IX).
484. . 985 F. Supp. 1458 (M.D. Fla. 1997).
485. . *Ollier v. Sweetwater High School District*, 858 F. Supp.2d 1093 (S.D. Cal. 2012); *Landow v. Sch. Bd. of Brevard County*, 132 F. Supp. 2d 958 (M.D. Fla. 2000); *Daniels v. School Board of Brevard County, Florida (Daniels I)*, 985 F. Supp. 1458 (M.D. Fla. 1997).
486. . *McCormick v. School District of Mamaroneck*, 370 F.3d 275 (2d Cir. 2004).
487. *Parker v. Franklin County Community School*, 667 F.3d 910 (7th Cir. 2012).

445. Consistent with the judicial view regarding equal athletic participation opportunities, courts accord significant deference to an educational institution's chosen means of remedying inequitable treatment and benefits based on gender. Rather than requiring a school to incur the costs of providing comparable benefits to the advantaged gender, a court will permit the school to proportionately disadvantage the favored gender to achieve gender equity. For example, to remedy a scheduling inequity depriving girls of the opportunity to compete for a state championship, the court gave the school the option to deprive each gender of the opportunity to compete for a championship in the sport in alternate years.[488]

446. Some courts have held that an educational institution's discrimination against student-athletes based on their sexual orientation or by gender stereotyping violates Title IX. In *Videckis v. Pepperdine University*,[489] a federal district court concluded:

> [S]exual orientation discrimination is a form of sex or gender discrimination, and that the actual orientation of the victim is irrelevant. It is impossible to categorically separate sexual orientation discrimination from discrimination on the basis of sex or from gender stereotypes; to do so would result in a false choice. Simply put, to allege discrimination on the basis of sexuality is to state a Title IX claim on the basis of sex or gender. . . .
>
> Coaches, trainers, and support staff repeatedly queried Plaintiffs about their sexual orientation, their private sexual behavior, and their dating lives. Plaintiffs allege that they were told lesbianism would not be tolerated on the women's basketball team. Plaintiffs further allege that they were not cleared to play basketball because of Pepperdine's discriminatory views against lesbianism. If the women's basketball staff in this case had a negative view of lesbians based on lesbians' perceived failure to conform to the staff's views of acceptable female behavior, actions taken on the basis of these negative biases would constitute gender stereotype discrimination. Consequently, Plaintiffs have stated a claim for discrimination because they allege that Pepperdine treated them differently due to their perceived lack of conformity with gender stereotypes, and further that Pepperdine discriminated against them based on stereotypes about lesbianism.

§4. Intentional Discrimination

447. Proof of intentional discrimination enables a plaintiff to recover compensatory damages for an educational institution's violation of Title IX, but not any punitive

488. . *McCormick v. School District of Mamaroneck*, 370 F.3d 275 (2d Cir. 2004).
489. 150 F.Supp.3d 1151 (C.D. Cal. 2015).

damages.[490] In *Pederson v. Louisiana State University*,[491] the Fifth Circuit held that the university had intentionally engaged in gender discrimination in the operation of its intercollegiate athletics program by refusing to provide equal athletic participation opportunities for women in violation of Title IX. It ruled that:

> alleged ignorance of the law does not preclude our finding that LSU acted intentionally. [LSU] need not have intended to violate Title IX, but need only have intended to treat women differently. … [Its] outdated attitudes about women amply demonstrate this intention to discriminate, and the district court squarely found that LSU's treatment of women athletes was remarkably outdated, archaic, and outmoded. Well-established Supreme Court precedent demonstrates that archaic assumptions such as those firmly held by LSU constitute intentional gender discrimination. We conclude that, because classifications based on archaic assumptions are facially discriminatory, actions resulting from an application of these attitudes constitute intentional discrimination.

448. In *Simpson v. University of Colorado Boulder*,[492] two women claimed that they were sexually assaulted by University of Colorado football players and recruits and brought an action against the university seeking damages under Title IX. The Tenth Circuit articulated the test for institutional liability:

> [Whether] a funding recipient can be said to have "intentionally acted in clear violation of Title IX, Davis, 526 U.S. at 642, 119 S. Ct. 1161, when the violation is caused by official policy, which may be a policy of deliberate indifference to providing adequate training or guidance that is obviously necessary for implementation of a specific program or policy of the recipient. Implementation of an official policy can certainly be a circumstance in which the recipient exercises significant "control over the harasser and the environment in which the harassment occurs.

449. After examining the facts, the Tenth Circuit concluded:

> [T]he evidence before the district court would support findings that by the time of the assaults on Plaintiffs, (1) Coach Barnett [the head coach], whose rank in the CU hierarchy was comparable to that of a police chief in a municipal government, had general knowledge of the serious risk of sexual harassment and assault during college-football recruiting efforts; (2) Barnett knew that such assaults had indeed occurred during CU recruiting efforts; (3) Barnett nevertheless maintained an unsupervised player-host program to show high-school recruits "a good time"; and (4) Barnett knew, both because of incidents reported to him and because of his own unsupportive attitude, that there had been no change in

490. . *Mercer v. Duke Univ.*, 50 Fed. Appx. 643 (4th Cir. 2002).
491. . 213 F.3d 858 (5th Cir. 2000). *See also Barrett v. West Chester University. of Pennsylvania*, 2003 WL 22803477 (E.D. Pa.) ("i]n the athletic realm of Title IX, intent is found on the face of most decisions").
492. 500 F.3d 1170 (10th Cir. 2007).

> the atmosphere since 1997 (when the prior assault occurred) that would make such misconduct less likely in 2001. A jury could infer that the need for more or different training [of player-hosts] so obvious, and the inadequacy so likely to result in [Title IX violations], that [Coach Barnett could] reasonably be said to have been deliberately indifferent to the need.

§5. Separate Sex Teams

450. Both the Equal Protection Clause of the U.S. Constitution, which applies only to public educational institutions, and Title IX's regulations permit "separate but equal" athletic teams in the same sport for both sexes. In *Hoover v. Meiklejohn*,[493] the court explained:

> Given the lack of athletic opportunity for females in past years, the encouragement of female involvement in sports is a legitimate objective and separation of teams promote that purpose. ... Separate soccer teams for males and females would meet the constitutional requirement of equal opportunity if the teams were given substantially equal support and if they had substantially comparable programs. There may be differences depending upon the effects of such neutral factors as the level of student interest and geographic locations. Accordingly, the standard should be one of comparability, not absolute equality.

451. Title IX's regulations generally prohibit exclusion from participation in any interscholastic, intercollegiate, club, or intramural sports or different treatment on the basis of gender.[494] However, they do not require that members of the opposite sex be permitted to try out for single sex contact sports:

> (b) Separate teams. Notwithstanding the requirements of paragraph (a) of this section, a recipient may operate or sponsor separate teams for members of each sex where selection for such teams is based upon competitive skill or the activity involved is a contact sport. However, where a recipient operates or sponsors a team in a particular sport for members of one sex but operates or sponsors no such team for members of the other sex, and athletic opportunities for members of that sex have previously been limited, members of the excluded sex must be allowed to try-out for the team offered unless the sport involved is a contact sport. For the purposes of this part, contact sports include boxing, wrestling, rugby, ice hockey, football, basketball and other sports the purpose or major activity of which involves bodily contact.[495]

452. For example, in *Barnett v. Tex. Wrestling Ass'n*,[496] the court held that Title IX was not violated when girls were denied permission to participate against boys at

493. . 430 F. Supp. 164, 170 (D. Colo. 1977).
494. . 34 C.F.R. §106.41(a).
495. . 34 C.F.R. §106.41(b).
496. . 16 F. Supp. 2d 690 (N.D. Tex. 1998).

a wrestling tournament. However, in *Yellow Springs Exempted Village School Dist. Bd. of Educ. v. Ohio High Sch. Athletic Ass'n,*[497] the Sixth Circuit held that a state high school athletics governing body's rule prohibiting mixed sex teams in contact sports violates Title IX by inhibiting its member schools' ability to provide equal athletic opportunity for girls.

453. On the other hand, Title IX does not prohibit mixed sex athletic competition in contact sports. Some states permit mixed sex teams or athletic competition in contact sports. If an educational institution permits a member of the opposite sex to try out for or participate in a single sex sport or athletic competition, it must comply with Title IX's gender equity and non-discrimination regulations. In *Mercer v. Duke University,*[498] the Fourth Circuit ruled that a female student-athlete's allegation that Duke University permitted her to try out for the football team as a kicker, made her a member of the team, and then discriminated against and excluded her from participation based on her gender stated a valid claim under Title IX.

454. In addition to Title IX claims, public high schools, colleges, and universities that engage in gender discrimination in their athletic program are subject to denial of equal protection claims under the U.S. Constitution.[499] Gender discrimination is examined under an intermediate level of judicial scrutiny, which requires that different treatment based on gender must serve important governmental objectives and that the discriminatory means are substantially related to achievement of those objectives.[500] In *Force v. Pierce City R-VI School District,*[501] the court enjoined a public school from refusing to allow a female student to compete for a place on its eighth-grade football team on the same basis as males. The court held the school's categorical exclusion of all girls regardless of their size and physically ability is not substantially related to its important governmental objective of protecting student-athletes' health and safety.

§6. Gender-Based Employment Discrimination in Athletics

455. Gender discrimination affects not only student-athletes; it can also adversely affect coaches and violate Title IX and employment discrimination laws. In the mid-1990s, two cases were decided that marked important victories for plaintiffs alleging gender-based employment discrimination in intercollegiate athletics. In *Tyler v. Howard Univ.,*[502] a women's basketball coach claimed that the disparity between her salary and that of the men's basketball coach and the difference in their office facilities violated Title IX, the Equal Pay Act, and state law. The Howard men's basketball coach was paid USD 34,500 more annually than Plaintiff and had a spacious office, while Plaintiff's office was in a storage room. The jury awarded plaintiff USD 2.34 million in damages, although the judge eventually reduced the award to USD 250,000. This case marked the first time a plaintiff had received a jury award based on such allegations. Similarly,

497. . 647 F.2d 651 (6th Cir. 1981).
498. . 190 F.3d 643 (4th Cir. 1999).
499. . *Fitzgerald v. Barnstable School Committee,* 555 U.S. 246 (2009).
500. . *United States v. Virginia*, 518 U.S. 515 (1996).
501. . 570 F. Supp. 1020 (W.D. Mo. 1983).
502. . *See* No. 91-CA11239 (D.C. 28 Jun. 1993).

in *Pitts v. Oklahoma State University*,[503] another jury awarded damages of USD 36,000 to a women's college golf coach because her salary was USD 28,000 a year less than the men's golf coach. She alleged that this disparity violated Title IX and other laws. However, in *Deli v. University of Minnesota*,[504] a federal district court rejected the alleged violation of Title IX claim by the plaintiff, a female who was the former head coach of the university's women's gymnastics team whose employment was terminated, because "[she] does not claim or provide any evidence to suggest that due to her receipt of a lower salary than that received by coaches of some men's athletic teams, Plaintiff's coaching services were inferior in 'quality, nature or availability' to those provided by men's teams, she has failed to make out a prima facie claim for violation of Title IX."

456. A coach expressing concern about gender inequity in athletics may bring a Title IX claim to recover damages for retaliation by an educational institution.[505] In *Lowrey v. Texas A&M University System*,[506] the women's basketball coach at Tarleton State University claimed she was terminated as Women's Athletics Coordinator for her role in the filing of a complaint with the OCR alleging Title IX violations in the university's women's athletics program. The Fifth Circuit ruled that her retaliation claim was actionable under Title IX because there was evidence her loss of an administrative position was based on her advocacy of the need to correct gender inequities in the university's athletics program.

503. . *See* No. CIV-93–1341-A (W.D. Okla. 1994).
504. 863 F. Supp. 958 (D. Minn. 1994).
505. . *Jackson v. Birmingham Board of Education*, 544 U.S. 167 (2005).
506. . 11 F. Supp. 2d 895 (S.D. Tex. 1998).

Chapter 7. Legal Protection Against Disability Discrimination

457. The U.S. Supreme Court has ruled that persons with a physical disability are not a suspect or quasi-suspect class justifying a heightened scrutiny of alleged discrimination in violation of the equal protection clause of the U.S. Constitution.[507] Because a professional league is not a state actor whose rules and conduct is subject to federal constitutional scrutiny, courts have rejected claims by physically impaired professional athletes (e.g., an athlete with blindness in one eye) that their exclusion from athletics violates the federal constitution.[508] In *Grube v. Bethlehem Area School District*,[509] the court expressed doubt that a public high school's exclusion of a student with one kidney from contact sports denies equal protection of the law. Such exclusion is constitutionally justifiable if the school's reliance on its team physician's medical recommendation that an athlete not play rationally furthers its permissible objective of ensuring students' health and safety.[510]

458. In *Neeld v. American Hockey League*,[511] the court enjoined enforcement of a professional league bylaw prohibiting one-eyed athletes from playing hockey. The court ruled that this bylaw violated New York's Human Rights Law prohibiting employees from discrimination based on disability unless the characteristic is a bona fide occupational qualification. There was no evidence that blindness in one eye substantially detracted from the plaintiff's ability to play hockey.[512]

459. Today, disability discrimination claims by U.S. athletes against sport leagues, sports governing bodies, or educational institutions generally are brought under the federal Rehabilitation Act of 1973 or the Americans with Disabilities Act of 1990 or similar state laws.

§1. Rehabilitation Act of 1973

460. The Rehabilitation Act[513] is primarily intended to provide persons with physical or mental impairments with an opportunity to participate fully in activities in which they have the physical capabilities and skills to perform. Qualified handicapped athletes must be given an "equal opportunity for participation" in interscholastic and intercollegiate athletics.

507. . *City of Cleburne v. Cleburne Living Ctr., Inc.*, 473 U.S. 432 (1985).
508. . *Neeld v. Am. Hockey League*, 439 F. Supp. 459 (W.D.N.Y. 1977).
509. . 550 F. Supp. 418, 423 (E.D. Pa. 1982).
510. . *See* generally Matthew J. Mitten, *Amateur Athletes with Handicaps or Physical Abnormalities: Who Makes the Participation Decision?*, 71 Neb. L. Rev. 987 (1992).
511. . 439 F. Supp. 459 (W.D.N.Y. 1977).
512. . However, in *Neeld v. NHL*, 594 F.2d 1297 (9th Cir. 1979), the Ninth Circuit rejected the same plaintiff's claim that this bylaw violates the federal antitrust laws because the bylaw's primary purpose of promoting safety outweighed any *de minimis* anticompetitive effect on excluded athletes.
513. . 29 U.S.C. A. §§701 et seq.

461. To prevail under the Rehabilitation Act, an athlete with a physical impairment must establish that he or she is: (1) an "individual with handicaps"; (2) "otherwise qualified" to participate; (3) subject to exclusion solely by reason of the handicap; and (4) excluded from a program or activity receiving federal funds.

462. The athletics program of most colleges and high schools generally do not receive direct federal funding, but they nevertheless are subject to the Act if any part of its educational institution receives federal financial assistance, which generally is the case. Professional sports leagues and governing bodies are not subject to the Rehabilitation Act unless they receive federal funding, which generally is not provided.

463. An athlete is an "individual with handicaps" entitled to the Act's protection if he or she has a physical impairment that substantially limits a major life activity. It is relatively easy for an athlete to establish the existence of a permanent physical impairment such as a heart condition, congenital back or spine abnormality, or loss of a paired organ (e.g., eye or kidney)—all of which are covered under the Act. It is more difficult to satisfy the requirement that the athlete's physical impairment substantially limits a major life activity. Some courts have held that exclusion of an impaired athlete from intercollegiate or interscholastic sports does not constitute a substantial limitation on a major life activity. In *Knapp v. Northwestern University*,[514] the Seventh Circuit held that a college basketball player is not protected by the Act because "[p]laying intercollegiate basketball obviously is not in and of itself a major life activity." Finding that learning was the affected major life activity, the court concluded that the plaintiff's "inability to play intercollegiate basketball at Northwestern foreclose[d] only a small portion of his collegiate [learning] opportunities" and did not substantially limit his college education, because his athletic scholarship continued in effect.

464. If the exclusion from athletics is deemed to impair a major life activity, the athlete must be "otherwise qualified" to participate in athletics (i.e., has the requisite physical ability and skills to play the sport in spite of his physical impairment) and excluded "solely by reason of handicap" (i.e., his ineligibility to participate in a sport is based entirely on consideration of his physical impairment or medical condition) to have a valid disability discrimination claim under the Act. Failure to select a disabled athlete for a position on a competitive sports team is not necessarily a violation of the Act. In *Doe v. Eagle-Union Community School Corp.*,[515] a federal district court held that a coach's decision not to select a disabled student for the varsity basketball team after a tryout did not violate the Act. The court found that the disabled student was given the same opportunity to try out for the team as students without disabilities, and was graded in a non-discriminatory manner based on the coach's same subjective and objective criteria. The court explained that "the term 'otherwise qualified' did not mean that the student must be selected for the basketball team despite his handicap; it prohibited the non-selection of the student when the student had the skills to make the team but was not selected."

465. An educational institution must make reasonable accommodations to enable physically impaired athletes to participate in its athletic program. An impaired athlete is "otherwise qualified" if able to meet a school's requirements with reasonable accommodations, such as medication, monitoring, or protective padding or braces,

---

514. . 101 F.3d 473 (7th Cir. 1996), *cert. denied*, 520 U.S. 1274 (1997).
515. . 101 F. Supp.2d 707 (S.D. Ind. 2000), *vacated on other grounds*, 248 F.3d 1157 (7th Cir. 2001).

that effectively reduce the risk of injury to himself or others. For example, in *Grube v. Bethlehem Area School District*,[516] the court ruled that the Act required a high school to permit a student-athlete with one kidney to play football if he wore a protective flak jacket, which it found to be was a reasonable accommodation.

466. Preventing a significant risk of harm to the health and safety of other participants is a valid ground for refusing to permit an athlete covered by the Act to play a particular sport if supported by valid medical evidence. In *Doe v. Woodford County Board of Education*,[517] the Sixth Circuit held that a public high school district's decision to place a member of its junior varsity basketball team, who suffered from hepatitis B, on "hold" status pending receipt of medical clearance from his physician, did not violate the Rehabilitation Act. Observing that one could be excluded from athletics if one's participation posed a direct threat to the health and safety of others, the court found that the school district was attempting to determine whether there was a significant risk of transmission of hepatitis B to other athletes. The student's membership on the team was never terminated, and the school district ultimately allowed him to participate fully on the team with no medical restrictions.

467. The Act permits the exclusion of a physically impaired athlete from a sport if necessary to prevent a significant risk of substantial harm to the athlete. In *Pahulu v. University of Kansas*,[518] a federal district court upheld the team physician's "conservative" medical disqualification of a college football player with an abnormally narrow cervical canal after an episode of transient quadriplegia during a scrimmage. After consulting with a neurosurgeon, the team physician concluded that the athlete was at extremely high risk for sustaining permanent, severe neurological injury, including permanent quadriplegia, if he continued playing football. The athlete wanted to resume playing because three other medical specialists concluded that he was at no greater risk of permanent paralysis than any other player. The university agreed to honor the athlete's scholarship, although he was not allowed to play football despite his willingness to sign a waiver absolving the university of legal liability if he were injured. The court held that university officials' adherence to the team physician's recommendation against playing does not violate the Rehabilitation Act, concluding that the university's medical disqualification decision "has a rational and reasonable basis and is supported by substantial competent evidence for which the court is unwilling to substitute its judgment."

468. Similarly, in *Knapp v. Northwestern University*,[519] the Seventh Circuit held that Northwestern University did not violate the Rehabilitation Act by accepting its team physician's recommendation that an athlete with idiopathic ventricular fibrillation not play intercollegiate basketball because doing so would expose him to a significant risk of or cardiac arrest during competitive athletics. The team physician's recommendation was based on Knapp's medical records and history, the 26th Bethesda Conference guidelines for athletic participation with cardiovascular abnormalities, and opinions of two consulting cardiologists. As a high school senior, Nicholas Knapp suffered sudden cardiac arrest while playing recreational basketball, which required cardiopulmonary

516. . 550 F. Supp. 418, 424 (E.D. Pa.1982).

517. . 213 F.3d 921 (6th Cir. 2000).

518. . 897 F. Supp. 1387 (D. Kan. 1995).

519. . 101 F.3d 473 (7th Cir. 1996), *cert. denied*, 520 U.S. 1274 (1997).

resuscitation and defibrillation to restart his heart. Thereafter, he had an internal cardioverter-defibrillator implanted in his abdomen. He subsequently played competitive recreational basketball without any incidents of cardiac arrest and received medical clearance to play college basketball from three cardiologists who examined him. Northwestern agreed to honor its commitment to provide Knapp with an athletic scholarship, although he was medically disqualified from playing intercollegiate basketball.

469. The court explained that Knapp's exclusion from Northwestern's basketball team was legally justified under the Act:

> We do not believe that, in cases where medical experts disagree in their assessment of the extent of a real risk of serious harm or death, Congress intended that the courts—neutral arbiters but generally less skilled in medicine than the experts involved—should make the final medical decision. Instead, in the midst of conflicting expert testimony regarding the degree of serious risk of harm or death, the court's place is to ensure that the exclusion or disqualification of an individual was individualized, reasonably made, and based upon competent medical evidence. So long as these factors exist, it will be the rare case regarding participation in athletics where a court may substitute its judgment for that of the school's team physicians.

§2. Americans with Disabilities Act of 1990

470. The Americans with Disabilities Act (ADA)[520] is patterned after the Rehabilitation Act and has similar policy objectives. The ADA's scope, however, is broader than that of the Rehabilitation Act because it covers entities that do not receive federal funding, such as professional sports leagues and their member teams. Depending on the particular sport, the ADA's provisions covering employers (Title I),[521] public entities (Title II),[522] and places of public accommodation (Title II)[523] may apply. The ADA applies to public entities such as public high schools, universities, and colleges; employers, such as professional leagues and clubs, with fifteen or more employees; and private persons or entities that own, lease, or operate a place of public accommodation, such as the PGA Tour, NCAA, youth sports leagues, and sports instructional schools.

471. In response to a June 2010 United States Government Accountability Office report finding that public elementary and secondary school students with disabilities do not have an equal opportunity to participate in extracurricular sports, the Department of Education's Office for Civil Rights (OCR), which is responsible for enforcing section 504 of the Rehabilitation Act and Title II of the ADA, issued January 25, 2013 written guidance regarding the obligations of covered elementary, secondary, and postsecondary educational institutions to provide students with disabilities to participate

520. . 42 U.S.C. §§12101 et seq.
521. . 42 U.S.C. §12111(5)(A).
522. . 42 U.S.C. §§12131–12132.
523. . 42 U.S.C. §12181(7)(L).

in interscholastic, intercollegiate, club, and intramural athletics.[524] It states that educational institutions must provide "qualified students with disabilities an equal opportunity for participation in extracurricular athletics in an integrated manner to the maximum extent appropriate to the needs of the student." An educational institution is required to create additional athletic participation opportunities (e.g., wheelchair basketball or tennis) for students with disabilities who are unable to participate in its existing extracurricular athletics program even with reasonable modifications thereto.

472. Courts generally construe the ADA in a manner consistent with judicial interpretations of the Rehabilitation Act. The factors governing the legality of excluding a physically disabled athlete from a sport under the ADA are similar to those relevant under the Rehabilitation Act.

473. The ADA requires a valid medical basis for excluding an athlete from competition on the ground that his physical condition exposes other participants to an increased risk of serious harm. In *Anderson v. Little League Baseball, Inc.*,[525] a federal district court held that a youth baseball league policy prohibiting coaches in wheelchairs from being on the field violated the ADA because the plaintiff's on-field coaching in a wheelchair did not pose a direct threat to the health and safety of others. It enjoined enforcement of the baseball league's policy because it unjustifiably discriminated against the plaintiff.

474. Courts have held it is legally permissible to exclude an athlete from participating in competitive sports with an infectious disease if no reasonable accommodation will prevent a direct threat to the health and safety of other participants. In *Montalvo v. Radcliffe*,[526] the Fourth Circuit ruled that a karate studio was permitted to exclude a Human Immunodeficiency Virus (HIV)-positive 12-year old boy from full contact karate classes, which involved frequent physical contact among students and instructors that resulted in bloody injuries. Relying on medical expert testimony that HIV can be transmitted through blood-to-blood contact and evidence that this type of contact frequently occurred in these karate classes, the court concluded that the plaintiff's participation would pose a direct threat to the health and safety of others by exposing them to the risk of HIV transmission. The court further found that there were no possible modifications that could effectively reduce the significance of this risk, while also maintaining the fundamental nature of the studio's "hard-style" Japanese karate. The studio's offer to give the plaintiff private karate lessons, which was rejected by him and his parents, was found to be a reasonable accommodation of the plaintiff's disability.

475. Consistent with judicial precedent recognizing harm to one's self as a valid justification for exclusion from athletics under the Rehabilitation Act, courts have recognized exclusion of a disabled intercollegiate athlete from a sport solely because of a potentially enhanced risk of injury is a legally valid justification under the ADA. Following *Knapp*,[527] in *Class v. Towson University*,[528] the Fourth Circuit upheld a university team physician's medical disqualification of a Towson University football

524. . Department of Education, Office for Civil Rights, Jan. 25, 2013 Directive.
525. . 794 F. Supp. 342 (D. Ariz. 1992).
526. . 167 F.3d 873 (4th Cir.), *cert. denied*, 528 U.S. 813 (1999).
527. 101 F.3d 473 (7th Cir. 1996), *cert. denied*, 520 U.S. 1274 (1997).
528. 806 F.3d 236, 251 (4th Cir. 2015).

player who suffered exertional heat stroke during practice that caused liver failure necessitating a liver transplant:

> [T]he standard for assessing [the team physician's] judgment not to clear Class for return to football under Towson University's Return-to-Play Policy is not whether we share that judgment or whether she had a better judgment than some other doctor. Rather, the standard is whether her judgment was reasonable—i.e., whether it was individualized to Class, was reasonably made, and was based on competent medical evidence. When applying that standard, we conclude that [her] decision was supported by legitimate health and safety concerns, manifested by the medical records, which were not eliminated by the proposed monitoring system. Therefore, we conclude that her decision was not unreasonable.

476. To date, there have not been any ADA cases in which a professional athlete with a physical abnormality has been denied an opportunity to play a sport solely on the ground that doing so would expose him to an enhanced risk of significant harm. Although the underlying medical issues may be the same, courts may develop a different legal framework for resolving participation disputes involving professional athletes than the one for college athletes established by the *Pahulu*, *Knapp*, and *Class* cases. An important distinction is that sports are a professional athlete's livelihood, rather than an extracurricular activity that is merely one component of an education.

477. In *Mobley v. Madison Square Garden LP*,[529] a New York federal district court ruled that Cutino Mobley, a former NBA basketball player, may have a valid state law disability discrimination claim against the New York Knicks for refusing to allow him to play basketball with hypertrophic cardiomyopathy during the 2008–2009 season based on his medical disqualification by two cardiologists. In his complaint, Mobley alleged that he had been medically cleared to play NBA basketball from 1999–2008 (subject to his signing a liability waiver) and that three other cardiologists examined him and concluded there was no material change in his heart condition and he was currently as medically fit to play basketball during the 2008–2009 season as he was during the prior nine seasons. The court held that Mobley pled sufficient facts to contradict the medical opinions of the two cardiologists who had disqualified him and that it is "plausible that he was qualified to perform safely the essential functions of a professional basketball player," which he ultimately must prove to prevail on his New York disability discrimination law claim against the Knicks.

478. The *Mobley* case suggests that some courts may be willing to adopt an "athlete informed consent model for professional athletes, which would enable a professional athlete to choose to participate, despite medical disqualification by the team physician, if other competent medical authority clears him to play."[530]

479. In *PGA Tour, Inc. v. Martin*,[531] the U.S. Supreme Court ruled that, although the essence of sports is that everyone plays by the same rules, a sport's governing body (including those that regulate professional sports) must make reasonable accommodations

---

529. . 2013 U.S. Dist. Lexis 46341 (S.D.N.Y.).

530. . Matthew J. Mitten, *Enhanced Risk of Harm to One's Self as a Justification for Exclusion from Athletics*, 8 MARQ. SPORTS L.J. 189, 222 (1998).

531. . 532 U.S. 661 (2001).

to provide a physically impaired athlete with an opportunity to compete in the subject sport. The PGA Tour had refused to provide Casey Martin, a professional golfer with a circulatory disorder that inhibits his ability to walk, with an exception to its rule that all golfers must walk the course during tournament play because of its position that walking injected an element of fatigue into championship golf. This decision effectively precluded him from playing in PGA tournaments, although his demonstrated golf skills qualified him to participate.

480. Title III of the ADA requires covered entities operating places of public accommodation (such as the PGA Tour) to make reasonable modifications to their policies when necessary to enable individuals with disabilities to have access to their facilities and services, unless doing so would "fundamentally alter" their nature. It was undisputed that using a golf cart was a reasonable modification necessary to enable Martin to participate in PGA tournaments.

481. The Court ruled that waiver of the PGA Tour's walking rule to allow Martin to use a cart did not fundamentally alter the nature of professional championship golf. The "essence of the game has been shot-making," according to the Court, and the "walking rule is not an essential attribute of the game itself." The Court recognized that "waiver of an essential rule of competition for anyone would fundamentally alter" the PGA's tournaments, but concluded that "the walking rule is at best peripheral to the nature of petitioner's athletic events, and thus it might be waived in individual cases without working a fundamental alteration."

482. Relying on undisputed trial testimony that "Martin easily endures greater fatigue even with a cart than his able-bodied competitors do by walking," the Court held:

> The purpose of the walking rule is therefore not compromised in the slightest by allowing Martin to use a cart. A modification that provides an exception to a peripheral tournament rule without impairing its purpose cannot be said to fundamentally alter the tournament. What it can be said to do, on the other hand, is to allow Martin the chance to qualify for and compete in the athletic events petitioner offers to those members of the public who have the skill and desire to enter. That is exactly what the ADA requires. As a result, Martin's request for a waiver of the walking rule should have been granted.

483. In *Barron v. PGA Tour, Inc.*,[532] a federal court held that the PGA Tour did not violate a professional golfer's rights under the ADA by suspending him for one year for testing positive for exogenous testosterone, a banned substance under its anti-doping program, and refusing to grant him a therapeutic use exemption. Plaintiff alleged he suffers from abnormally low testosterone, which causes him to have a reduced sex drive, experience fatigue, and have a compromised immune system, and that by refusing to allow him to take medically prescribed exogenous testosterone and suspending him for using it, the PGA Tour discriminated against him in violation of the ADA. The court concluded that he had not shown a likelihood of success on his claim:

532. . 670 F. Supp.2d 674 (W.D. Tenn. 2009).

> Barron has not shown that the reasonable accommodation he has requested (allowing him to continue taking exogenous Testosterone) is necessary in order for him to continue playing golf in PGA Tour events. His complaint and post-hearing brief, at most, claim that he needs these Testosterone shots to address specific medical concerns relating to a reduced sex drive, fatigue, and a compromised immune system-not to play golf. While Barron's abnormally low Testosterone may in some way cause him to be a less competitive golfer than he would be if he were permitted to take the Testosterone injections, [the ADA] simply does not provide a remedy under those circumstances.

484. After his suspension ended, the PGA Tour granted Barron a therapeutic use exemption to use testosterone while attempting to qualify for the 2011 PGA Tour, which was based on new medical information he submitted.[533]

485. In *Kuketz v. Petronelli,* [534] the Massachusetts Supreme Judicial Court ruled that the ADA does not require that a wheelchair-bound paraplegic, who is a nationally ranked player in wheelchair racquetball competitions, be permitted to play in a health club's men's A-level league with footed players and be given two bounces to hit the ball. He was permitted in play in nonleague matches with footed racquetball players, but wanted to compete against the best footed players in league competition to prepare for an upcoming international wheelchair racquetball tournament. The official rules of racquetball require the ball to be returned on one bounce in a game between footed players, but allow for two bounces if both participants are playing in wheelchairs. The court explained:

> Unlike the use of carts in golf, the allowance for more than one bounce in racquetball is inconsistent with the fundamental character of the game. The essence of the game of racquetball, as expressly articulated in the rules, is the hitting of a moving ball with a racquet before the second bounce. Giving a wheelchair player two bounces and a footed player one bounce in head-to-head competition is a variation of the official rules that would alter such as essential aspect of the game . . . that it would be unacceptable even if it affected all competitors equally. The modifications sought by [plaintiff] create a new game, with new strategies and new rules. The club certainly is free to establish or enter into a league that plays this variation of racquetball, but it is not required by the ADA to do so.[535]

486. Judicial decisions illustrate that high school student-athletes with the same disability (e.g., a learning disability) may not have the same athletic participation rights

---

533. . *See* generally Travis Tygart & Anthony R. Ten Haagen, *The Americans With Disabilities Act, The United States Anti-Doping Agency, and the Effort Toward Equal Opportunity: A Case Study of the United States Anti-Doping Agency v. George Hartman Matter*, 2 Harv. J. Sports & Ent. L. 199 (2011) (discussing ADA's reasonable accommodation requirement as applied to athlete's therapeutic use of synthetic testosterone).
534. 821 N.E. 2d 473 (2005).
535. *See* generally Paul M. Anderson, *A Cart That Accommodates: Using Case Law to Understand the ADA, Sports, and Casey Martin*, 1 Va. Sports & Ent. L.J. 211 (2002).

under the ADA. For example, in determining whether granting a waiver of a state high school athletic association eligibility rule (e.g.,19-year-old maximum age rule) would fundamentally alter the nature of a sport by providing a competitive advantage or would adversely affect other participants' safety, the student-athlete's individual size, skills, and athletic prowess are the dispositive factors. This is a fact-specific inquiry; whether the ADA requires that a disabled student-athlete be given an opportunity to participate depends on the individual's physical characteristics and athletic abilities as well as the subject sport.

487. In *Cruz v. Pennsylvania Interscholastic Athletic Assn.*,[536] a federal district court ruled that a 19-year-old public school special education student who was classified as "educable mentally retarded" could not be excluded from participation in any high school sports without an individualized evaluation of whether doing so was necessary to prevent a threat to the health and safety of other participants or to prevent competitive unfairness. The court noted that he is five foot three inches tall and weighs 130 pounds and is not a "star" player in any of his interscholastic sports. Observing that there is a no "cut" policy for both teams, the court suggested he should be permitted to continue playing football because there he is only "a marginal player" and participating in track because he "is not a fast runner." However, it implied that he could be excluded from wrestling because "he may have a competitive advantage based on his outstanding dual meet record."

488. Similarly, in *Baisden v. West Virginia Secondary Schools Activities Commission*,[537] the West Virginia Supreme Court concluded:

> While we decide, through this opinion, that individualized assessments are required in cases of this nature and that reasonable accommodations may be made through waiver of the age nineteen rule under certain circumstances, we do not believe that the facts of this case justify waiver as an accommodation. Mr. Baisden turned nineteen on July 27, 2001. He is six feet four inches tall and weighs 280 pounds. He runs the forty-yard-dash in 5.3 seconds. His participation in high school football would permit him to compete in this contact sport against students approximately five years younger. The safety of younger, smaller, more inexperienced students would be unreasonably compromised. In our view, this would fundamentally alter the structure of the interscholastic athletic program, a result which is not required by reasonable accommodation standards in anti-discrimination law.

489. Although courts have ruled that the ADA applies to the National Collegiate Athletic Association, there are relatively few reported cases applying *Martin's* reasonable accommodation/fundamental alteration legal framework to intercollegiate athletics. In *Matthews v. NCAA*,[538] a Washington federal district court held that a request by a student-athlete with a learning disability for a waiver of an NCAA rule requiring student-athletes to earn at least 75% of their annual required credit hours during the

536. 157 F. Supp. 2d 485 (E.D. Pa. 2001).
537. 568 S.E.2d 32 (W. Va. 2002).
538. 179 F. Supp. 2d 1209 (E.D. Wash. 2001).

regular academic year would not fundamentally alter its academic eligibility requirements.[539]

539. *See* generally Maureen A. Weston, *Academic Standards or Discriminatory Hoops? Learning-Disabled Student-Athletes and the NCAA Initial Academic Eligibility Requirements*, 66 Tenn. L. Rev. 1049 (1999).

Chapter 8. Legal Protection of Privacy, Reputation, and Publicity Rights

§1. Historical Background and Overview

490. Today's professional athlete is a celebrity. The truly gifted athlete probably is a celebrity, at least locally, much earlier than the onset of his or her professional career. Astounding amounts of money can be made from the utilization of a celebrity's name and likeness. Well-known athletes have entered into lucrative deals to promote and endorse a wide variety of products and services. Income earned from the licensing of a player's identity to sell products and services may be greater than that derived from his or her athletic ability or success. For example, Michael Jordan signed his first Nike endorsement contract in 1985 for USD 2.5 million, and he has earned more money from endorsement deals than from playing NBA basketball. Before ever playing in a NBA game, LeBron James signed a five-year, USD 5 million endorsement deal with Upper Deck trading cards and a seven-year shoe endorsement deal with Nike worth more than USD 90 million. In 2015, NBA superstar Kevin Durant earned USD 35 million in endorsement income, and tennis player Serena Williams earned USD 13 million. In June 2016, Ben Simmons, the number one overall pick in the NBA draft, signed a USD 20 million endorsement contract with Nike, prior to being drafted.

491. In the U.S., the body of law protecting the reputation, privacy, and publicity rights of athletes, which is primarily state law, varies by jurisdiction. Federal trademark and unfair competition law under the Lanham Act also provides some protection to athletes' commercial endorsement and sponsorship rights.

I. Defamation

492. The tort of defamation includes both oral (slander) and written (libel) statements. The scope of its legal protection is not limited to celebrities such as well-known athletes, but defamation assumes special significance in this context. Professional athletes are written about all the time in various forms of media, including online publications, blogs, Twitter, and many others. Their lives, both professionally and personally, are scrutinized, at times to excruciating degrees and media statements may give rise to false statements that harm an athlete's reputation.

493. Although there are variations in state law definitions and approaches to defamation, a general definition of defamation is set forth in the Restatement (Second) Torts, §558, which provides:

> To create liability for defamation, there must be: (a) a false and defamatory statement concerning another; (b) an unprivileged communication to a third party; (c) fault amounting at least to negligence on the part of the publisher; and

(d) either actionability of the statement irrespective of special harm or the existence of special harm caused by the publication.

494. Statements must be both false and defamatory, meaning they tend to damage the reputation of the person identified by the statement in the minds of others. Not included in the definition but generally accepted as a part thereof is that the false statement must be one of fact, not merely opinion. Most of what is written about the professional performance of athletes or coaches is opinion, which is not legally actionable even if it harms his or her reputation.[540] For example, a statement in newspaper article that a coach "usually finds a way to screw things up" and "[t]his season will be no different" is nonactionable opinion regarding team's potential for upcoming season and coach's ability.[541] On the other hand, asserting that an athlete "fixed" a boxing match and used cocaine with his opponent thereafter, or unknowingly used "loaded" gloves are statements of fact that harm one's professional reputation and may cause resulting economic loss.[542] False factual statements about an athlete's personal life such as alleged criminal conduct are also defamatory.

495. Since the U.S. Supreme Court's 1964 landmark decision, *New York Times v. Sullivan*,[543] the traditional state law elements of defamation have been modified by federal constitutional law; therefore, First Amendment free speech issues must also be considered. A prominent athlete is considered to be a "public figure" who must prove by clear and convincing evidence that a defamatory statement was made with "actual malice," meaning the defendant had knowledge of its falsity or a reckless disregard regarding whether or not it was true.[544] Thus, although athletes are protected by the laws of defamation, it is difficult for them to prove the necessary elements of this tort.

II. Right of Privacy

496. The right of privacy was first enunciated in a famous law review article by Samuel Warren and Louis Brandeis that was published in the Harvard Law Review in 1890, in which they argued that a distinct tort protecting a person's right to privacy existed at common law and should be recognized.[545] A further impetus to the development

540. . *Time, Inc. v. Johnston*, 448 F.2d 378, 380 (4th Cir. 1971) ("as a paid performer," professional athlete "assumed the risk of publicity, good or bad, … so far as it concerned his public performance."). *See also Parks v. Steinbrenner*, 520 N.Y.S.2d 374 (N.Y. App. Div. 1987) ("rhetorical hyperbole" that generally accompany the communication of displeasure at an umpire's "calls" is statement of opinion, not fact).
541. . *Washington v. Smith*, 893 F. Supp. 60 (D.D.C. 1995), *aff'd*, 80 F.3d 555 (D.C. Cir. 1996).
542. . *Cobb v. Time, Inc.*, 278 F.3d 629 (6th Cir. 2002); *Dempsey v. Time Inc.*, 252 N.Y.S.2d 186 (N.Y. Sup. Ct. 1964). *See also Faigin v. Kelly*, 978 F. Supp. 420 (D. N.H. 1997), *aff'd*, 184 F.3d 67 (1st Cir. 1999) (pro football player's charge that former agent engaged in untrustworthy conduct in handling his business affairs).
543. 376 U.S. 254 (1964).
544. . *See* e.g., *Cobb v. Time, Inc.*, 278 F.3d 629 (6th Cir. 2002); *Cepeda v. Cowles Magazines and Broadcasting*, 392 F.2d 417 (9th Cir. 1968).
545. . Samuel D. Warren & Louis D. Brandeis, *The Right to Privacy*, 4 Harv. L. Rev. 193 (1890).

of the right of privacy occurred many years later through the various writings of Professor William Prosser. He advocated four separate torts should be subsumed under a general concept of privacy: (1) protection against intrusion into one's private affairs; (2) avoidance of disclosure of one's embarrassing private facts; (3) protection against publicity placing one in a false light in the public eye; and (4) remedies for appropriation, usually for commercial advantage, of one's name or likeness.[546] All or some of these four categories of torts have largely been adopted in all states, although there is no unanimity as to the nature and scope of their common law development by courts. In some states, statutes have codified these torts.

497. The first three torts provide legal remedies for intrusions into one's private life and affairs, frequently accompanied by widespread public disclosure. Athletes (and other sports celebrities) have relied on one or more of these legal theories in asserting various invasions of privacy claims. Former professional wrestler Hulk Hogan was awarded USD 115 million in compensatory damages and USD 25 million in punitive damages against the website Gawker Media for publishing an unauthorized videotape of him having sex.[547] A Nashville, Tennessee jury awarded sports broadcaster Erin Andrews USD 55 million in damages arising out of a 2008 peeping Tom incident and posting of a video of her naked body on the internet.[548]

498. Courts have recognized claims for public disclosures placing an athlete in a false light in the public eye. In *Spahn v. Julian Messner, Inc.*,[549] the court held that publication of an unauthorized fictionalized biography of well-known baseball player violates New York's statutory privacy law. In *Chuy v. Philadelphia Eagles Football Club*,[550] an NFL club was found liable for its team physician's known false statement to the media that a player had a fatal blood disease, which caused him severe emotional distress.

499. The fourth privacy tort is distinguishable from the others because of its recognition of the commercial value in one's name or likeness. In some early cases, athletes asserted that the unauthorized use of their name or likeness in connection with the advertising or sale of products violated their common law privacy rights. *O'Brien v. Pabst Sales Co.*[551] illustrates that courts generally were not receptive to these claims. In *O'Brien*, a famous professional football player alleged that the unauthorized use of his photograph in a calendar advertising defendant's beer invaded his right of privacy. Because he was not a private person and "the publicity he got was only that which he had been constantly seeking and receiving," the Fifth Circuit adopted the reasoning of the district court in holding: "Considered from the standpoint merely of an invasion of plaintiff's right of privacy, no case was made out, because plaintiff was an outstanding national football figure and had completely publicized his name and his pictures."

Now it is the basis for a separate right of publicity or commercial misappropriation claim that is recognized in many states by common law or statute. Unlike the rights

546. . William Prosser, *Privacy*, 48 Cal. L. Rev. 383 (1960).
547. *Terry Gene Bollea v. Gawker Media LLC*, (Fla. Cir. Ct. 2016).
548. *Erin Andrews v. Marriott International Inc.* (Tenn. Cir. Ct. 2016).
549. . 286 N.Y.S.2d 832 (N.Y. 1967).
550. . 595 F.2d 1265 (3d Cir. 1979).
551. . 124 F.2d 167 (5th Cir. 1941).

of reputation and privacy, the right of publicity is a property right that may be transferred and is descendible in many states.

III. Right of Publicity

500. Courts initially refused to characterize celebrity names and likenesses as protectable property rights. In *Hanna Mfg. Co. v. Hillerich & Bradsby Co.*,[552] the Fifth Circuit held that "fame is not merchandise." It concluded that an athlete has a valid claim for unauthorized commercial use of his name only if such usage falsely suggests that he uses or endorses the product, thereby constituting unfair competition.

501. In 1953, a U.S. court recognized the right of publicity for the first time. *Haelan Laboratories, Inc. v. Topps Chewing Gum, Inc.*[553] involved a dispute over the rights to use baseball players' images on bubblegum trading cards. One company had been assigned these rights by the players; however, the defendant produced its own cards without the players' permission. One of the central issues was whether the players' rights, if any, were assignable—or were they strictly personal to the player. The Second Circuit held that New York law recognized a common law right of publicity, which is a freely transferable property right, not just a personal right. The court explained "in addition to and independent of the right of privacy ... a man has a right in the publicity value of his photograph, i.e., the right to grant the exclusive privilege of publishing his picture."

502. Since the *Haelan* decision, there has been a lot of litigation to determine if a common law right of publicity exists in a particular jurisdiction.[554] A perplexing aspect is that most cases have been brought in federal courts, not state courts. Thus, it is federal courts that have determined if such state law protections exist and, if so, their nature and scope. There is always the possibility that a state's highest court subsequently may rule that a federal court's decision was erroneous. As a result, the common law development of the right of publicity has been fraught with uncertainty and continues to be today. Several states have attempted to remedy conflicting judicial interpretations of the right of publicity by the enactment of specific legislation.[555]

IV. Lanham Act

503. The unauthorized misappropriation of an athlete's *persona* (i.e., name, likeness, or other well recognized aspects of one's identity) violates §43(a) of the Lanham Act[556] if it causes consumer confusion regarding whether he or she has endorsed

---

552. . 78 F.2d 763 (5th Cir. 1935).
553. . 202 F.2d 866 (2d Cir. 1953), *cert. denied* 346 U.S. 816 (1953). *See* generally J. Gordon Hylton, Baseball Cards and the Birth of the Right of Publicity: *The Curious Case of Haelan Laboratories v. Topps Chewing Gum,* 12 MARQ. SPORTS L. REV. 273 (2001).
554. . *See* generally 1 J. Thomas McCarthy, *The Rights of Publicity and Privacy* (2d ed.) §§6:1–6:9 (West Group 2012) (overview of state common law publicity rights).
555. . McCarthy, *supra* , §6:6–6:7 (overview of state statutory publicity rights).
556. . 15 U.S.C. § 1125(a).

or sponsored particular products and services. This federal statutory claim provides a consumer protection-based cause of action, and various state laws establish a similar consumer protection standard. As the Ninth Circuit has observed, "Many people may assume that when a celebrity's name is used in a television commercial, the celebrity endorses the product advertised."[557]

504. In *Hillerich & Bradsby v. Christian Brothers,*[558] defendant was selling its Pro-Rite hockey blades with the name "Messier" clearly affixed on the blade and product label without the permission of Mark Messier, one of professional hockey's most recognized players who led the Edmonton Oilers and the New York Rangers to a total of six Stanley Cup championships and was twice voted the most valuable player in the NHL. The court ruled that this unauthorized commercial use of Messier's name creates the false impression that he endorses defendant's hockey blades in violation of §43(a) and enjoined defendant from using his name on its products or in connection with their advertising and sale with his express permission.

505. If an athlete's name or likeness is used without authorization in an artistic or expressive work, it is difficult to establish a §43(a) violation. In *Brown v. Electronic Arts, Inc.,*[559] the Ninth Circuit rejected a famous former professional football player's claim that Electronic Arts" unauthorized use of his likeness in its *Madden NFL* football video games violated §43(a). Observing that §43(a) protection "is limited by the First Amendment, particularly if the product involved is an expressive work," the court relied on the test developed in *Rogers v. Grimaldi,* 875 F.2d 994 (2d Cir.1989) "to balance the public's First Amendment interest in free expression against the public's interest in being free from consumer confusion about affiliation and endorsement." Under the *Rogers* test, §43(a) will not be applied to expressive works "unless the [use of the trademark or other identifying material] has no artistic relevance to the underlying work whatsoever, or, if it has some artistic relevance, unless the [use of trademark or other identifying material] explicitly misleads as to the source or the content of the work. Applying this test, the Ninth Circuit found that EA's video game is an expressive work and that there was no evidence EA "explicitly misled consumers about Brown's endorsement of the game," which requires more than "a survey demonstrating that consumers of the *Madden NFL* series believed that Brown endorsed the game."[560]

506. An athlete may use his or her name as a trademark or service mark, and it may be federally registered under the Lanham Act after acquiring secondary meaning as the source or origin of goods or services (i.e., it is a brand name for a product or service the public associates with an identifiable athlete). For example, the name "Tiger Woods" has been federally registered as a trademark for art prints, calendars, mounted photographs, notebooks, pencils, pens, posters, trading cards, and unmounted photographs. Unauthorized usage of an athlete's federally registered name that creates a likelihood of consumer confusion regarding the source or sponsorship of goods or services

557. . *Abdul-Jabbar v. Gen. Motors Corp.*, 85 F.3d 407, 413 (9th Cir. 1996).

558. . 943 F.Supp. 1136 (D. Minn. 1996).

559. . 724 F.3d 1235 (9th Cir. 2013).

560. *See also ETW Corp. v. Jireh Publishing, Inc.*, 332 F.3d 915 (6th Cir. 2003) (adopting and applying *Rogers* in rejecting Tiger Woods" §43(a) false endorsement claim arising out of unauthorized painting depicting him winning the 1997 Masters golf tournament).

constitutes trademark infringement and unfair competition in violation of the Lanham Act and various state laws.

507. Courts require that a person's photo, image, or likeness actually function as a trademark to be protected by the Lanham Act's provisions prohibiting trademark infringement. In *ETW Corp. v. Jireh Publishing, Inc.*,[561] In *ETW Corp.*, the Sixth Circuit observed:

> Here, ETW claims protection under the Lanham Act for any and all images of Tiger Woods. This is an untenable claim. ETW asks us, in effect, to constitute Woods himself as a walking, talking trademark. Images and likenesses of Woods are not protectable as a trademark because they do not perform the trademark function of designation. They do not distinguish and identify the source of goods. They cannot function as a trademark because there are undoubtedly thousands of images and likenesses of Woods taken by countless photographers, and drawn, sketched, or painted by numerous artists, which have been published in many forms of media, and sold and distributed throughout the world. No reasonable person could believe these images all originated with Woods.

508. However, in *Pirone v. Macmillan, Inc.*,[562] the Second Circuit acknowledged that "[u]nder some circumstances, a photograph of a person may be a valid trademark—if, for example, a particular photograph was consistently used on specific goods."

§2. Athlete's Right of Publicity

509. By common law or statute, a majority of states (but not all) recognize a right of publicity property-based claim for unauthorized commercial use of an athlete's identity. As one court observed:

> a celebrity has a legitimate proprietary interest in his public personality. A celebrity must be considered to have invested his years of practice and competition in a public personality which eventually may reach marketable status. A name is commercially valuable as an endorsement of a product or for use for financial gain only because the public recognizes it and attributes good will and feats of skill or accomplishments of one sort or another to that personality.[563]

510. Although college and high school student-athletes have the same legally protectable publicity rights as professional athletes, the NCAA and state high school athletics governing bodies generally prohibit its individualized exercise in order to be eligible to participate in intercollegiate or interscholastic sports competition as an "amateur" athlete.[564] For example, to retain his eligibility to play college football for

561. . 332 F.3d 915, 922 (6th Cir. 2003).
562. . 894 F.2d 579 (2d 1990).
563. . *Uhlaender v. Henricksen*, 316 F. Supp. 1277, 1282–1283 (D. Minn. 1970).
564. . *See* generally Sean Hanlon & Ray Yasser, J.J. Morrison and His Right of Publicity Lawsuit Against the NCAA, 15 Vill. Sports & Ent. L.J. 241 (2008).

the University of Colorado, the NCAA prohibited U.S. Olympic moguls skier Jeremy Bloom from commercially exploiting his right of publicity to earn future endorsement and modeling contract income needed to finance his training.[565] In 2003, the Ohio High School Athletic Association (OHSAA) declared LeBron James ineligible to continue playing high school basketball for violating its rule prohibiting "capitalizing on athletic fame by receiving money or gifts of monetary value." James had accepted two "throwback" jerseys worth a combined USD 845 from an Akron, Ohio sporting goods store for posing for photos to be displayed on its walls. Although an Ohio trial court ultimately enjoined the OHSAA from enforcing its rule, James was required to serve a two-game suspension for his conduct. "

511. In *Newcombe v. Adolph Coors Co.*,[566] the Ninth Circuit held that Don Newcombe, a well- known former MLB pitcher, had California common law and statutory right of publicity claims against a brewery for using an identifiable likeness of his distinctive pitching style without his permission in a magazine advertisement for one of its products. The court observed:

> Having viewed the advertisement, we hold that a triable issue of fact has been raised as to whether Newcombe is readily identifiable as the pitcher in the advertisement. Initially, we note that the drawing in the advertisement and the newspaper photograph of Newcombe upon which the drawing was based are virtually identical. The pitcher's stance, proportions and shape are identical to the newspaper photograph of Newcombe; even the styling of the uniform is identical, right down to the wrinkles in the pants. It may be the case that Newcombe's stance is essentially generic, but based on the record before us, Newcombe is the only one who has such a stance. The record contains pictures of other pitchers in the windup position but none of these pitchers has a stance similar to Newcombe's, thus giving us no basis to reach the conclusion proposed by the defendants that the pitcher in the advertisement is generic . . . [T]here is a genuine issue of material fact as to whether Newcombe's stance was so distinctive that the defendants used his likeness by using a picture of Newcombe's stance.

512. Consistent with *Newcombe*, courts have broadly defined the protected aspects of an athlete's identity to encompass more than merely his or her name or photo, including one's birth name even after it was changed after conversion to Islam,[567] voice,[568] robotic caricature,[569] distinctive car driven by professional racer,[570] facial

565. . *Bloom v. NCAA*, 93 P.3d 621 (Colo. App. 2004) (upholding NCAA bylaws prohibiting student-athletes from being paid for advertisements and product endorsements).
566. . 157 F.3d 686 (9th Cir. 1998).
567. . *Abdul-Jabbar v. Gen. Motors Corp.*, 85 F.3d 407 (9th Cir. 1996).
568. . *Ventura v. Titan Sports, Inc.*, 65 F.3d 725 (8th Cir. 1995).
569. . *White v. Samsung Elecs. Am., Inc.*, 971 F.2d 1395 (9th Cir. 1992).
570. . *Motschenbacher v. R.J. Reynolds Tobacco Co.*, 498 F.2d 821 (9th Cir. 1974).

features and moniker "The Greatest,"[571] player names and game statistics,[572] and "Crazy Legs" nickname.[573]

513. A state statutory or common law right of publicity may even protect an athletic performance; for example, a human cannonball act.[574] However, federal copyright law preempts a state law right of publicity claim that is equivalent to any of the exclusive rights within the general scope of copyright protection. In *Baltimore Orioles, Inc. v. Major League Baseball Players Assn.*,[575] the MLB players union claimed that the clubs" unauthorized telecasts of games in which they played violated their publicity rights. Finding that the clubs owned the copyright to televised baseball games, the Seventh Circuit held that the players" publicity rights in their game performances are preempted by the Copyright Act. The court explained:

> [O]nce a performance is reduced to tangible form, there is no distinction between the performance and the recording of the performance for the purpose of preemption under § 301(a). Thus, if a baseball game were not broadcast or were telecast without being recorded, the Players' performances similarly would not be fixed in tangible form and their rights of publicity would not be subject to preemption. By virtue of being videotaped, however, the Players' performances are fixed in tangible form, and any rights of publicity in their performances that are equivalent to the rights contained in the copyright of the telecast are preempted.

514. Infringement of an athlete's right of publicity occurs if an aspect of his identity was used without permission to advertise and sell a product or service.[576] Other examples of infringing commercial usage include incorporating an athlete's photo into a product such as sports trading cards,[577] drinking glasses,[578] or clothing.[579] Courts generally refuse to characterize the use of a famous athlete's name or identity in connection with the sale of a product as legally permissible incidental or informational use. Rather, such usage is unauthorized commercial appropriation of the athlete's

---

571. . *Ali v. Playgirl, Inc.*, 447 F. Supp. 723 (S.D.N.Y. 1978).
572. . *Uhlaender v. Henricksen*, 316 F. Supp. 1277 (D. Minn. 1970).
573. . *Hirsch v. S.C. Johnson & Son, Inc.*, 280 N.W.2d 129 (Wis. 1979).
574. . *Zacchini v. Scripps-Howard Broadcasting Co.*, 433 U.S. 562 (1977).
575. . 805 F.2d 663 (7th Cir. 1986).
576. . *See* e.g., *Hillerich & Bradsby v. Christian Brothers*, 943 F. Supp. 1136 (D. Minn. 1996) (selling its Pro-Rite hockey blades with the name "Messier" clearly affixed on the blade and product label without the permission of Mark Messier, one of the NHL's most accomplished and recognized players).
577. . *Haelan Labs., Inc. v. Topps Chewing Gum*, 202 F.2d 866 (2d Cir. 1953).
578. . *Vinci v. Am. Can Co.*, 459 N.E.2d 507 (Ohio 1984).
579. . *Shamsky v. Garan, Inc.*, 632 N.Y.S.2d 930 (N.Y. Sup. Ct. 1995).

persona. In *Abdul-Jabbar v. General Motors Corp.*,[580] the Ninth Circuit held that, although such information is newsworthy, an auto manufacturer's use of Lew Alcindor's name and college basketball records in a television advertisement is commercial usage. The auto manufacturer gained a commercial advantage from the advertisement, which attracted the attention of television viewers of the 1993 NCAA men's basketball tournament.

515. Unauthorized usage of an athlete's identity is a necessary element of a claim for misappropriation or infringement of publicity rights. An athlete's consent to the use of his or her identity for commercial purposes may be either express or implied under the circumstances. The nature and scope of such consent is necessarily determined on a case-by-case basis and requires careful contract drafting to delineate which rights are conferred.[581]

516. Available remedies for violation of one's publicity rights are damages and injunctive relief.[582] In 2015, a Chicago, Illinois jury awarded Michael Jordan USD 8.9 million in damages for violation of his right of publicity by Dominick's, a Chicago grocery store chain that ran an ad with a coupon for discounts on steaks in a Sports Illustrated commemorative issue recognizing his induction into the pro basketball hall of fame.

I. First Amendment Limitations

517. The First Amendment of the United States Constitution limits the protection of publicity rights under state law. In *Titan Sports, Inc. v. Comics World Corp.*,[583] the Second Circuit explained there is an "inherent tension between the protection of an individual's right to control the use of his likeness and the constitutional guarantee of free dissemination of ideas, images, and newsworthy matter in whatever form it takes." Courts have struggled to draw the line between unauthorized commercial use of one's identity that may be prohibited by state law and communicative or expressive use protected by the First Amendment.

---

580. . 85 F.3d 407 (9th Cir. 1996). *See also Jordan v. Jewel Food Stores, Inc.*, 743 F.3d 509 (7th Cir. 2014) (grocery store ad in magazine issue congratulating former player on induction into pro basketball hall of fame is commercial speech subject to right of publicity claim). But *see Jordan v. Jewel Food Stores, Inc.*, 83 F. Supp. 3d 761 (N.D. Ill. 2015) (grocery store ad does not necessarily satisfy the "commercial purpose" element of the Illinois Right of Publicity Act as a matter of law, which defines it as "the public use or holding out of an individual's identity (i) on or in connection with the offering for sale or sale of a product, merchandise, goods, or services; (ii) for purposes of advertising or promoting products, merchandise, goods, or services; or (iii) for the purpose of fundraising").

581. . *See* , e.g., *Cepeda v. Swift & Co.*, 415 F.2d 1205 (8th Cir. 1969); *O'Brien v. Pabst Sales Co.*, 124 F.2d 167 (5th Cir. 1941); *Sharman v. C. Schmidt & Sons, Inc.*, 216 F. Supp. 401 (E.D. Pa. 1963); *Andretti v. Rolex Watch U.S.A., Inc.*, 437 N.E.2d 264 (N.Y. 1982).

582. *See* generally Laura L. Stapleton and Matt McMurphy, *The Professional Athlete's Right of Publicity*, 10 Marq. Sports L. Rev. 23, 53–62 (1999).

583. . 870 F.2d 85, 88 (2d Cir. 1989).

518. In *Zacchini v. Scripps-Howard Broadcasting, Inc.*,[584] the U.S. Supreme Court held that the media's right to report newsworthy events does not permit the unauthorized broadcast of a performer's entire act, which threatens harm to its economic value. A local Ohio television station sent a news crew to film the act of Hugo Zacchini, the "human cannonball," who was performing at a county fair. This was done despite Zacchini's request that his performance not be filmed. His entire fifteen-second performance was shown on the evening news. The Supreme Court ruled that showing his entire act is not permitted by the First Amendment's protection of news reporting. The television station's broadcast is not protected by the US Constitution, because it reduces the commercial value of Zacchini's entertainment product and corresponding economic incentive to produce his performance.

519. The *Zacchini* case is notable, not for the clarity of its line-drawing, but for its clear demonstration that such line-drawing regarding the scope of First Amendment protections is one that is often difficult and likely to be criticized, whatever the result reached. When the usage of an athlete's identity moves from the purely commercial, as is most likely the case in the advertising or sale of a product, to more of a mixed medium—such as films, television, radio, newspapers and other literary works—the more likely that First Amendment issues will arise.

520. It is important to recognize another aspect of the First Amendment's influence on the development of privacy and publicity rights. At times, the nature and scope of protectable publicity rights are defined by state law in such manner as to avoid violating the First Amendment. For example, New York's right of publicity statute defines illegal commercial misappropriation as use "for advertising purposes or for the purposes of trade."[585] New York courts have held that the unauthorized use of athlete's names and photos in publications, even though done for profit, are not for "purposes of trade."[586] In other words, such activity falls outside the basic definition of the tort, thereby avoiding any potential conflict with the First Amendment. The California publicity statute is even more explicit and provides: "For purposes of this section, a use of a name, voice, signature, photograph, or likeness in connection with any news, public affairs, or sports broadcast or account, or any political campaign, shall not constitute a use for which consent is required."[587]

521. The media may use a celebrity's name, photograph, and other aspects of his or her identity in connection with truthful news reporting. The First Amendment immunizes the media from state law liability for infringement of publicity rights, even though media publications and broadcasts usually are for-profit commercial activity. Courts generally extend constitutional protection to media republications of news

---

584. . 433 U.S. 562 (1977).

585. . N.Y. Civ. Rights Law §§ 50–51.

586. . *See* , e.g., *Finger v. Omni Publ'ns Int'l, Ltd.*, 566 N.E.2d 141 (N.Y. 1977); *Koussevitsky v. Allen, Towne & Heath, Inc.*, 68 N.Y.S.2d 779 (N.Y. Sup. Ct. 1947), *aff'd*, 69 N.Y.S.2d 432 (N.Y. App. Div. 1947); *Jeffries v. N.Y. Evening Journal Publ'g Co.*, 124 N.Y.S. 780 (N.Y. Sup. Ct. 1910).

587. . California Civil Code § 3344(d).

coverage of sporting events and athletic accomplishments even if used for advertising purposes.[588]

522. Historical accounts of player records and accomplishments as well as video depictions of their athletic performances may remain newsworthy despite the passage of time, and the First Amendment protects their usage by third parties. In *Gionfriddo v. Major League Baseball,*[589] a group of retired professional baseball players claimed the unauthorized use of their names and likenesses in for-profit print and video publications providing historical information about MLB players violated their right of publicity. The court found that "[t]he public has an enduring fascination in the records set by former players and in memorable moments from previous games, ... [which] are the standards by which the public measures the performance of today's players." Affirming summary judgment for defendants, it concluded: "Balancing plaintiffs" negligible economic interests against the public's enduring fascination with baseball's past, we conclude that the public interest favoring the free dissemination of information regarding baseball's history far outweighs any proprietary interests at stake."

523. Similarly, in *C.B.C. Distribution and Marketing, Inc, v. Major League Baseball Advanced Media,*[590] the Eighth Circuit ruled that the unauthorized use of MLB players' names and statistics in online fantasy baseball games is protected by the First Amendment. The court explained that "the information used in CBC's fantasy baseball games is all readily available in the public domain, and it would be strange law that a person would not have a first amendment right to use information that is available to everyone." The court found the *Gionfriddo* court's views "persuasive": "recitation and discussion of factual data concerning the athletic performance of [players on MLB's website] command a substantial public interest, and, therefore, is a form of public expression due substantial constitutional protection."

524. In *Cardtoons, L.C. v. Major League Baseball Players Assn.,*[591] the Tenth Circuit recognized a First Amendment parody defense to a right of publicity claim challenging Cardtoons' production of a series of baseball cards lampooning readily identifiable individual MLB players. The court explained:

> Cardtoons' parody trading cards receive full protection under the First Amendment. The cards provide social commentary on public figures, major league baseball

588. . *Montana v. San Jose Mercury News, Inc.*, 34 Cal. App. 4th 790, 40 Cal. Rptr. 2d 639 (Cal. Ct. App. 1995) (newspaper may contemporaneously reproduce a full-page account of the San Francisco Forty-Niners" four Super Bowl victories in the 1990s in poster form for public sale without violating the publicity rights of Joe Montana, the team's quarterback, whose name and likeness appeared therein because these were newsworthy sports events in which he had played a prominent role); *Namath v. Sports Illustrated*, 371 N.Y.S.2d 10 (N.Y. App. Div. 1975), *aff'd*, 352 N.E.2d 584 (N.Y. 1976) (dismissing athlete's right of publicity claim against magazine for using his photograph in advertisements to promote subscriptions).
589. . 94 Cal. App. 4th 400, 114 Cal. Rptr. 2d 307 (Cal. Ct. App. 2001).
590. . 505 F.3d 818 (8th Cir. 2007), *cert. denied*, 553 U.S. 1090 (2008). *See also CBS Interactive Inc., v. National Football League Players Ass'n Inc.*, 259 F.R.D. 398 (D. Minn. 2009) (unauthorized use of NFL players' names and statistics in connection with a fantasy football game does not violate players' publicity rights).
591. . 95 F.3d 959 (10th Cir. 1996).

players, who are involved in a significant commercial enterprise, major league baseball. While not core political speech (the cards do not, for example, adopt a position on the Ken Griffey, Jr., for President campaign), this type of commentary on an important social institution constitutes protected expression.

525. In *ETW v. Jireh Publishing, Inc.*,[592] the Sixth Circuit held that the First Amendment protects a sports artist's freedom of expression to include the likenesses of famous professional athletes (e.g., Tiger Woods and other legendary professional golfers) in a painting commemorating Woods' historic victory in the 1997 Masters Tournament, reprints of which were sold to the public. The court explained that the First Amendment protects expressive materials "including music, pictures, films, photographs, paintings, drawings, engravings, prints, and sculptures," which is not limited even if it is sold. Observing that famous athletes, "through their pervasive presence in the media, have come to symbolize certain ideas and values in our society and have become a valuable means of expression in our culture," the court concluded:

> While the right of publicity allows celebrities like Woods to enjoy the fruits of their labours, here Rush has added a significant creative component of his own to Woods's identity. Permitting Woods's right of publicity to trump Rush's right of freedom of expression would extinguish Rush's right to profit from his creative enterprise.

526. On the other hand, the use of news coverage of an athletic event incorporating an athlete's name or likeness to advertise or sell unrelated products is not constitutionally protected. In *Pooley v. National Hole-in-One Association*,[593] the defendant made a videotape of a professional golfer's hole-in-one and used his name to promote its hole-in-one fund-raising competitions. Denying defendant's motion to dismiss plaintiff's right of publicity claim, the court ruled:

> [W]hile Plaintiff's hole-in-one at the Bay Hill Classic was open to national observation and public videotaping, its subsequent unauthorized reproduction was not automatically privileged simply because the hole-in-one continued to be a newsworthy event. Defendant did not create the videotape in connection with a news account. Defendant did not include Plaintiff's name and videotape footage simply to communicate an idea. It capitalized on Plaintiff's name, reputation, and prestige in the context of an advertisement. The promotional videotape went one step further and implied a false connection between the Plaintiff and its business. The Court finds that the use of Plaintiff's identity was strictly commercial and not protected by the First Amendment.

---

592. . 332 F.3d 915 (6th Cir. 2003).
593. . 89 F. Supp. 2d 1108 (D. Ariz. 2000). *See also Gridiron.com, Inc. v. Nat'l Football League Players Assn., Inc.*, 106 F. Supp. 2d 1309 (S.D. Fla. 2000) (First Amendment does not provide immunity from right of publicity claim arising out of operation of Web site using NFL players' identities for commercial purposes, rather than merely conveying news).

527. Courts have held that the unauthorized use of college and professional athletes' "likenesses in video games may be challenged under state right of publicity laws. In *In re NCAA Student-Athlete Name & Likeness Licensing Litigation,*[594] the Ninth Circuit ruled that EA Sports" usage of former NCAA football and men's basketball players' likenesses in video game avatars without their consent "does not qualify for First Amendment protection as a matter of law because it literally recreates [them] in the very setting in which [they] achieved renown." It determined that EA's conduct did not satisfy the requirements of the "transformative use defense," which is "a balancing test between the First Amendment and the right of publicity based on whether the work in question adds significant creative elements so as to be transformed into something more than a mere celebrity likeness or imitation." The court explained:

> EA is the producer of the NCAA Football series of video games, which allow users to control avatars representing college football players as those avatars participate in simulated games. In NCAA Football, EA seeks to replicate each school's entire team as accurately as possible. Every real football player on each team included in the game has a corresponding avatar in the game with the player's actual jersey number and virtually identical height, weight, build, skin tone, hair color, and home state … . In the 2005 edition of the game, the virtual starting quarterback for Arizona State wears number 9, as did Keller, and has the same height, weight, skin tone, hair color, hair style, handedness, home state, play style (pocket passer), visor preference, facial features, and school year as Keller … . [W]e conclude that EA's use of Keller's likeness does not contain significant transformative elements such that EA is entitled to the defense as a matter of law … . Given that NCAA Football realistically portrays college football players in the context of college football games, the district court was correct in concluding that EA cannot prevail as a matter of law based on the transformative use defense …

528. Similarly, in *Electronic Arts v. Davis,*[595] the Ninth Circuit ruled that the "historic teams" feature in Madden NFL games, which allows gamers to control avatars resembling retired NFL players, is not an "incidental use" protected by the First Amendment because their likenesses are "central to the creation of an accurate virtual simulation of an NFL game."

529. In *In re NCAA Student–Athlete Name & Likeness Licensing Litigation,*[596] a California federal district court held that a right of publicity claim by college football and basketball players arising out of the unauthorized use of their images in televised games is not preempted by the First Amendment or Copyright Act and may be recognized in other jurisdictions, although such a claim is not viable under California's statutory right of publicity law. However, the Sixth Circuit subsequently affirmed the dismissal of a claim that "college players have a 'right of publicity' in their names and images

594. . 742 F.3d 1268 (9th Cir. 2013). *See also Hart v. Electronic Arts, Inc.*, 717 F.3d 141 (3d Cir.2013) ("the *NCAA Football* … games at issue … do not sufficiently transform [Hart]'s identity to escape the right of publicity claim").

595. 775 F.3d 1172 (9th Cir. 2013), *cert. denied*, 136 S. Ct. 1448 (2016).

596. 990 F. Supp. 2d 996 (N.D. Cal. 2013).

as they might appear in television broadcasts of football or basketball games in which the plaintiffs participate," characterizing it as "a legal fantasy" under Tennessee law.[597] Most courts have ruled that the Copyright Act preempts athletes' claims that unauthorized telecasts of games or athletic competitions in which they participated violates their publicity rights.[598]

---

597. *Marshall v. ESPN, Inc.*, 111 F. Supp. 3d 815 (M.D. Tenn. 2015), *aff'd*, 2016 WL 4400358 (6th Cir. 2016).

598. See e.g., *Dryer v NFL*, 814 F.3d 938 (8th Cir. 2016); *Ray v. ESPN, Inc.*, 783 F.3d 1140 (8th Cir. 2015); *Baltimore Orioles, Inc. v. Major League Baseball Players Assn.*, 805 F.2d 663 (7th Cir. 1986); *Somerson v. McMahon*, 956 F. Supp. 2d 1345 (N.D. Ga. 2012). See also *Baiul v. NBC Sports*, 118 USPQ2d 1641 (S.D.N.Y. 2016) (figure skater's state law accounting, unjust enrichment, and conversion claims based on allegation that she has been deprived of royalties to which she is entitled based on television broadcaster's use and exploitation of motion picture recordings of her performance are preempted by the Copyright Act).

Part III. Doping and Sport

Chapter 1. Introduction

530. The Executive Summary, *What Sport Means in America: A Study of Sport's Role in Society*, a 2010 research report commissioned by the USADA, states:

> Ethics violations and the desire to win at all costs threaten the inherent value of sport in America. A majority of adults (75%) agree that athletes' use of performance-enhancing substances is a violation of ethics in sport. This is further underscored by the fact that Americans rank the use of performance-enhancing drugs as the most serious problem facing sport today, closely followed by the focus on money and the criminal behavior of well known athletes.[599]

531. In the U.S., federal and state laws strictly regulate the usage of controlled substances, including anabolic steroids, which have been federally regulated since 1990. These laws prohibit a physician from prescribing, and a person's usage or possession of, anabolic steroids for the purpose of enhancing athletic performance. Although there currently are no US laws specifically prohibiting or criminalizing "sports doping" (i.e., the impermissible use of drugs by athletes to enhance their sports performance), the federal government recently has taken steps to restrict athletes' access to performance-enhancing drugs to protect their health and safety (particularly youthful ones). To prevent athletes' usage of steroid precursors (the functional equivalent of anabolic steroids after entering the body), which formerly were sold as legal over-the-counter dietary supplements under a 1994 federal law, most steroid precursors now are regulated by the Anabolic Steroid Control Act of 2004.

532. As evidenced by the 2003 Bay Area Laboratory Cooperative (BALCO) grand jury investigation into the illegal sale and distribution of the designer steroid THC and resulting criminal proceedings against the involved individuals, the U.S. government will prosecute those who provide performance-enhancing drugs to athletes for illegal usage. To date, there have been no prosecutions of U.S. athletes for using controlled substances for non-therapeutic purposes in violation of general federal drug laws. However, since 2000, some well-known professional and Olympic sport athletes have been investigated or prosecuted for perjury for lying to federal grand juries or investigators about their usage of anabolic steroids or other controlled substances to enhance their athletic performance (e.g., Marion Jones, Barry Bonds, and Roger Clemens).

599. . *See* www.usada.org/outreach-research/executive-summary.

533. On August 4, 2008 the U.S. ratified the International Convention Against Doping in Sport (Convention), a treaty under the auspices of the United Nations Educational, Scientific, and Cultural Organization, pursuant to which the signatory countries undertake to adopt national anti-doping measures consistent with the WADA Code. Under U.S. law, specific federal legislation is required for the provisions of the Convention adopting the WADA Code to become enforceable domestic law. Thus far, the U.S. Congress has not enacted enabling legislation. Even if it were to do so, the flexible terms of Article 5 of the Convention would not require Congress to compel all U.S. sports leagues and governing bodies to comply with the WADA Code. Because different levels of professional and amateur athletic competition are separately regulated by autonomous governing bodies, there are differing drug testing programs and applicable sanctions for athletes at various levels of sports competition in the U.S.

534. Courts and arbitration panels generally have upheld the legal authority of a U.S. sports league, governing body, or educational institution to randomly drug test athletes subject to its jurisdiction. These tribunals have concluded that protecting the integrity of athletic competition and athletes" health and safety outweighs their legitimate privacy interests that may be infringed by sports drug testing, which authorizes them to condition an athlete's eligibility to participate in competitions under its auspices on compliance with its anti-doping rules. If given appropriate notice and a fair hearing, an athlete who uses banned performance-enhancing substances such as anabolic steroids may be sanctioned appropriately and proportionately for violating these rules.

Chapter 2. Interscholastic Sports

535. For health and safety reasons, the U.S. Supreme Court has upheld mandatory random testing of student-athletes for recreational drugs such as marijuana and cocaine by public high schools. In *Vernonia School Dist. 47J v. Acton,*[600] the Court ruled that a public school district's requirement that all students choosing to participate in interscholastic athletics must agree to submit to random, suspicion-free testing for illegal recreational drugs does not violate the U.S. Constitution. Although student-athletes have legally recognized privacy interests, they have a lessened expectation of privacy and voluntarily subject themselves to greater regulation by choosing to participate in high school sports. As minors, they are entrusted by their parents or guardian to the custodial care of school officials who have a legal duty to protect their health and safety while engaged in interscholastic athletics. The Court held that the school district's legitimate interests in deterring illegal drug use, preventing disruption of the educational process, and protecting minor student-athletes' health outweighed the "not significant" infringement of their privacy, thereby justifying its mandatory random drug testing program.

536. *Vernonia* suggests that steroids testing of interscholastic athletes would not violate the U.S. Constitution.[601] However, very few state high school athletic associations or individual schools currently test for performance-enhancing substances because of the significant costs of testing the thousands of boys and girls who participate in numerous high school sports. In 2006 New Jersey became the first state to institute random steroids testing of high school student-athletes whose schools qualify for state championship games. After spending USD 6 million since February 2008 to randomly test more than 50,000 high school athletes, which resulted in fewer than thirty positive tests, Texas significantly reduced funding for the state's high school drug testing program. In February 2009 Florida's high school drug testing program was eliminated for financial reasons. Florida's pilot program cost the state over USD 100,000 and found only one steroid user among 600 students tested at fifty-three high schools. The Florida High School Athletic Association still maintains a formal policy prohibiting the use of performance-enhancing drugs, but now there is no testing program in place to detect violations. In June 2012, the Illinois High School Association's Board of Directors approved continuation of the association's steroid testing program. Any

600. . 515 U.S. 646 (1995). *See also Board of Education of Indep. Sch. Dist. No. 92 of Pottawatomie County v. Earls*, 536 U.S. 822 (2002) (upholding the constitutionality of mandatory suspicionless drug testing of all students participating in high school extracurricular activities such as the Academic Team, Future Farmers of America, band, choir, pom-pom, cheerleading, and athletics).

601. . However, the Washington Supreme Court subsequently ruled that a similar public high school drug testing program violated the Washington state constitution, which provides stronger legal protection of an individual's privacy rights than the federal constitution. *York v. Wahkiakum School Dist. No. 200*, 178 P.3d 995 (Wash. 2008). But *see Hageman v. Goshen County School Dist. No. 1*, 256 P.3d 487 (Wyo. 2011) (holding that a public school system's policy requiring all students who participate in extracurricular activities to submit to random drug and alcohol testing does not violate the Wyoming constitution, which the court find to be more like the federal constitution than the Washington state constitution).

student who participates in an IHSA-sponsored or sanctioned athletic event is subject to steroids testing.

Chapter 3. Intercollegiate Sports

537. The National Collegiate Athletics Association's drug testing program was initiated in 1986 "[s]o that no one participant might have an artificially induced advantage, so that no one participant might be pressured to use chemical substances in order to remain competitive, and to safeguard the health and safety of participants."[602] The current list of banned substances consists of performance-enhancing drugs, including anabolic steroids and steroid precursors, recreational drugs, and agents that mask drug use. As a condition of being eligible to participate in inter-collegiate athletics at an NCAA member institution, each student-athlete must consent to submit to random, suspicion-free drug testing during all NCAA championships, Division I Football Bowl Series games, and out-of-season (NCAA Divisions I and II only). With approximately 480,000 student-athletes subject to testing, the NCAA's protocol is currently the world's largest sports drug testing program.

538. The NCAA drug testing program provides for strict liability and a one-year suspension from participation in all NCAA sports (along with the loss of one year of intercollegiate athletics eligibility) for the first positive test for a banned substance (rather than the standard two-year or four-year suspension the WADA Code provides the first doping offence). A student-athlete has the right to an administrative appeal before members of the NCAA's Competitive Safeguards and Medical Aspects of Sports Drug Education and Testing Subcommittee. Consistent with the WADA Code, the subcommittee may reduce the standard one-year suspension based on extenuating circumstances. Based on the student-athlete's degree of fault for a doping violation, it may reduce the length of the suspension to one-half season of competition in the particular sport or determine that no suspension is appropriate. A student-athlete under a drug testing suspension from a national or international sports governing body that has adopted the WADA Code is ineligible to participate in NCAA intercollegiate competition for the duration of the suspension even if it exceeds one year, but his or her NCAA eligibility is not otherwise affected.[603]

539. The NCAA is a private association rather than a governmental entity or "state actor."[604] Therefore, it is not subject to the constraints of the U.S. Constitution which prohibit its member public universities from subjecting student-athletes to unreasonable searches (which includes the collection and analysis of bodily fluids to determine the presence of prohibited substances) or otherwise infringing their privacy rights.

540. Courts have rejected student-athletes' state constitutional law challenges to the NCAA's drug testing program. In *Hill v. NCAA*,[605] the California Supreme Court ruled that it is necessary to further the NCAA's legitimate and important objectives of maintaining the integrity of intercollegiate athletics competition and protecting student-athletes' health. The court initially recognized that sports competition requires a "special set of social norms" and that student-athletes "normally and reasonably forgo a measure

602. . Chapter IV, 2013–14 NCAA Drug Testing Program.
603. . NCAA Bylaw 18.4.1.5.3.
604. . *NCAA v. Tarkanian*, 488 U.S. 179 (1988).
605. . 865 P.2d 633 (Cal. 1994).

of their privacy in exchange for the personal and professional benefits of extracurricular activities." It explained:

> A student athlete's already diminished expectation of privacy is outweighed by the NCAA's legitimate regulatory objectives in conducting testing for proscribed drugs. As a sponsor and regulator of sporting events, the NCAA has self-evident interests in ensuring fair and vigorous competition, as well as protecting the health and safety of student athletes. These interests justify a set of drug testing rules reasonably calculated to achieve drug-free athletic competition.

541. Adopting the *Hill* court's reasoning, in *Brennan v. Bd. of Trustees for Univ. of Louisiana Systems*,[606] a Louisiana appellate court held that the NCAA's drug testing program does not violate the Louisiana constitution.

606. . 691 So.2d 324 (La. App. 1997).

Chapter 4. Olympic Sports

542. All U.S. athletes, including college, high school, and professional athletes, who participate in the Olympic Games or other international competitions under the auspices of an international sports federation (IF) that is part of the Olympic Movement are subject to the requirements of the World Anti-Doping Code (WADA Code). Virtually all IFs have adopted and implemented the WADA Code, which applies to their respective U.S. member national governing bodies (NGBs) and U.S. athletes.

543. The WADA Code, which was originally approved in 2003 (with 2009 and 2015 revisions), seeks to harmonize regulations regarding anti-doping across all sports and all countries of the world. It creates a uniform system of drug testing procedures, establishes a strict liability regime, and fixes sanctions for violations, which may be reduced in "exceptional circumstances" if the athlete bears "no fault or no negligence" or "no significant fault or no significant negligence."

544. The United States Anti-Doping Agency (USADA) was formed in 2000 and is an independent private anti-doping agency for Olympic sports in the United States.[607] USADA, which is not subject to the control of the USOC, provides drug education, conducts drug testing of U.S. athletes, investigates positive results, and recommends charges and sanctions for violations. USADA handles the initial adjudication procedure that an IF requires its U.S. member NGB to undertake when a U.S. athlete tests positive for a banned substance.[608]

545. Applying the IF's rules (which are based on the WADA Code), a USADA review board considers written submissions to determine whether there is sufficient evidence of doping to warrant a hearing. If so, USADA proposes doping charges and sanctions against the athlete consistent with the IF's rules. WADA or an IF may challenge USADA's disposition of a doping matter by appealing to the CAS. If the athlete does not accept USADA's proposed sanction, he or she may request a hearing before an American Arbitration Association (AAA) panel (a right provided by the federal Amateur Sports Act because it affects his or her opportunity to participate in "protected competitions"[609]), whose members are also U.S. CAS arbitrators. Special AAA Supplementary Procedures apply to USADA doping arbitrations, including rules that provide the panel with broad discretion to "determine the admissibility, relevance, and materiality of evidence offered" (Rule R-28) and that permit the panel to 'consider the evidence of witnesses by declaration or affidavit'," but shall give it only such weight as [it] deems it entitled to after consideration of any objection made to its

607. . The USADA web site is at http://usantidoping.org.

608. . Prior to 2000, the U.S. athlete's NGB conducted the initial doping investigation and internal adjudication. Externalizing this process through USADA has enhanced the credibility of the U.S.'s Olympic sports anti-doping efforts within the international community and has resulted in the disposition of doping cases in a manner more acceptable to all concerned parties. Anne Benedetti & Jim Bunting, *There's a New Sheriff in Town: A Review of the United States Anti-Doping Agency*, [2003] I.S.L.R. 19 (concluding that "USADA has laid a strong foundation to combat doping at the national level" and "is achieving international and national respect for its commitment to eradicate doping among U.S. athletes").

609. *See* Part II, Ch. 3, supra.

admission" (Rule R-29).[610] In the arbitration proceeding, USADA and the athlete are adverse parties. The IF may observe the proceeding or participate as a party. The athlete, USADA, the IF, or WADA may appeal the AAA arbitration award to the CAS, whose review is de novo and whose decision is final and binding.

546. USADA has adopted an aggressive stance in its efforts to combat doping by U.S. athletes, as illustrated by its investigation and successful proceedings against several athletes for doping offences based on circumstantial evidence of usage of banned substances (i.e., non-analytical positives).[611] These proceedings arose out of federal grand jury indictments of BALCO (a San Francisco Bay Area company that customized supplements for professional athletes), including two of the company's principals, a track coach and a personal trainer, for possession and distribution of anabolic steroids (including THG), human growth hormone, and misbranded drugs to athletes. In 2008, Latasha Jenkins, a sprinter who tested positive for the steroid nandrolone, became the first U.S. athlete to win an arbitration appeal of a USADA doping charge.[612] USADA had prevailed in all thirty-six prior AAA arbitrations.

547. In a widely publicized case, a AAA arbitration panel upheld a USADA doping charge against Floyd Landis, the winner of the 2006 Tour de France bicycle race, based on a French laboratory's finding of exogenous testosterone in his urine. Although Landis proved that the French lab deviated from the international standards for laboratory analysis, USADA proved to the comfortable satisfaction of the panel that the lab's departure from the standards did not cause the positive test results.[613] In its review of the AAA award based on Landis's appeal, a CAS panel unanimously agreed and awarded USADA USD 100,000 in costs, to be paid by Landis, because, all he proved were "some minor procedural imperfections" by the French lab and all his multiple defenses were "unfounded" and "barely arguable."

548. Armstrong v. Tygart,[614] arose out of USADA's July 2012 charges that Lance Armstrong, although he had not tested positive for a banned substance, had committed several anti-doping rule violations including use or attempted use of EPO, blood transfusions, testosterone, corticosteroids, and masking agents. USADA also alleged that Armstrong possessed banned substances, engaged in their trafficking, and had been involved in a doping conspiracy with five others beginning in January 1998 and continuing until he retired from cycling in 2009. It sought to invalidate all of his

610. . *Jacobs v. USA Track & Field*, 374 F.3d 85 (2d Cir. 2004) (rejecting athlete's petition to compel arbitration pursuant to AAA Commercial Rules).

611. . *See* , e.g., *USADA v. Kirk* O'Bee, AAA Award No. 77 190 00515 09 JENF (Oct. 1, 2010) (finding violation of UCI anti-doping rules based on athlete's admissions and email communications); *USADA v. Tim Montgomery*, CAS 2004/O/645 (Dec. 13, 2005) (finding a violation of the IAAF's anti-doping rules based on sprinter Tim Montgomery's admission to fellow sprinter Kelli White that he had used prohibited substances); *USADA v. Michelle Collins*, AAA No. 30 190 00658 04 (Dec. 10, 2004) (despite not testing positive for any banned substances, sprinter Michelle Collins found guilty of doping through the use of prohibited substances and techniques for more than a year').

612. . *USADA v. Latasha Jenkins*, AAA 30 190 00199 07 (Jan. 25, 2008) (because the mandatory international standard for laboratory operations requiring that tests be run by two different scientists was violated, USADA was unable to rely on laboratory's positive findings).

613. . *USADA v. Landis*, AAA 30 190 00847 06 (Sep. 20, 2007).

614. . 886 F. Supp.2d 572 (W.D. Tex. 2012).

competition results from August 1, 1998 (including his seven Tour de France cycling titles) to the present and to impose a lifetime period of ineligibility for future competitions sanctioned by sports governing bodies that are signatories to the WADA Code.

549. The court rejected Armstrong's allegations that USADA's arbitration procedures violated his federal constitutional due process rights. Acknowledging "it is very possible" that USADA is not a state actor, and therefore not subject to the constraints of the federal constitution, the court concluded that "the USADA arbitration rules, which largely follow those of the American Arbitration Association (AAA) are sufficiently robust to satisfy the requirements of due process."

550. Observing that "Armstrong is asking a court of the United States to decide matters which are designed to be resolved by, and with direct input from, members of the international community," the court ruled that it lacked subject matter jurisdiction over Armstrong's state common law due process and tortious interference with contract claims:

> The Court agrees … that federal courts should not interfere with an amateur sports organization's disciplinary procedures unless the organization shows wanton disregard for its rules, to the immediate and irreparable harm of a plaintiff, where the plaintiff has no other available remedy. To hold otherwise would be to turn federal judges into referees for a game in which they have no place, and about which they know little.[615]

551. Armstrong then refused to participate in the USADA arbitration process. On October 10, 2012, USADA published its 200-page "reasoned decision" with numerous exhibits, including testimony from eleven of Armstrong's former U.S. Postal Service cycling teammates, detailing its evidence that Armstrong was the central figure in the "most sophisticated, professionalized and successful doping program that sport has ever seen" and imposed the foregoing sanctions. After reviewing USADA's report, the Union Cycliste Internationale (UCI), the international governing body for cycling, recognized these sanctions.

552. U.S. courts will enforce a valid CAS doping award against a U.S. athlete (which is a Swiss arbitration award regardless of where the arbitration occurred) and preclude re-litigation of its merits in subsequent litigation. In *Slaney v. International Amateur Athletic Association*,[616] the Seventh Circuit refused to permit U.S. middle-distance runner Mary Decker Slaney to re-litigate claims against the IAAF arising out of her positive result for exogenous testosterone based on the IAAF's use of a test showing her ratio of testosterone to epitestosterone (T/E ratio) exceeded the permissible 6:1 maximum level. An IAAF arbitration panel in London had previously rejected

615. . *See also Graham v. USADA*, 2011 WL 1261321 (E.D.N.C.) (court lacks jurisdiction over coach's claims against USADA challenging his lifetime suspension from coaching Olympic athletes in amateur sports).

616. . 244 F.3d 580 (7th Cir.), *cert. denied*, 534 U.S. 828 (2001). *See also Gatlin v. U.S. Anti-Doping Agency, Inc.*, 2008 WL 2567657 (N.D. Fla. 2008) at *1 ("Pursuant to the United Nations Convention on the Recognition and Enforcement of Foreign Arbitral Awards (New York Convention), claims that have been properly submitted to arbitration and ruled upon by entities such as CAS are barred from re-litigation in this forum").

these same claims. The court ruled that the United Nations Convention on the Recognition and Enforcement of Foreign Arbitral Awards[617] (New York Convention), a treaty to which the U.S. is a signatory, barred Slaney's subsequent state law claims against the IAAF. The court determined that Slaney was given a fair opportunity to present her legal claims in the IAAF arbitration proceeding, that the IAAF arbitration award was valid, and that none of the New York Convention's defenses to enforcement of a foreign arbitration award were applicable. Concluding that Slaney's lawsuit seeks to re-litigate the identical issues decided by a foreign arbitration panel in violation of New York Convention, the court stated: "Our judicial system is not meant to provide a second bite at the apple for those who have sought adjudication of their disputes in other forums and are not content with the resolution they received."

617. . 9 U.S.C. §201.

Chapter 5. Professional Sports

§1. Team Sports

553. Two major issues differentiate the legal framework governing drug testing in professional team sports as contrasted with high school, college, and Olympic sports. First, professional sports leagues and associations are private in nature. There are no public professional sports leagues, in contrast to public universities and public school systems. Thus, the U.S. Constitution does not constrain professional sports drug testing programs because no governmental or state action is involved.[618]

554. Second, drug testing programs, which are terms and conditions of employment, are mandatory subjects of collective bargaining that generally require the agreement of the players union before they may be lawfully implemented. Unlike the U.S. governing bodies for Olympic, college, and non-unionized team or individual performer professional sports, MLB and the NBA, WNBA, MLS, NFL, and NHL must comply with federal labor law, which prohibits them from unilaterally impose a drug testing program on their players before collectively bargaining with their respective players union to impasse.[619]

555. Players unions often are as concerned about the effects of drug testing programs on their members' privacy and economic interests as protecting their health and safety. Because of pressure from their member athletes and their agents, players unions historically have been reluctant to agree to random drug testing of players without reasonable suspicion of performance-enhancing or recreational drug usage and severe sanctions for even the inadvertent the usage of banned substances. A great deal is at stake in economic terms, certainly more so than at the interscholastic and intercollegiate levels, and usually more than at the Olympic level of athletic competition. A suspension imposed for non-compliance with a league's drug testing program may cost a professional athlete thousands or even millions of dollars in lost salary, bonuses, and endorsement opportunities.

556. As part of the BALCO grand jury investigation into the illegal sale and distribution of the designer steroid THC, several prominent MLB players were called to testify before the U.S. Congress in December 2003 regarding whether they used anabolic steroids to enhance their athletic performance. In the wake of this scandal, President George Bush, in his 2004 State of the Union Address, urged professional sports leagues to voluntarily adopt more stringent drug policies that will effectively eliminate steroid usage and set a better example for America's youth.

557. In 2005, the U.S. Congress held extensive hearings regarding performance-enhancing drug use by professional athletes and proposed federal legislation that would establish a uniform random drug testing policy for professional athletes, with substantial fines imposed on professional sports leagues and organizations for failing to implement and comply with this policy. Faced with this threatened stringent federal legislation,

---

618. . *Long v. National Football League*, 66 F. 3d 311 (3rd Cir. 1994).

619. . *See* Part II, Ch. 4, §2, I, A.

the major professional leagues and their respective players unions reached agreements establishing more extensive drug testing programs and stiffer penalties for usage of banned substances. Each league's drug testing program is subject to renegotiation when its current CBA expires.

558. A 2013 survey of Americans found that "63% of the public believe steroid use is a big problem among professional athletes" in comparison to 46% and 17% believing it is "big problem" for college and high school athletes, respectively.[620]

I. MLB Drug Policy

559. Historically, several MLB commissioners attempted to deal with players' usage of recreational drugs (e.g., cocaine) without agreement by the MLB Players Association. Because of concerns about player privacy and the reliability of drug testing, the players union was reluctant to agree to widespread drug testing and successfully challenged the commissioner's disciplinary action against players for recreational drug usage.[621] Therefore, drug testing programs applicable to MLB players historically were very minimal unless based on their union's voluntary acquiescence. However, the MLB commissioner unilaterally instituted drug testing programs for minor league players (who are not unionized) as well as MLB club managers and coaches (management officials who not permitted to unionize under federal labor law).

560. In January 2005, in response to proposed federal legislation, MLB and the players union agreed to a comprehensive system of enhanced penalties for steroid and methamphetamines usage. First-time offenders now face an eighty-game suspension for testing positive for the use of banned performance-enhancing substances and are ineligible to play in the postseason for the year in which the suspension ends. This rises to a season-long 162 game suspension for a second positive test, and a lifetime ban for a third. The sanctions are more severe if a player is criminally convicted of possession or distribution of steroids. An arbitrator may reduce a suspension for a first or second violation by up to 50% if a player proves by "clear and convincing evidence" that a positive test was not caused by his "significant fault or negligence" except for the use of defined muscle-building substances.

561. MLB has expanded its drug testing program to include testing for human growth hormone (HGH). Major League Baseball previously had unilaterally implemented random blood testing to detect HGH usage by minor league baseball players, but under the new CBA, beginning with the 2012 season, all MLB players are to be tested for HGH during Spring Training and are otherwise subject to testing "for reasonable cause" throughout the year. Beginning with the offseason following the 2012 season, all major league players are to be subject to random, unannounced testing.

---

620. . The American Public's Perception of Illegal Steroid Use: A National Survey at 9 (2013) available at https://www.umb.edu/editor_uploads/images/centers_institutes/center_social_development_education/SteroidReport_000.pdf.

621. . *See* , e.g., In the Matter of Arbitration Between Major Baseball Players Association (Steve Howe) and Fay Vincent, Commissioner of Baseball (1992); In the Matter of Arbitration Between Major Baseball Players Association (Pascual Perez) and Bowie Kuhn, Commissioner of Baseball (1992).

562. In 2011, Barry Bonds, MLB's all-time home run leader, was tried for perjury and obstruction of justice in relation to a governmental investigation of steroid use in MLB. Several years earlier, federal authorities had seized drug testing information for approximately 100 MLB players who tested positive for performance-enhancing drugs in 2003, reportedly including Bonds, David Ortiz, Manny Ramirez, Alex Rodriguez, and Sammy Sosa. The Ninth Circuit held that the seizure violated the players' federal constitutional rights,[622] and as a result, federal authorities were ordered to return the seized information to the MLBPA for destruction. The government, however, was permitted to retain Bonds' positive test results, and those results were presented at his 2011 trial as evidence that his performance-enhancing drug use denials were false. Ultimately, a San Francisco jury convicted Bonds of obstruction of justice, but it failed to reach a verdict on the perjury charges. Although Bonds was found guilty of obstructing justice, he never admitted knowingly using performance enhancing drugs and has not been sentenced to any jail time.

563. MLB Roger Clemens was prosecuted twice by federal prosecutors for perjury and obstruction of justice. The first case against him, brought in 2011, ended in a mistrial on the second day of testimony due to a prosecutorial error. Prosecutors tried Clemens again in 2011, and he was acquitted of all charges.

564. During the months between Clemens' two 2011 trials, National League MVP Ryan Braun was suspended for fifty games because of a positive drug test revealing he had an extremely high testosterone-to-epitestosterone level, but his suspension was overturned because MLB's drug testing protocol was not followed.

565. In 2013, another MLB performance-enhancing drug scandal erupted. After a lengthy investigation and lawsuit against him and his company, MLB persuaded Anthony Bosch, the founder of the Biogenesis "anti-aging" clinic located in Coral Gables, Florida to "turn over a cache of material, including emails, ledgers and phone records, that allegedly confirmed ballplayers were doping."[623] Several MLB players were suspended for fifty games. After being confronted with substantial evidence that he had used performance enhancing drugs, Ryan Braun admitted his PED use and was suspended for sixty-five games. MLB suspended New York Yankees superstar Alex Rodriguez for 211 games, but he played the rest of the 2013 season after appealing to an arbitrator, who ultimately reduced his suspension to 162 games covering the 2014 season.

II. NBA Drug Policy

566. The initial steps taken in the NBA to curb player usage of recreational drugs were tentative, even though there were perceptions that drug usage, particularly cocaine, was at epidemic proportions in the early 1980s. The 1983 NBA CBA provided only for player drug testing when there was reasonable cause, not the mandatory random testing of all players sought by the NBA. However, it did provide for graduated

622. . *U.S. v. Comprehensive Drug Testing, Inc.*, 621 F.3d 1162 (9th Cir. 2010).

623. . Julie K. Brown, *A-Rod, 12 others suspended in Biogenesis scandal*, Miami Herald, Aug. 6, 2013, http://www.miamiherald.com/2013/08/06/3543980/a-rod-12-others-suspended-in-biogenesis.html.

sanctions and for possible permanent suspension of players guilty of violating the drug policy. In the 1988 drug testing agreement, rookies were added to the list of players to be tested after Len Bias of the University of Maryland, the Boston Celtics' first-round draft pick, died of an overdose of cocaine one day after the 1986 NBA draft. However, it did not require random testing of veteran NBA players, and marijuana was not on the list of prohibited drugs.

567. In general, the NBA's collectively bargained drug policy includes the following provisions:

(1) Prohibited drugs include marijuana, steroids, HGH, amphetamines, cocaine, opiates (such as heroin, codeine, and morphine), and PCP.
(2) Sanctions vary depending on the drug detected in the tests. Steroids and marijuana are separated from the others. In general, the NBA is tougher on "recreational" or "street" drugs than on "performance-enhancing" drugs such as steroids. Marijuana has the lightest penalties, starting with no penalty on the first offence and increasing to five-game suspensions. Steroid use has a five to twenty-five game suspension. All NBA players are subject to three random, unannounced HGH tests annually (two in-season, one off-season), and players will also be subject to reasonable cause testing for HGH. A player's first violation will result in a 20-game suspension, his second violation will result in a 45-game suspension, and his third violation will result in expulsion from the NBA.
(3) Drug testing procedures provide safeguards through a two-sample testing method.
(4) Veteran players can be randomly tested during training camp and at other times for reasonable cause. First-year players are subject to drug testing once during training camp and three times during the regular season. All tests are at the discretion of the appropriate league officials. Players cannot be tested on days during which they have games.

III. WNBA Drug Policy

568. The WNBA has a drug testing program, which is part of the CBA between the league and the NBPA, the union that represents both NBA and WNBA basketball players. AWNBA player's use of steroids is subject to significant fines and penalties, including a USD 1,000-per-day fine if a player enters the WNBA Steroid Program and fails to comply with its dictates. Suspensions for steroids abuse begin with a five-game suspension, then ten games, then one year. If a player has run the gamut of those suspensions, the next step is disqualification for a period of not less than two years, and the player's contract shall be voided. Reinstatement is discretionary after the mandatory two-year suspension.

IV. NFL Drug Policy

569. In 1982, after earlier unilateral actions taken by Commissioner Pete Rozelle in response to the convictions of NFL players Randy Crowder and Don Reese for cocaine possession and distribution, the NFL implemented a regularized drug program through its newly entered CBA. However, the CBA drug testing provisions were limited in their scope, and Commissioner Rozelle unilaterally established additional prohibitions after becoming dissatisfied with their effectiveness. These were challenged by the National Football League Players Association (NFLPA), the players union, in 1986. Arbitrator Sam Kagel agreed that Commissioner Rozelle had the unilateral authority to implement drug policies because the overall problem posed threats to the "integrity of the game," but he held that these policies could not contradict the provisions in the CBA. As a result, if specific drug program issues were not covered in the CBA, Commissioner Rozelle could take unilateral action. At the time, these included such items as which drugs were on the prohibited list and the severity of the sanctions that could be imposed. However, Rozelle's attempts to institute random mandatory testing of all NFL players were held to contradict the CBA and, therefore, were nullified in arbitration.

570. The NFL's drug policies have steadily evolved since 1982, with the 1994 CBA presenting the first truly comprehensive approaches to drug testing, sanctions, and treatment. The major aspects of the NFL's drug testing program under that CBA and as subsequently revised can be summarized as follows:

(1) A first time offence for steroids results a four-game suspension (one-quarter of the sixteen-game NFL season). This sanction was expanded to include ephedra, a dietary supplement, after the 2001 death of NFL player Korey Stringer. For steroids, the sanction is six games for a second offence and one year or more subsequent violations. Recreational drugs (such as marijuana, opiates, PCP, and amphetamines) are dealt with more leniently, with no penalty until the third offence (four-game suspension), and at least a one-year suspension thereafter.
(2) There are also sanctions for alcohol abuse and for drug offences involving criminal prosecutions that result in either a guilty or no-contest plea to criminal charges.
(3) The NFL commissioner has the authority to impose more stringent sanctions if drug trafficking is involved. The standard NFL Player Contract stipulates that the commissioner has the right "to suspend Player for a period certain or indefinitely; and/or to terminate this contract ... " if he "provides other players with stimulants or other drugs for the purpose of attempting to enhance onfield performance."

571. In August 2008, Minnesota Vikings players Kevin Williams and Pat Williams along with New Orleans Saints players Charles Grant, Deuce McAllister, and Will Smith were notified they had tested positive for bumetanide, a prescription diuretic banned because it may mask the presence of steroids. This violation of the NFL's drug testing policy subjected each player to a four-game suspension. During an arbitration hearing before Jeffrey Pash, the NFL's chief legal officer, (the appeals proceeding established by the NFL CBA), the players established that they unknowingly ingested bumetanide as an unlisted ingredient in "StarCaps" weight-loss pills. The players argued that their violations should be excused on grounds that both NFL personnel and Dr. John Lombardo, the independent administrator of the NFL's drug testing policy, knew as early as 2006 that StarCaps might contain bumetanide and that they failed to advise NFL players and team doctors accordingly. On December 2, 2008, Pash upheld the suspensions and reaffirmed the NFL's commitment to strict liability for banned substance violations.

572. Rejecting the players' effort to have their suspensions judicially vacated, a federal district court confirmed the Pash arbitration award on the ground that NFL players are strictly liable for violations of the NFL's collectively bargained drug policy.[624] Although it found the NFL's failure to inform players about the presence of bumetanide in StarCaps was "baffling," the court ruled this did not breach any legal duty the NFL owed to the players. However, the court ruled that the claims of Vikings' players Kevin Williams and Pat Williams that the NFL's drug testing policy and four-game suspensions violated Minnesota's Drug and Alcohol Testing in the Workplace Act (DTAWA) and its Consumable Products Act (CPA), which impose limits on employer drug testing and prohibitions on employee discipline for using a legal substance offsite during non-working hours, are not pre-empted by federal labor law pursuant to which the NFL's drug testing policy was collectively bargained. In *Williams v. NFL*,[625] the Eighth Circuit affirmed the district court's confirmation of the Pash arbitration award and its ruling that the players' DATWA and CPA claims are not pre-empted.

573. A Minnesota appellate court subsequently held that the NFL's drug testing program does not violate Minnesota law.[626] The Minnesota Supreme Court subsequently declined to review the appellate court's decision, thereby ending this lengthy federal and state court litigation and permitting the NFL to impose the original four-game suspensions on the players for violating its drug testing policy. In May 2011, legislation was enacted in Minnesota that effectively precludes Minnesota's employer drug testing laws from interfering with a collectively bargained professional sports league's drug testing program.[627] In September 2011, the NFL imposed two-game suspensions on the four players to be served once the season commenced.

574. In 2012 D.J. Williams, a player for the Denver Broncos, challenged his six-game suspension for attempting to manipulate a urine specimen taken in conjunction with the League's drug policy. He argued that a gap in the chain of custody of the specimen and a failure to collect and handle the specimen in accordance with established protocol violated the integrity of the test, but the league arbitrator upheld the suspension noting that in two previous cases Williams' collected specimens were determined to not be human urine and that all told there existed with respect to Williams' drug tests a "compelling picture of deceit and evasion." Thereafter he unsuccessfully sought to have the arbitrator's decision judicially vacated. Affirming the federal district court's refusal to do so, the Tenth Circuit stated that "a court's role in these types of arbitration cases is simply to determine whether the arbitrator strayed from the collective-bargaining agreement," which it concluded he did not.[628]

---

624. . *NFLPA v. NFL*, 2009 WL 1457007 (D. Minn.).
625. . 582 F.3d 863 (8th Cir. 2009).
626. . *Williams v. NFL*, 794 N.W.2d 391 (Minn. App. 2011).
627. . The provision states that no aspect of DATWA shall "be construed to interfere with the operation of a drug and alcohol testing program if: (1) the drug and alcohol testing program is permitted under a contract between the employer and employees; and (2) the covered employees are employed as professional athletes. Minn. Stat. §181.955(3).
628. . *Williams v. Nat'l Football League*, 495 Fed. Appx. 894 (10th Cir. 2012).

V. NHL Drug Policy

575. The NHL has experienced basically the same union and player reactions to its drug testing proposals as have occurred in MLB. In 1986, reports of widespread cocaine use by NHL players caused then-NHL president John Ziegler and Alan Eagleson, head of the NHL Players Association, to announce a mandatory drug testing program. This was subsequently rejected by the players and never implemented.

576. In 1996, the players union approved a four-step drug testing program that began with in-patient treatment for a first offence and escalated after each subsequent offence to a fourth stage that involves a minimum one-year suspension of a player with no guarantee of reinstatement. The specifics of this program were not set forth in the NHL CBA, and few details regarding its actual operation were released by either the NHL or the players union out of concern for the privacy of the players.

577. The 205 NHL CBA established a substantially different drug testing program, penalties, and the procedures that focuses on performance-enhancing substances. For a first positive test, a player is suspended for twenty games without pay. For a second positive test, the suspension is sixty games without pay. There is also a mandatory referral to the NHL substance abuse program for both a first and second offence. For a third positive test, there is a "permanent" suspension without pay, although the player can reapply for reinstatement after a minimum period of two years, which is a discretionary decision to be made by a special NHL committee. These provisions are essentially the same in the NHL's 2011–2020 CBA.

§2. Individual Performer Sports

578. Individual performer sports such as golf, tennis, and auto racing are not unionized because the players are independent contractors rather than "employees"; therefore, their respective drug testing program may be unilaterally imposed by each sport's governing body (a private entity) rather than being collectively bargained. In recent years, organizations such as the PGA, Ladies PGA, and National Association of Stock Car Racing have adopted random drug testing programs that are internally administered. Thus far, there have been only a few reported positive tests, although some have generated litigation against the sport's governing body.

579. In *Mayfield v. National Stock Car Auto Racing, Inc.*,[629] a federal district court ruled that under Florida law a contractual release signed by professional stock car driver Jeremy Mayfield barred his tort and breach of contract claims against NASCAR arising out of his positive test for methamphetamines, a banned substance. The court also rejected Mayfield's North Carolina Persons With Disabilities Protection Act claim because he is not a NASCAR employee or a "qualified person with disability" as required by the statute.

580. In *Barron v. PGA Tour, Inc.*,[630] the court held that the PGA Tour did not violate a professional golfer's rights under the Americans with Disabilities Act (ADA), a federal law, by suspending him for one year for testing positive for exogenous

629. . 713 F. Supp.2d 527 (W.D. N. C. 2010), *aff'd*, 674 F.3d 369 (4th Cir. 2012).
630. . 670 F. Supp.2d 674 (W.D. Tenn. 2009).

testosterone, a banned substance under its anti-doping program, and refusing to grant him a therapeutic use exemption. Doug Barron alleged he suffers from abnormally low testosterone, a physical disability that causes him to have a reduced sex drive, experience fatigue, and have a compromised immune system, and that by refusing to allow him to take medically prescribed exogenous testosterone and suspending him for using it, the PGA Tour discriminated against him in violation of the ADA.

581. The court concluded that he had not shown a likelihood of success on his claim:

> Barron has not shown that the reasonable accommodation he has requested (allowing him to continue taking exogenous Testosterone) is necessary in order for him to continue playing golf in PGA Tour events. His complaint and post-hearing brief, at most, claim that he needs these Testosterone shots to address specific medical concerns relating to a reduced sex drive, fatigue, and a compromised immune system-not to play golf. While Barron's abnormally low Testosterone may in some way cause him to be a less competitive golfer than he would be if he were permitted to take the Testosterone injections, [the ADA] simply does not provide a remedy under those circumstances.

582. After his suspension ended, the PGA Tour granted Barron a therapeutic use exemption to use testosterone while attempting to qualify for the 2010 PGA Tour, which was based on new medical information he submitted.

583. Singh v. PGA Tour, Inc.[631] arose out of VJ Singh's use of a product called "deer antler spray" to remedy his knee and back problems for approximately one month while he was not golfing on the PGA Tour. Singh instituted an arbitration proceeding to challenge the PGA's initial determination that he committed an anti-doping violation by using the spray and imposition of a sanction, which he discontinued after the PGA ceased its disciplinary action against him. In his subsequent lawsuit asserting several causes of action, he alleged that the PGA inconsistently and recklessly administered its anti-doping program, thereby exposing him to ridicule and humiliation. A New York trial court dismissed his breach of fiduciary duty claim against the PGA because "the nature of the parties" relationship as set forth in the complaint, that of an individual member subject to the oversight of a governing body, does not support the conclusion that [it] was "'under a duty to act for or to give advice for [his] benefit' . . . upon matters within the scope of the relation." However, the court refused to dismiss his breach of the implied covenant of good faith and fair dealing claim because the PGA has a legal duty not to act arbitrarily or irrationally in exercising its contractual discretion under the anti-doping program.

631. 2014 WL 641311 (N.Y. Sup. Ct.).

Part IV. Sports and Commerce

Chapter 1. Legal Protection of Sports Intellectual Property and Sponsorship Rights

584. Sports-related intellectual property rights such as trademarks, service marks, and copyrights generate billions of dollars in annual revenues for professional leagues and clubs, the USOC, and the NCAA as well as universities and high schools that participate in interscholastic athletics. These revenues are derived from various sources, such as the sale of television, radio, and Internet broadcasting rights for sports events; trademark and team logo licensing agreements; and league, team, or event sponsorship deals with advertisers. In addition, popular athletes and coaches license various aspects of their identity, such as their name or photo, to others for commercial purposes, thereby earning a substantial amount of money for endorsing various products and services.

585. Sports event broadcasting rights are a multibillion-dollar source of revenue. For example, the NFL's television contracts with Fox, CBS and NBC that will took effect after the 2013 football season will pay the NFL an average of USD 3.1 billion a year in rights fees over the life of these nine-year deals through 2022. Major League Baseball's television contracts with three media entities (Fox; Turner Sports, specifically TBS; and ESPN) will generate approximately USD 12.4 billion through 2021. In April 2010 the NCAA entered into an agreement with CBS and Turner Sports pursuant to which they will pay almost USD 11 billion for the television rights to the "Final Four" men's basketball tournament for fourteen-years.

586. The licensing and merchandising of sports brands (i.e., trademarks and logos) also generate billions of dollars in aggregate revenues for professional sports leagues, clubs, and organizations, the USOC, and the NCAA and its member universities. The estimated annual value of collegiate sports licensing revenues alone is more than USD 3.5 billion. Plunkett Research estimates that companies and businesses spend approximately USD 35 billion annually for sports-related advertising in the U.S., which includes naming rights and sponsorship of professional, Olympic, and intercollegiate sports events and organizations, professional leagues and their member clubs, colleges and universities, and others.

§1. Sports Sponsorships

587. Arena and stadium naming rights contracts, presenting sponsorships, and other sports sponsorship agreements generate hundreds of millions of dollars in revenue annually for professional sports events, leagues, and clubs,[632] the USOC and its member NGBs, and the NCAA and its member colleges and universities[633] as well as other organizers of athletic events in the U.S.

588. There are voluntary industry and/or legal limits on sports event sponsorships or advertising by producers of alcoholic beverages and tobacco products. The alcoholic beverage industry has adopted voluntary guidelines stating that alcohol advertising and marketing efforts should not be directed to an audience that is primarily underage (i.e., more than 50% of the advertising audience is less than 21 years old, the legal drinking age in the U.S.). A November 1998 Master Settlement Agreement, which settled litigation by private plaintiffs and forty-six states against the major U.S. tobacco companies, prohibits brand name sponsorships of sports events in which the intended audience would have a significant percentage of youths, or any athletic event between opposing teams in any football, basketball, baseball, soccer or hockey league.

589. The federal Bureau of Alcohol, Tobacco, Firearms and Explosives (ATF) has the authority to prohibit false, deceptive, or misleading alcoholic beverage labeling or advertising, but there are no specific prohibitions regarding alcoholic beverage companies' sponsorship of sports events. However, ATF Ruling 95-2 expresses concern that the usage of athletes to endorse alcoholic beverages may create the deceptive or misleading impression that consuming alcohol is conducive to athletic performance (or least does not harm it).[634]

590. The Federal Trade Commission (FTC) has broad authority to protect consumers against "unfair or deceptive acts or practices." To prevent consumer deception, the FTC has promulgated *Guides Concerning the Use of Endorsements and Testimonials in Advertising*,[635] which are applicable to athletes' endorsements of products and services. The *Guides* require that all endorsements "must reflect the honest opinions, findings, beliefs, or experience of the endorser" and must not be otherwise deceptive. An athlete must be a bona fide user of the subject product if the advertisement in which he or she appears represents his or his usage of it.

---

632. . To maximize the revenues from its national sponsorship agreements, which generally are distributed pro rata to its member clubs, a sports league may have exclusive agreements with its official sponsors and corresponding limits on its member clubs' individual sponsorships with other companies. A club that violates league restrictions on its local sponsorship agreements may be liable for breach of contract and fiduciary duty, tortious interference with contractual relationships, and trademark infringement. *See NFL Properties, Inc. v. Dallas Cowboys Football Club, Ltd.*, 922 F. Supp. 849 (S.D.N.Y. 1996).

633. . Sports sponsorship payments to universities and organizers of intercollegiate sports events such as the NCAA and college football bowl games, which generally are structured as non-profit entities, may be tax deductible. *See* James L. Musselman, Recent Federal Income Tax Issues Regarding Professional and Amateur Sports, *13 Marq. Sports L. Rev.* 195, 203–208 (2003).

634. . *See* generally Michael Devlin, *Alcohol-Endorsing Athletes Can Join Joe Camel and the Marlboro Man on the Bench*, 27 Ent. & Sport L. 15 (2009).

635. . 16 C.F.R. Part 255.

§2. TRADEMARKS, LOGOS, AND OTHER IDENTIFYING SPORTS INSIGNIA

I. Trademark Infringement and Unfair Competition

591. Common law trademark and service mark rights are acquired by first usage of a name, logo, or other symbol to identify one's products or services and to distinguish them from those of others. In *White v. Board of Regents of University of Nebraska at Lincoln,*[636] the court determined that a university acquired rights in "Husker Authentics" by virtue of its first use of this mark in connection with the advertising and sale of products to season ticket holders, alumni, and boosters. Professor Thomas McCarthy observes that "the exclusive 'property' right of a trademark is defined by consumer perception."[637] In other words, the nature and scope of one's property interest in a trademark generally is only the right to prevent consumer confusion. As the Seventh Circuit explained: "the trademark laws exist not to 'protect' trademarks, but … to protect the consuming public from confusion, concomitantly protecting the trademark owner's right to a non-confused public."[638]

592. A sports team's name functions as a trademark and/or a service mark by virtue of public association of that name with a particular team. Sports team names generally are either inherently distinctive or have acquired "secondary meaning," therefore entitling them to trademark protection. An inherently distinctive mark is one that is coined or arbitrary in relation to the goods or services it identifies such as "Miami Dolphins" for an NFL club, or suggestive of the club's desired characteristics such as "Tennessee Titans."[639] As one court explained, "Secondary meaning is the consuming public's understanding that the mark, when used in context, refers, not to what the descriptive word ordinarily describes, but to the particular business that the mark is meant to identify."[640] Courts have recognized that the popularity of NFL football combined with its extensive media coverage and advertising creates a public association of its team names with its member clubs,[641] which also is true of any of the other US major professional leagues. Sports team logos such as the Oakland Raiders" pirate and The Ohio State University's "Brutus Buckeye" function as trademarks that identify

636. . 614 N.W.2d 330 (Neb. 2000).

637. . 1 J.T. Mccarthy, McCarthy on Trademarks and Unfair Competition (4th ed.), § 2:14 (West 2012).

638. . *James Burrough, Ltd. v. Sign of the Beefeater, Inc.*, 540 F.2d 266, 276 (7th Cir. 1976).

639. . *See In re WNBA Enterprises LLC*, 70 U.S.P.Q.2d 1153 (TTAB 2003) (finding "Orlando Miracle" to be an inherently distinctive mark for Women's National Basketball Association club in Orlando).

640. . *Md. Stadium Auth. v. Becker*, 806 F. Supp. 1236, 1241 (D. Md. 1992) (finding that public identifies "Camden Yards" with a Baltimore baseball stadium).

641. . *NFL Properties, Inc. v. N.J. Giants, Inc.*, 637 F. Supp. 507 (D. N. J. 1986).

particular teams. Distinctive helmet and uniform designs and colors also can function as trademarks.[642]

593. Trademark rights exist indefinitely as long as the mark continues to be used and serves these functions.[643] However, such rights are lost if usage of the mark to identify, advertise, or promote the seller's goods and services is discontinued.

594. The Lanham Act[644] provides nationwide legal protection for federally registered trademarks. Federal registration provides prima facie evidence of the registrant's ownership and exclusive right to use of the mark for the subject goods or services as well as the validity of the registration. Legal proceedings to prevent and remedy infringement of federally registered marks may be brought in federal courts. It permits the filing of an "intent to use application" for a mark, which "shall constitute constructive use of the mark, conferring a right of priority, nationwide in effect, on or in connection with the goods or services specified in the registration" if it is subsequently federally registered.[645] The applicant generally must adopt and use the mark in connection with the described goods or services within two years after filing of the application.

595. Infringement of the prior user's rights occurs if another's use of the same or similar mark creates a likelihood of consumer confusion regarding the source, affiliation, endorsement, or sponsorship of sports-related products or services. For example, in *Champions Golf Club, Inc. v. Champions Golf Club, Inc.*,[646] the court found a likelihood of consumer confusion regarding the (non-existent) affiliation between two independently owned and operated golf courses located in Nicholasville, Kentucky, and Houston, Texas that were concurrently using the "Champions" mark.

A. Name of Sports Team or Event

596. Courts have held that a professional sports club retains the right to continue using its name with a different geographical identifier if it relocates to another city. In *Johnny Blastoff, Inc. v. L.A. Rams Football, Co.*,[647] the Seventh Circuit held that the NFL's Los Angeles Rams club retained its rights to continue using "Rams" to identify the team name although it was relocating to St. Louis. Observing that the franchise was founded in 1937 as the Cleveland Rams, it moved to become the Los Angeles

642. . *Bd. of Supervisors of the La. State Univ. v. Smack Apparel Co.*, 550 F.3d 465 (5th Cir. 2008) (finding that well-known and long-used color schemes, logos and designs identify university's sports teams); *Dallas Cowboys Cheerleaders, Inc. v. Pussycat Cinema, Ltd.*, 604 F.2d 200, 204 n. 5 (2nd Cir. 1979) (finding trademark rights in uniform "universally recognized as the symbol of the Dallas Cowboys Cheerleaders").

643. . *Boston Prof'l Hockey Assn. v. Dallas Cap & Emblem Mfg., Inc.*, 510 F.2d 1004, 1011 (5th Cir. 1975) ("[T]here is no reason why trademarks should ever pass into the public domain by the mere passage of time.").

644. . 15 U.S.C. § 1051, et seq.

645. 15 U.S.C. §1057(c).

646. . 78 F.3d 1111 (6th Cir. 1996).

647. . 188 F.3d 427 (7th Cir. 1999). *See also Indianapolis Colts, Inc. v. Metropolitan Baltimore Football Club Ltd Ptshp*, 34 F.3d 410 (7th Cir. 1994) ("A professional sports team is like Heraclitus's river: always changing, yet always the same. [T]he record discloses there is as much institutional continuity between the Baltimore Colts of 1984 and the Indianapolis Colts of 1994 as there was between the Baltimore Colts of 1974 and the Baltimore Colts of 1984.").

Rams in 1946, and was again moving to become the St. Louis Rams in 1995, the court concluded: "[T]he Rams organization and the NFL had a long-established priority over the use of the 'Rams' name in connection with the same professional football team, regardless of urban affiliation."

597. Legal considerations aside, business reasons may justify treating the favorable goodwill developed by a popular local sports franchise over the years as "a non-transportable cultural institution." For example, the NFL decided to leave the "Browns" identity in Cleveland when the franchise relocated to Baltimore in 1996. The franchise formerly named the "Cleveland Browns" established a new identity as the "Baltimore Ravens." The NFL expansion club that began playing in Cleveland in 1999 is named the "Cleveland Browns."

598. However, the use of the same mark by different teams, even if playing the same sport, does not inevitably create a likelihood of consumer confusion. Rather, a fact-specific inquiry must be made on a case-by-case basis. In *Harlem Wizards Entertainment Basketball, Inc. v. NBA Properties, Inc.*,[648] the court held that a NBA club's proposed name change to the "Washington Wizards" would not infringe a "show basketball" team's prior use of "Harlem Wizards." Unlike the Washington NBA club, the Harlem club is not a competitive sports team that plays in a professional league. The Harlem Wizards combine trick basketball and comedic basketball in a form of entertainment similar to that of the world famous Harlem Globetrotters. Although the Harlem club has the right to use "Wizards" for its entertainment services, the court concluded that the NBA club's concurrent use of the same mark will not create a likelihood of confusion among basketball fans. The teams do not compete with each other for fan patronage. The Harlem club markets its games to event organizers at high schools, colleges, and charitable organizations through direct mail, trade shows, and trade magazines; whereas, the NBA club advertises its games directly to fans. Survey results evidenced that consumer familiarity with the Harlem Wizards team "is almost non-existent." There is a significant disparity between the parties' respective ticket prices, and the court found "it unlikely that consumers will attend a Harlem Wizards" game expecting to see NBA basketball or purchase NBA tickets expecting to see the Harlem Wizards perform show basketball."

B. Unauthorized Affixation of Sports Team Mark to Merchandise

599. US consumers annually purchase billions of dollars' worth of merchandise bearing the names and logos of their favorite teams. In *National Football League Properties, Inc. v. Consumer Enterprises, Inc.*,[649] the court observed that the NFL's "trademarks are associated with highly successful football teams that enjoy tremendous notoriety. Through the extensive licensing arrangements developed and perpetuated

648. . 952 F. Supp. 1084 (D. N. J. 1997).

649. . 26 Ill. App.3d 814, 327 N.E.2d 242, 246 (Ill. App. 1975). *See also Univ. Bookstore v. Bd. of Regents of the Univ. of Wis. Sys.*, 33 U.S.P.Q.2d 1385, 1405 (TTAB 1994) ("[T]he mark of a university on clothing can signify that the university endorses and licenses the sale of such wearing apparel by the manufacturer. … It is a question of fact as to whether consumers view such indicia as "merely ornamental" or as symbols that identify a secondary source of sponsorship.").

by [the NFL] and its licensees, the buying public has come to associate the trademark with the sponsorship of the NFL or the particular member team involved." It concluded "that the trademarks of the teams copied by defendant indicate sponsorship or origin in addition to their ornamental value."

600. Major professional leagues such as the NFL, NBA, NHL, and MLB currently market, license, and enforce their clubs' trademark rights collectively through a central league operated entity.[650] Similarly, many NCAA member universities now utilize Collegiate Licensing Company, a private company, to market and license their respective marks for use by third parties.

601. To avoid weakening valuable trademark rights that may be licensed and generate substantial revenues, professional teams and educational institutions must carefully monitor unauthorized third party usage of their trademarks and take timely, necessary steps to prevent infringement of its marks. The affirmative defense of laches may bar or limit monetary recovery for infringement if a mark owner's delay in asserting its trademark rights prejudices an infringer that detrimentally relied on such inaction. In *University of Pittsburgh v. Champion Product, Inc.*,[651] the court ruled that a university's thirty-six-year delay in objecting to unauthorized sale of clothing and novelty items bearing its name and panther mascot barred an accounting for past infringement, but not an injunction against future unauthorized use.

602. Under the Lanham Act or similar state laws, a "likelihood of confusion" must be shown to prove trademark infringement or unfair competition. The existence of actual confusion of consumers is a factor to be considered, but is not a required element. In *Board of Governors of the University of North Carolina v. Helpingstine*,[652] the court observed:

> While cases have indicated at one extreme that an alleged infringer's use of a mark with the knowledge that the public will be aware of the mark's origin is enough to establish likelihood of confusion, ... and at the other that likelihood of confusion occurs only where there would be confusion as to the origin of the goods themselves, ... the majority of courts have taken the middle ground on this issue. This middle position, which both parties recognize in this case, is that the requisite likelihood of confusion will exist where there is likelihood of confusion as to source, sponsorship or endorsement of the goods.

603. Several factors, in addition to others, are relevant in determining whether the unauthorized usage of a sports team mark creates a likelihood of confusion:

> The degree of similarity between the owner's mark and the alleged infringing mark; the strength of the owner's mark; the price of the goods and other factors indicative of the care and attention expected of consumers when making a purchase; the length of time the defendant has used the mark without evidence

650. . *See* Part I, Ch. 5, §3, I, D *supra* , for a discussion of antitrust law challenges to a professional league's exclusive control and licensing of its member clubs' trademarks.
651. . 686 F.2d 1040 (3d. Cir. 1982), *cert. denied*, 495 U.S. 1087 (1982).
652. . 714 F. Supp. 167, 172 (M.D. N.C. 1989).

of actual confusion; the intent of the defendant in adopting the mark; and the evidence of actual confusion.[653]

604. Whether the requisite likelihood of confusion exists is a question of fact decided on a case-by-case basis. Examples of infringement include: unauthorized use of "St. Louis Rams" for a fictional, cartoon sport team;[654] advertising Coors beer as "Official Beer of the NFL Players" without NFL's permission;[655] unauthorized use of "Boston Marathon" to sell T-shirts;[656] use of University of Georgia bulldog mark and logo portraying an English bulldog for "Battlin" Bulldog Beer";[657] unauthorized use of golf club manufacturers' marks on counterfeit golf equipment;[658] and unauthorized use of Auburn University's trademarks on six-finger foam hands.[659] In contrast, defendants' unauthorized use of "The Brooklyn Dodger" for its Brooklyn, New York, restaurants was found not to infringe the Los Angeles Dodgers mark for a MLB club because it did not create any likelihood of consumer confusion.[660]

605. In addition to trademark infringement and unfair competition, the intentional and unauthorized use of a mark known to be "identical with, or substantially indistinguishable from" a federally registered mark that creates a likelihood of confusion constitutes trademark counterfeiting,[661] which may enable the mark owner to recover statutory damages and attorneys" fees under the Lanham Act. For example, in *Ohio State University v. Skreened, Ltd.*,[662] the court held that the defendant's unauthorized sale of shirts bearing marks identical to or substantially indistinguishable from The Ohio State University's federally registered marks sold by its licensees constitutes trademark counterfeiting.

606. The fair use of a trademark does not constitute infringement. In *WCVB-TV v. Boston Athletic Association*,[663] the First Circuit explained: "In technical trademark jargon, the use of words for descriptive purposes is called a 'fair use',and the law usually permits it even if the words themselves also constitute a trademark." The court held that a television station's use of "Boston Marathon" to describe its unlicensed broadcast of the event is not trademark infringement,[664] although another local television

653. . *National Football League Properties, Inc. v. New Jersey Giants, Inc.*, 637 F. Supp. 507 (D.N. N. 1986).
654. . *Johnny Blastoff, Inc. v. L.A. Rams Football Co.*, 188 F.3d 427 (7th Cir. 1999).
655. . *NFL v. Coors Brewing Co.*, 205 F.3d 1324 (2nd Cir. 1999) *NFL v. Coors Brewing Co.*, 205 F.3d 1324 (2nd Cir. 1999).
656. . *Boston Athletic Ass'n v. Sullivan*, 867 F.2d 22 (1st Cir. 1989).
657. . *Univ. of Ga. Athletic Assn. v. Laite*, 756 F.2d 1535 (11th Cir. 1985).
658. . *Acushnet Co. v. 100GolfClubs.com*, 2012 WL 692187 (S.D. Fla.).
659. . *Auburn Univ. v. Moody*, 2008 WL 4877542 (M.D. Ala.).
660. . *Major League Baseball Props., Inc. v. Sed Non Olet Denarius, Ltd.*, 817 F. Supp. 1103 (S.D.N.Y. 1993).
661. 15 U.S.C. § 1114.
662. 16 F. Supp. 3d 905 (S.D. Ohio 2014).
663. . 926 F.2d 42, 46 (1st Cir. 1991).
664. . *See also Dream Team Collectibles, Inc. v. NBA Props., Inc.*, 958 F. Supp. 1401, 1421 (E.D. Mo. 1997) (use of NBA team name on framed collage of trading cards depicting players in team uniforms "not likely to cause confusion, but is a simply a way to identify a particular NBA team").

station was exclusively authorized to broadcast this event. This was judicially characterized as fair use of the Boston Marathon mark merely to describe the event defendant was broadcasting that did not create any viewer confusion.

607. For the same reason that underlies the fair use defense, the parody of a trademark is not infringing. In *Cardtoons, L.C. v. Major League Baseball Players Association.*,[665] the Tenth Circuit held that parody trading cards with caricatures of baseball players and critical commentary does not create public confusion regarding the source of the cards. The court explained that "as with all successful parodies, the effect of the cards is to amuse rather than confuse." In *Ohio State University v. Skreened, Ltd.*,[666] the court observed: "[A]n allegation of parody is but one consideration to be considered in the larger context of possible infringement. The evidence here does not . . . suggest that Defendants are seeking to be ironic commentators on academia or college athletic culture [simply by selling shirts bearing a university's trademarks without authorization]; the only evidence before this Court is that Defendants are trying to make a buck by appropriating marks for commercial use."

608. In *University of Alabama Bd. of Trustees v. New Life, Inc.*,[667] the University of Alabama alleged that an artist's paintings, prints, and calendars infringed its trademarks because his unauthorized inclusion of the university's crimson and white uniforms and helmets therein created a likelihood of consumer confusion that it sponsored or endorsed these products. Characterizing the paintings, prints, and calendars as expressive speech protected by the First Amendment, the Eleventh Circuit held it "should construe the Lanham Act narrowly when deciding whether an artistically expressive work infringes a trademark." Such usage does not violate the Lanham Act "unless the use of the mark has no artistic relevance to the underlying work whatsoever, or, if it has some artistic relevance, unless it explicitly misleads as to the source or the content of the work."

609. Applying this standard, the court concluded:

> The depiction of the University's uniforms in the content of these items is artistically relevant to the expressive underlying works because the uniforms' colors and designs are needed for a realistic portrayal of famous scenes from Alabama football history. Also there is no evidence that Moore ever marketed an unlicensed item as endorsed or sponsored by the University, or otherwise explicitly stated that such items were affiliated with the University … . Even if some members of the public would draw the incorrect inference that [the University] had some involvement with [Moore's paintings, prints, and calendars,] … that risk of misunderstanding, not engendered by any overt [or in this case even implicit] claim … is so outweighed by the interest in artistic expression as to preclude any violation of the Lanham Act.

665. . 95 F.3d 959 (10th Cir. 1996).
666. 16 F. Supp. 3d 905 (S.D. Ohio 2014).
667. . 683 F.3d 1266 (11th Cir. 2012).

II. Trademark Dilution

610. The Trademark Dilution Revision Act of 2006 (TDRA), which is part of the Lanham Act, protects the owner of a "famous mark" from unauthorized use of its mark or similar mark that is likely to cause dilution of the mark's distinctiveness.[668] Proof that the defendant's unauthorized usage creates an actual or likelihood of confusion or actual economic injury is not required. The statute provides a remedy for tarnishing the goodwill associated with a famous mark by using it in a disparaging manner outside the context of permissible parody, or a blurring of the mark's distinctiveness because it is used to identify a wide range of unrelated goods and services.

611. To be "famous," the mark must be "widely recognized by the general consuming public of the United States as a designation of source of the goods or services of the mark's owner."[669] The trademarks and logos of major U.S. sports events such as the Indianapolis 500 auto race, Kentucky Derby horse race, and Masters golf tournament as well as those of major league professional teams, sports governing bodies such as the USOC, NCAA and NASCAR, and many universities with successful football and basketball teams are well known among sports fans and may be considered "famous" marks. A court has ruled that the "New York City Triathlon," "NYC Triathlon," and "NYC Tri" marks are famous because of their extensive national and international promotion and recognition.[670] However, mere niche market fame is insufficient to establish that a particular mark is "famous." Some courts have suggested the mark must be "a household name" among members of the general consuming public to be protected by the federal dilution law. For example, in *University of Texas v. KST Electric*,[671] the court held that, even though its athletic teams are nationally prominent, the University of Texas did not prove that its longhorn silhouette logo is "like those few truly famous marks like Budweiser beer."

612. A court ruled that the unauthorized use of "America's Team" on apparel "blurs the uniqueness" of the mark and tarnishes it because it is used in connection with the defendant's inferior goods.[672] Another court held that defendant's unauthorized usage of the "New York City Triathlon" marks as the name of its athletic club blurred and tarnished their distinctiveness in violation of the dilution statute by creating a negative association because of defendant's reputation for poor customer service.[673] The following cases, which were decided prior to the TDRA, provide clear examples of usages that tarnish sports marks. In *NBA Properties v. Untertainment Records LLC*,[674] a federal district court held that the unauthorized use of an altered NBA logo showing

668. . 15 U.S.C. § 1125(c).
669. . 15 U.S.C. § 1125(c)(2)(A).
670. . *New York City Triathlon LLC v. NYC Triathlon Club Inc.*, 95 U.S.P.Q.2d 1451 (S.D.N.Y. 2010). *See also Dallas Cowboys Football Club, Ltd. v. America's Team Properties*, 616 F. Supp.2d 622 (N.D. Tex. 2009) (Dallas Cowboys' "long duration and geographic reach" of "America's Team" mark in connection with various products advertised and sold to public combined with survey.
671. . 550 F. Supp. 2d 657, 679 (W.D. Tex. 2008).
672. . *Dallas Cowboys Football Club, supra.*
673. . *New York City Triathlon, supra.*
674. . 1999 WL 335147 (S.D.N.Y. 1999).

a silhouetted basketball player dribbling a basketball with a handgun in his other hand to advertise a rap album violates the federal dilution statute. Because "linking the NBA Logo with violence and drugs will adversely color the public's impressions of the NBA," the court concluded that "[a]ny suggestion that the NBAP or the NBA endorses violence, gunplay or drug use, or that they have chosen to associate themselves with those who do, will likely tarnish their reputation with their corporate customers and partners, as well as the public at large." Similarly, in *Dallas Cowboys Cheerleaders, Inc. v. Pussycat Cinema, Ltd.*,[675] the Second Circuit ruled that the unauthorized use of female actors wearing well-known Dallas Cowboys Cheerleaders uniforms in a "sexually depraved film … has 'tendency to impugn (plaintiff's services) and injure plaintiff's business reputation'"

III. Anticybersquatting Consumer Protection Act of 1999

613. The significant expansion and use of the Internet in recent years gave rise to "cybersquatting," which is the registration of well-known trademarks (including those of sports teams and events) as domain names (i.e., Web site addresses) by non-trademark holders. Their objective frequently is to try to sell rights to the domain names back to the trademark owners at a profit or to attract Internet users to their websites, such as online sports gambling. Cybersquatting that creates a likelihood of consumer confusion constitutes trademark infringement and unfair competition.[676] It also may constitute trademark dilution and violate the Anticybersquatting Consumer Protection Act (ACPA) of 1999.[677]

614. The ACPA provides a trademark owner with a cause of action against a defendant for bad faith registration or use of a domain name that is (1) identical to or confusingly similar to a distinctive mark; or (2) identical to or confusingly similar to, or dilutes, a famous mark. 15 USC. §1125(d)(1).[678] In addition to available remedies under the Lanham Act, the ACPA provides for statutory damages for bad faith registration of domain names after the November 29, 1999, effective date of the statute.[679] The ACPA also authorizes an in rem action against the domain name itself for forfeiture or transfer to the trademark owner if the domain name registrant cannot be located or is not subject to personal jurisdiction by an American court.[680]

675. . 604 F.2d 200, 205 (2nd Cir. 1979).

676. . *See* , e.g., *March Madness Athletic Assn. v. Netfire, Inc.*, 2003 WL 22047375 (N.D. Tex. 2003) (www.marchmadness.com infringes NCAA's federally registered March Madness mark for basketball tournament); *Quokka Sports, Inc. v. Cup Int'l Internet Ventures*, 99 F. Supp. 2d 1105 (N.D. Cal. 1999) (defendants' www.americascup.com Web site "masquerading as an official site associated with the America's Cup event" located at www.americascup.org and infringes registered mark "America's Cup").

677. . 15 U.S.C. § 1129.

678. . *See March Madness Athletic Assn. v. Netfire, Inc.*, 2003 WL 22047375 (N.D. Tex.) (finding that defendants" registration and use of www.march-madness.com violates ACPA, entitling NCAA to injunctive relief).

679. . 15 U.S.C. § 1117(d).

680. . 15 U.S.C. § 1125(d)(2)(A).

615. As a faster and less expensive alternative to litigation against a cybersquatter under the Lanham Act and/or ACPA, a mark owner may choose to instead utilize arbitration procedures under the Uniform Domain Name Dispute Resolution Policy (UDRP). The domain name registration agreement incorporates the terms of the UDRP, which governs disputes between the domain name registrant and others concerning the registration and use of a domain name. Several sports-related domain name disputes have been resolved by UDRP proceedings, including the first decided case under this procedure.[681] For example, in *June Bug Enterprises v. Kyamko*,[682] the operator of a pornography site was ordered to transfer its "magicjohnson.com" domain name to plaintiff June Bug Enterprises, the owner of former NBA player Earvin Johnson's federally registered "MAGIC JOHNSON" mark.

IV. Olympic Marks

616. The USOC owns the exclusive right to use and license the Olympic marks within the United States.[683] The Ted Stevens Olympic and Amateur Sports Act (ASA) prohibits the unauthorized usage of the Olympic name and marks, including the five-ring Olympic symbol, "for the purpose of trade, to induce the sale of any goods or services, or to promote any theatrical exhibition, athletic performance, or competition."[684] The ASA extended the USOC's exclusive property rights to include the "Pan-American" and "Paralympiad" marks, which are now protected to the same extent as the Olympic marks.[685]

617. The Olympic marks have a broader scope of protection under federal law beyond that generally provided to other trademarks and service marks. In *San Francisco Arts & Athletics, Inc. v. United States Olympic Committee*,[686] the U.S. Supreme Court held that the ASA's language and legislative intent evidenced Congress's intent to grant the USOC exclusive rights to control use of the Olympic marks regardless of whether their unauthorized usage creates a likelihood of confusion. It concluded that defendant's unauthorized use of "Gay Olympic Games" for an athletics competition

681. . *See World Wresting Fed'n Entm't, Inc. v. Bosman*, WIPO, Case No. D99-0001, Jan. 14, 2000, available at http://pub.bna.com/ptcj/d990001.htm (finding bad faith registration and use of worldwrestlingfederation.com domain name, which is identical or confusingly similar to federally registered World Wrestling Federation trademark and service mark, and ordering transfer of domain name registration to owner of marks).

682. . 73 U.S.P.Q.2d 1310 (2004).

683. . *United States Olympic Comm. v. Intelicense Corp., S.A.*, 737 F.2d 263 (2d. Cir. 1984), *cert. denied*, 469 U.S. 982 (1984).

684. . 36 U.S.C. § 220506(c). See *USOC v. Xclusive Leisure & Hospitality Ltd.*, 2008 WL 3971120 (N.D. Cal.) (enjoining unauthorized usage of Olympic marks in United States to advertise and sell tickets and hospitality packages to the Beijing Olympics).

685. . *United States Olympic Comm. v. Toy Truck Lines, Inc.*, 237 F.3d 1331 (Fed. Cir. 2001).

686. . 483 U.S. 522 (1987).

in San Francisco was infringing regardless of whether it tends to cause any confusion.[687] The Court explained:

> One reason for Congress to grant the USOC exclusive control of the word Olympic, as with other trademarks, is to ensure that the USOC receives the benefit of its own efforts so that the USOC will have an incentive to continue to produce a quality product, that, in turn, benefits the public. See 1 J. McCarthy, Trademarks and Unfair Competition § 2:1, pp. 44–47 (1984). But in the special circumstance of the USOC, Congress has a broader public interest in promoting, through the activities of the USOC, the participation of amateur athletes from the United States in the great four-yearly sport festival, the Olympic Games. … Olympic Charter, Rule 1 (1985). The USOC's goal under the Olympic Charter, Rule 24(B), is to further the Olympic movement, that has as its aims: to promote the development of those physical and moral qualities which are the basis of sport; to educate young people through sport in a spirit of better understanding between each other and of friendship, thereby helping to build a better and more peaceful world; and to spread the Olympic principles throughout the world, thereby creating international goodwill. Congress interests in promoting the USOC's activities include these purposes as well as those specifically enumerated in the USOC's charter. Section 110 directly advances these governmental interests by supplying the USOC with the means to raise money to support the Olympics and encourages the USOC's activities by ensuring that it will receive the benefits of its efforts.

618. The ASA "grandfathers" the rights of those who lawfully used the Olympic marks prior to 1950 (the date the Act's predecessor was enacted) to advertise and sell their goods or services. However, such users may not expand the scope of their goods or services sold under the Olympic mark, or adopt new marks with the word "Olympic" therein. In *O-M Bread, Inc. v. United States Olympic Committee*,[688] a federal appellate court held that the proposed use of "Olympic Kids" for bakery products is not a permitted extension of a prior user's grandfathered right to use the Olympic mark for bakery products. The court found these "different marks present a different commercial impression and are not legal equivalents." It concluded that:

> commercial growth into new Olympic-based marks is outside the letter of the statute, as well as outside its spirit. The statutory balance that limited prior users to the words, marks, goods and services in use before enactment, and thus limited potential expansion, is not an unreasonable implementation of the legislative policy.

687. . *See also USOC v. Tobyhanna Camp Corp.*, 2010 WL 4617429 (M.D. Pa.) (use of "Camp Olympik" and non-interlocked five-ring Olympic symbol for children's summer camp infringing); *USOC v. Xclusive Leisure & Hospitality Ltd.*, 2008 WL 3971120 (N.D. Cal.) (enjoining unauthorized usage of Olympic marks in United States to advertise and sell tickets and hospitality packages to the Beijing Olympics).

688. . 65 F.3d 933 (Fed. Cir. 1995).

619. The ASA does not prohibit all unauthorized uses of the Olympic marks. In *United States Olympic Committee v. American Media, Inc.*,[689] the court observed, "because the Amateur Sports Act grants the USOC rights over and above both the common law and [the Lanham Act], the language and scope of the Act must be strictly construed." For example, the media may report about Olympic sports competitions, which would include use of the word "Olympic" and competition photographs containing Olympic marks in news reporting. It ruled that the mere publication of an Olympic preview magazine titled "Olympics USA" is non-commercial speech that does not infringe the USOC's rights under the Amateur Sports Act. However, the publisher's usage of the Olympic marks in a manner falsely suggesting that the USOC officially endorses or authorizes its magazine would violate the Lanham Act.

620. Unless a likelihood of public confusion as to origin, sponsorship, or affiliation is created, the Olympic mark may be used for purely expressive purposes. In *Stop the Olympic Prison v. United States Olympic Committee*,[690] the court found that publication and distribution of a poster with the words "Stop the Olympic Prison" to marshal public opposition to the planned conversion of the Lake Placid Olympic Village into a prison after the 1980 Olympics does not violate the ASA. The publisher was not using the Olympic mark to make a profit; its only purpose was to disseminate its political views in an effort to change future plans for the Olympic Village. The poster is not likely to be viewed as a commercial advertisement for the sale of any goods or services, and it was not used to promote any theatrical exhibition or athletic competition.

V. Ambush Marketing

621. Ambush marketing is a creative advertising practice by a business other than an official sponsor that seeks to create an association with a sports event without using the event's name, trademarks, or logos. It encompasses "a company's intentional efforts to weaken its competitor's official association with a sport organization, which has been acquired through the payment of sponsorship fees" as well as seeking "to capitalize on the goodwill, reputation and popularity of a particular sport or event by creating an association without the authorization or consent of the necessary parties."[691]

622. Official event sponsors claim that ambush marketing dilutes the value of their sponsorships. Ambush marketing may harm event organizers, which need sponsorship money to fund production of a sporting event. When ambush marketers receive commercial benefits by free-riding on an event's popularity or goodwill, the value of an official sponsorship may be significantly reduced. This creates an economic disincentive to be an official event sponsor, with a corresponding incentive to engage in ambush marketing instead. This in turn reduces the value of official sponsorships

689. . 156 F. Supp. 2d 1200, 1209 (D. Col. 2001).
690. . 489 F. Supp. 1112 (S.D.N.Y. 1980).
691. . Steve McKelvey & John Grady, *Ambush Marketing: The Legal Battleground for Sports Marketers*, 21 Ent. & Sports L. 8, 9 (2004).

and causes sports event organizers to lose sponsorship revenues.[692] Successful ambush marketing campaigns also may harm consumers of sporting events. A decrease in sponsorship revenues could force event organizers to find new revenue sources (e.g., pay-per-view television broadcasts rather than free-to-air telecasts), or possibly result in the discontinuance of sports events that lack adequate commercial sponsorship support.

623. Under current U.S. law, ambush marketing is illegal only if it creates a likelihood of consumer confusion. In *Federation Internationale De Football v. Nike, Inc.*,[693] the court refused to preliminarily enjoin Nike's use of "USA 03" to advertise and sell various products in connection with its sponsorship of the U.S. Women's National Soccer Team. Plaintiff Federation Internationale De Football (FIFA) used "USA 2003" in connection with its 2003 women's soccer World Cup held in the United States. Nike was not a World Cup sponsor and was not authorized to use FIFA's marks. Although Nike did not use FIFA's name or refer to the World Cup, FIFA alleged that Nike's usage of "USA 03" is infringing and illegally interfered with its official sponsorship contracts.

624. Holding that FIFA has not shown a substantial likelihood of success on the merits of its claims, the court observed:

> Nike argues that its use of USA 03 (or United States 2003) is innocent, given the company's sponsorship of the Women's National Team. After all, the team that Nike is backing is the United States team for the year 2003, and therefore, USA 03 is an appropriate and understandable way for Nike to associate itself with that group of players. The Court agrees that Nike's preexisting and entirely legitimate relationship with the Women's World Cup provides an important context for its use of the disputed marks. For there can be little doubt, in light of the success that the U.S. women enjoyed in the 1999 World Cup, that the team and the event are already linked in the public mind. As such, Nike's careful use of a mark that might be affiliated with both is not necessarily an indication of bad faith, but instead of savvy marketing. Whenever that team plays in this country, it is to be expected that the sponsors of both the team and the event would want to use trademarks that reflect the United States and that emphasize this year's date. Nike's doing so here thus may not indicate a deliberate attempt to deceive the buying public.

625. Even if there currently are only limited legal remedies for combating ambush marketing, a sports event organizer can minimize its successful use and resulting detrimental effects by developing a comprehensive anti-ambush marketing plan. For example, it can contractually prohibit broadcasters from selling commercial time to the competitors of official sponsors. Non-sponsor advertisements and signage

---

692. . *See United States Olympic Comm. v. Am. Media, Inc.*, 156 F. Supp. 2d 1200, 1204 (D. Colo. 2001) (alleging that defendant's ambush marketing will encourage other companies to do so, which will adversely affect USOC's ability to fund United States' participation in the Olympic Games).

693. . 285 F. Supp. 2d 64 (D.D.C. 2003).

in connection with a sporting event should be carefully monitored to ensure that the event's name, marks, and logos are not included therein.

626. Courts will enforce contract rights to prevent unfair competition that causes a likelihood of consumer confusion. In *Mastercard International, Inc. v. Sprint Communications Co.*,[694] an international soccer federation granted exclusive rights to Mastercard to use the 1994 World Cup Soccer Tournament trademarks on "all card-based payment and account access devices." The court held that Mastercard's contract rights precluded the United States Local Organizing Committee from authorizing Sprint Communications to use and imprint those marks on phone cards. Finding that Sprint's conduct violated the Lanham Act, the court concluded:

> Sprint wishes to use the World Cup marks to convey to the world the false impression that its use of the marks on calling cards is officially sanctioned by the World Cup organization. Clearly, that is not the case, and Mastercard, which has the exclusive right to use the mark for such purposes, is entitled to enjoin this deceptive use.

§3. Game Accounts, Sports Statistics, and Broadcasting Rights

I. Historical Background and Overview

627. Historically, producers of sporting events sought to protect live game accounts and play-by-play descriptions from unauthorized viewer usage under state misappropriation, unfair competition, and contract laws. The then-current federal copyright laws did not provide any legal protection for sporting events or simultaneously recorded broadcasts. Relying primarily on the misappropriation doctrine established by the Supreme Court in *International News Service v. Associated Press*,[695] courts broadly held that the creator of a game or athletic event has an exclusive property right in its commercial value. Recognizing that the production of athletic events requires the expenditure of substantial time, effort, and money, these courts prohibited observers and listeners—whether inside or outside the facility in which the event occurred—from unauthorized transmission of live game accounts to the public for commercial benefit.[696]

628. In *Pittsburgh Athletic Co. v. KQV Broadcasting Co.*,[697] the court held:

> the Pittsburgh Athletic Company [owner of the Pittsburgh Pirates professional baseball club], by reason of its creation of the game, its control of the park, and its restriction of the dissemination of news therefrom, has a property right in

694. . 1994 WL 97097 (S.D.N.Y.), *aff'd*, 23 F.2d 397 (2d. Cir. 1994).

695. . 248 U.S. 215 (1918).

696. . *See* generally Bruce P. Keller, *Condemned to Repeat the Past: The Reemergence of Misappropriation and Other Common Law Theories of Protection for Intellectual Property*, 11 Harv. J.L. & Tech. 401 (1998) (tracing historical reliance on state misappropriation law to protect sports-related intellectual property rights).

697. . 24 F. Supp. 490 (W.D. Pa. 1938).

such news, and the right to control the use thereof for a reasonable time following the games.

629. The Pittsburgh Athletic Company sold the exclusive rights to broadcast Pirates games played at Forbes Field to General Mills, Inc. The defendant broadcast play-by-play accounts of Pirates games as described by observers stationed outside of Forbes Field who were able to see them being played. Finding that the defendant's conduct violated the baseball club's property rights, the court ruled that its unauthorized broadcast of Pirates games constitutes misappropriation, unfair competition, and unlawful interference with the parties' contract rights.

630. Today, federal copyright law prohibits the unauthorized broadcast of sports events. The Copyright Act of 1976 grants a copyright owner the exclusive right to use and authorize others to use the work in five statutorily defined ways, including the right to perform publicly an audiovisual work such as the broadcast of a sports event.[698] The act provides that anyone who violates any of these exclusive rights engages in copyright infringement.[699] The owner of a copyright has a variety of available remedies for infringement including injunctive relief and the recovery of actual or statutory damages, the infringer's profits, and attorneys' fees.[700] The act also establishes certain defenses to claimed infringement of broadcast.

631. A threshold issue is who owns the copyright to the broadcast of a sporting event—the clubs playing the particular game, the league, the broadcaster of the game, and/or the players participating in the game? In general, ownership of a copyright initially vests in the author(s) of the work.[701] The Copyright Act recognizes that a work may be jointly authored and its copyright co-owned.[702] Within a sports league, broadcasting rights and copyright ownership of broadcast games generally are determined by contract. A broadcaster's camera angles, types of shots, use of instant replays, split screens, special effects, and commentary supplies the creativity necessary for "authorship" of a broadcast sports event.[703] Ownership of the copyright for a sports broadcast vis-à-vis the league/clubs and the broadcaster generally is contractually determined.[704]

632. In *Baltimore Orioles, Inc. v. Major League Baseball Players Association*,[705] the Seventh Circuit held:

698. . 17 U.S.C. § 106.
699. . 17 U.S.C. § 501(a).
700. . 17 U.S.C. §§ 502–505.
701. . 17 U.S.C. § 201(a).
702. . 17 U.S.C. § 201(a).
703. . *Baltimore Orioles, Inc. v. Major League Baseball Players Assn.*, 805 F.2d 663, 668–69 (7th Cir. 1986); *Nat'l Assn. of Broadcasters v. Copyright Royalty Tribunal*, 675 F.2d 367, 377–79 (D.C. Cir. 1982).
704. . *See* , e.g., *NFL v. Insight Telecomm. Corp.*, 158 F. Supp. 2d 124, 128 (D. Mass. 2001) ("The NFL owns the copyright in all regular season and postseason NFL game telecasts, as confirmed by the League's contracts with the networks").
705. . 805 F. 2d 663, 670 (7th Cir. 1986). See also *Big Fights Inc. v. Ficara*, 40 U.S.P.Q.2d 1377, 1378 (S.D.N.Y. 1996) (promoter of a professional boxing match, not boxers, owns copyright in film of the match).

> Because the Players are employees and their performances before broadcast audiences are within the scope of their employment, the telecasts of major league baseball games, which consist of the Players' performances, are works made for hire within the meaning of § 201(b). … Thus, in the absence of an agreement to the contrary, the Clubs are presumed to own all of the rights encompassed in the telecasts of the games. The district court found that there was no written agreement that the Clubs would not own the copyright to the telecasts, and, therefore, that the copyright was owned by the Clubs.

II. Nature and Scope of Legal Rights in a Sports Event

633. Although copyright law protects the broadcast of a sports event, it does not protect ideas, procedures, systems, or methods of operation "regardless of the form in which it is described, explained, illustrated, or embodied."[706] As a result, neither the underlying idea for a type of athletic event nor a system or method of playing a sport is copyrightable.[707] In *Hoopla Sports and Entertainment, Inc. v. Nike, Inc.*,[708] the court held that the concept of an international high school all-star basketball game is not copyrightable and plaintiff cannot prevent defendant from using its idea to conduct a similar event. The court observed that "the methods or rules of playing basketball games are not generally copyrightable."

634. Similarly, in *Seltzer v. Sunbrock*,[709] the court rejected the plaintiff's claim that his idea of staging a transcontinental roller-skating race is protected by copyright law. It held: "What [plaintiff] really composed was a description of a system for conducting races on roller skates. A system, as such, can never be copyrighted. If it finds any protection, it must come from the patent laws." For example, the Arena Football League obtained U.S. Patent No. 4,911,433, which was issued on March 27, 1990, for its unique system for playing indoor professional football. The Patent Office also issued U.S. Patent No. 5,616,089 for a particular method of golf putting.

635. In *NBA v. Motorola, Inc.*,[710] the Second Circuit ruled that athletic events are not copyrightable and explained:

> In our view, the underlying basketball games do not fall within the subject matter of federal copyright protection because they do not constitute original works of authorship under 17 U.S.C. § 102(a). Section 102(a) lists eight categories of works of authorship covered by the act, including such categories as literary works, musical works, and dramatic works. The list does not include athletic events, and, although the list is concededly non-exclusive, such events are neither similar nor analogous to any of the listed categories.

---

706. . 17 U.S.C. § 102(b).
707. . 1 M. Nimmer & D. Nimmer, *Nimmer on Copyright* § 2.18[H][3][a] (2004).
708. . 947 F. Supp. 347 (N.D. Ill. 1996).
709. . 22 F. Supp. 621, 639 (S.D. Cal. 1938).
710. . 105 F.3d 841 (2d Cir. 1997).

> Sports events are not authored in any common sense of the word. There is, of course, at least at the professional level, considerable preparation for a game. However, the preparation is as much an expression of hope or faith as a determination of what will actually happen. Unlike movies, plays, television programs, or operas, athletic events are competitive and have no underlying script. Preparation may even cause mistakes to succeed, like the broken play in football that gains yard-age because the opposition could not expect it. Athletic events may also result in wholly unanticipated occurrences, the most notable recent event being in a championship baseball game in which interference with a fly ball caused an umpire to signal erroneously a home run.

> What authorship there is in a sports event, moreover, must be open to copying by competitors if fans are to be attracted. If the inventor of the T-formation in football had been able to copyright it, the sport might have come to an end instead of prospering. Even where athletic preparation most resembles authorship—figure skating, gymnastics, and, some would uncharitably say, professional wrestling—a performer who conceives and executes a particularly graceful and difficult—or, in the case of wrestling, seemingly painful—acrobatic feat cannot copyright it without impairing the underlying competition in the future. A claim of being the only athlete to perform a feat doesn't mean much if no one else is allowed to try.

636. The *Motorola* court held that the defendants' reproduction of real-time NBA basketball game statistics (e.g., teams playing, score, time in possession of the ball, time remaining in game) which information was obtained from broadcast games "did not infringe the NBA's copyright because they reproduced only facts from the broadcasts, not the expression or description of the game that constitutes the [copyrighted] broadcast." Because this information was already in the public domain, the court rejected the NBA's state law commercial appropriation claim because the defendants' collection and dissemination of "strictly factual information about the games" did not have an adverse economic effect on the production or broadcasting of NBA games.

637. In *National Football League v. Governor of the State of Delaware*,[711] the court reached a similar result. The NFL sought to enjoin the unauthorized use of its game schedules and scores as the basis for a Delaware state football lottery. Although defendants profited from public popularity generated by NFL games, the court found no misappropriation of the league's property because this information was "obtained from public sources and are utilized only after plaintiffs have disseminated them at large and no longer have any expectation of generating revenue from further dissemination." However, it cautioned that defendants could not use NFL game scores in a manner that creates a likelihood of consumer confusion regarding the NFL's authorization or sponsorship of its lottery.

638. In *Morris Communications Corp. v. PGA Tour, Inc.*[712] a federal district court held that producer of sports event may limit access to real-time scores and game

711. . 435 F. Supp. 1372, 1377 (D. Del. 1977).
712. . 235 F. Supp. 2d 1269 (M.D. Fla. 2002), *aff'd*, 364 F.3d 1288 (11th Cir.), *cert. denied*, 543 U.S. 919 (2004).

information by contract (e.g., by allowing admission only if ticket holders or members of the media agree to comply with certain conditions). The court stated:

> The PGA Tour's property right does not come from copyright law, as copyright law does not protect factual information, like golf scores. See Feist Publications v. Rural Tel. Serv. Co., 499 U.S. 340, 348, 111 S.Ct. 1282, 113 L.Ed.2d 358 (1991). However, the PGA Tour controls the right of access to that information and can place restrictions on those attending the private event, giving the PGA Tour a property right that the Court will protect. … [T]he instant case deals with facts that are not subject to copyright protection. The compiler of the information … collects information, which it created, at a cost. Also the events occur on private property to which the general public does not have unfettered access, and the creator of the event can place restrictions upon those who enter the private property. The vastly increased speed that the Internet makes available does not change the calculus or the underlying property right. Accordingly, the PGA Tour … has a property right in the compilation of scores, but that property right disappears when the underlying information is in the public domain.

III. Infringement of a Sports Broadcast

639. The *Motorola* court ruled that the Copyright Act of 1976 protects the broadcast of a sporting event, even though it does not protect the underlying event itself:

> [R]ecorded broadcasts of NBA games—as opposed to the games themselves—are now entitled to copyright protection. The Copyright Act was amended in 1976 specifically to insure that simultaneously-recorded transmissions of live performances and sporting events would meet the Act's requirement that the original work of authorship be fixed in any tangible medium of expression. 17 U.S.C. § 102(a). … Congress specifically had sporting events in mind: [T]he bill seeks to resolve, through the definition of fixation in section 101, the status of live broadcasts—sports, news coverage, live performances of music, etc.—that are reaching the public in unfixed form but that are simultaneously being recorded. H.R. No. 94–1476 at 52, reprinted in 1976 U.S.C.C.A.N. at 5665. The House Report also makes clear that it is the broadcast, not the underlying game, that is the subject of copyright protection. …

640. In *NFL v. McBee & Bruno's, Inc.*,[713] the court ruled that the unauthorized interception of the broadcast of a sports event through the use of satellite dish antennae by a commercial establishment, which occurred in the mid-1980s, constitutes copyright infringement. This was an unauthorized public performance of a copyrighted sports broadcast, which violates federal copyright law.

641. Today, the Internet provides a modern means for infringing copyrighted sports event broadcasts, including by transmissions originating outside of the United

713. . 792 F.2d 726 (8th Cir. 1986).

States, and enables unauthorized webcasts to occur throughout the world. In *NFL v. TVRadioNow*,[714] defendants captured sports broadcasts and other copyrighted programming from U.S. television stations, converted them into computerized data, and streamed them over the Internet to viewers in the U.S. from a website in Canada. The court ruled that "defendants are unlawfully publicly performing plaintiffs" copyrighted works in the U.S. by transmitting (through use of "streaming" technology) performances of the works to the public, over the Internet, which violates plaintiffs' exclusive rights to perform their works publicly and to authorize others to do so.[715]

642. In *WPIX, Inc. v. IVI, Inc.*,[716] a significant case protecting the ability of producers of broadcast sports events to maximize their economic value, the Second Circuit ruled that the unauthorized streaming of copyrighted television programming over the Internet does not constitute non-infringing retransmission of copyrighted programming protected by § 111 of the Copyright Act's compulsory licensing provisions for cable television systems. Section 111 permits "cable systems to publicly perform and retransmit signals of copyrighted television programming to its subscribers, provided they pay royalties at government-regulated rates and abide by the statute's procedures." The court concluded that Congress "has not codified a statutory provision for Internet retransmissions, nor has it included the "Internet" as an acceptable communication channel under §111" and "did not ... intend for §111's compulsory license to extend to Internet transmissions." It expressed concern that the plaintiffs" "desire to create original television programming surely would be dampened if their creative works could be copied and streamed over the Internet in derogation of their exclusive property rights." It affirmed the district court's preliminary injunction against defendant's unauthorized streaming because this infringing conduct irreparably harms plaintiffs.

643. Effectively characterizing this as an unauthorized form of Internet streaming, in *American Broadcasting Companies, Inc. v. Aereo, Inc.*,[717] the U.S. Supreme Court ruled that a system combining the functionality of a standard TV antenna, a DVR, and a Slingbox-like device, which enabled users to watch live television programs broadcast over the public airwaves, including sports events, over the Internet in real-time constitutes copyright infringement. The Court held that this technologically complex system of retransmitted television broadcasts is analogous to a cable television system, which publicly performs the copyrighted programs it broadcasts to its subscribers. The Copyright Act permits a cable television system to do so without infringement liability pursuant to a compulsory license requiring payment of statutorily determined fees, which are distributed to owners of the copyrighted broadcasts. On remand, the

---

714. . 53 U.S.P.Q.2d 1831 (W.D. Pa. 2000). *See also Live Nation Motor Sports, Inc. v. Davis*, 2006 WL 3616983 (N.D. Tex. 2006) (providing unauthorized access to motorcycle racing producer's live webcasts through defendant's website is copyright infringement). *See* generally Michael J. Mellis, *Internet Piracy of Live Sports Telecasts, 18 Marq. Sports L. Rev.* 259 (2008).

715. . *See also Wisconsin Interscholastic Athletic Ass'n v. Gannett Co., Inc.*, 658 F.3d 614 (7th Cir. 2011). (implicitly recognizing high school athletic association has property right in its state championship tournament games by ruling that its exclusive contract to stream games over the internet does not violate the First Amendment of the U.S. Constitution).

716. . 691 F.3d 275 (2d. Cir. 2012).

717. 134 S. Ct. 2498 (2014).

district court determined that the Supreme Court "did not imply, much less hold, that simply because an entity performs publicly in much the same way as a CATV system, it is necessarily a cable system entitled to a §111 compulsory license." The court issued a preliminary injunction "barring Aereo from retransmitting programs to its subscribers while the programs are still being broadcast."[718].

644. In *Fox Broadcasting Co., Inc. v. Dish Network LLC,*[719] a federal district court held that a satellite television provider's Dish Anywhere service (which includes a DVR and built-in Sling device) that enables its subscribers to view copyrighted television programming, such as sports events, on their computers and mobile devices does not violate copyright law. Distinguishing *Aereo*, the court concluded that the subscribers' use of this service to access their individual live or recorded programming and transfer it to these Internet-connected devices does not result in a public performance of copyrighted programming because the provider has a license for initial retransmission of this programming to its subscribers.

645. The unauthorized commercial usage of taped broadcasts of sports events constitutes copyright infringement. In *New Boston Television, Inc. v. Entertainment Sports Programming Network, Inc.*,[720] ESPN, a cable television network, contended that its rebroadcast of taped sports event highlights is permissible fair use. Rejecting this defense and finding copyright infringement, the court stated:

> While protection of the public right of access to [newsworthy] information is a primary justification for the fair use defense, this right is sufficiently protected merely by enabling defendants to report the underlying facts which the plaintiff's videotapes record. It does not however permit defendants to appropriate the plaintiff's expression of that information by copying the plaintiff's films themselves.

646. However, tape recording of televised sports broadcasts for solely in-home, personal use is not copyright infringement. In *Sony Corp. of America v. Universal City Studios, Inc.*,[721] the U.S. Supreme Court characterized this activity as time-shifting for private home use that is non-infringing fair use of a copyrighted broadcast pursuant to §107 of the Copyright Act.

---

718. *American Broadcasting Companies, Inc. v. Aereo, Inc.*, 112 U.S.P.Q.2d 1582 (S.D.N.Y. 2014).
719. 114 U.S.P.Q.2d 1100 (C.D. Cal. 2015).
720. . 215 U.S.P.Q. 755, 756 (D. Mass. 1981).
721. . 464 U.S. 417, 449 (1984).

Chapter 2. Regulation of Athlete Agents

§1. Introduction

647. The use of agents by U.S. professional athletes can be traced back to as early as the mid-1920s, when Charles Pyle negotiated a football contract along with endorsement and movie deals for NFL player Harold "Red" Grange. The proliferation in the number and use of agents by athletes did not occur until the 1960s and 1970s, as a result of the demise of reserve and option clauses in standard-form contracts between players and clubs; competition for players between rival major professional leagues; the growing strength of labor unions and their positive impact on players' salaries; the increased income of athletes that necessitated advice on matters such as financial investments, taxes, and estate planning; and the increase in players' opportunities to generate outside income through endorsement contracts.

648. The rise in the use of agents has been accompanied by an expansion in the range of services that they perform for the players they represent. A breadth of substantive expertise is required in order for agents to effectively represent athletes. The role of agents extends beyond simply negotiating a player's contract with his or her club and frequently includes financial, tax, and estate planning, money management and investment advice, solicitation and negotiation of endorsement contracts, playing career, personal, and post-career guidance, and general legal representation.

649. The relationship between an agent and the athlete he represents is consensual in nature (i.e., the athlete agrees to permit the agent to act on his or her behalf, and the agent agrees to do so). The parties' relationship is generally formalized by a written contract. An agent has a common law fiduciary relationship with the player, which means he has a legal duty of undivided loyalty and good faith to act primarily for the player's benefit in all matters within the scope of his representation.[722] An agent must act as a reasonably prudent agent would do on the player's behalf in similar circumstances, consistent with a player's best interests.[723] As a general rule, an agent must follow the player's instructions (which requires him to be fully informed of the pros and cons of his available options) unless doing so would be illegal.

650. There is a multi-layered legal regulatory framework that governs agent representation of professional athletes in the U.S. consisting of federal and state laws as well as players' union regulation of agents who represent their members.

722. . *Detroit Lions, Inc. v. Argovitz*, 580 F. Supp. 542 (E.D. Mich. 1984); *Brown v. Woolf*, 554 F. Supp. 1206 (S.D. Ind. 1983).

723. . *Zinn v. Parrish*, 644 F.2d 360 (7th Cir. 1981).

§2. Federal Law: Sports Agent Responsibility Trust Act

651. In September 2004, President George W. Bush signed into law the Sports Agent Responsibility Trust Act (SPARTA),[724] the first federal legislation that specifically regulates sports agents. SPARTA is modeled after key provisions of the Uniform Athlete Agents Act (UAAA), which more than forty states adopted and is discussed *infra*. SPARTA does not preempt but rather supplements state law requirements imposed by the UAAA. SPARTA states that it is the "sense of Congress that States should enact the Uniform Athletes Agents Act … to protect student-athletes and the integrity of amateur sports from unscrupulous sports agents."[725]

652. Like the UAAA, SPARTA prohibits agents from using improper inducements (e.g., cash payments and gifts) and providing misleading information to recruit student-athletes, predating or postdating agency contracts, and not providing certain disclosures. The agency agreement must conspicuously notify student-athletes, and parents or guardians of athletes under the age of 18 of the potential loss of eligibility to compete as an amateur in interscholastic or intercollegiate athletics. Within seventy-two hours of signing an agency contract or before the next athletic event in which the athlete is eligible to participate, both the student-athlete and agent must inform the athletic director of the educational institution at which the athlete is enrolled of the agency agreement.

653. Violations of SPARTA, which constitute unfair and deceptive acts or practices under the FTC Act and will be enforced by the FTC, are punishable by fines up to USD 10,000 per incident.[726] SPARTA specifically authorizes state attorney generals to bring civil actions in federal court seeking injunctive relief and damages if there is reason to believe the interests of that state's resident have been "threatened or adversely affected" by a violation of SPARTA. SPARTA also permits individuals, to seek "remedies available under existing Federal or State law or equity."[727] Thus far, there are no reported cases of any government or private party enforcement of SPARTA.

§3. State Law

654. Two bodies of state law may be available to regulate the athlete agent profession. One level consists of general common law contract and tort law that defines the legal relationship between an agent and an athlete[728] as well as criminal laws that

724. . 15 U.S.C. §§ 7801–7807 (2011).

725. . 15 U.S.C. § 7807.

726. . 15 U.S.C. § 45 (l) & (m).

727. . 15 U.S.C. § 7806.

728. . *See* , e.g., *Hilliard v. Black*, 125 F. Supp. 2d 1071 (N.D. Fla. 2000) (NFL players asserted breach of fiduciary duty, breach of contract, conversion, negligence, and civil conspiracy claims against agent Tank Black and his company contending they improperly induced them to invest millions in investment schemes); *Detroit Lions v. Argovitz*, 580 F. Supp. 542 (E.D. Mich. 1984) (agent's conflict of interest and self dealing in contract negotiations breaches fiduciary duty to player); *Brown v. Woolf*, 554 F. Supp. 1206 (S.D. Ind. 1983) (agent breached fiduciary duty by failing to investigate club's financial stability and obtain guarantees or collateral to protect player's contract rights, including receipt of deferred compensation).

might be invoked to penalize agents for fraud and other crimes. The other level consists of agent-specific legislation. Prior to the year 2000, agent-specific legislation was in effect in twenty-eight states (the state of Washington had adopted such legislation, but repealed it in 1999).

655. In 2000, the National Conference of Commissioners on Uniform State Laws drafted the UAAA and presented it to the states for adoption. The UAAA has been adopted in more than forty states and two U.S. territories. From a regulatory perspective, the primary goal of the UAAA is to protect the interests of student-athletes and institutions of higher education by regulating the activities of sports agents, whose dealings with student-athletes may cause them to lose their eligibility to play intercollegiate sports and their athletic scholarships before earning their college degrees. NCAA rules provide that an individual is ineligible to participate in an intercollegiate sport "if he or she ever has agreed (orally or in writing) to be represented by an agent for the purpose of marketing his or her athletics ability or reputation in that sport"[729] or has accepted any benefits from an agent.[730]

656. The UAAA's other critical goal is to achieve uniformity in state regulation of athlete agents. The Prefatory Note to the UAAA states:

> The statutes differ greatly. About two-thirds of the statutes impose registration requirements. There are substantial differences in the registration procedures, disclosure required, and requirements relating to record maintenance, reporting, renewal, notice, warning and security. The term of the registration is one year in thirteen States, two years in four states, and two States do not specify a term. Most States require notification to States or educational institutions and athletes of certain matters, but the matters vary widely. Conscientious agents operating in more than a single State must have nightmares caused by the lack of uniformity in the existing statutes, and the difficulties in compliance and the severity of penalties which may be imposed for violations.[731]

657. The UAAA requires an individual to register as an athlete agent with the appropriate state agency before entering into an agency contract with a student-athlete or soliciting a student-athlete to enter into an agency contract. A certificate of registration may be denied if the applicant "has a significant adverse effect on the applicant's fitness to act as an athlete agent." In making this determination, the state agency that administers and enforces the UAAA, which generally is the secretary of state's office, may consider factors such as whether the applicant has been convicted of a crime involving moral turpitude or a felony; made misrepresentations in the application for certification; engaged in conduct that would disqualify the agent from serving in a fiduciary capacity; engaged in conduct prohibited by the UAAA; had an agent license revoked, suspended or denied; or engaged in conduct that adversely affected a student-athlete's eligibility or resulted in an educational institution being sanctioned.

658. The UAAA prohibits an athlete agent, with the intent to induce a student-athlete to enter into an agency contract, from giving any materially false or misleading

729. . NCAA Bylaw 12.3.1.
730. . NCAA Bylaw 12.3.1.2.
731. . *Prefatory Note*, Uniform Athlete Agents Act 5–6 (2000).

information or making a materially false promise or representation or furnishing anything of value to a student-athlete before the student-athlete enters into the agency contract. An athlete agent also is prohibited from engaging in the following conduct: intentionally initiating contact with a student-athlete unless registered; failing to register; providing false information in the application for registration; predating or postdating an agency contract; or failing to inform a student-athlete of the eligibility implications of signing an agency agreement. An athlete agent is required to notify the athletic director of the educational institution at which the student-athlete is enrolled within the earlier of seventy-two hours after entering into an agency contract or before the next scheduled intercollegiate athletic event in which the student-athlete would otherwise be eligible to participate.

659. An athlete agent who violates the UAAA may be fined by the state and is subject to criminal prosecution. An agency contract between an unregistered athlete agent and student-athlete is void. An educational institution may recover damages against an athlete agent for harm caused by his violation of the UAAA (e.g., sanctions imposed by the NCAA for permitting an ineligible student-athlete to participate, which may preclude the institution from participating in NCAA postseason championship competition in the student-athlete's sport and/or adverse financial consequences).

660. A 2010 study conducted by the Associated Press revealed that over half of the forty-two states that had enacted the UAAA had "yet to revoke or suspend a single license, or invoke penalties of any sort."[732] According to the Associated Press:

> [t]wenty four states reported taking no disciplinary or criminal actions against sports agents, and were unable to determine if state or local prosecutors had pursued such cases. Others described the laws as being enforced a few times, or rarely, an indication of what a low priority they are.

661. Texas is one of the few states that consistently enforced the UAAA. The Associated Press study found that Texas had disciplined thirty-one agents and levied fines totaling USD 17,500 between 2008 and 2010.

662. Some states are beginning to enforce the UAAA more aggressively in response to athlete agent conduct that results in the imposition of NCAA sanctions against in-state public universities. For example, in 2010, the North Carolina Secretary of State's office began a three-year investigation in connection with the NCAA's probe of the University of North Carolina at Chapel Hill (UNC)'s football program. As a result, it charged former NFL agent Terry Watson with 13 violations of its version of the UAAA for giving UNC players Robert Quinn, Marvin Austin and Grey Little roughly USD 24,000 in cash and travel accommodations to induce them to enter into agency contracts with him. In April 2017, Watson pled guilty to these charges and was fined USD 5,000 and placed on probation for thirty months.

663. In 2015, the UAAA was revised in response to concerns regarding its lack of uniformity because several states adopted variations to the Act, its limited deterrence effect arising from under-enforcement and weak penalties, and its perceived failure to adequately protect the interests of student-athletes. Prior to its revision, the UAAA had been adopted in forty-three states, territories, and Washington, D.C. The revised

732. . Alan S. Zagler, *US Sports Agents*, ASSOCIATED PRESS (Aug. 17, 2010).

UAAA (RUAAA) has been enacted in Alabama, Idaho and Washington and introduced for state legislative approval in several other states, including Colorado and Michigan.

664. The RUAAA's Preface states:

> . . . It became evident that the variations from state to state put uniformity at risk and may have discouraged reputable agents from complying with the act. To deal with these issues, the Uniform Law Commission adopted the Revised Uniform Athlete Agents Act (RUAAA) in July of 2015.
>
> The purposes of the RUAAA include providing enhanced protection for student athletes and educational institutions, creating a uniform body of agent registration information for use by the state agencies registering agents, and simplifying the registration process for agents.

Specifically, the RUAAA:

- Revises the definition of "athlete agent" to include an individual who, for compensation or the anticipation of compensation, serves the athlete in an advisory capacity on a matter related to finances, business pursuits, or career management decisions or manages the business affairs of the athlete by providing assistance with bills, payments, contracts, or taxes, and an individual who gives something of value to a student-athlete or another person in anticipation of representing the athlete for a purpose related to the athlete's participation in athletics.
- Contains two alternatives for athlete agent registration. Alternative A includes a true reciprocal registration requirement in that if an individual is issued a certificate of registration by one state, the registration is in good standing and no disciplinary proceedings are pending against the registration, and the law in that state is the same or more restrictive as the law in another state, the other state would be required to register the individual. Alternative B would adopt an interstate compact when the act is enacted by at least five states. The compact would create the Commission on Interstate Regulation of Athlete Agents to provide a single registration site where an individual could register to act as an athlete agent in the states that are members of the compact.
- Adds additional requirements to the signing of an agency contract. . . .
- Requires an agent to notify the educational institution at which a student athlete is enrolled before contacting a student athlete and requires an athlete agent with a preexisting relationship with a student athlete who enrolls at an educational institution and receives an athletic scholarship to notify the institution of the relationship if the agent knows or should have known of the enrollment and the relationship was motivated by the intention of the agent to recruit or solicit the athlete to enter an agency contract or the agent actually recruited or solicited the student athlete to enter a contract.
- Adds criminal penalties for athlete agents who encourage another individual to take on behalf of the agent an action the agent is prohibited from taking and gives student athletes a right of action against an athlete agent in violation of the act.

§4. Players Union Regulation

665. Players unions are an important part of the web of regulation that governs the relationship between athlete agents and the players they represent. Pursuant to U.S. labor law, the union is the exclusive bargaining representative of its members. In most industries, the union negotiates all terms and conditions of employment for its members, including their individual wages. However, the professional team sport industries are unique because each players union permits each of its member players to individually negotiate with a club his compensation and other terms and conditions of employment such as contract length, bonus provisions, no trade clauses, etc. As a result, players are permitted (but not required) to hire agents to represent them in their contract negotiations with their respective clubs within the parameters of the league's CBA and UPC.

666. In *Collins v. National Basketball Players Association*,[733] the court described the abuses that prompted players unions to exercise regulatory authority over agents who represent their players:

> Specifically, players complained that the agents imposed high and nonuniform fees for negotiation services, insisted on execution of open-ended powers of attorney giving the agents broad powers over players' professional and financial decisions, failed to keep players apprised of the status of negotiations with NBA teams, failed to submit itemized bills for fees and services, and, in some cases had conflicts of interest arising out of representing coaches and/or general managers of NBA teams as well as players. Many players believed that they were bound by contract not to dismiss their agents regardless of dissatisfaction with their services and fees, because the agents had insisted on the execution of long-term agreements. Some agents offered money and other inducements to players, their families, and coaches to obtain player clients.

667. In 1983, the NFL players union required that agents representing its member players in contract negotiations with league clubs be certified, which was based on its asserted inherent authority to regulate agents acting on behalf of players .and In 1986, in response to player complaints regarding the above-described abuses by agents, the NBA players union established a comprehensive system of agent certification. The MLB and NHL players unions also require agents to be certified.[734]

668. Each players union establishes its own certification requirements for agents, which generally require a prospective agent to satisfy certain character standards such as not having engaged in any conduct that significantly impacts adversely on his/her credibility, integrity or competence to serve in a fiduciary capacity on behalf of players. Prospective player agents also may have to satisfy competency requirements such as passing a written examination administered by the players union and/or fulfilling particular education or experience criteria. For example, the NFL Players Association (NFLPA) requires a postgraduate degree from a college or university or at least seven

733. . 850 F. Supp. 1468, 1471 (D. Colo. 1991).

734. . *See* generally Kenneth L. Shropshire, Timothy Davis, and N. Jeremi Duru, *The Business of Sports Agents* (3d ed. 2016).

years of "sufficient negotiation experience" to be eligible for certification as a "contract advisor" (i.e., agent). In addition to paying an annual fee to the players union, agents may be required to satisfy particular requirements to maintain their certification. National Basketball Players Association (NBPA) regulations provide that an agent's certification will automatically expire if he or she does not represent a player under contract with an NBA club for a five-year period. The NFLPA requires agents to attend of its annual seminars on individual contract negotiations, and to negotiate at least one player contract during a three-year period to retain his certification.

669. Federal labor law empowers player unions to regulate fees for agent services, and the statutory labor exemption immunizes this regulatory authority from antitrust challenge by agents.[735] For example, NFLPA's regulations generally limit the maximum fee an agent can charge for negotiating an NFL player contract to 3% of the compensation that a player receives during the playing season covered by the contract the agent negotiates, although agents are allowed to charge less than the maximum. The NBPA allows an agent to charge a maximum fee of up to 4% for the negotiation of a player/team contract; 2% is the maximum allowable fee for negotiating a contract for an NBA player who receives the minimum compensation pursuant to the CBA. The MLB Players Association allows the market to determine agent's fees and sets no maximum on the amount of the fee an agent can earn for negotiating a player's contract with a club.

670. The players union establishes a code of conduct that agents must comply with as a condition of their certification to represent players in contract negotiations with their respective clubs. For example, relevant provisions of the NFL player union standards of conduct are as follows:

A. General Requirements

671. A Contract Advisor shall be required to:

(1) Disclose on his/her Application and thereafter upon request of the NFLPA all information relevant to his/her qualifications to serve as a Contract Advisor . . . ;

(5) Comply with the maximum fee schedule and all other provisions of these Regulations and any amendments thereto;

(6) Execute and abide by the printed Standard Representation Agreement with all players represented . . . ;

(9) Provide on or before May 1, each year, to every player who he/she represents, with a copy to the NFLPA, an itemized statement covering the period beginning March 1 of the prior year through February 28 or 29 of that year, which separately

735. . *Collins v. National Basketball Players Ass'n*, 976 F.2d 740 (10th Cir. 1992).

sets forth both the fee charged to the player for, and any expenses incurred in connection with, the performance of the following services: (a) individual player salary negotiations; (b) management of the player's assets; (c) financial, investment, legal, tax and/or other advice to the player; and, (d) any other miscellaneous services.] … ;

(14) Fully comply with applicable state and federal laws … ;

(17) Act at all times in a fiduciary capacity on behalf of players.[736]

B. Prohibited Conduct

672. Contract Advisors are prohibited from:

(1) Representing any player in individual contract negotiations with any Club unless he/she (i) is an NFLPA Certified Contract Advisor; (ii) has signed the Standard Representation Agreement with such player; and (iii) has filed a copy of the Standard Representation Agreement with the NFLPA along with any other contract(s) or agreement(s) between the player and the Contract Advisor.

(2) Providing or offering money or any other thing of value to any player or prospective player to induce or encourage that player to utilize his/her services.

(3) Providing or offering money or any other thing of value to a member of the player's or prospective player's family or any other person for the purpose of inducing or encouraging that person to recommend the services of the Contract Advisor.

(4) Providing materially false or misleading information to any player or prospective player in the context of recruiting the player as a client or in the course of representing that player as his Contract Advisor … .

(7) Holding or seeking to hold, either directly or indirectly, a financial interest in any professional football club or in any other business entity when such investment could create an actual conflict of interest or the appearance of a conflict of interest in the representation of NFL players.

736. The complete NFLPA Regulations Governing Contract Advisors (as amended through June 2012) can be found at http://nflparesources.blob.core.windows.net/mediaresources/files/PDFs/SCAA/2012_NFLPA_Regulations_Contract_Advisors.pdf.

(8) Engaging in any other activity which creates an actual or potential conflict of interest with the effective representation of NFL players. …

(10) Negotiating and/or agreeing to any provision in a player contract which deprives or purports to deprive that player of any benefit contained in any collectively bargained agreement between the NFL and the NFLPA. …

(14) Engaging in unlawful conduct and/or conduct involving dishonesty, fraud, deceit, misrepresentation, or other activity which reflects adversely on his/ her fitness as a Contract Advisor or jeopardizes his/her effective representation of NFL players.

(15) Failure to comply with the maximum fee provisions contained in section 4 of these Regulations. …

(21) (a) Initiating any communication, directly or indirectly, with a player who has entered into a Standard Representation Agreement with another Contract Advisor and such Standard Representation Agreement is on file with the NFLPA if the communication concerns a matter relating to the: (1) Player's current Contract Advisor; (2) Player's current Standard Representation Agreement; (3) Player's contract status with any NFL Club(s); or (4) Services to be provided by prospective Contract Advisor either through a Standard Representation Agreement or otherwise.

(b) If a player, already a party to a Standard Representation Agreement, initiates communication with a Contract Advisor relating to any of the subject matters listed in section 3(B)(21)(a) the Contract Advisor may continue communications with the Player regarding any of those matters.

(c) Section 3(B)(21) shall not apply to any player who has less than sixty days remaining before his NFL Player Contract expires, and he has not yet signed a new Standard Representation Agreement with a Contract Advisor within the sixty day period.

(d) Section 3(B)(21) shall not prohibit a Contract Advisor from sending a player written materials which may be reasonably interpreted as advertising directed at players in general and not targeted at a specific player. …

> (26) Directly or indirectly soliciting a prospective rookie player for representation as a Contract Advisor if that player has signed a Standard Representation Agreement prior to a date which is thirty days before the NFL Draft and if thirty days have not elapsed since the Agreement was signed and filed with the NFLPA . . .[737]

673. An agent who violates a players union's regulations is subject to discipline, which may include a fine, suspension, or decertification. In *Collins v. National Basketball Players Association,*[738] the Tenth Circuit upheld the authority of a players union to discipline agents, including the power to refuse to recertify an agent. Former NBA basketball superstar Kareem Abdul-Jabbar filed a lawsuit accusing his agent of financial improprieties. Prior to the settlement of this lawsuit, the agent had been decertified by the NBA players union for violating its regulations. After his application for recertification was denied, the agent sued the players union. Rejecting his claims, the court ruled:

> [The agent] maintains his attack on the Committee's decision to deny his certification because it was based in part on its finding that he had breached his fiduciary duty as an investment agent and money manager. He argues that his conduct outside of negotiations between players and their teams is not a legitimate interest of the union because it has no bearing on the union's interest in the wage scale and working conditions of its members.
>
> The [union] established the Regulations to deal with agent abuses, including agents' violations of their fiduciary duties as labor negotiators. It was entirely fair for the Committee to conclude that a man who had neglected his fiduciary duties as an investment agent and money manager could not be trusted to fulfill his fiduciary duties as a negotiator. The integrity of a prospective negotiating agent is well within the [union]'s legitimate interest in maintaining the wage scale and working conditions of its members.

674. In *White v. NFL,*[739] the court impliedly affirmed the authority of a players union (e.g., the NFLPA) to police agents and discipline them for violating its regulations. The NFL charged that the San Francisco Forty-Niners club and certain agents violated the NFL's CBA and a stipulation and settlement (SAS) by entering into undisclosed agreements concerning player compensation. The NFL sought to discover information regarding these agreements from the involved agents, who objected to doing so because they were "not signatories to the CBA and SSA and were not subject to any penalty scheme provided in those agreements." A special master had dismissed the agents from the underlying proceeding, but ruled the agents could be subject to penalties if the court subsequently determined the agents were required to comply with the CBA and SSA. The court concluded that the NFL CBA and the SSA contractually bound these agents, even though they were not signatories. It reasoned that certified agents

737. . *Ibid.*
738. . 976 F.2d 740 (10th Cir. 1992).
739. . 92 F. Supp. 2d 918 (D. Minn. 2000).

give implied consent to adhere to the NFL CBA by accepting the NFLPA's permission to negotiate player contracts; "player agents enjoy significant and ongoing economic benefits" that result directly from the CBA; and "agents have expressly agreed to be bound by NFLPA agent regulations which include specific provisions (1) requiring each certified player agent to become familiar with "applicable CBAs and other governing documents," and (2) prohibiting certified agents from "negotiating and/or agreeing to any provision in any agreement involving a player which directly or indirectly violates any stated policies or rules established by the NFLPA."

675. Players union regulations typically provide that arbitration before a union-selected arbitrator is the sole procedure available to challenge the union's refusal to certify an agent or its disciplinary action against an agent for rules violations. Courts have held that this form of arbitration system is consistent with the Federal Arbitration Act, which provides for limited judicial review of arbitration awards, including agent claims that the arbitrator was biased in favor of the union.[740]

740. . *Black v. NFLPA*, 87 F. Supp. 2d 1 (D. D.C. 2000).

Chapter 3. Commercial Integrity of Sport

676. Unlike in Europe, sports betting is generally prohibited in the U.S. under a variety of federal laws,[741] although some U.S. states have grandfathered rights to permit certain forms of licensed and regulated sports betting in their respective jurisdictions. Sports betting is prohibited because of the negative social effects of gambling addictions (particularly among youths who engage in online gambling), the threat it poses to the integrity of sport, and the inability of sports governing bodies to eradicate gambling.[742]

677. One commentator has summarized three of the most significant federal laws prohibiting sports betting as follows:

> [T]he Interstate Wire Act of 1961 (Wire Act) prohibits gambling businesses from transmitting bets or information via wire communications between states or countries. To violate the Wire Act, a person must be in the business of betting and knowingly use a wire communication to transmit information for gambling purposes. Using wire communications includes use of the telephone and the Internet. However, a bet placed via wire communication between bettors in two states that have legalized gambling is a legal act under the Wire Act. Additionally, the Wire Act has other limitations, like a lack of punishment for individual bettors. [because]. Congress never intended that the federal government should thus invade the criminal jurisdiction that properly belongs to the states. The Wire Act has broad application to gambling, and thirty-one years after the Wire Act was passed, Congress decided to address sports gambling with specific legislation.
>
> This sports specific legislation, [the Professional and Amateur Sports Protection Act (PASPA)], was enacted in 1992 in order to regulate sports gambling. PASPA states that it is unlawful for (1) a governmental entity to sponsor, operate, advertise, promote, license, or authorize by law or compact, or (2) a person to sponsor, operate, advertise, or promote, pursuant to the law or compact of a government entity, a lottery, sweepstakes, or other betting, gambling, or wagering scheme

741. . *See* , e.g., The Interstate Wire Act of 1961 (The Wire Act), 18 U.S.C.S. § 1084. The Professional and Amateur Sport Protection Acts (PASPA), 18 U.S.C. §3702; Unlawful Internet Gambling Enforcement Act of 2006 (UIGEA), 31 U.S.C. §5363 ; The Transportation in Aid of Racketeering Enterprises Act of 1961 (The Travel Act), 18 U.S.C. §1952; The Illegal Gambling Business Act of 1970, 18 U.S.C. §1955; the Racketeer Influenced and Corrupt Organizations Act of 1970 (RICO), 18 U.S.C. §1962; and the Bribery in Sporting Contests Act, 18 U.S.C §224. For a discussion of these and other laws impacting the sports betting and gambling industry *see* Paul Anderson, "*The Regulation of Gambling Under U.S. Federal and State Law," Int'l Sports L. J. 68 (2009); Erica N. Reib, Comment, Ante Up or Fold: What Should Be Done About Gambling in College Sports*?, 21 Marq. Sports L. Rev. 621 (2011).

742. . *See* generally John W. Kindt & Thomas Asmar, *College and Amateur Sports Gambling: Gambling Away Our Youth?*, 8 Vill. Sports & Ent. L.J. 221 (2002); Lori K. Miller & Cathryn L. Claussen, *Online Sports Gambling – Regulation or Prohibition?*, 11 J. Leg. Aspects Sport 99 (2001).

based, directly or indirectly (through the use of geographical references or otherwise), on one or more competitive games in which amateur or professional athletes participate, or are intended to participate, or on one or more performances of such athletes in such games.

However, there are exceptions to PASPA. These exceptions include gambling schemes in states to the extent that they occurred legally between January 1, 1976 and August 31, 1990. These existing schemes are grandfathered in and not subject to PASPA the way that a new form of gambling would be. This exception applies to only a few states, namely Nevada, Oregon, Washington, New Mexico, Delaware, and Montana, and the gambling allowed in each varies greatly. At the time of the Act, Nevada had the most extensive sports betting scheme that was run through casino books. Oregon had a lottery based on the National Football League (NFL). In even more limited situations, Washington permitted one-dollar bets on racecars, and New Mexico allowed gambling on bicycle races. Although Delaware and Montana had state statutes that allowed for sports gambling, neither of them actually had state-endorsed sports gambling at the time the PASPA was enacted. Another important exception to PASPA was the fact that there was a one-year window of opportunity for any state to legalize casino gambling, which could have included sports betting. No state capitalized on this opportunity during the time frame.

An interesting caveat of the PASPA is that it forbids sports gambling that is established by a State or person, but it provides no way to punish the gambling of individual bettors. This enforcement issue is similar to that found in the Wire Act. . . .

Since the proliferation of the Internet and its use by large contingents of the population, online sports betting has exploded. . . . In the United States, the Unlawful Internet Gambling [Enforcement] Act of 2006 [UIGEA] was passed as a part of the Safe Accountability for Every Port Act of 2006. The bill prohibits anyone engaged in the business of betting or wagering, knowingly accept[ing], in connection with the participation of another person in unlawful Internet gambling, credit, an electronic fund transfer, any check, draft, or similar instrument, or the proceeds of any other financial transaction. [which] involves a financial institution as a payor or financial intermediary. However, the law has received criticism because it is unclear what unlawful internet gambling is, and it has the potential to be difficult to implement because of a lack of jurisdiction over foreign entities.[743]

743. . Reib, *supra* n. 652 (internal citations omitted).

678. In *NCAA v. Governor of New* Jersey,[744] the Third Circuit, in an en banc rehearing, affirmed a three-judge panel's holding that a 2014 New Jersey statute to partially repeal certain prohibitions on sports gambling in order to generate revenues for the state's casinos and horse racing tracks, violated PASPA. The court ruled that "Under PASPA, it shall be unlawful for 'a governmental entity to sponsor, operate, advertise, promote, license, or authorize by law or compact' sports gambling. 28 U.S.C. § 3702(1). We conclude that the 2014 Law violates PASPA because it authorizes by law sports gambling." In June 2017, the U.S. Supreme Court agreed to review the Third Circuit's ruling, which precludes individual states from effectively legalizing sports gambling to increase business and tax revenues within their respective jurisdictions, and will issue its opinion in 2018.

679. U.S. professional sports governing bodies strictly prohibit their respective players, coaches, umpires, referees, and administrators from engaging in sports gambling or match fixing.[745] Severe internal disciplinary sanctions have been imposed on those who violate these prohibitions. In the so-called "Black Sox Scandal," eight players from the Chicago White Sox baseball club were accused of intentionally allowing the Cincinnati Reds team to win the 1919 World Series. Although all eight players were acquitted of criminal charges, the sport's governing authority banned them from baseball for life for their involvement in this match fixing scandal.

680. Pete Rose, MLB's all-time hits leader, bet on a reported fifty-two baseball games during the 1987 season as the Cincinnati Reds' manager. Although he never bet against the Reds, Commissioner Bart Giamatti placed Rose placed on baseball's permanently ineligible list on August 24, 1989, which precludes him from being considered for election to baseball's Hall of Fame.

681. Even absent any allegations or proof of match fixing or efforts to improperly influence the outcome of a sports event, U.S. courts have upheld the authority of a sports league to impose severe discipline on a professional athlete for betting on league games. In *Molinas v. National Basketball Association,*[746] the NBA indefinitely suspended Jack Molinas from playing in the league (which effectively constituted a lifetime suspension) after he admitted to placing bets on his own team to win games. Rejecting his antitrust claim, a New York federal court held that " … a disciplinary rule invoked against gambling seems about as reasonable a rule as could be imagined" and is "necessary for the survival of the league." The court explained:

> when he [Molinas] chose to place a bet this would indicate to the book- makers that a member of the Fort Wayne team believed that his team would exceed its expected performance. Similarly, when he chose not to bet, bookmakers thus would be informed of his opinion that the Pistons would not perform according to expectations. It is certainly reasonable for the League … to conclude that this conduct could not be tolerated and must, therefore, be eliminated. The reasonableness

744. 832 F.3d 389 (3d Cir. 2016).

745. Nevertheless, the NHL and NFL have approved the operation of league clubs in Las Vegas, Nevada, which is the only U.S. state in which casino sports gambling is legal. The Vegas Golden Knights will begin play during the 2017–2018. The Oakland Raiders will relocate to Las Vegas and begin playing home games there in 2019 or 2020.

746. . 190 F.Supp. 241 (S.D.N.Y. 1961).

of the League's action is apparent in view of the fact that at the time, the confidence of the public in basketball had been shattered, due to a series of gambling incidents. Thus, it was absolutely necessary for the sport to exhume gambling from its midst for all times in order to survive. The league could reasonably conclude that in order to effectuate its important and legitimate policies against gambling, and to restore and maintain the confidence of the public vital to its existence, it was necessary to apply its rules strictly and to apply the most stringent sanctions. One can certainly understand the reluctance to permit an admitted gambler to return to the league, and again to participate in championship games, especially in light of the aura and stigma of gambling which has clouded the sports world in the past few years. Viewed in this context, it can be seen that the league was justified in determining that is was absolutely necessary to avoid even the slightest connection with gambling, gamblers, and those who had done business with gamblers, in the future.

682. Because the U.S. major professional sports leagues currently are unionized, the scope of a league's authority to discipline players for gambling and match fixing is defined by the terms of the CBA and/or uniform player contract negotiated between the players union and league clubs. For example, under paragraph 5(e) of the NBA Uniform Player Contract:

> the Player agrees that if the Commissioner, in his sole judgment, shall find that the Player has bet, or has offered or attempted to bet, money or anything of value on the outcome of any game participated in by any team which is a member of the NBA, the Commissioner shall have the power in his sole discretion to suspend the Player indefinitely or to expel him as a player for any member of the NBA, and the Commissioner's finding and decision shall be final, binding, conclusive, and unappealable.

683. Article 35(b) of the NBA Constitution, which is incorporated into the NBA Uniform Player Contract, states that:

> The Commissioner shall direct the dismissal and perpetual disqualification from any further association with the [NBA] or any of its Members, of any Player found by the Commissioner after a hearing to have been guilty of offering, agreeing, conspiring, aiding or attempting to cause any game of basketball to result otherwise than on its merits.

684. In 2007, NBA referee Tim Donaghy, who had placed bets on the point spread of NBA games that he refereed, pled guilty to conspiracy to engage in wire fraud and transmitting wagering information through interstate commerce. Donaghy received USD 30,000 for giving tips based on players' physical conditions and player/referee relations. Donaghy was fined USD 500,000, ordered to pay USD 30,000 in restitution, and sentenced to fifteen months in prison.

685. On January 30, 2017, MLB Commissioner Rob Manfred permanently banned former St. Louis Cardinals scouting director Chris Correa from baseball for hacking into the Houston Astros" team database and accessing it forty-eight times over two and a half years, thereby obtaining confidential information about Astros" player statistics, trade discussions, and scouting reports. In 2016, Correa pled guilty to twelve counts of corporate espionage (a federal crime) and was sentenced to four years in prison. Based on his belief that the Cardinals gained a competitive advantage from Correa's actions even if the club did know how he obtained this information, Commissioner Manfred required the Cardinals to pay USD 2 million in compensation and to give its top two picks in the 2017 MLB draft to the Astros.

686. In the U.S., Daily Fantasy Sports (DFS) contests operated by private parties via the Internet, which are based on the daily points earned by a gamer's selected players' statistical performances in predetermined categories for a particular major league sport, have become very popular, but must comply with applicable federal and state laws. The UIGEA makes it illegal for those "engaged in the business of betting or wagering" to "knowingly accept" funds "in connection with the participation of another person in unlawful Internet gambling."[747] It defines "unlawful Internet gambling" as to "knowingly transmit a bet or wager by any means . . . of the Internet where such a bet or wager is unlawful" under the laws of the state where the wager is "initiated, received, or otherwise made." Although the UIGEA is inapplicable to fantasy sports contests that comply with certain requirements, one commentator has observed, "the legality of [DFS] is very much unsettled, and the ultimate issue of legality seems to depend on each individual contest's game rules and states of operation."[748] In general, under state gambling laws, the legality of a particular DFS contest depends upon whether it is characterized judicially or statutorily as a game of "skill," which generally is legal, or "chance," which usually is not. In March 2016, Virginia became the first of several states (including New York) to legalize and regulate DFS contests. Although U.S. professional sports leagues historically opposed DFS contests, MLB has promoted "a play-for-cash [DFS] contest on its website" and the NBA "owns an equity stake in FanDuel Inc.—the marketplace leader in [DFS],"[749] which reduced the likelihood of being challenged as illegal gambling under PASPA.

687. Like the U.S. professional sports leagues, the NCAA also prohibits sports betting and gambling. NCAA Bylaw 10.3 prohibits its member educational institution's athletics department staff members, non-athletics staff member with athletics responsibilities, conference staff member, and student-athletes from knowingly participating in "sports wagering activities" or providing information to those involved in or associated "with any type of sports wagering activities concerning intercollegiate, amateur or professional athletics competition." NCAA Bylaw 10.2.1 states: "Sports wagering includes placing, accepting or soliciting a wager (on a staff member"s or student-athlete's own behalf or on the behalf of others) of any type with any individual or organization on any intercollegiate, amateur or professional team or contest. Examples of sports wagering include, but are not limited to, the use of a bookmaker or parlay card; Internet sports wagering; auctions in which bids are placed on teams, individuals or contests; and pools or fantasy leagues in which an entry fee is required and there

747. 31 U.S.C. §5363.

748. *See* generally, Marc Edelman, *Navigating the Legal Risks of Daily Fantasy Sports: A Detailed Primer in Federal and State Gambling Law*, 2016 U. Ill. L. Rev. 117.

749. *Ibid.*

is an opportunity to win a prize." In February 2017, the NCAA suspended five University of Richmond baseball players for violating this rule by participating in a Fantasy football league that required payment of an entry fee pending completion of the process for reinstating their intercollegiate athletics eligibility.

Selected Bibliography

§1. Books

Abram, Roger I, *Sports Justice: Law and the Business of Sports* (2010).

Greenberg, Martin J. & James T. Gray, *Sports Law Practice* (2002).

Herz, Gerald, *Professional Athletes and the Law of Workers' Compensation: Rights and Remedies in Law of Professional and Amateur Sports*, 17–1 (Gary A. Uberstine ed., West Group, 2002).

Korr, Charles P, *The End of Baseball As We Knew It: The Players Union*, 1960-81 (2002).

Kuhn, Bowie, *Hardball: The Education of a Baseball Commissioner* (1987).

Miller, Marvin, *A Whole Different Ballgame: The Sport and Business of Baseball* (1991).

Nafziger, James A.R, *International Sports Law* (2d. Ed., Transnational Publishers, Inc., 2004).

Shropshire, Kenneth L, *In Black and White: Race and Sports in America* (1996).

Shropshire, Kenneth L, *The Sports Franchise: Cities in Pursuit of Sports Franchises, Events, Stadiums, and Arenas* (1995).

Shropshire, Kenneth L, Timothy Davis & N. Jeremi Duru, *The Business of Sports Agents* (3d ed. 2016).

Szymanski, Stefan & Stephen F. Ross, Fans of the World, Unite! A (Capitalist) *Manifesto for Sports Consumers* (2008).

Weiler, Paul, *Leveling the Playing Field: How the Law Can Make Sports Better for Fans* (2000).

Weistart, John C. & Cym H. Lowell, *The Law of Sports* (1979).

§2. Law Review Articles

Abram, Roger I, *Inside Baseball's Salary Arbitration Process*, 6 U. Chi. L. Sch. Roundtable 55 (1999).

Anderson, Paul & Barbara Osborne, *A Historical Review of Title IX Litigation*, 18 J. L. Aspects Sport 128 (2008).

Selected Bibliography

Anderson, Paul M, *A Cart That Accommodates: Using Case Law to Understand the ADA, Sports, and Casey Martin*, 1 Va. Sports & Ent. L. J. 211 (2002).

Bard, Robert L. & Lewis Kurlantzick, "*Knicks-Heat and the Appropriateness of Sanctions in Sport*, 20 Cardozo Arts & Ent. L.J. 507 (2002).

Barlett, Stephen J, *Contract Negotiations and Salary Arbitration in the NHL: An Agent's View*, 4 Marq. Sports L.J. 1 (1993).

Barner, Tamara L, *Show Me the ... Ethics?: The Implications of the Model Rules of Ethics on Attorneys in the Sports Industry*, 16 Geo. J. Legal Ethics 519 (2003).

Bean, Lori L, *Ambush Marketing: Sport Sponsorship Confusion and the Lanham Act*, 75 B.U. L. Rev. 1099 (1995).

Benedetti, Anne & Jim Bunting, *There's a New Sheriff in Town: A Review of the United States Anti-Doping Agency*, I.S.L.R. 19 (2003).

Berry, Carole C, *Taxation of U.S. Athletes Playing in Foreign Countries*, 13 Marq. Sports L.R. 1 (2002).

Berry, Robert C. & William B. Gould, *A Long Deep Drive to Collective Bargaining: Of Players, Owners, Brawls, and Strikes*, 31 Case W. Res. L. Rev. 685 (1981).

Brake, Deborah L. & Verna L. Williams, *The Heart of the Game: Putting Race and Educational Equity at the Center of Title IX*, 7 Vir. Sports & Enter. L.J. 199, 210–211 (2008).

Bridgeman, Jacquelyn, *The Thrill of Victory and the Agony of Defeat: What Sports Tell Us About Achieving Equality in America*, 7 Vir. Sports & Ent. L.J. 248 (2008).

Burton, Bruce W. & Matthew J. Mitten, *New Remedies For Breach of Sports Facility Use Agreements: Time For Marketplace Realism*, 88 Iowa L. Rev. 809 (2003).

Byrnes, Jaime D. & Alison B. Prout, *Major League Baseball Players Association v. Garvey: Revisiting the Standard for Arbitral Review*, 7 Harv. Negot. L. Rev. 389 (2004).

Carter, W. Burlette, *Introduction: What Makes a "Field" a Field?* 1 Va. J. Sports &L. 235 (1999).

Champion, Walter T. Jr., *Attorneys Qua Sports Agents: An Ethical Conundrum*, 7 Marq. Sports L.J. 349 (1997).

Cozillio, Michael, *The Athletic Scholarship and the College National Letter of Intent: A Contract by Any Other Name*. 35 Wayne L. Rev. 1275 (1989).

Davis, Timothy, *Absence of Good Faith: Defining a University's Educational Obligation to Student-Athletes*, 28 Hous. L. Rev. 743 (1991).

Davis, Timothy, *Avila v. Citrus Community College District: Shaping the Contours of Immunity and Primary Assumption of the Risk*, 17 Marq. Sports L. Rev. 259 (2006).

Davis, Timothy, *Intercollegiate Athletics: Competing Models and Conflicting Realities*. 25 Rutgers L.J. 269 (1994).

Davis, Timothy, *Race and Sports in America: An Historical Overview*, 7 Vir. Sports & Enter. L.J. 291 (2008).

Selected Bibliography

Davis, Timothy, *Regulating the Athlete-Agent Industry: Intended and Unintended Consequences*, 42 Willamette L. Rev. 781 (2006).

Davis, Timothy, *Tort Liability of Coaches for Injuries to Professional Athletes: Overcoming Policy and Doctrinal Barriers*, 76 UMKC L. Rev. 571 (2008).

Davis, Timothy, *What is Sports Law?*, 11 Marq. Sports L. Rev. 211 (2001).

Edelman, Marc, *Navigating the Legal Risks of Daily Fantasy Sports: A Detailed Primer in Federal and State Gambling Law*, 2016 U. Ill. L. Rev. 117.

Feldman, Gabriel A, *The Puzzling Persistence of the Single Entity Argument for Sports Leagues: American Needle and the Supreme Court's Opportunity to Reject a Flawed Defense*, Wis. L. Rev. 835 (2009).

Goplerud, C. Peter III & Nicolas P. Terry, *Allocation of Risk Between Hockey Fans and Facilities: Tort Liability After the Puck Drops*, 38 Tulsa L. Rev. 445 (2003).

Gould, William B, *Labor Issues in Professional Sports: Reflections on Baseball, Labor and Antitrust Law*, 15 Stan. L. & Pol'y Rev. 61 (2004).

Grauer, Myron C, *Recognition of the National Football League As a Single Entity Under Section 1 of the Sherman Act: Implications of the Consumer Welfare Model*, 82 Mich. L. Rev. 1 (1983).

Grow, Nathaniel, *Defining the "Business of Baseball*": A Proposed Framework for Determining the Scope of Professional Baseball's Antitrust Exemption, 44 UC Davis L. Rev. 557 (2010).

Hanlon, Sean M. & Ray Yasser, *J.J. Morrison and His Right of Publicity Lawsuit Against the NCAA*, 15 Vill. Sports & Ent. L.J. 241 (2008).

Harary, Charles, *Aggressive Play or Criminal Assault? An In-Depth Look at Sports Violence and Criminal Liability*, 25 Colum. J.L. & Arts 197 (2002).

Holden, John T., et. al, *The Future Is Now: Esports Policy Considerations and Potential Litigation*, 27 J. Legal Aspects Sport 46 (2017).

Hurst, Thomas R. & James N. Knight, *Coaches Liability for Athletes' Injuries and Deaths*, 13 Seton Hall J. Sport L. 27 (2003).

Hylton, Joseph G, *A Foul Ball in the Courtroom: The Baseball Spectator Injury as a Case of First Impression*, 38 Tulsa L. Rev. 485 (2003).

Hylton, Joseph G, *The Haelan Decision and the Origins of the Right of Publicity*, 12 Marq. Sports L. Rev. 273 (2001).

Idleman, Scott, *Religious Freedom and the Interscholastic Athlete*, 12 Marq. Sports L. Rev. 295 (2001).

Kahn, Mark A, *May the Best Merchandise Win: The Law of Non-Trademark Uses of Sports Logos*, 14 Marq. Sports L. Rev. 283 (2004).

Karcher, Richard T, *The Use of Players' Identities in Fantasy Sports Leagues: Developing Workable Standards for Right of Publicity Claims*, 111 Penn. St. L. Rev. 557, 572 (2007).

Karcher, Richard T, *Fundamental Fairness in Union Regulation of Sports Agents*, 40 Conn. L. Rev. 355 (2007).

Keller, Bruce P, *Condemned to Repeat the Past: The Reemergence of Misappropriation and Other Common Law Theories of Protection for Intellectual Property*, 11 Harv. J.L. & Tech. 401 (1998).

Kircher, John J, *Golf and Torts: An Interesting Twosome*, 12 Marq. Sports L. Rev. 347 (2001).

Koller, Dionne L., *Putting "Public Law" Into Private Sport*, 43 Pepp. L. Rev. 681 (2016)

Lazaroff, Daniel E, *The Influence of Sports Law on American Jurisprudence*, 1 Va.Sports & Ent. L.J. 1, 2 (2001).

Lazaroff, Daniel E, *The NCAA in Its Second Century: Defender of Amateurism or Antitrust Recidivist?*, 83 Ore. L. Rev. 329 (2007).

Marburger, Daniel R. & Nancy Hogshead-Makar, *Is Title IX Really to Blame for the Decline in Intercollegiate Men's Nonrevenue Sports?*, 14 Marq. Sports L. Rev. 65 (2003).

Marsh, Gene & Marie Robbins, *Weighing the Interests of the Institution, the Membership and Institutional Representatives in an NCAA Investigation*, 55 Fla. L. Rev. 667 (2003).

Mathewson, Alfred D, *Major League Baseball's Monopoly Power and the Negro Leagues*, 35 Am. Bus. L.J. 291, 292 (1998).

McCann, Michael, *American Needle v. NFL: An Opportunity to Reshape Sports Law*, 119 Yale L. J. 726 (2010).

McCormack, Robert A, *Labor or Antitrust? Let the Players Choose*, 4 Vill. Sports & Ent. L.J. 39 (1997).

McCormick, Robert A, & Amy Christian McCormick. *Myth of the Student-Athlete: The College Athlete as Employee*, 81 Wash. L. Rev. 71 (2006).

McKelvey, Steve & John Grady, *Ambush Marketing: The Legal Battleground for Sports Marketers*, 21 Ent. & Sports Law 8 (2004).

McLaren, Richard H, *The Court of Arbitration for Sport: An Independent Arena for the World's Sports Disputes*, 35 Val. U. L. Rev. 379, 381 (2001).

Mellis, Michael J, *Internet Piracy of Live Sports Telecasts*, 18 Marq. Sports L. Rev. 259 (2008).

Mishkin, Jeffrey A, *Dispute Resolution in the NBA: The Allocation of Decision Making Among the Commissioner, Impartial Arbitrator, System Arbitrator, and the Courts*, 35 Val. U.L. Rev. 449 (2001).

Mitten, Matthew J, *Why and How the Supreme Court Should Have Decided O'Bannon v NCAA*, 62 Antitrust Bull. 62 (2017)

Mitten, Matthew J & Stephen F. Ross, *A Regulatory Solution to Better Promote the Educational Values and Economic Sustainability of Intercollegiate Athletics*, 92 Ore. L. Rev. 837 (2014)

Selected Bibliography

Mitten, Matthew J, *Baseball: An Illustration of How Professional Sports Are Structured, Internally Governed, and Legally Regulated in the USA*, 9 J. Comp. L. (Dongguk U.) 141 (2008).

Mitten, Matthew J, *Drug Testing of Athletes – An Internal, Not External, Matter*, 40 New Eng. L. Rev. 797 (2006).

Mitten, Matthew J, *Emerging Legal Issues in Sports Medicine: A Synthesis, Summary, and Analysis*, 76 St. John's L. Rev. 5 (2002).

Mitten, Matthew J, *Enhanced Risk of Harm to One's Self as a Justification for Exclusion from Athletics*, 8 Marq. Sports L.J. 189 (1998).

Mitten, Matthew J, *A Triple Play For The Public Domain: From Delaware Lottery to Motorola to C.B.C*, 11 Chapman L. Rev. 569 (2008).

Mitten, Matthew J & Bruce W. Burton, *Professional Sports Franchise Relocations From Private Law and Public Law Perspectives: Balancing Marketplace Competition, League Autonomy, and the Need for a Level Playing Field*, 56 Md. L. Rev. 57 (1997).

Mitten, Matthew J. & Hayden Opie, *"'Sports Law': Implications for the Development of International, Comparative, and National Law and Global Dispute Resolution"*, 85 Tul. L. Rev. 269 (2010).

Mitten, Matthew J. & Timothy Davis, *Athlete Eligibility Requirements and Legal Protection of Sports Participation Opportunities*, 8 Va. Sports & Ent. L. J. 71 (2009).

Nafziger, James A. R, *Arbitration of Rights and Obligations in the International Sports Arena*, 35 Val. U. L. Rev. 357 (2001).

Oates, Eli D, *Cureton v. NCAA: The Recognition of Proposition 16's Misplaced Use of Standardized Tests in the Context of Collegiate Athletics as a Barrier to Educational Opportunity for Minorities*, 35 Wake Forest L. Rev. 445 (2000).

Parkinson, Jerry R, *Scoundrels: An Inside Look at the NCAA Infractions and Enforcement Processes*, 12 Wyo. L. Rev. 215 (2012).

Parlow, Matthew, *Professional Sports League Commissioners' Authority and Collective Bargaining*, 11 Tex. Rev. Ent. & Sports L. 179 (2010).

Piraino, Thomas A. Jr., *The Antitrust Rationale for the Expansion of Professional Sports Leagues*, 57 Ohio St. L.J. 1677 (1996).

Potuto, Josephine (Jo) R. & Mitten, Matthew J., *Comparing NCAA and Olympic Athlete Eligibility Dispute Resolution Systems in Light of Procedural Fairness and Substantive Justice*, 7 Harv. J. Sports & Ent. L. 1 (2016)

Potuto, Josephine (Jo) R. & Parkinson, Jerry R, *If It Ain't Broke, Don't Fix It: An Examination of the NCAA Division I Infractions Committee's Composition and Decision-Making Process*, 89 Neb. L. Rev. 437 (2011).

Rapp, Geoff, *Affirmative Injunctions in Athletic Employment Contracts: Rethinking the Place of the Lumley Rule in American Sports Law*, 16 Marq. Sports L. Rev. 261 (2006).

Roberts, Gary R, *The Legality of the Exclusive Collective Sale of Intellectual Property Rights by Sports Leagues*, 3 Va. J. Sports & L. 52 (2001).

Roberts, Gary R, *The NCAA, Antitrust, and Consumer Welfare*, 79 Tul. L. Rev. 2631 (1996).

Roberts, Gary R, *Sports Leagues and the Sherman Act: The Use and Abuse of Section 1 to Regulate Restraints on Intraleague Rivalry*, 32 UCLA L. Rev. 219 (1984).

Rogers, Mike & Rory Ryan, *Navigating the Bylaw Maze in NCAA Major-Infractions Cases*, 37 Seton Hall L. Rev. 749 (2007).

Ross, Stephen F, *Antitrust Options to Redress Anticompetitive Restraints and Monopolistic Practices by Professional Sports Leagues*, 52 Case W. Res. L. Rev. 133 (2001).

Ross, Stephen, *Monopoly Sports Leagues*, 73 Minn. L. Rev. 643 (1989).

Ross, Stephen F. & Stephan Szymanski, *Open Competition in League Sports*, Wis.L. Rev. 625 (2002).

Samuels, Jocelyn & Kristen Galles, *In Defense of Title IX: Why Current Policies Are Required to Ensure Equality of Opportunity*, 14 Marq. Sports L. Rev. 11, 31 (2003).

Sangree, Suzanne, *Title IX and the Contact Sports Exemption: Gender Stereotypes in a Civil Rights Statute*, 32 Conn. L. Rev. 381 (2000).

Smith, Rodney K, *When Ignorance Is Not Bliss: In Search of Racial and Gender Equity in Intercollegiate Athletics*, 61 Mo. L. Rev. 329, 335–336, 339 (1996).

Smith, Rodney K. & Robert D. Walker, *From Inequity to Opportunity: Keeping the Promises Madeto Big-Time Intercollegiate Student Athletes*, 1 Nev. L.J. 160 (2001).

Stiglitz, Jan, *Player Discipline in Team Sports*, 5 Marq. Sports L.J. 167 (1995).

Sudia, Diane & Rob Remis, *Athlete Agent Legislation in the New Millennium: State Statutes and the Uniform Athlete Agents Act*, 11 Seton Hall J. Sport L. 263 (2001).

Tygart, Travis T, *Winners Never Dope and Finally, Dopers Never Win: USADA Takes Over Drug Testing of United States Olympic Athletes*, 1 DePaul J. Sports L. & Contemp. Probs. 124 (2003).

Wall, Anne M, *The Game Behind the Games*, 12 Marq. Sports L. Rev. 557 (2002).

Weston, Maureen A, *NCAA Sanctions: Assigning Blame Where It Belongs*, 52 B.C. L. Rev. 551 (2011).

Williams, Phoebe, *Racially Hostile Environments*, 6 Marq. Sports L.J. 287 (1996).

Wilson, Darryl C, *The Legal Ramifications of Saving Face: An Integrated Analysis of Intellectual Property and Sport,* 4 Vill. Sports & Ent. L.J. 227 (1997).

Wolohan, John T, An Ethical and Legal Dilemma: Participation in Sports by HIV Infected Athletes, 7 Marq. Sports L.J. 373 (1997).

Index

The numbers here refer to paragraph numbers.

Index

Index

Index

www.ingramcontent.com/pod-product-compliance
Lightning Source LLC
Chambersburg PA
CBHW071434230926
51846CB00001B/223
9789041192257